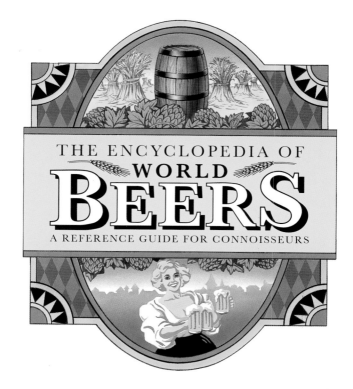

THE ENCYCLOPEDIA OF
WORLD
BEERS
A REFERENCE GUIDE FOR CONNOISSEURS

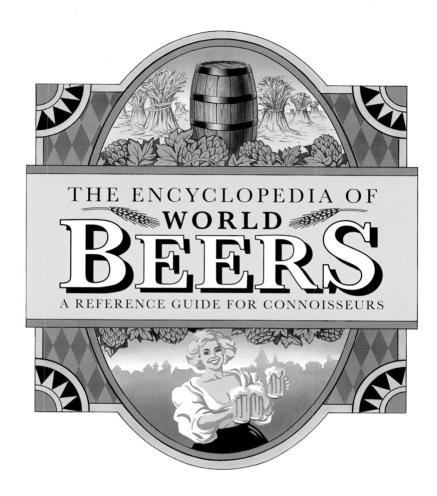

THE ENCYCLOPEDIA OF WORLD BEERS

A REFERENCE GUIDE FOR CONNOISSEURS

BENJAMIN MYERS & GRAHAM LEES

CHARTWELL
BOOKS, INC.

Credits

Commissioning editor:
Will Steeds

Design and project management:
Stonecastle Graphics Ltd., Marden, Kent

Copy editor:
Philip de Ste. Croix

Picture research:
Steve Kirkby, Leora Kahn; Brooks Krikler
Research

Location photography:
Neil Sutherland

Production:
Neil Randles, Ruth Arthur

Color reproduction:
Emirates Printing Press, Dubai, United Arab
Emirates

THIS EDITION PUBLISHED BY:

CHARTWELL BOOKS
A division of Book Sales, Inc.
114 Northfield Avenue
Edison, N.J. 08837, USA

CLB 4934
© 1997 CLB International,
a division of Quadrillion Publishing Ltd.,
Godalming, Surrey, U.K.

All rights reserved

Printed and bound in the United Arab Emirates

ISBN 0-7858-0799-3

Acknowledgments

Benjamin Myers
Dedication
To my parents, Hyman and Sandra Myers, whose encouragement and support have made it possible for me to avoid law school (so far).

My sincere thanks (and the promise of a pint) to the numerous brewers, editors, journalists, and others who have helped me with beery explorations over the years, as well as with the writing of this book: In Britain, Iain Loe of CAMRA, Susan Nowak, the dependable Denis Palmer, Mark 'White Horse' Dorber, Richard Larkin, Rupert Ponsonby (publicist extraordinaire), Mark Hughes-Morgan of *The Sunday Telegraph*, Matthew Boucher, Tim Webb (for Belgian tour advice), Graham Lees and Will Steeds, Barrie Pepper, and my colleagues in the British Guild of Beer Writers. In America, Liz Rozin (for helping me develop a book), Don Burdick (for helping me develop a book contract), Pat Hagerman and Mark Silva of RealBeer.com, George Rivers of *BarleyCorn*, Tony Forder of *Ale Street News*, Ken Spolsino and Don Gosselin of *Yankee Brew News*, the incomparable Tom Dalldorf of *Celebrator Beer News*, John Forbes, Phil and Sara Doersam of *Southern Draft*, Lucy Saunders, Phyllis Richman and Nancy McKeon of *The Washington Post*, Jane Daniels and Gerald Asher of *Gourmet*, Lew Bryson, Tom Bedell, Mike Hennick, Jim Dorsch, Jim Anderson, Larry '*Pint Post*' Baush, Tom Peters (for Philadelphia's best darn beer bar), Nick Funnell (for great brewin'), Rob Haiber, my co-workers from Pyramid Breweries (especially Rande Reed and Clay Biberdorf), and my colleagues in the North American Guild of Beer Writers. Special thanks to Roger Protz for jump-starting this project; to John '*Malt Advocate*' Hansell and Stephen Beaumont for their generous proofing expertise (not to mention beer knowledge); and to Julie and Daniel '*All About Beer*' Bradford for good advice, good beer, and good companionship. And, finally, a 'permanent pint' offer to Michael Jackson both for his support and for blazing the beer-writing trail.

Graham Lees
This book would not have been possible without the generous assistance of numerous people associated with brewing and beer, but in particular I would like to thank the following: Mike Rayner, Allied Brewery Traders' Association; *Brewing & Distilling International*; Desmond Bradley, for help in Asia; Nigel Bath, for help in the Ukraine; Dave Cunningham and Peter Dyer for help in Eastern Europe and Germany; Conrad Seidl for help in Austria; Mark Dorber and Rupert Reeves at the White Horse, Parson's Green, London; John Bass/Roger Sherman, Brewing Technology Services; *China-Britian Trade Review*; Thomas Lange, Brewers Imports, London; Iain Loe, Research Manager of CAMRA; Bill Mellor, Managing Editor, *Asia, Inc.* magazine, for help in China; Mikko Montonen, in Finland; William Taylor of Lion Nathan Australia; Karen Wise, Oddbins, London; Peter Zizkovsky, director of the Plzen Brewery Museum; and, last but not least, Will Steeds and Steve Kirkby at CLB for enduring the struggle.

Finally, the Publishers would like to thank...
Tony Stanton, Marcus and everyone else at the Hog's Back Brewery, Tongham, Surrey; Mark Dorber and Rupert Reeves at the White Horse, Parson's Green, Fulham, London; Kim Adams at Brewers Publications; Frank Baillie; Peter Barnes; John Conen; Michael Cook at Premier Worldwide Brands; Dennis Cox at Ryan & Cox PR; Dave Cunningham; Peter Dyer; Greg at the Hop Back Brewery; Denise Hunn at the Beer Cellar; Thomas Lange; Don Mansell; Hans Nordlov; Alfonso Ornelas of Grupo Modelo; Keith Osborne; Hugh Shipman of Bierlijn; Nick Sholley of *All About Beer* magazine; Conrad Seidl; Ed Strohmaier of the Stichting Promotie Uitzonderlijk Bier, Holland; Keith Taylor of Keith Taylor Trading; Jef van den Broeck; Joanne Walker at Beer Paradise. Particular thanks to: The Bridgewater Book Company for working on the original design concept; Tim Murphy for location photos in Colorado; Larry C. Volk for location photos in the northeastern US; Neil Sutherland for taking location and still photos in California and England; Leora Kahn; and Roger Protz for his help and advice at the beginning of this project.

CONTENTS

Entries in *italics* denote a feature

Acknowledgments and picture credits appear on page 4

FOREWORD

It's no coincidence that as the world's largest brewing conglomerates seek to capitalize from the so-called global marketplace, we see more microbreweries and brewpubs being established. The reason is simple: the bigger a brewing combine grows, the blander its beers become. Out of necessity to reach a mass market, the brewing giants must make their products acceptable to the lowest common denominator of taste.

Such a policy, backed by huge advertising budgets, will always win new converts - the under-developed taste buds of the young, for example. But such a policy is also alienating growing numbers of more discerning beer drinkers - people whose taste buds have matured to demand something more flavorsome and satisfying than Miller Lite, or Budweiser, or Foster's to round off the day or to accompany lunch or dinner.

In the past ten years, more than 1,000 microbreweries and brewpubs have been created across the globe to quench this growing thirst for beers of taste and character. From its revolutionary beginnings in Britain and North America, the trend has spread across Europe, into Africa and now also through Asia.

The interesting phenomenon is that demand for the brews of the micros is occurring not only in countries where consumer choice was being squeezed by the domination of the brewing giants, but also in countries where there had never been a particularly wide choice of beers. This signals more than a renaissance in craft brewing. It suggests a new and vigorous interest in beer choice and variety which the globalizing giants, with their economies of scale, do not wish to nurture. If Europeans or North Americans travel to Asia, they naturally seek out the local cuisine. They should also be able to find local beers to match, not the uniform blandness of Carlsberg, Heineken or Interbrew (Stella Artois), whose anodyne Asian versions of their European flagship brands are an insult to their own great brewing heritage. Of course, the total capacity of the small breweries is only a drop compared with the output of the giants, but the impact of the minnows is greater today than at any time since the arrival of the multinational brewers.

Informing beer drinkers about choice and variety, and where to find them, is the central aim of this book. We hope our selections will whet many appetites, and encourage people to cross the street or travel the extra mile to drink the world's favorite and most enduring beverage. Only by doing that can the globalizing giants be kept in check. Only that way can consumers hope to continue enjoying real choice and diversity.

Graham Lees

Graham Lees
Manchester, England

From left to right: Conditioning a cask of beer. The cask is a kilderkin, holding 18 UK gallons (21.6 US gallons, 81.8 liters). First, the cellarman prepares to vent the cask by hammering home a porous bamboo spile (above). As the spile pierces the seal (right), beer is forced . . .

. . . from the cask with the escaping gas (left); the cellarman watches this flow (above) – if, when wiped, the spile top stays clean for from three seconds to a minute, (depending on the level of carbonation required) a non-porous hard spile can be inserted in the cask.

INTRODUCTION

Just as today's beer consumer confronts an expanding choice of flavorful ales and lagers, today's reader faces what seems an ever-growing selection of beer books. Territory once only covered by brewing journals or other technically-oriented works now is inhabited by volumes of advice on everything from home brewing to beer-based cooking. *The Encyclopedia Of World Beers* was written to stand out from the crowded shelf.

Graham and I were determined to find a way to present the best of world brewing in a practical, accessible form. We immediately realized that an exhaustive study of global breweries was beyond our scope. Indeed, even exhaustive coverage of American craft breweries and brewpubs seemed impossible (especially considering how rapidly they continue to proliferate!). So instead we decided to concentrate on those breweries that we considered most distinctive – in terms of their beers, their reputations, or, usually, both.

Our goal, in short, was to present a thorough review of noteworthy worldwide brewers. That's why the following pages contain profiles of creative brewpubs in British Columbia and Hong Kong, for example, but rather little mention of what Graham calls 'the globalizing giants.' To help direct readers towards the top beers, each profile provides a list of 'recommended' brews that particularly are worth sampling (in the North American section, where many brewers make a wide range of distinguished beers, this list was limited to three).

We have organized the entries according to a geographic (and sometimes regional) focus. Although areas of production generally influence a wine's character more than a beer's, many breweries still reflect local or regional tastes – either because of the ingredients they use or because of the markets to which they try to appeal. Examining a region's brewers as a whole not only proves interesting from a historical perspective, but also helps reveal why individual beers have specific aromas or flavors. It's easy to understand why America's Pacific northwest makes beers bursting with citrusy hops, after all, when you know that nearby Yakima Valley is famous for growing hop varieties with that character. At the end of each region's entries, an 'Also Worth Trying' section explores worthwhile breweries and beers that, either for space or other considerations, did not receive full treatment.

Finally, we are particularly excited to have compiled a unique resource in our opening 'A-Z of Beer.' Over twenty-eight pages this glossary covers everything from technical terms to beer styles, and famous brewing regions – all in a detailed yet straightforward fashion. We hope that, like the book overall, it provides an exciting introduction for new beer lovers and a reliable reference for experienced fans.

Cheers!

Benjamin Myers
Seattle, Washington

Once the hard spile has been inserted, the cask is left for about two days, allowing the beer time to settle (above). The beer should be kept at a temperature of 52-55°F (11-15°C) throughout this period.

When the beer has finally settled, a plastic tap is hammered into place by the cellarman, using a heavy wooden mallet (above). With the tap in place, a glass is drawn off to test for clarity, aroma, flavor, and condition (right).

A glass of fine, bright ale – thanks to the skills of the brewer – and cellarman!

AN A-Z OF BEER

60/- (SIXTY SHILLING)

Designation based on shillings, an old unit of British currency, which identifies the lowest-strength, at least today, 'variety' of 'Scottish ale' (see entry). The shilling system refers to the fact that Scottish ales once were priced and taxed based on their strength – the stronger the beer, the higher its shilling designation. A sixty-shilling ale also can be referred to in Scotland as 'Light' ale (describing potency, not color). Overall, Scottish sixty-shillings (3-3.5%) tend to be sweeter than the light-colored mild ales of England. A trend towards stronger, more flavorful beers means few remain in production.

70/- (SEVENTY SHILLING)

Designation for a medium-bodied Scottish ale (3.5-4%), based on the old pricing/taxing system (see 60/-). A seventy-shilling ale sometimes also is called a 'Heavy.' Several Scottish independent breweries – Alloa's Maclay, Edinburgh's Caledonian – still offer ales in this style, which tend to be amber to light bronze in color with the country's sweetish-malt accents (distinct from England's hoppier low-strength ales).

80/- (EIGHTY SHILLING)

As above, the designation for another variety of Scottish ale – in this case the most popular, 'standard' strength brews (4-4.5%) also known as 'Export.' Edinburgh's Caledonian offers a beautifully balanced amber example that might define the modern style. Other versions come from Scotland's Maclay, Carlsberg/Tetley (Archibald Arrol), and Belhaven.

90/- (NINETY SHILLING)

Scottish designation for the highest-strength variety of ale – also can be known as a 'wee heavy' or 'Scotch ale.' Although few examples remain in production under the ninety-shilling name, Scotland's Belhaven offers an occasional 90/- (8%) that ranks among the absolute best (deep ruby color, big-bodied and chewy, sweet and full of caramel-fruity notes, exceedingly vinous). A handful of new North American specialty brewers (such as Colorado's Odell) attempt the style.

ABBEY ALE

Belgian (or Belgian-style) beer brewed to replicate a Trappist variety. The practice seems to have begun when monasteries, lacking either the financial or physical means to brew their own beers, licensed commercial breweries to produce under their name. Belgium's Affligem monastery ceased brewing its own beers during World War II, for example, but subsequently licensed their production to the De Smet brewery. Several companies today offer abbey-style beers that have no monastic connections whatsoever: witness America's New Belgium Brewing and its Abbey (dubbel) Ale.

ADJUNCT

Frequently derogatory term for fermentable materials used to supplement barley malt and other classic brewing ingredients (wheat, rye). The world's largest breweries commonly use corn (maize) and rice as adjuncts: rice tends to create a crisp, 'clean-tasting' brew, while corn imparts a sweetish character. Sugar, a traditional ingredient in British and Belgian ales (especially in its 'candi' form), is considered an adjunct by both many new-wave specialty brewers and the Reinheitsgebot-standard Germans.

ALCOHOL

Colorless, volatile, flammable liquid (C_6H_6O) that provides the intoxicating agent in fermented and distilled beverages. Alcohol is produced as a by-product of the process in which a yeast cell consumes a molecule of sugar. The human body also produces a tiny amount of alcohol each day as part of its natural processes. Despite the health problems created by overconsumption of alcohol, a growing amount of medical evidence suggests that, when consumed in moderation, beverages containing alcohol can help reduce a person's risk of heart disease.

ALCOHOL BY VOLUME (ABV)

A percentage measure of the amount of pure alcohol in a given volume of liquid. For example, a 12-fluid ounce (355ml) bottle of a beer listed as containing five percent alcohol by volume holds exactly 0.6 fluid ounces (17.75ml) of alcohol. Most beers range between three and 12 percent alcohol by volume. Extremely strong beers have been produced with alcohol contents of up to 17.5 percent by volume! Alcohol by volume is becoming the standard figure by which the world measures alcohol content. Unless otherwise noted, all measurements of alcohol in this book are given by volume (e.g., 5.5%).

Below: Tray chic? Barmaids and weissbier draw drinkers to Bavaria.

ALCOHOL BY WEIGHT (ABW)

The alcohol contained in a given amount of liquid, expressed (as a percentage) as a comparison of the weight of the amount of alcohol compared to the total weight of the liquid. Because alcohol weighs less than water, measurements of alcohol by weight are always lower than measurements of alcohol by volume. For example, a 12-fluid ounce (355ml) bottle of beer at five percent ABV would contain approximately four percent ABW. Measurements of alcohol by weight once were standard among American brewers, fostering the misconception that American beers were weaker than Canadian and European brews (which listed alcohol by volume).

ALE

Any beer fermented with yeast that 'works' at warm temperatures (approximately 60-75°F, 15-24°C). Natural 'wild' yeasts – those found in orchards, vineyards, etc. – thrive in this temperature range, meaning that all of mankind's early beers (and today's Belgian lambics) are classified as ales. Warm temperatures encourage both yeast activity, creating

fairly rapid fermentations, and the production of aromatic and/or flavor compounds (esters) in addition to carbon dioxide and alcohol.

As a result, most ales undergo relatively short production cycles (around two weeks) and many possess distinctive, often fruity, flavors. In addition to those with 'ale' in their names (pale ale, brown ale, etc.), beers that traditionally are ales include porters, stouts, Bavarian wheat beers, Belgian 'specialty' beers (abbey beers, white beers), German altbiers, and Kölsch.

ALE BOCK

A warm-fermented beer designed to replicate the smooth, sweet, malty character of a German-style bock – both in terms of flavor profile and, occasionally, extended periods of cold conditioning after fermentation. The style arose in North America during the past decade, as ale-making specialty brewers have attempted to recreate classic bock styles using their standard yeasts. In general, ale bocks lack the finessed, rounded notes of a true cool-fermented bock.

ALL MALT

Designation given to a beer brewed entirely from malted grain – usually barley, but also specialty grains such as wheat or rye. Any beer that meets the Reinheitsgebot is 'all malt.' Specialty brewers generally see 'all malt' as a hallmark of quality. The companion term 'all grain,' though less specific, at least reveals that sugar has not been used as an adjunct.

ALTBIER

German for 'old beer' – not in the sense of being past its prime, but rather brewed according to older methods. In the land of lagers, this means warm fermentation with 'ale' yeast. Today, altbier specifically refers to a dry, hoppy, German ale style (generally 4.5-5%) whose production is centered around Düsseldorf.

Many German alts are mashed by the decoction method, and most have a restrained fruitiness created by fermentation with 'pure' single-strain yeasts and lager-like periods of cold conditioning. Their copper color comes from adding specialty malts to the mainly Pilsner malt grist. Classic Düsseldorf examples include Zum Uerige, Frankenheim, Hannen, and Diebels (the most successful independent). The style also has taken root as a specialty in nearby Hanover and Münster, as well as farther-flung Austria, Japan, the Netherlands, and North America.

AROMA HOPS

Varieties of hops whose primary function is to impart aroma, as opposed to bitterness, to a finished beer. Aroma hops always are added towards the end of a beer's boil period because their aromatic 'essential oils' are particularly volatile (and would boil off). They also frequently are used in 'late hopping' or 'dry hopping.' Classic European varieties (Hallertau, Saaz, Tettnang, Spalt, Styrian Goldings) display floral, herbal aromas. English brewers favor domestic varieties such as spicy Goldings and

earthy Northdowns. In addition to growing derivatives of German (Liberty, Mt Hood) and English (Willamettes, B.C. Goldings) aroma hops, North America offers indigenous varieties (Cascade, Chinook, Centennial) with trademark 'piney,' citrusy notes.

AUSTRALIA

Known worldwide as the home of megabrands such as Castlemaine XXXX and Foster's Lager. Commercial brewing arrived with the first British settlers, some of whom came under less than wholesome conditions: Tasmania's Cascade Brewery, for example, was designed by an Englishman serving a prison term for bankruptcy.

Given the warm Australian climate, it is not surprising that lager became the country's main beer style. Nevertheless, in a curious remnant of English tradition, many of Australia's domestic lagers are labelled as 'bitter.' A handful of traditional ales survive from long-established breweries such as Cooper's, as well as the megabrewer-owned Tooth's (Sheaf Stout) and Toohey's (Hunter Old brown ale). Over the past several years, microbrewers such as Perth's Matilda Bay (now owned by Fosters) have 'fostered' a new interest in specialty beers.

AUSTRIA

Central European country best known to beer enthusiasts for originating the 'Vienna lager' style. Austria's breweries today make mainly golden lagers that, overall, lack the panache of Germany's best examples. This may be due to the fact that, unlike their Bavarian neighbors, Austrian brewers do not feel compelled to follow the Reinheitsgebot. The brand best known in foreign circles, appropriately, is Gösser Export. A few breweries offer distinctive specialties: the Eggenburg brewery, for example, brews MacQueen's Nessie (a potent whiskey-malt 'red' beer) and the long-lagered (nine months!) Urbock 23° (9.3%). Since 1986, the country's biggest brewing group, Brau A.G., has produced highly-regarded Bavarian-style weizenbiers under the Edelweiss label at its brewery in the Salzburg region.

BALLING

Brewers see nothing naughty in this term: it refers to a scale, indicated in degrees, for measuring the density (due to malt-derived sugars) of wort prior to fermentation. The higher a beer's Balling rating, the more sugars in its wort, and therefore the greater its potential alcohol content. The scale was developed in 1843 by Carl Joseph Napoleon Balling of Bohemia, and still is used today by brewers in that region. Multiplying a beer's Balling rating by four provides an approximation of the last two digits of the brew's 'original gravity.' Thus, a beer listed as 16 degrees Balling would approximate an original gravity of 1064 – or approximately 6.4% alcohol by volume.

BARLEY

A cereal grass (of the genus *Hordeum*, the most common variety being *Hordeum vulgare*) whose seed, or grain, in its malted form serves as the main source of a beer's fermentable sugar. There are two varieties of brewing barley: six-row (which has six 'rows' of grain in each ear), and two-row. Most large brewers use less expensive six-row barleys. Traditional and specialty brewers, however, tend to prefer two-row (believing that six-row barley, which has thicker husks, imparts a 'grainy' character to beer).

Like all crops, barley differs in character depending on the climate and conditions in which it grows. Moravia in the Czech Republic is renowned for barley that produces a 'sweet' malt, for example, while hardy winter barleys (planted in fall) are thought to give beer a more robust flavor than spring varieties. Brewers even swear by specific barley types. Maris Otter, a traditional English variety, remains a favorite of ale makers for its soft, nutty flavors.

BARLEY WINE

An ale so rich and fruity in flavor, so warming and potent in character, that it seems wine-like. Barley wines generally range from 8-12% – beers in the lower 6-7% range perhaps are better called 'strong ales' – and display a vinous, sweetly malty character (sometimes balanced by generous amounts of hops). They can be light or dark in color.

Although traditionally a British style, barley wines have found new champions among North America's specialty brewers. The best examples mellow and become more delicious with bottle-age like fine wines. Excellent versions include Fuller's Golden Pride, Whitbread Gold Label, and Lee's Harvest Ale from England; Scaldis/Bush and winter's Bush Noel from Belgium; and Anchor Old Foghorn, Sierra Nevada Bigfoot, and Rogue Old Crustacean from America.

BARREL

Any large container of beer. Also, and more often, the term for a 'standardized' container (with a defined capacity) that is used to measure brewery production. In America, a 'barrel' holds 31 US gallons (117.3 liters) of beer: a brewery with an annual production of 1,000 barrels, then, makes 31,000 US gallons of beer per year. In Britain, a 'barrel' holds 36 Imperial gallons (163.7 liters, approximately 42.6 US gallons) of beer.

As consumption has fallen, in both America and Britain, smaller containers have become the norm. The standard American 'keg' actually is a half-barrel (15.5 gallons, 58.7 liters). The typical British cask now is a kilderkin (18 gallons, 81.8 liters). Still smaller containers – America's quarter-barrel or 'pony keg' (7.75 gallons, 29.3 liters) and Britain's firkin (9 gallons, 40.9 liters) – also are used.

BAVARIA

State in southeastern Germany, bordering the Czech Republic and Austria. Home to many of the country's most important breweries and beer styles. Munich, the Bavarian capital, played a crucial role in the development of cold-fermented lager beers: its brewers pioneered the dunkel style, and popularized the helles and, later, Pilsner and Oktoberfest/Märzen styles. As the state's royal seat, Munich also drove the development of Bavarian wheat beers (once the privileged drink of royalty), now popular throughout Germany.

Franconia, a northern Bavaria region, also hosts famous brewers and beers: extremely dark lagers named after the city of Kulmbach; specialties like rauchbier (smoked beer) and rye beer; examples of highly-hopped, lowly-carbonated kellerbier (cellar beer); and the ultra-potent bock variety called eisbock (ice bock). Famous Bavarian breweries include Paulaner/Hacker-Pschorr, Spaten, Schneider, Ayinger, Erdinger, Maisel, and Tucher.

Above: Despite Pittsburgh's association with steel, the Penn Brewery chose classic copper for its German-built brewhouse in the Pennsylvania city.

BEER

Any fermented beverage made from grain. Almost all modern beers are seasoned with hops. But for much of civilization's brewing history, alternative flavorings – dates, honey, nutmeg, pepper, and far stranger substances – were employed (a tradition that survives in spiced 'winter warmers' and Belgian witbier). Unhopped brews such as Africa's sorghum beers also still exist.

Beer divides into two basic categories, ales and lagers, much like wine can be split into reds and whites. Because of its low alcohol content compared to wines or spirits, beer historically has been seen as 'the beverage of moderation.'

BEER ENGINE

See 'Hand Pump.'

BEER FESTIVAL

An organized exhibition and/or celebration of beer, usually with brands from many different breweries across (at least) several styles. The majority encourage sampling rather than overconsumption. Munich's annual Oktoberfest perhaps is the best-known and longest-running example (although it barely meets the aforementioned criteria). Most are more modern, coinciding with the renaissance in specialty beers. The pioneer surely is the annual Great British Beer Festival, organized by Britain's Campaign For Real Ale (CAMRA) every year since 1978 (now usually in London during early August). Other popular examples include the Great American Beer Festival (every October in Denver, Colorado), Amsterdam's bock beer festival (organized by Dutch beer-consumer group PINT each November), and the Great Canadian Beer Festival (each November in Victoria, British Columbia).

BELGIAN RED ALE

Distinctive sour Belgian ale style (4.5-5.5%) almost wholly local to western Flanders. Examples traditionally are brewed with Vienna (and other specialty) malts for a deep red color, fermented with complex ale yeasts (even by Belgian standards) for a rich malty-fruity flavor, and aged up to 18 months in unlined wooden vessels (usually huge tuns) to acquire a refreshing tart acidity from lactobacilli and other microorganisms. The wooden-tun process suggests that Belgian red ales, along with the country's sour brown ales, may be related to early English porters. Top examples include Rodenbach (three versions), Petrus, and Vichtenaar.

BELGIUM

Small European country bordered by the North Sea (west), France (south), Germany and Luxembourg (east), and the Netherlands (north). Although its everyday beers tend to be Pilsners – Stella Artois, for example, from Belgian brewing giant Interbrew – Belgium has maintained a vibrant tradition of specialty ales. In fact, Belgium's significance in the brewing renaissance now rivals that of its capital Brussels in European business or its cuisine (waffles and sprouts aside) in international cookery.

Belgian culture appreciates specialty beers much as French culture elevates wine: many styles and brands are served in unique glasses, and even the finest restaurants and hotels stock highly-regarded brews. Most small specialty brewers cluster in Flanders, the Flemish-speaking northern region. Here you will find lambics, fruit beers, spiced beers, brown ales, red ales, pale ales, strong golden ales, spiced ales, and more – all with a unique Belgian touch. Wallonia, the French-speaking south, hosts the distinctive saison style and three of the most famous Trappist brewers (Chimay, Rochefort, Orval).

BERLINER WEISSE

Extremely tart, low-alcohol (2.5-3.5%) wheat beer developed around the German city of Berlin. Because these sour brews traditionally are sweetened (and colored) at the bar prior to drinking with syrups such as green-hued woodruff or red raspberry, the name 'weisse' (white) seems somewhat ironic. Hop rates are extremely low: the beer's character comes from the interplay of tart wheat flavor and the sourness created by fermentation (and some warm maturation) with deliberately-introduced lactobacillus cultures.

The centuries-old style may have been developed by Berlin-bound Huguenots who migrated through Belgium (the sour beer connection). Whatever the case, the beers became so popular that Napoleon's troops, occupying Berlin, called them 'the Champagne of the North' – a reference not only to the beers' effervescence, perhaps, but also to their tartness. Today, although in decline, the style is kept alive by Berlin's Kindl and Schultheiss breweries. Bremen's Haacke-Beck brewery also offers an example, and several North American microbrewers have experimented with versions.

BIÈRE BLANCHE

French term for 'white beer.' Used in French-speaking regions to denote a Belgian-style witbier.

BIÈRE DE GARDE

French for 'beer to keep,' implying a 'farmhouse' brew of the variety made in northern France (French Flanders). The style's roots parallel those of neighboring Belgium's saisons: farmer-brewers made a higher-strength beer in early spring that was bottled and stored ('kept') for summer drinking. The best blend ale fruitiness with malty depth and a touch of 'cellar character' that reveals the style's origins.

Bières de garde have been 'rediscovered' thanks to new interest in specialty brews. Today's versions (6-8%) are malt accented, sometimes with toasty or spicy notes from darker 'Vienna' malts. They traditionally are ales, but several large producers now ferment (sometimes at warm temperatures) with lager yeasts for 'stability.' Few bières de garde are pasteurized; a handful are bottle-conditioned. Breweries offer up to three varieties (pale, amber, brown/dark) and occasionally a seasonal version. Top brands include Jenlain, Castelain's organic Jade, La Choulette/Sans Culottes, and St Sylvestre's highly-regarded range (especially the Trois Monts family).

BIERGARTEN

Outdoor area set aside for beer consumption; literally a 'beer garden' (in German). The term is most associated with Bavaria, which hosts hundreds of biergartens affiliated with specific breweries. In other countries, the term simply indicates an outside drinking space.

The biergarten concept probably developed before commercial refrigeration: brewers, who protected their beers from summer's heat by storing them in cool caves or areas cut into rural hillsides, would open a barrel or two on site to check quality. Word spread, and the bucolic biergarten was born! In 1995, visitors to Munich's 100 or so biergartens hoisted a few steins in celebration after a Bavarian court overturned an early closing-time law (established in response to complaints about noise).

BITTER

Basic taste sensation perceived mainly on the back or rear of the tongue. The bitter flavors in beer traditionally are derived from hops. In Britain, the term 'bitter' also indicates a draft ale of moderate strength (3.5-4%), generally somewhat dry and well-hopped. Versions branded 'best bitter' or 'special bitter' have a higher strength (4-5%) and intensity of flavor. An 'extra special bitter' (ESB) is yet more potent (5-5.5%) and flavorsome.

British examples abound, from Fuller's ESB to Brakspear's Bitter. American specialty brewers also offer versions – Blue Ridge ESB, Hale's Special Bitter, etc. – although most have found that drinkers recoil from any beer named 'bitter.' Perhaps because of their country's ties to England, Canadian micros have fared better: Conners Best Bitter, Wellington County's Arkell Best Bitter, and Shaftebury ESB are all popular. Australian brewers apply the term (nostalgically?) to mainstream lagers such as Victoria Bitter.

BITTERING HOPS

Hops whose primary function is to impart bitterness, as opposed to aroma, to beer (balancing its malt-derived sweetness). Hops get their bitterness from a resinous substance called lupulin, stored in glands at the base of a blossom's leaves. More specifically, bitterness comes from two components of lupulin: alpha acids (the primary bittering component) and beta acids (secondary). Alpha acid content is rated on a percentage scale – the traditional British hop variety called Fuggles has an alpha content of 4-5.5%, for example, while newer 'high alpha' varieties (such as England's Target and America's Nugget) offer 10-14%.

Some bittering hops, particularly North American ones, impart distinctive flavors as well as basic bitterness. Others (like England's Challenger and America's Columbus) work as both bittering and aroma hops (see entry), matching high alpha contents with high levels of essential oils.

Above: The Sudwerk Hübsch brewpub in Davis, California – just add drinkers!

BLACK BEER

See 'Schwarzbier.'

BLACK MALT

Malted barley that has been heated in a 'roasting machine' (like a coffee roaster) to the point where it blackens in color and takes on a burnt, roasted character. As a result, it sometimes is also known by the generic term 'roasted malt.' Brewers traditionally use black malt not only to darken a beer's color, but also to impart 'bittersweet' flavors and sometimes a perceptible dry character. Black malt creates a somewhat less 'dry' character than 'roasted barley' (see entry).

BOCK

Potent lager style, associated with springtime, that developed in Germany. The style encompasses *helles* (pale), *Mai* (May), and *doppel* (double) bocks. When bock stands alone, it usually denotes a *dunkles* (dark) example. All share a richly malty, even sweetish, character. By German law, they must have an original gravity of at least 16° Plato (approximately 6.4%). A finessed, rounded character (the product of lengthy lagering) separates bocks from other high-strength lagers.

Because *bock* is also the German word for 'billy goat,' that virile animal long has symbolized the style. Bock's roots probably rest in the north German city of Einbeck, famous as early as the 14th century for exporting powerful beers. Einbeck's brews proved popular in Bavaria, where local producers, whose regional dialect corrupted the city's name to

'Einbock,' dropped a syllable and began making their own 'bock' beers. Originally an ale style, bocks evolved into lagers along with most German beers. Today bocks also are brewed in many other regions, particularly the Netherlands, Austria, Scandinavia, and North America.

BOHEMIA

Central European region, today the principal region of the Czech Republic. It has been famous as a brewing center since at least the 13th century, and probably earlier. Bohemia left an indelible mark on worldwide brewing when, in 1842, a brewery in its city of Pilsen introduced the first golden lager beer. (Bohemian brewers earlier had adopted the dunkel lagers introduced by their Bavarian brethren). Today, when applied to beer, 'Bohemian' refers to the character of brews from the region: for Pilsners, this implies something of a soft, malty character; for dark lagers, perhaps a slightly more simple, caramel-accented character than Bavarian examples.

BOK

Traditional Dutch spelling, and interpretation, of German bock beer. When simply called 'bok,' the style implied is a red-brown brew (around 6.5%) with a character both sweeter and 'simpler' than most German examples. In addition, while Teutonic versions are associated with springtime, Dutch boks tend to be released in the autumn – a tradition that suggests their early production may have had more in common with Germany's Märzen beers.

Inspired by Germany's late-spring Maibocks (see entry), the Dutch also offer (with typically tweaked spelling) their own sweetish Meibocks. In recent years, microbrewers in the Netherlands, like their American counterparts, have introduced ale boks (generally darker in color and fuller in flavor than standard boks). A specialty sub-category of tarweboks (wheat boks), sweeter and cleaner-tasting than standard versions, also is developing.

BOTTLE CONDITIONING

The process whereby a beer undergoes a refermentation in the bottle from which it will be served. This fermentation might occur with a different yeast than that used for primary fermentation (the Trappist ale Orval, for example, is bottled with a multi-strain yeast after fermentation with a single-strain culture). In some cases, bottles are primed with sugar as a yeast food source; in others, beer is 'kräusened' (see entry) in the bottle.

Bottle conditioning usually generates complexity in addition to pleasant natural

carbonation. The presence of oxygen-absorbing yeast in the bottle also reduces the chances that the beer will oxidize. On the down side, bottle conditioning is a difficult process to control and sometimes produces an unappealing hazy, yeasty brew. Beer that is bottle-conditioned qualifies as 'real ale.'

BOTTOM FERMENTATION

Somewhat outdated term for fermentation with lager yeast, which tends to settle out towards the bottom of the fermenting vessel after finishing its 'work.' The term also appears, variously, as an adjective (bottom-fermenting) and noun (a bottom fermenter). Because many breweries now employ tall conical fermenters – which cause even ale yeasts to settle toward the bottom – the more accurate term for denoting standard production with a lager yeast is 'cool' or 'cold fermentation.'

BREW KETTLE

The vessel used to boil wort, usually with hops, prior to fermentation. It is traditionally known as 'the copper' in Britain, where many were constructed from that heat-conducting metal. Now generally made of stainless steel. Although many breweries once used open brew kettles – which look like large cauldrons – almost all today have switched to closed vessels.

BREWERIANA

Material related to beers and/or breweries. The overall term encompasses everything from coasters to logo-painted trucks. Many collectors specialize in this type of material.

BREWPUB

Now common term for a pub or restaurant with an on-premises brewery that serves the majority of its beer to customers 'at the source.' Alternatively spelled 'brew-pub' or 'brew pub.' A 'brewery tap' – a restaurant or pub serving the products of the brewery to which it is attached – should not be termed a brewpub unless its beers are made on a separate, on-site system.

Although hundreds of examples have opened across the

world as a result of the beer renaissance, the concept is not new: England's Blue Anchor brewpub in Cornwall, for example, and Bohemia's U Fleků brewery-tavern in Prague both have been operating for centuries. In fact, before the Industrial Revolution, many small local breweries actually were brewpubs.

BREWSPAPER

Punning name for the monthly or bi-monthly newspapers, targeted at beer consumers and enthusiasts, that arose relatively recently as part of the brewing renaissance. Also sometimes known as 'beeriodicals.' Primarily a phenomenon in the United States, where examples tend to be regionally focused: *Southwest Brewing News* and *Southern Draft Brew News*, for example. Other well-regarded American examples include *Ale Street News, Yankee Brew News, Great Lakes Brewing News, BarleyCorn, Midwest Beer Notes*, and *The Celebrator Beer News*. Beer-organization organs, such as CAMRA's *What's Brewing*, also can fit the description.

BRITAIN

Country traditionally associated with ale brewing, and particularly famous for the 'real ales' (see entry) served at its many pubs. Perhaps because of the British reverence for tradition, lager beers never wholly supplanted ales: even today, a national brewery partially owned by Carlsberg produces a top-selling 'session' ale, Tetley Bitter.

Over the last decade, British drinkers and brewers alike have

rediscovered the joys of classic ale styles: mild ales, pale ales, porters, stouts, barley wines, and more. Many new micros have sprung up to quench this thirst. At the same time, however, the country's biggest producers have been merging their brewing empires – subsequently closing breweries and discontinuing brands. Coupled with increasing European pressure to abolish 'the tie' (brewery ownership of pubs), this trend could foreshadow darker times for the lover of traditional ales.

BROWN ALE

At its most basic, an ale with a brown color from specially toasted or roasted malts. Depending on its point of stylistic origin, 'brown ale' denotes different types of beer. Northern England is famous for caramel-accented, quaffable brews of standard strength (4-5%) – Newcastle Brown Ale, Vaux Double Maxim, Samuel Smith Nut Brown Ale, etc. – that probably developed as a regional response to the popular copper-colored pale ales of England's Midlands. Southern England has nearly lost its tradition of bottling dark 'mild ales' (see entry) as 'brown ales.'

Elsewhere, 'English style' brown ales approximate the northern category (Australian examples tend to be sweeter in flavor). Craft-brewed 'American brown ales' blend the northern English style's nutty flavors with liberal doses of citric North American hops. And in Belgium, East Flanders brewers (Liefmans, Clarysse/Felix, etc.) have preserved a tradition of sour, complex, dark 'old brown' ales

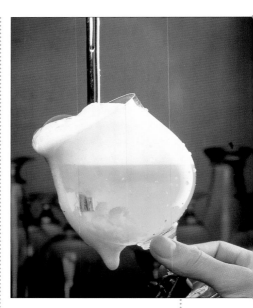

(6-8%) which may be related, historically, to early porters.

BRUNE

French for 'brown,' denoting the above-average strength (6-6.5%) dark lagers produced by France's breweries. These display a more aromatic, fuller-bodied character than many Bavarian/Bohemian dunkels or other generic 'dark lagers' (see entry). Examples include Kronenbourg's 1664 Brune, Pelforth Brune (Heineken-owned), and Ackerland Brune.

BURTON

City in England's Midlands that became and remains famous for brewing pale ales: Bass, which rose to international heights on pale ale production, is head-quartered there. The local 'hard' water, rich in gypsum (calcium sulfate), enhances the style's crisp character and clarity. Brewers sometimes describe adding gypsum to their brewing water as 'Burtonization' (beers made this way have been 'Burtonized').

BUs (BITTERNESS UNITS)

A scale for recording the bitterness of beer. Alternatively called International Bitterness Units (IBUs) or European Bitterness Units (EBUs). Because the BU figure is based on an analysis of the parts per million of 'isomerized' alpha acids in a beer (see 'Bittering Hops'), it does not directly correlate to perceived bitterness – the level of bitterness tasted by a drinker. A hoppy pale ale may seem substantially 'bitter' at 39 BUs, for example, while a rich barley wine still may taste malty at 70 BUs. Also, the measurement gives no indication of hop aroma or flavor.

CAMRA
(CAMPAIGN FOR REAL ALE)

British consumer organization. The world's first beer drinkers' group successfully to confront the brewing industry with demands for choice and quality. After being founded in northern England in 1971, CAMRA quickly developed into a national movement. Its primary goal was the survival of British cask-conditioned 'draught' ales, as well as traditional methods of brewing and beer dispensing, at a time when they were under threat from industry changes (pasteurization, artificial carbonation, etc.).

From its four founding members, CAMRA now boasts around 50,000 members, with branches in Europe, North America, and Australia. Among its achievements, CAMRA forced brewers routinely to disclose beer strengths and ingredients. It also is credited with inspiring the

microbrewing revolution in Britain and (to a lesser degree) other countries. It publishes the monthly beer newspaper *What's Brewing*, and has a sister group (Apple) that campaigns for traditional cider.

CANADA

North American country whose dubious contributions to world brewing include 'ice beer' and a host of bland lagers from national producers Molson and Labatt. The country's single legitimate beer style may be 'Canadian ale' – a pale golden, soft, restrained variety of standard strength, neither as sweet as American cream ales nor as hoppy as many new-wave golden ales. Examples today include such brews as Molson's Golden and Export, but the style was recognized at least as far back as the 1930s.

Considering its smaller population, Canada has made substantial contributions to North America's specialty brewing scene. English-style ales are popular in the eastern regions, particularly (and somewhat ironically) in French-speaking Quebec. The central and western areas tend towards softer, maltier

Above: The ad touts its 'delicious clear' flagship, but Heineken also offers special brews.

brews. A few producers even offer some of the continent's best Belgian-style witbiers and Bavarian-style bocks. Both Molson and Labatt (now owned by Belgian giant Interbrew) have launched specialty beers of their own, although with somewhat less vigor than their big American counterparts.

CARBONATION

The level of carbon dioxide (CO_2) gas dissolved in a beer. A natural by-product of fermentation, carbon dioxide gives beer its 'fizz.' Some beers display an all-natural carbonation that comes from a process like bottle conditioning. Others are 'force carbonated' prior to bottling and kegging, meaning that CO_2 is added back to the brew at this stage.

Whatever the case, an appropriate level of carbonation is crucial for a beer's perceived body and mouthfeel. Describing a beer as 'carbonic' implies that it is over-carbonated to the point of having a fizzy bite on the tongue.

CASK

A large beer container, usually barrel-shaped, with a removable

bung and an area for inserting a manual tap. The term chiefly is used in Britain, where it generally refers to an 18-gallon (81.8-liter) kilderkin. Most modern casks are made from metal (aluminum). Only a handful of British breweries – Mitchell's of Lancaster, for example, and Samuel Smith's of Tadcaster (in its home areas) – still regularly use wooden casks. Beers called 'cask ales' have experienced a process known as 'cask conditioning' (see entry).

CASK CONDITIONING

Process whereby a beer undergoes a refermentation in the container (a cask) from which it will be served. This final fermentation generally occurs with the same yeast as primary fermentation. In most cases, casks are primed with sugar as a yeast food source; only rarely is beer kräusened in the cask. Overall, the process seems to impart extra complexity to beers, especially lower-strength examples. It also generates a gentle carbonation that some drinkers wrongly consider 'flat.'

Cask conditioning is a time-honored practice in Britain, where almost every brewery offers at least one such beer (thanks, in large part, to the success of CAMRA). It occasionally is attempted by specialty brewers in other countries, particularly America and Canada. Cask-conditioned beer qualifies as 'real ale' (see entry). Also see 'Keg Conditioning.'

CELLARMAN

The worker in a British pub charged with looking after the beer, particularly cask-conditioned ales. The term comes from the fact that most British pubs store their beer in cool cellars. To perform the job properly, a cellarman (cellarperson?) must master a range of skills involved in the handling of cask ales. These include everything from proper tapping techniques to the ability to tilt a cask without disturbing its yeast sediment. Many British breweries hold courses to teach correct 'cellarmanship.'

CHOCOLATE MALT

Malt that has been roasted to a deep brown color and character, though not to the higher 'burnt' degree of 'black malt' (see entry). Chocolate malt imparts (as its name suggests) a chocolatey, cappuccino-like character to beers. It is used to provide depth and 'roundness' in porters and stouts.

COLOGNE

City in northern Germany on the Rhine river, capital of the surrounding Rhineland region. It is known in German as Köln, and its local beer style is called

'Kölsch' (see entry). Some 20 breweries in and around the city brew Kölsch, making it one of the world's most dense brewing regions. Cologne's Guild of Brewers, established at the end of the 14th century, is the city's oldest existing trade organization.

CONDITIONING

The varying period of maturation a beer undergoes prior to being offered to consumers. In Britain, the term also refers to a beer's level of carbonation: a beer that is 'highly conditioned' displays strong carbonation, for example. Beers that are matured and carbonated at their producing facility sometimes are called 'brewery-conditioned.'

COOL SHIP

A broad, shallow, open vessel in which hopped wort is left to cool before fermentation. The shape and depth of the vessel are designed to release as much heat as possible, lowering the brew's temperature so that it can provide a hospitable environment for yeast. Before the advent of modern cooling techniques, most breweries processed their wort in this fashion. Nowadays, only a handful (including Belgian's lambic brewers) still do.

In fact, lambic brewers continue to use cool ships precisely for the reasons that other brewers abandoned them: the vessels promote 'infection' of the wort by airborne wild yeasts and other micro-organisms. In the few non-lambic breweries where cool ships still exist – Germany's Schumacher brewery (home of

Schumacher Alt), for example, and Scotland's Traquair House – they produce a 'house character' for the same reason.

COOPER

A person who builds or repairs wooden barrels. The worldwide shift to metal casks and kegs has severely curtailed this work, at least in the brewing industry (wine and spirits makers still require wooden casks). A small number of breweries – including English companies like Young's, Theakston's, and Samuel Smith's – still employ on-site coopers, sometimes solely 'for show.'

COPPER

Heat-conductive metal historically used to construct brewing equipment, especially kettles. Today, when most successful brewers employ newer stainless steel equipment, copper remains positively associated with 'traditional' brewing methods. See 'Brew Kettle.'

CORIANDER

An herb in the carrot family. In its green leafy state, used as a flavoring or garnish, it is called cilantro or Chinese parsley. Brewers (particularly Belgian brewers) use coriander seeds, either in whole or crushed form, to provide an aromatic, lemony note to witbiers and other spiced brews.

CRAFT BREWER(Y)

Many of America's successful small brewers, who began as 'microbreweries' (see entry), now vastly exceed that official production level. At the same time, they have not abandoned

their original 'micro-outlook' and brewing philosophy. Such companies have adopted the term 'craft brewery' to distinguish themselves from mainstream major and/or regional producers.

CREAM ALE

Once popular North American (particularly American) beer style, developed by ale brewers to compete with golden lagers. Extremely pale golden in color, cream ales (4-5%) display a faint fruitiness, light body, and sweetish character. Some were stand-alone ales brewed with a significant percentage of adjuncts. Others were a blend of such an ale with a brewery's lightest lager.

A handful of examples still exist. The best-known American version comes from New York's Genesee Brewery. Canada's top example, Sleeman's Cream Ale, comes from an Ontario regional that closed in 1930 and was resurrected more than 50 years later by a micro-minded family member. Ohio's Hudepohl-Schoenling, brewers of Little Kings Cream Ale, had the 'good humor' to cash in on the ice beer fad with Little Kings Ice Cream Ale.

CRYSTAL MALT

Sometimes called 'caramel malt.' Malt that is kilned while still moist from the germination process. The effect is like conducting a 'mini mash' inside every grain: the hot temperature of the kiln activates enzymes in the moist malt that convert each kernel's starch to liquid sugar. When kilning ends, this malt sugar crystallizes into caramel-ish 'nuggets' inside the reddish-tinged kernels. A traditional ingredient in British bitters, crystal malt creates an amber color and provides a distinctive toasty, nutty flavor. Because it contains a high degree of non-fermentable sugars, crystal malt also imparts residual sweetness to a finished beer. Crystal malt is extremely similar to 'Vienna malt.'

CURAÇAO

Small south Caribbean island in the Dutch Antilles. It lends its name not only to a variety of liqueur flavored with island-grown oranges, but also to the oranges themselves. Their tangy-bitter peels, dried and 'fermented' like tobacco leaves, are a traditional seasoning in Belgian witbiers and other spiced brews. (Curaçao orange peel probably found its way to Belgium when that country was under the control of the neighboring Netherlands).

CZECH REPUBLIC

Central European country (see 'Bohemia') with a long brewing tradition. Not only home to some of the world's best golden lagers, such as Pilsner Urquell and Budweiser Budvar, but also some of its top brewing

Above: Unusual flavorings such as dried orange peel help give specialty beers character.

ingredients: barley from the state of Moravia is renowned for its 'sweetness,' while hops from the town of Žatec (Saaz) are prized for their herbal, floral qualities.

The fall of Communist rule has helped Czech brewers find a broader international customer base. But the arrival of the free market has had two unfortunate effects: first, a few colorful older breweries, who have lost the Communist cushion, are struggling; second, some of the most successful brewers, in their rush to modernize, may be sacrificing the character that made them famous. The Pilsner Urquell brewery, which replaced its age-old wooden fermenters with new stainless steel conicals, sadly fits the latter category.

DARK (DUNKEL) LAGER

A lager of moderate strength (4.5-5.5%) with a reddish-brown to black color. The style developed from Munich's original lager beers of the early 19th century, whose brown color reflected the period's primitive malting standards. The Munich *dunkel* ('dark') style soon was adopted by brewers across Bavaria and in neighboring 'Bohemia' (see

entry). Today's Bavarian dunkels are smooth and rich with hints of coffee and chocolate from specially-toasted malts. Bohemia's versions (Trebon's Regent Brewery makes the best known) unfortunately have acquired an image as 'women's beer.'

Generic 'dark lagers' from international brewers seldom match the character of these classics. During the post-Prohibition period, many American brewers made dark lagers simply by adding caramel to their main brand – a practice that may continue, in some quarters, today.

DECOCTION

Mashing technique preferred by classic lager breweries, particularly those of central Europe (Bavaria, Bohemia, Austria, etc.). The process developed in the late 19th century as a means of coping with Continental Europe's poorer-quality malts. In short, decoction mashing works as follows: the temperature of the mash is raised, in several stages, by pumping portions of it into a secondary vessel, boiling them, and returning them to the main

mash. The result is a thorough conversion of malt starches to sugars. Decoction mashing also includes a low-temperature rest that breaks down malt-derived proteins, a process that helps clarify the finished beer. Finally, the decoction process can increase malt-derived compounds called 'melanoidins' that darken a beer's color (this effect is particularly notable in dunkel lagers).

DOPPELBOCK

German for 'double bock.' An extra-potent bock, though rarely twice as strong as standard versions. According to German law, doppelbocks must be brewed to a gravity of at least 18° Plato (around 7.5%). They generally are reddish-brown to near-black in color, with a sweetish flavor and rich, rounded character. The style was developed by medieval monks, who consumed thickly caloric, nourishing brews during Lenten fasts – as a result, doppelbocks remain directly associated with springtime.

Munich's Paulaner brewery, which evolved from a monastery, emphasized its doppelbock's religious origins by naming the beer Salvator ('savior' in Latin). Competitors responded with doppelbocks whose names also ended in '-ator.' Examples with amusing titles like Animator, Celebrator, and Operator now are brewed across Bavaria. Specialty producers in many other countries also brew the style.

DORTMUNDER EXPORT

Golden lager style developed in the industrial German city of Dortmund, and frequently shipped elsewhere (hence 'export'). Slightly above-average in strength (5-5.5%), Dortmunder lagers traditionally are malty in character with a 'firm' body from residual unfermented sugars. They at once are neither as sweet as Munich's helles lagers, nor as hoppy and bitter as Pilsners (especially north German versions).

Exported to the nearby Netherlands, Dortmunder lagers proved popular enough that domestic brewers adopted them: Dutch versions, bearing the shortened title 'Dort,' tend to be somewhat stronger (6-7%). The top German examples come from Dortmund's large Actien Brauerei (DAB) and Union Brauerei (DUB). Established brewers from Spain to Japan also offer interpretations, and several of North America's smaller producers have embraced the style.

DRY BEER

Beer thoroughly fermented to the point where it contains extremely few residual sugars – it therefore seems 'dry' (as opposed to sweet). The lack of residual sugars may make the beer seem thinner in body and cleaner in flavor. It also reduces the beer's lingering flavors, or 'finish' (see entry). The Dry Beer 'style' of pale lager offered by major brewers from Japan to Britain was designed to minimize such characteristics.

DRY HOPPING

The practice of adding unused hops, either in whole or pelletized form, to a maturing beer. The hops used for such a purpose are called 'dry hops.' As they steep, their essential oils give the beer a notable 'fresh' hop aroma and, to a lesser degree, flavor. British real ales traditionally are dry-hopped in their casks. Specialty brewers in other countries, faced with sealed kegs, frequently add dry hops to beer in the maturation tanks before bottling or kegging.

DRY (IRISH) STOUT

Variety of stout, developed in Ireland, with a 'burnt' roasted-coffee flavor and, usually, notable hop bitterness. The style's 'dry' character comes from both thorough fermentation and the taste imparted by highly-roasted grain. Many examples are made with roasted barley, others with black malt, and a handful with both. Despite the heft suggested by their powerful flavors and black color, classic Irish dry stouts (Beamish, Murphy's, Guinness) are all moderate in strength (around 4.2%). Irish-style stouts brewed in other countries, including Australia and North America, tend to be stronger (5-6%).

DUBBEL

Flemish for 'double,' implying a dark Trappist-style or abbey-style brew of notable strength (usually 6-8%). 'Dubbel' originally may have referred to markings on the sides of wooden barrels that revealed the strength and character of the beer within: a single mark denoted the standard brew, while two marks ('dubbel') suggested a richer, more potent drink. Three marks ('tripel') suggested an even more distinctive beer.

The best dubbels balance complex fruitiness with rich, dark malt character. Top Belgian examples include Westmalle Dubbel, Chimay Red, Affligem's dark version, and range-capping Rochefort 8° (9.2%). The style also is popular with specialty brewers in other countries, including America and the Netherlands.

DUNKEL

See 'Dark.'

DUNKEL-WEIZEN

German for 'dark wheat.' A wheat beer, frequently unfiltered and Bavarian in style,

made with a percentage of toasted and/or specially-roasted barley malts. In addition to darkening the beer's color, these specialty malts impart a nutty, even chocolatey, taste and greater complexity of flavor. Examples come from many German wheat beer brewers (Paulaner, Erdinger, Munich's Hofbrau) and specialty producers in other countries. Some of America's microbrewers offer dark interpretations of the tamer 'American wheat' style (see 'Wheat Beer').

DÜSSELDORF

City on the Rhine in western Germany, north of Cologne. Like the latter, it has preserved one of the country's few remaining ale styles, 'altbier' (see entry). Altbier production – in brewery-pubs (Zum Schlüssel, Zum Uerige, Schumacher and Im Füchschen) – and appreciation is centered in Düsseldorf's Altstadt. This charming 'Old Town' region, with its twisty streets, stands in pleasant contrast to the modern center city area (full of skyscrapers that reflect Düsseldorf's modern status as a capital of international finance).

EBCU (EUROPEAN BEER CONSUMERS' UNION)

A loose federation of beer-drinkers' groups from different European countries, which work together as a lobbying body on behalf of Europe's beer consumers. The EBCU was established in 1990 by Britain's CAMRA, Belgium's Objective Bier Proevers, and the Netherlands' PINT (Promotie Informatie Traditioneel Bier) – all three groups remain key members. Beer-drinkers' organizations from France, Finland, Sweden, and Switzerland also are involved.

The EBCU's role has become increasingly important as the European Union expands and seeks to standardize Europe's brewing industry. In particular, it lobbies two key arms of the Union: the unelected Commission, and the elected European Parliament. A basic objective is to require all European brewers to divulge their beers' ingredients. The group successfully worked to create legal definitions in Belgium for the lambic and gueuze beer styles.

EISBOCK

'Ice bock' in German. An extremely potent brew produced by partially freezing a bock and separating the ice (water freezes before alcohol) from the remaining liquid. The result is a powerful 'concentrated' brew – rich, warming, and mellow with layers of character. Legend suggests that an apprentice brewer accidentally discovered eisbock after leaving kegs of bock outside during winter.

The classic example (10%) – clearly labelled Eisbock, with the subtitle *Bayrisch G'frorns* (Bavarian frozen), and a snowflake-decorated label – used to come from Reichelbräu, a sizable brewery in the Bavarian town of Kulmbach. Canada's Niagara Falls Brewing offers a famous annual 'vintage' version (somewhat lighter in color and lesser in strength). A few specialty brewers elsewhere, including western Canada's Vancouver Island Brewery and New York's Zip City brewpub, have attempted the style.

ENGLAND

See 'Britain.'

ENTIRE

Early name for the dark ale – later called porter – that supposedly incorporated all the qualities of a popular blend of well-matured, 'stale' brown ale and fresher brews. It was developed in early 18th century London. Credit for its creation traditionally rests with Ralph Harwood, a pub-brewer in the eastern London region of Shoreditch.

ESTER

A flavor compound, also usually aromatic, that frequently is created by yeast as by-product during warm (ale) fermentation. Most esters are 'fruity' – reminiscent of bananas, apples, pineapples, etc. They help give ales their characteristic complexity and fullness of flavor.

FARO

A lambic sweetened with sugar (usually Belgian candi sugar), occasionally for the purpose of starting a secondary fermentation in the bottle or cask. Faro developed from lambic brewers' attempts to create more 'drinkable' versions of their sour beers. Towards this end, spices sometimes also were used in addition to, or in place of, sugar. Today's best-known Belgian example, Frank Boon's Pertotale, is both sweetened with sugar and spiced with Curaçao and gentian. Critical opinion divides on this curious style.

FERMENTATION

The process in which yeast cells feed on sugar, converting it into alcohol and carbon dioxide. In brewing terms, 'primary' fermentation refers to the initial period of conversion, when yeasts hungrily work their way through sugars in the wort: this can last as long as seven days for an ale, up to twice that for a lager. A 'secondary' fermentation, or refermentation, denotes a subsequent – and generally much less significant – stage of activity when yeast cells consume any residual sugars (sometimes added by brewers for just such a purpose).

FERMENTER

Vessel in which fermentation occurs, ranging from a homebrewer's plastic bucket to a megabrewery's 500+ barrel, sealed, stainless-steel tank. A fermentation vessel that is not totally sealed (like the topless square or circular vessels traditionally used to produce English-style ales) can be called an 'open fermenter.' Many modern breweries have replaced dedicated fermenters with conical vessels known as unitanks, in which fermentation is followed directly by maturation – as opposed to maturing the beer in a separate tank. Whether beer (particularly ale) ferments 'better' in open or closed vessels, in conicals or unitanks, remains a subject of some debate.

FESTBIER

German term for a special brew, frequently made for some kind of event (a 'fest'). Festbiers usually have a fuller flavor, higher strength (5.5-6%), and sometimes deeper color (rich golden to red-bronze) than a brewery's standard offering. Specialty brewers in America occasionally offer examples in this broad style, but most are made in Germany. Toward the upper end of their colors and potency, festbiers share territory with Oktoberfest/Märzen brews – perhaps the earliest organized 'special event' beers.

Above: Carved hops decorate the facade of Toner's, a traditional Dublin pub.

FILTRATION

Clarifying a beer by passing it through one of several varieties of filtering devices. Filtration also can improve beer's shelf-life and stability. Filters with extremely tiny openings actually will remove all yeast and any bacteria (always rare) from a brew – hence the phrase 'sterile filtration' (sometimes billed in marketing lingo as 'cold filtration' because the beer is kept cool during the process). Most brewers believe that sterile filtration affects flavor less notably than heat pasteurization. Nonetheless, many small brewers feel that sterile filtration also strips beer of flavor and color (compounds responsible for both are too big to pass through the tight filters).

FINING

Clarifying a beer by adding a substance that attracts particulate matter such as yeast and encourages it to settle out. Such a substance, or substances, are called 'finings.' The classic fining agent is an all-natural gelatinous material made from the swim bladders of fish (sturgeon is common). This substance, also known as isinglass, naturally holds an

electric charge opposite to that of yeast and other brewing leftovers: it attracts them together, forming bigger 'globs' that settle to the bottom of a beer's tank or container. Secondary fining agents, with an opposite charge, sometimes also are employed. British brewers traditionally rely on finings to clarify their cask-conditioned ales. Followers of the Reinheitsgebot, on the other hand, consider finings an illegal beer additive.

FINISH

Tasting term – usually modified with descriptors such as 'lingering,' 'short,' 'bitter,' 'sweet,' 'malty,' 'dry,' etc. – for the perceived body and flavor of a beer after the drinker has swallowed it. Also known as 'aftertaste.' This is a natural and desired component of a beer's character.

FLEMISH BROWN ALE

The sour variety of 'old brown' ale traditionally brewed in eastern Flanders, Belgium. See 'Brown Ale.'

FOREIGN STOUT

Rich, strong (7-9%) stout variety found throughout Caribbean, Asian, and Pacific regions. Like 'Imperial stouts' (see entry), these hearty brews are derived from potent stouts exported around the globe by British (and Irish) brewers: in fact, most of the countries where 'foreign stouts' are popular once belonged to the British Empire.

Foreign stouts tend to be more winey – a faint sourness is refreshing in hotter climates – and perhaps less complex (many

are fermented with lager yeasts) than classic Imperial stouts. Examples include the deep, deliberately-soured Guinness Foreign Extra Stout, Sri Lanka's bottle-conditioned Lion Stout, and New Guinea's phonetic Niugini Gold Extra Stout.

FRAMBOISE/FRAMBOZEN

French and Flemish words, respectively, for 'raspberry.' Denotes a raspberry or raspberry-flavored 'fruit beer' (see entry), generally of a Belgian variety (frequently lambic-based). Belgium's famous examples include Liefmans Frambozen, Boon's Mariage Parfait Framboise, and Lindemans Framboise. While many microbrewers in other countries make raspberry fruit beers, only a few name them with the traditional terms.

FRANCE

Like many of its European neighbors, France has joined the beer renaissance. Then again, despite the country's fascination with wine, beer has always played an important role in French culture – the popular restaurants called 'brasseries' actually take their name from yesteryear's small brewery-pubs.

French beer divides broadly into two camps: German-influenced brewers in Alsace-Lorraine make moderately flavorful golden lager beers; the northern farming region called 'French Flanders' offers characterful bières de garde (see entry), traditionally ales. But even the large Alsatian brewers are embracing specialties. Their tasty 'brune' lagers (see entry) are becoming more popular, and

they have revived once-traditional seasonal beers – bières de Noël for Christmas, for example, and bières de Mars (March) for spring. The French also seem to have a small fascination with whiskey-malt 'Scottish' beers.

FRUIT BEER

Beer refermented with, or flavored with, fruit. A specialty of Belgian lambic brewers, who began adding fruit to their beers in an effort to round out the rough flavors produced by wild fermentation. Fresh raspberries or Belgium's native sour cherries – a few lambic producers have switched to fruit juice or sweeter syrups – traditionally are placed into oak casks of maturing lambic, where their sugars spark a refermentation. They also color the base lambic, aromatize it, and impart varying degrees of fruit flavor.

Inspired by this process, a few specialty brewers in other countries now offer beers flavored with real fruit. Most, however, rely on fruit concentrates or extracts; raspberry and blackberry are perhaps the most popular. In either case, the brews tend to be based on clean-tasting wheat beers (although a small number, as in Belgium, are made from brown ales and other beers). Fruit beers are increasingly popular in North America.

Above: Stirring in the hops at San Francisco's famous Anchor Brewing Co.

GERMANY

The world's top beer country, not in terms of production but rather in the number of breweries (around 1,400, with half in Bavaria) and the highly-held place of beer in German culture. Germans are among the biggest beer drinkers, per capita, in the world. Perhaps they are celebrating their country's crucial role in the development and promotion of lager (which today is the national beer 'style').

Germany's brewers conform to regional tastes: the northern areas produce dry, hoppy Pilsners; Berlin has its tart weisse beers, while the eastern regions retain pitch-black schwarzbier; Bavaria offers popular weizenbiers, many lager styles (from dunkel to doppelbock), and specialties such as rauchbier; to the west, Cologne's Kölsch and Düsseldorf's altbier keep ale alive. This regional orientation has helped slow the rise of truly national breweries and megabrands – a situation that shows signs of ending as modern competition (and falling consumption) puts long-established small brewers out to pasture.

GOLDEN ALE

Any ale approximating the golden color of a Pilsner or other 'standard' pale lager. Most styles (Kölsch, cream ale, etc.) that fit this description were developed by ale-brewers as a way to compete in a world increasingly embracing lager beers. Today, many specialty brewers offer a golden ale as an introductory or 'training wheels' beer (designed to appeal to drinkers used to mass-market brands). While most deliberately are mild, others can be much more flavorful – usually through the generous use of hops. The best achieve a subtle complexity by blending an ale's fruitiness with a soft, rounded malt character and balancing hop flavor.

GRIST

Term for grain that has been crushed in a mill, prior to mixing with hot water to form a 'mash' (see entry). More generally, the term denotes the grain ingredients of a given brew (sometimes alternatively called the 'grain bill').

GUEUZE

A sparkling, blended 'lambic' (see entry), usually packaged in a corked Champagne-style bottle. To make gueuze, a brewer blends a portion of old, well-matured lambic with a younger lambic (which has not fermented fully). Residual sugars in the young version spark a refermentation, creating a lively bottle-conditioned brew. Most gueuzes are moderate in strength (5-5.5%).

HAND PUMP

A manually-operated pump, usually mounted on a bar, used to draw beer from its container (usually a cask or keg). Also known as a 'beer engine.'

HEAT EXCHANGER

Water-cooled, radiator-type device used to chill wort (before fermentation) after it has been boiled in the brew kettle. Modern heat exchangers are totally sealed, allowing the wort to cool in a sterile, oxygen-free environment. The water, which absorbs the wort's heat, is frequently used to start the next mash.

HEFE

German for 'yeast' (pronounced 'hay-fuh'). When applied to a beer's name, it implies that the brew contains unfiltered yeast. The classic examples are hefeweizens, unfiltered wheat beers like those popular throughout Bavaria. Also sometimes appears as the phrase *mit hefe* ('with yeast').

HEFEWEIZEN

German for 'yeast-wheat' (pronounced 'Hay-fuh-vy-'tzen'), denoting an unfiltered wheat beer. Although the style has been adopted by specialty brewers around the world, hefeweizen's homeland is Bavaria, where examples today account for around 30 percent of the beer market. This popularity comes after a dramatic mid-century decline, when the centuries-old style was viewed as 'old fashioned.'

To qualify as hefeweizen under Bavarian law, at least 50 percent of a beer's grist must be malted wheat; the rest is barley malt. Bavarian hefeweizens traditionally ferment with special ale yeasts that give them a fruity 'bananas and bubble-gum' character. Bottle-conditioning imparts a powerful effervescence to classic examples, although in recent years major producers have begun re-seeding pasteurized

beer with lager yeast (to enhance stability). Brewers in America's Pacific northwest have made a successful specialty of 'hefeweizens' fermented with standard ale or lager yeasts. These lack the complexity of Bavarian examples.

HELL(ES)

Nothing infernal about this term, which is German for 'pale.' It usually refers to the golden lager style introduced by Munich brewers around the turn of the century to compete with Bohemia's Pilsners. Helles lagers tend to be paler in color and slightly lower in strength (4.5-5%) than Pilsners. They also are more malty (less hoppy) and 'softer' in character – although a handful of brewers to Munich's north and west offer notably hoppy, dry examples. Today, despite the encroaching popularity of Pilsners, helles lagers remain the everyday beers of Munich. In other Germanic-language regions (Scandinavia, Austria, etc.), the word 'hell' most frequently is used in a generic fashion to signify a golden-colored brew.

HELLES BOCK

A pale variety of bock, usually golden to amber in color.

HERB/SPICE BEER

Any beer flavored with herbs or spices in addition to, or occasionally instead of, hops. Many medieval beers were so flavored, especially in Britain (where hops were not widely used by brewers until the 16th century). Today, small Belgian brewers remain the chief producers of herb and/or spice beers: popular seasonings include coriander seed and dried orange peel, while more exotic ingredients range from anise to medicinal lichens. Specialty brewers in other countries sometimes offer beers that have been seasoned with herbs or spices – these appear most frequently as higher-strength

'winter warmers.' In America, additionally, there is a fad for chili-pepper beers.

HONEY BEER

Beer either fermented or flavored with honey. Probably because it offers a natural source of fermentable sugar, honey long has been used as a supplementary ingredient in beer. Its resurgence as part of the specialty beer renaissance reflects both its historic brewing role and its 'wholesome' connotations in the minds of consumers. Small brewers across the world now offer everything from honey porters to unfiltered honey-wheat beers. In most cases, honey is added prior to fermentation, imparting a faint residual sweetness and slight honey flavor to the finished brew.

HOP BACK

A traditional brewing vessel used to separate wort from spent hop flowers after the boil. It has been replaced by a whirlpool in modern breweries that use hop pellets. Many traditional British breweries still employ hop backs.

HOP PELLETS

Made by pulverizing whole hop blossoms and extruding the results as small, thin pellets (held together by the hops' naturally sticky lupulin). Because less of their surface area is exposed to air – and because they frequently are vacuum packed – hop pellets oxidize (go 'off') less quickly than whole hops. Many modern brewers prefer them for this reason. Others feel that pellets impart a tannic character to beer.

HOPS

Flowers – frequently called 'blossoms' or 'cones' – of a climbing vine (*Humulus lupulus*) that give beer its bitter flavors and herbal aromas. Hop vines are perennials: they are cut down to ground level during each fall's harvest, and grow back the following spring to heights of up to 18ft (5.5m) (supported by a network of twine, wires, and poles). Their roots, in addition to extending more than 10ft (3m) below ground, stretch back into ancient history – the Romans wrote about hops, for example.

Modern brewers use the female hop plant's seedless blossoms, which store a complex resinous substance called lupulin in glands at the base of their petals. Lupulin contains both aromatic oils, noticeable in beers that have been dry-hopped, and 'alpha acids.' The latter are compounds that impart bitterness to beer and also help preserve it (they have anti-bacterial properties). Just like grapes, different varieties of hops have different flavor and aroma characteristics.

IMPERIAL (RUSSIAN) STOUT

Extra-hearty, extremely potent (7-12%) variety of stout. British brewers developed the style during the late 18th century for export to northern Europe and the Baltic regions. After donating 5,000 bottles to Russian hospitals, one famous shipper received an Imperial warrant from that country's Empress. Similar beers subsequently became known as 'Imperial' stouts (the originally-warranted version, called Imperial Russian Stout, still is produced by Britain's Scottish Courage group).

The style has remained a specialty in Baltic and Scandinavian countries, where it frequently is sold under the more pedestrian name 'porter.' Examples have been re-popularized by the beer renaissance, and brewers in several countries now make versions. The best are true ales (some of the 'porters' ferment with lager yeast) that blend a rich 'burnt' fruit character with dark malt depth and alcoholic warmth. Also see 'Foreign Stout.'

IPA (India Pale Ale)

Highly hopped, above-average strength (5.5%-7.5%) pale ale style that was popularized during the early 19th century by British brewers for export to India. Generous hopping made the beers particularly refreshing in warmer climates, and also helped protect them from spoilage during shipping (as did their higher alcohol content). IPAs soon caught on in their homeland and other export regions such as North America.

Over time, however, beers in the style (including America's famous Ballantine IPA) progressively declined in character and strength. Several British breweries today offer tame 'IPAs' that, well, pale in comparison with the original brews. Thankfully, the beer renaissance has prompted specialty brewers to reintroduce India pale ales made to 'historic' specifications. North America's small brewers, for example, have pioneered robust, powerful IPAs brewed with their continent's citric hop varieties.

Infusion

Mashing technique preferred by classic ale brewers (in Britain, America, Canada, Australia, etc.). In a similar process to brewing tea, crushed grain is steeped in hot water at a constant temperature. (Sometimes, in a process called 'step infusion,' the temperature will be raised at given intervals). Many brewers believe infusion mashing helps create a fuller-bodied beer than the 'decoction' technique (see entry).

Irish Ale

Vague style denoting a malt-accented ale, usually with a copper-reddish hue and 'soft' character. The color comes from the Irish practice, notable in the country's stouts, of brewing with a portion of roasted barley. The mellow malty character of Irish ales reflects Ireland's cool climate, which is more suited to growing grain than hops.

Guinness owns three Irish breweries (Cherry's, Macardle, and export-oriented Smithwick's) that all make beers which fit the profile. Ireland's now-defunct Killian brewery has licensed its name to 'red' beers, broadly in the Irish style, brewed by Coors (for America) and Heineken (for France and the Netherlands, under the spelling Kylian). Specialty brewers in both North America and Britain are helping to preserve the style's more characterful extremes.

Japan

The fact that Japanese brewers focus almost exclusively on lagers can be attributed to the influence of Germans, who helped found the modern Japanese brewing industry. Although their emphasis on Pilsner styles is apparent in export markets, the Japanese brewers also have maintained hard-to-find specialties. Each of Japan's four megabrewers (Asahi, Kirin, Sapporo, Suntory) offers 'black beer,' for example, a variety of dark lager stylistically related to eastern Germany's schwarzbiers. Kirin, Sapporo, and Suntory also offer foreign-strength stouts, and all have experimented with the likes of altbiers and wheat beers. Japan recently legalized microbrewing, giving rise to a growing number of small producers.

Juniper

An evergreen of the pine family, with tangy-flavored berries. Juniper branches (formed into a rough filter) and berries (for flavor) commonly were used in brewing the traditional rustic beers of northern Europe, particularly Scandinavia.
See 'Sahti.'

Keg

A metal (usually aluminum) beer container designed for gas-pressure dispense. See 'Barrel.'

Keg Conditioning

Term used by American specialty brewers to denote beer (usually ale) in a keg, as opposed to a cask, that undergoes a process otherwise similar to 'cask conditioning' (see entry).

Kellerbier

German for 'cellar beer,' denoting an amber-red lager

Above: Hop heritage. This museum in Toppenish, Washington, traces the history of hops in the Pacific northwest.

style peculiar to the Franconia area of northern Bavaria in Germany. Although fermented with lager yeast, kellerbier (4.5-5%) is rather aleish in character. Its method of maturation – a relatively short six-week period of conditioning, sometimes involving the venting of natural carbon dioxide – creates a low level of carbonation similar to that of a cask-conditioned ale.

In addition, kellerbier traditionally is unfiltered and heavily hopped. To maintain its mellow, soft-bodied character, kellerbier frequently is racked into wooden casks and – in another similarity to cask-conditioned ales – served by gravity dispense. Classic examples come from two breweries south of Bamberg, St Georgen and Löwenbräu.

Above: Anchor's away! From Steam Beer to barley wine, every pitcher tells a story.

KÖLSCH

Pale golden ale style (4.6–5%) that is a regional specialty around the city of Cologne (Köln), Germany. To combat the rise of Pilsner-style lagers, Cologne's long-time ale brewers introduced Kölschbier: made from pale Pilsner malts (and sometimes a portion of wheat), fermented with single-strain ale yeast, and cold-conditioned for extended periods like lager. The best examples are fairly dry but 'soft' in body, with subtle ale fruitiness and notable herbal hop character.

According to German law, beer brewed outside Köln cannot be labelled as Kölsch (with a few exceptions). Top German examples come from Früh, Malzmühle, and the Päffgen brewpub.

Before the rise of Kölschbier, Cologne was famous for unfiltered pale ales known as wiess (a local variant of the German weiss, or 'white'). In recent years, a few brewers have reintroduced this 'sub-style.'

KRÄUSENING

German-favored technique of sparking a secondary fermentation (to generate natural carbonation) by adding a small amount of partially- (or un) fermented wort to beer. While this typically occurs in the maturation tank prior to filtration and packaging, some beers are 'kräusened' in casks, kegs, or bottles.

KRIEK

Flemish for 'cherry.' Denotes a cherry or cherry-flavored 'fruit beer' (see entry), generally the lambic-based Belgian variety. Belgium's famous examples include the sweet Boon Kriek, syrupy Lindemans Kriek, and tart, complex Liefmans Kriek (actually based on a sour brown ale). Several specialty brewers in other countries make cherry fruit beers, but only a few name them with this traditional term.

KRUIDENBIER

Flemish (Belgian) term, sometimes used in the Netherlands, for a beer seasoned with herbs or spices.
See 'Herb/ Spice Beer.'

LAGER

Any beer fermented with yeast that 'works' at relatively low temperatures (approximately 40–50°F, 4–10°C). Such cool temperatures discourage both yeast activity, creating fairly lengthy fermentations, and the production of ale-like aromatic and/or flavor compounds. As a result, most lagers undergo long production cycles that include extended periods of cold-maturation (sometimes up to a year!), emerging with clean-tasting flavors and a 'rounded' character.

Lager beers were developed by Bavarian brewers, who empirically discovered that storing their brews in cool caves – the word *lager* actually derives from the German verb meaning 'to store' – produced a more consistent product. Credit for the first modern lager, designed with an understanding of the process, rests with Munich's Spaten brewery. Most of the world's mainstream beers fit the 'lager' category, as do Pilsners, schwarzbiers, bocks, Dortmund's 'Export' styles, and Vienna-style ambers.

LAGER (VERB)

To subject a beer to a period of cold maturation. Such a brew is said to be 'lagered.' The period of cold maturation can be called 'lagering.' Confusingly, the beer so treated need not be a lager.

LAMBIC

Centuries-old Belgian beer style, brewed with a significant amount of unmalted wheat, that is spontaneously fermented with airborne 'wild' ale yeasts and traditionally matured (usually up to five years) in unlined wooden barrels. The resulting tart, sour brew (around 5%) seems more like farmyard cider than standard beer. Lambic is local to Belgium's 'Senne Valley' (see entry) and probably takes its name from the regional brewing town of Lembeek. Brews spontaneously fermented elsewhere should not be called 'lambic.'

Lambics most often are blended to make gueuze (see entry) or refermented with fruit such as cherries or raspberries. Only rarely are they served 'straight.' Classic producers include Belgium's Frank Boon, Lindemans, Cantillon, Girardin, Vandervelden, and Belle Vue (Vandenstock).

LATE HOPPING

Adding unused hops to wort in either the whirlpool or hop back, in order to impart extra hop aromas to the finished beer.

LAUTER TUN

A brewing vessel designed to separate the wort from 'spent' grain after the mash (*läutern* means 'to clarify' in German). Lauter tuns typically are have 'false' slotted bottoms that allow liquid to drain through while keeping grain behind. They also usually possess a system of rotating metal 'rakes' that stir the grain, enhancing the sparging process and encouraging drainage.

LIGHT BEER/ALE

Traditional British term for low-strength ale (3–4%), the bottled counterpart of standard draft 'bitter.' Today, describing a beer as light (or 'lite') more frequently denotes a low-calorie brew – especially in America, and certainly whenever the beer in question is a lager.

MAIBOCK

German for 'May bock,' a bock variety brewed to celebrate springtime. Most Maibocks are designed to look and taste 'fresh.' They generally are deep golden to amber in color, with a moderate bock strength (6.5-7%). They also tend to have a lightly fruity character from relatively short lagering times (especially compared to standard bocks). Along with their seasonal availability, usually from March to May, this shortened maturation separates them from pale (helles) bocks.

Many German breweries, including Munich's Hofbräuhaus and Einbeck's Einbecker Brauhaus, offer popular examples. The style has been embraced by lager brewers in several other countries, including the Netherlands (see 'Bok' above). A handful of North American specialty brewers produce 'ale bocks' (see entry) in the style.

MALT

Any cereal grain that has been partially germinated and then dried by heat to a 'toasty' consistency. Barley, wheat, and other grains are malted as follows: grain is soaked in water until it begins to sprout, starting a natural enzyme reaction that will turn its starch into sugar. Germination and the reaction are halted by drying the grain, usually with hot air. Depending on the level and duration of heat applied, the grain will take on anything from a pale to deep-amber color. Darker 'roasted malts' also can be made. Mixing malt with hot water to create a 'mash' reactivates the starch-to-sugar reaction that began during germination.

MALT LIQUOR

American term for extra-strong beer (5.5-7.5%), usually lager, meant to serve as a 'cheap high' (frequently brewed with a high percentage of adjuncts). Strange post-Prohibition laws in some American states require any high-strength beer – whether it is a robust barley wine or rich doppelbock – to be labelled a malt liquor.

MÄRZEN/OKTOBERFEST

Malty, reddish-brown, hearty lager style (5.5-6%). The best examples balance rich malty sweetness with nutty, toasty flavors from the specially-roasted malts used to brew them. Many Bavarian breweries (Paulaner, Hofbräu, Spaten, etc.) offer versions, although the beer itself is less popular than in previous years. The style also is popular with lager breweries (particularly micros) in other countries.

März is German for 'March' – a reference to the last month, in the days before commercial refrigeration, before hot summer temperatures made fermentation impossible. This was the time when German brewers made a robust final beer that was stored in cool caves and consumed as needed over the summer. Any remaining beer was drained at a festival in the fall, when cooler weather allowed brewing to resume. Such beers naturally were the ones served at the first institutionalized Oktoberfest. Brewers today typically label year-round examples of the style as Märzen, and seasonal specialties as Oktoberfest (see entries).

MASH (TUN)

The mixture of hot water (around 150°F, 66°C) and grain that starts the brewing process. A 'mash tun' (or mash cooker) is the vessel where these materials mix and steep. The 'mashing' process converts the grains' starch into sugars which are absorbed into the water, creating a sugary liquid called 'wort.' The wort also picks up color and character (flavor, aroma) from the grains. Overall, mashing generally lasts one to two hours.

MEXICO

Like many Latin and Central American countries, Mexico maintains a low-level tradition of 'aleish' brews such as pulque (fermented agave plant juice) and chicha (indigenous, unhopped corn-based beer). Its modern brewing industry, however, is devoted wholly to German-style lagers – testimony to the fact that Mexicans did not really embrace European-style beers until the advent of commercial refrigeration, which went hand-in-hand with lager production, during the mid-19th century.

Most modern Mexican beers are pale Pilsner-style brews, sometimes made with high proportion of adjuncts (rice, corn, etc.). Nevertheless, the country's brewers also have preserved a handful of amber and darker-colored lagers that fall broadly between the Vienna and dunkel styles. Dos Equis (from the Moctezuma brewing group) exemplifies the former, while Negra Modelo (from the Modelo group) is closer to the latter. Special Christmas-time lagers occasionally are produced.

MICROBREWERY

A relatively small brewery (compared to regional, national, or international companies). Also sometimes known as a 'boutique' or 'cottage' brewery. America's Association of Brewers has defined 'microbrewery' as a facility producing fewer than 15,000 US barrels (10,750 UK barrels, 17,600hl) of beer per year. In general, microbreweries produce beers across a broad range of historic and/or innovative styles using only natural ingredients (barley malt, specialty grains, water, yeast, hops, etc.). The modern microbrewery movement arose over the last 25 years as a response to the limited choice of beers and beer styles offered by larger producers.

MILD ALE

Lightly hopped, malt-accented British ale style, almost always with a relatively low strength (3-3.5%). Usually ruby to brown in color, although a few pale examples are made. Unfermented sugars give most milds extra body to compensate for their lack of alcoholic heft (specialty malts also give darker versions extra flavor). Examples are mainly brewed in Britain (Highgate, Banks', etc.), although specialty ale brewers elsewhere occasionally offer milds.

The style's name initially referred only to its low hopping compared to pale ales and porters. (In fact, mild ales were one of the original varieties of beer blended to make early porters). Milds' strength fell over time as they became increasingly popular as a refresher among Britain's laboring class – particularly miners in England and Wales. Mild itself fell from favor during the last two decades after acquiring an 'old fashioned'

Above: 3.30pm in Ryan's pub in Dublin, but pints of beer are the preferred teatime drink!

blue-collar image. Nevertheless, modern concern about alcohol consumption has helped renew interest in the style.

MILK STOUT

see 'Sweet Stout.'
German for 'from/of Munich.' Across the brewing world, the term signifies a dark lager of the variety first developed in Munich during the 19th century. In Bavaria, such beers are identified with the word 'dunkel' (see entry) to distinguish them from the city's pale helles lagers.

MUNICH

see 'Bavaria.'

MUNICH MALT

Highly-kilned malt that imparts a rich pumpkin-orange color (and corresponding toasty, caramel-ish character) to beer, named after its traditional use in Munich's dunkel lagers.

NETHERLANDS, THE

Western European country best known as the home of international brewers such as Heineken and Grolsch. Although the country's beer scene remains dominated by these large companies and their Pilsner-style brews, the past two decades have seen a significant surge of microbreweries and specialty beers.

Many of the new Dutch brewers, inspired by their Belgian neighbors, offer witbiers and abbey-style ales. On the other hand, the beer renaissance also has resurrected traditional Dutch styles such as German-inspired 'bok' beers. Today, even Heineken offers domestic specialties such as a wheat bock,

stout, and Vienna-style lager. A few of the most characterful Dutch beers, including the La Trappe family of ales (brewed at the only Trappist monastery outside of Belgium) and St Christoffel's hoppy Pilsner, are gaining a positive international reputation.

NEW ZEALAND

As with Australia, British settlers brought modern brewing to New Zealand. And just like its neighbor, New Zealand today has abandoned British ales for mainly pale Pilsner-style lagers. (In fact, its main Lion Nathan brewing group now owns Australia's Castlemaine, Swan/Emu, and Toohey's brands in addition to its own Steinlager). The country has preserved a tradition of slightly more colorful beers, including 'browns' – sweetish, fuller-bodied lagers brewed with darker malts and sometimes fermented at 'ale' temperatures.

A handful of micros and brewpubs also has sprung up in recent years. Although many offer beers not so far removed from the mainstream, they slowly are increasing awareness of specialty brews. Like Australia's Tasmania (which grows the country's 'Pride of Ringwood' hops), parts of New Zealand are good hop-growing regions: 'Green Bullet' is the main bittering variety.

'NEAR BEER'

Generic term for extremely low-alcohol beers (0.5% or less) produced largely during Prohibition in North America.

NITROGEN

Elemental gas increasingly used in addition to, or in place of, carbon dioxide to create 'fizz' in beer and to dispense it. Because nitrogen dissolves into smaller, finer bubbles than carbon dioxide, it creates a smoother-tasting beer whose mouthfeel seems more 'draft-like.' It also generates a seething 'cascade' effect when the beer is poured. Mixed CO_2-nitrogen dispense (commonly known as 'mixed gas') was popularized by Guinness. Guinness also took the lead in developing the nitrogenated 'draft-in-a-can' beers (Pub Draught, Draughtflow, etc.) that are becoming standard among most British breweries.

OATMEAL STOUT

A stout, usually sweetish in character, brewed from a portion of oatmeal (rolled oats) in addition to standard ingredients. Oatmeal imparts a notably smooth, sometimes even 'oily' character to the black brew (and most other beers in which it is used). The style developed in Britain during the early 20th century as

an offshoot of sweet stouts (see entry) promoted for their health-giving, 'nutritious' value. But it had died out completely by 1980, at which time Britain's independent Samuel Smith Brewery reintroduced an example at the request of American beer importer Charles Finkel. Several other British brewers (Maclay, Young's, Broughton) today make beers in the style, frequently inspired by old recipes. Many North American specialty brewers (California's Anderson Valley, Oregon's Rogue Ales, Montreal's McAuslan) also have adopted the style.

OKTOBERFEST (EVENT)

The world's biggest (in size, not in variety of beers available), bawdiest beer festival, held annually in Munich, Germany. Despite its name, the festival takes place over two weeks in September, always ending on the first Sunday in October. Although predated by rural harvest festivals, the Oktoberfest originated in 1810 as a celebration of the marriage of Bavaria's Crown Prince. It is still held on the same city-center site today. Its 14 wood-and-canvas beer halls – which house almost 100,000 people, along with a giant 'fun fair' – sprawl over an area the size of 50 football (soccer) fields. The Oktoberfest attracts around 6,000,000 visitors who drink more than 10,000,000 pints of beer (all produced by the city's six largest breweries) and eat 830,000 sausages, 750,000 chickens, 65,000 pork knuckles, and 50-60 whole oxen. Outside Bavaria, 'Oktoberfest' generally

denotes any fall-themed event where beer is a focus.

OKTOBERFEST (BEER)

Term traditionally used – along with 'Märzen' (see entry) – to describe a reddish-copper lager (5-6%) with a predominantly malty, nutty, sweetish flavor and perhaps a spicy German hop character. The style evolved from the copper-colored 'Vienna lagers' (see entry) created in Vienna by Anton Dreher. Impressed with Dreher's brews, Josef Sedlmayr of Munich's Spaten Brauerei introduced a robust example at the 1871 Oktoberfest (in place of the traditional old-style Märzenbier) that became the festival's favored beer.

Today, unfortunately, Munich's brewers tend to produce 'Oktoberfests' that are paler and thinner-tasting than classic examples. Paulaner's export version is perhaps the most traditional. The style has found new favor among specialty brewers in America and other countries. A handful of ale-making micros in the United States, such as Oregon's Portland Brewing, even offer interpretations that approximate the style's spicy maltiness.

OLD ALE

Not related to 'Altbier.' In Australia, the term (common throughout Sydney and New South Wales) describes a dark beer, usually an ale. Examples come from Toohey's (Old Black) and Tooth (Kent Old Brown). The British use the term to describe a variety of red-brown brews: it generally designates a darkish, sweetish,

top-fermented ale of above average strength (5.5-8.5%) – Theakston's Old Peculier, Marston's Owd Roger, Robinson's Old Tom, etc..

The term may derive from brewers' traditional practice of maturing strong brews for lengthy periods (perhaps as stocks for the summer, when warm temperatures made brewing impossible). Britain's Greene King still produces a beer in this fashion, maturing it up to five years in oak tuns. Gale's of Hampshire, England, similarly ages its Prize Old Ale for six months to a year.

ORGANIC BEER

Beer brewed from organically-grown (i.e., free of chemicals and other artificial agents) materials, usually with a certification from one of several 'organic' organizations. The greatest difficulty, apparently, comes in finding organic hops, which enjoy neither the availability nor the character of traditional varieties. Popular examples include Golden Promise ale (named for the barley variety) from Scotland's Caledonian Brewery, and Pinkus Spezial lager from German's Pinkus Müller.

ORIGINAL GRAVITY (OG)

The 'original' (before fermentation) specific gravity of a beer, measuring its density compared to that of pure water (1.000, or 1000 on the British scale). The higher a beer's original gravity, the greater the amount of fermentable material it initially contains – and thus the higher the potential alcoholic strength of the finished brew. The final two figures of an 'OG' reading correspond roughly to an alcohol-by-volume figure: for example, OG 1055 approximates 5.5% ABV. This relationship is not as direct at higher original gravities.

Comparing a beer's original gravity to its finished alcohol content can help determine how much fermentable material has been converted to alcohol (and thus the brew's 'sweetness' or 'dryness'). A stout with OG 1064 but finished alcohol of 5.6% by volume, for instance, should be slightly sweet because not all of the potential fermentables (1064) have been converted to alcohol (5.6%).

OYSTER STOUT

Literally, a stout made ('enriched') with oysters or the essence thereof. Much like 'oatmeal stout,' this style became popular in Britain during the mid-20th century, when brewers emphasized the nutritious aspects of stout. (At a much earlier date, speculates beer-writer Michael Jackson, ground oyster shells may have been used as finings to clarify beer). One of the best-known examples came from the Isle of Man's Castletown Brewery; the island's small Bushy Brewery has toyed with producing a version.

In 1996, Britain's large Whitbread brewing group introduced an oyster-ized stout in connection with Ireland's Murphy's. Several years earlier, America's creative Pike Place Brewery (now Pike Brewing) concocted a version of their roasty regular stout wherein one-sixth of the brewing water was replaced by the salty liquid found inside oyster shells. Homebrewers also seem to enjoy experimenting with the style.

PALE ALE

Originally a term describing the hoppy, copper-red ales made popular by the brewers in Burton-on-Trent, England, during the 1800s. These beers were 'pale' compared to the dark porters and stouts that were the period's standard brews. As the style developed, and was toned down from its 'India Pale Ale' extremes (see entry), 'Pale Ale' became the term applied to bottled versions of beer known on draft as 'bitter.' Nowadays the term is applied around the world to beers in a broad range

of 'pale' colors and strengths (generally 3.5-6%).

Classic British pale ales still come from three Burton brewers – Bass, Marston's, and Ind Coope/Carlsberg Tetley – but versions now are made by almost every English brewery. Belgian and Belgian-style pale ales (Palm, De Koninck, etc.) tend to be more malt-accented and spicy-fruity, thanks to complex yeasts, than British versions. In North America, eastern breweries generally offer pale ales that approach the British profile, while west coast American micros have developed truly pale ales (brewed with light-colored malts) that burst with citric hop character.

PALE (ALE) MALT

Lightly-toasted variety of malt with, as its name implies, a pale color – although not so pale as Pilsner malt. It provides the majority of fermentable material for most ales.

PASTEURIZATION

Sterilizing a liquid by heating it

to a temperature (140-180°F, 60-82°C) that destroys objectionable organisms (bacteria, etc.) without substantially altering the liquid itself. The process is named after French scientist Louis Pasteur, who researched beer spoilage at London's Whitbread brewery during the late 19th century.

In brewing, the standard practice involves slowly heating bottles of beer to the desired temperature over an extended period (say, 20 to 30 minutes). In 'flash pasteurization,' beer is rapidly raised to this temperature by running it through a heated pipe before bottling or kegging. Some brewers feel that flash pasteurization imparts less of a 'cooked' character to beer.

Brewers originally embraced pasteurization as a means of giving their products extra stability. Most modern craft-brewers believe that any kind of pasteurization negatively affects a beer's flavor (and perceived 'freshness') – as do the larger brewers who have switched to sterile filtration.

Above: If 'Guinness is good for you,' this bar could carry a doctor's endorsement!

PILS(E)NER

Golden lager style named after the place in which it first was brewed (in 1842): the city of Pilsen (Plzeň) in 'Bohemia' (see entry). A beer from Pilsen was a 'Pilsner' in the same way that examples from the rival brewing city of Budweis became known as 'Budweisers.' The style quickly proved popular throughout Europe, both because of its sparkling clarity – until this time, thanks to more primitive malting technologies, all European beers were darker in color – and its refreshing, well-hopped character. Almost every modern mainstream golden lager is a derivative of this style.

Bohemian Pilsners are moderate in strength (around 5%) with a soft, malty body, an herbal/flowery aroma (from traditional hop varieties like Saaz), and a hoppy finish. Classic examples in this style include the Czech Pilsner Urquell and its neighbor Gambrinus. Pilsners brewed in northern Germany tend to be extremely dry and hoppy, while Bavaria's southern examples are more malty. Elsewhere, small specialty brewers are helping to revitalize a style that has become the world's most widely-copied beer variety.

PILSNER MALT

Extremely pale variety of malt of the type used to brew golden Pilsner beers. Sometimes used by ale brewers who want to create a notably pale-colored beer. Technological advances that allowed the production of extremely pale malts in turn allowed the introduction of Pilsner beers in 1842.

PLATO

A scale favored by lager brewers around the world for measuring the amount of fermentable material in wort. Named for Dr. Fritz Plato, who refined it from Bohemia's 'Balling scale' (see entry) for use in Germany. As with figures in Balling, multiplying a beer's Plato rating by four provides an approximation of the last two digits of the beer's 'original gravity.' Thus, a beer listed as 16 degrees Plato would approximate an original gravity of 1064 – or approximately 6.4% alcohol by volume.

PORTER

Dark ale style that was Britain's first beer variety to be produced and distributed on a commercial level. Originally known as 'entire,' its rise coincided with the 18th-century Industrial Revolution, when it proved popular with manual laborers – including many working porters (it probably was named after these highly visible customers). Early porter brewers matured their beers in huge wooden vats: the vatted red and 'old brown' ales of Flanders may be modern vestiges of this tradition. Extra strong porters originally were called 'stout porters,' and, over time, stouts eclipsed the original style to the point where porter wholly disappeared (excepting northern Europe's Imperial-style versions).

Porter was resurrected during the last two decades by new-wave specialty brewers in both North America and Britain. Today's porters (which, excepting Imperial examples, generally range from 4.5-5.5%) tend to fall into two categories: hoppy, dry 'robust' porters, and sweetish, mellow 'brown' porters. Overall, the style typically is brewed with less roasted barley or black malt than stout.

PRIMING

Encouraging a secondary or other refermentation in beer by adding sugar (and sometimes fresh yeast). The process differs from 'kräusening' (see entry) in that pure sugar, not sugary wort, is added. Britain's cask-conditioned and bottle-conditioned ales frequently are primed in this fashion.

PROHIBITION

Early 20th-century period when America and Canada, in the grip of the Temperance (anti-alcohol) movement, enforced laws that prohibited the manufacture, sale, and distribution of alcoholic beverages. Understandably, Prohibition severely damaged both countries' brewing industry. Many brewers failed to re-open after the anti-alcohol laws were repealed; those that did faced a highly competitive industry rife with buy-outs and takeovers.

In America, specifically, the period of national Prohibition (some states and regions enforced Prohibition earlier) officially lasted from 1920 through its Repeal in 1933. Canada's Prohibition became effective across different areas of the country before achieving a national presence by 1920 – although Quebec sensibly opted out of the arrangement altogether, and certain regions allowed the sale of low-strength 'temperance brews.'

RAUCHBIER

German for 'smoke beer,' denoting a lager brewed with a proportion of malt that has been smoked, usually over burning beechwood logs. Rauchbier is local to the city of Bamberg in the northern Bavarian region of Franconia. Before the advent of indirect-heat malting techniques, all beer had a lightly smoky character from the drying of malt over direct fires. The brewers of Bamberg, surrounded by plentiful beechwood forests, never wholly abandoned this practice.

Bamberg rauchbiers usually are of standard strength (5%), although bock versions are offered during winter. The classic example is the Heller brewery's Aecht Schlenkerla, brewed entirely from smoked malt in the Märzen style. Versions also come from the Bürgerbräu brewery (Kaiserdom) and Maisel's brewery. A handful of specialty brewers elsewhere, including

New York's Zip City, have offered credible interpretations of the style.

REAL ALE

'Live' (unpasteurized) ale which experiences a secondary (or subsequent) fermentation in the container from which it is dispensed. All bottle-conditioned and cask-conditioned ales, then, qualify as 'real ales.' The term was developed by Britain's Campaign for Real Ale (CAMRA) to emphasize the authenticity of the country's traditional cask-conditioned beers.

REGIONAL BREWERY

Any sizable brewery whose primary market is a definable surrounding region, from a large city to several states or provinces. The term is frequently used to describe older mid-size American brewers. A successful 'craft brewer' can qualify as a regional brewery – but most eschew the latter term in favor of the former.

Above: Take me to your lederhosen! Chopping wood and slapping thighs is thirsty work in Mayrhofen in the Austrian Alps, but plenty of refreshing beer is at hand.

REINHEITSGEBOT

Bavaria's famous 'Beer Purity' law of 1516. Introduced by the royal family, it mandated that only barley malt, water, and hops – yeast, because its nature was not understood, was not listed explicitly – could be used to make beer. The Reinheitsgebot later was expanded to allow wheat-beer brewing (originally a privilege reserved by the Bavarian royalty) and ultimately was adopted by producers across Germany.

In 1987, the European Court (petitioned by French brewers) ruled that Germany could not use the Reinheitsgebot standard to restrict imports of foreign beers. Virtually all German brewers still follow it voluntarily - although not always for their export brands - and it remains a legal requirement for Bavarian breweries.

While many brewers and consumers value the Reinheitsgebot for its basic 'purity,' others (perhaps rightly) feel it is an uncomfortable limit on brewing creativity: classic beer styles such as spiced Belgian wheat beers, for example, are illegal under its terms. Whatever the case, the Reinheitsgebot clearly only defines beer ingredients, not finished 'quality.'

ROASTED BARLEY

Unmalted barley that literally has been roasted (just like a coffee bean) until it is blackened and burnt. It imparts a drier, perhaps more 'acidic' character to beer than does similar 'black malt' (see entry). Roasted barley

commonly is used in brewing porters, stouts, and, in smaller quantities, Irish ales (it helps create their reddish color). Irish brewers probably began using roasted barley in all these brews as a means of avoiding a 19th-century tax on malted barley.

ROASTED MALT

Generic term for dark malts – amber malt, brown malt, 'chocolate' malt, black malt – that have been roasted at high temperatures to varying degrees of color and character.

RYE BEER

Beer brewed with a portion of rye grain, which imparts a spicy, lightly fruity character. Because rye lacks a husk and readily absorbs water – both traits that make mashing difficult – it is not commonly used in modern brewing. Nevertheless, the grain is a traditional ingredient in the indigenous beers (such as Finland's rustic sahti) of eastern Europe, a region that accounts for one-third of the world's rye production.

A few of today's brewers have introduced rye beers as specialties: Bavaria's Schierlinger Roggen ('rye' in German), made from a whopping 60 percent rye malt, perhaps is the most famous. Rye beers are becoming popular in America, where Pacific northwestern breweries (Steelhead, Big Time, Nor'Wester, Pyramid, Redhook, Thomas Kemper) have helped pioneer versions.

SAHTI

Rustic ale style, indigenous to Finland and Estonia, brewed from a mixed-grain mash of barley malt, rye (malted or 'raw'), and sometimes oats. Rye traditionally has accounted for up to half of the grist, but modern producers generally use lesser amounts because of the grain's brewing difficulties. Juniper is the classic sahti seasoning – the brew is filtered through juniper branches and flavored with juniper berries – although today small quantities of hops also are used (for preservative properties). Fermentation with rough baker's yeasts or other 'farmhouse' varieties gives the finished beer a winey, extremely fruity character.

While Estonian sahti effectively remains rural homebrew, Finland's versions have benefited from renewed interest in specialty beers. A handful of brewers now offer commercial examples: the best-known is Lammin Sahti, a potent brew (about 8%) sold in a 'wine box.'

SAISON

French for 'season,' denoting an ale style local to Wallonia, the French-speaking region of Belgium. Like 'bières de garde' (see entry), saisons are rooted in the agrarian days when summertime temperatures made brewing difficult. Just before the weather warmed, Wallonia's farmer-brewers produced strong, hoppy ales (pale to dark amber in color) that were bottled, stored in cool cellars, and consumed over the summer. High alcohol content and hop rates prevented these beers from spoiling, while their fruity flavors (from complex 'farmhouse' ale yeasts) and herbal hop character made them refreshing enough to slake a midsummer thirst. Some of today's still-potent (5.5-8.5%) versions, such as Saison de Pipaix, are spiced for extra flavor. Top examples include Saison Dupont (and its winter brother Bons Voeux), La Gauloise, and La Moneuse. Most are bottle-conditioned.

SAKE

The 'rice wine' of Asia technically is a beer (brewed from unmalted rice). After rice has been soaked in water and steamed (to break down its cell walls), it is inoculated with a variety of fungus that converts its starch to sugar. As this process progresses, yeast is added to ferment the sugar to a wine-like alcohol content (15-20%).

SCANDINAVIA

Denmark, Sweden, Norway, and Finland share a long brewing history. In fact, the words 'øl' and 'öl' – used, respectively, in Norway and Sweden as the generic term for beer – reveal the old Germanic-language origins of the English term 'ale.' While Scandinavia's ale-brewing traditions have not disappeared totally (witness Finland's sahti and similar Norwegian homebrews), the region was among the first to embrace lager beer. The roots of Denmark's Carlsberg/ Tuborg, one of the world's largest lager brewers, actually extend back to the pioneering lager work of Munich's Spaten brewery.

Scandinavian brewers specialize in Pilsner-style lagers, but they also have maintained – and perhaps lately revived – a tradition of Munich-style dunkels, Vienna-style ambers, pale and dark bocks, and special Christmas beers ('Jule-øl'). The region also has preserved a taste for 'Imperial stouts' (see entry), sometimes labelled as 'porters' (and frequently fermented with lager yeast).

SCHWARZBIER

Particularly dark (literally 'black beer' in German) lager style – although early in its history it was an ale – associated with eastern Germany and northern Bavaria. The style (4.5-5%) is distinguished from Munich dunkels by its darker color, 'bittersweet' chocolate flavors, and dry character.

The most famous example, from the spa town of Köstritz, is known appropriately as Köstritzer Schwarzbier. Consumers traditionally sweetened this bittersweet beer with sugar before drinking. A stronger, 'pre-sugared' version also was produced. Since the reunification of Germany, the Köstritzer brewery has offered only one version of intermediate character.

SCOTCH ALE

The strongest variety of Scottish ale (6.5-10%), sometimes also called '90/-' (see entry) or 'wee heavy' (after the small bottles in which it traditionally is packaged). The Scottish equivalent of England's barley wines, Scotch ales tend to be richly malty and complex. Their sweetish character is balanced either by dark specialty malts or, for a genuine Scotch touch, peat-smoked 'whiskey' malt (more frequent in new-wave examples such as that from America's Samuel Adams).

The beer renaissance has renewed interest in Scotch ales both in their homeland and other ale markets (England, America, Canada, etc.). Additionally, the style has been a popular specialty in Belgium since World War I, when the country's breweries reportedly introduced examples to nourish British soldiers. Top examples include Scotland's McEwan's Scotch and Belgium's Gordon's Highland Scotch (and wintertime 'Xmas' brew). The classic Scottish 'wee heavy,' Fowler's, actually is bottled Belhaven 90/-.

SCOTTISH ALE

Any malty ale of moderate strength (3.2-6.5%), usually amber to deep bronze in color, of the variety found throughout Scotland. See also '60/-,' '70/-,' '80/-,' '90/-.' Like its westerly cousin Ireland, Scotland has a cool, damp climate better suited to growing barley than hops. And Scots have a reputation for thriftiness that perhaps explains why the country's brewers never imported large quantities of English hops. (Instead, the Scots historically used a variety of hop-substitutes to bitter their beers). As a result, Scotland's ales (like Ireland's) tend to be malt-accented in character.

SEASONAL BEER

Any beer specifically designed in character to complement one of the year's four seasons – or, at the most basic, offered during only one of those seasons. The concept has its roots in agrarian times when brewing was a seasonal pursuit. It has been reinvigorated by new interest in specialty beers. The most common seasonals are 'winter warmers,' stronger brews made to warm more than just the hearts of drinkers during cold weather. A number of once-seasonal beers – from Germany's Märzens to Belgium's saisons – now are offered year-round.

SENNE VALLEY

A valley in Belgium, encompassing Brussels, that surrounds the Senne River (Zenne in Flemish). The wild yeasts and other microorganisms supported by its climate give 'lambic beers' (see entry) their distinctive character.

SMOKED BEER

Beer brewed with smoked malt or grain, giving it varying amounts of smoky aroma and flavor (also see 'Rauchbier'). While malt traditionally is smoked over wood, recent years have seen an increase in avant-garde brews made with a portion of peat-smoked 'whiskey' malt (witness France's interest in beers such as Fischer's Adelscott and Meteor's Mortimer). America's Alaskan Brewing makes a famous wintertime Smoked Porter from malt 'treated' at a nearby fish smokehouse. Specialty brewers around the world commonly experiment with beers in the broad 'smoked' style.

SPARGING

Spraying hot brewing water over spent grains (usually in the lauter tun) in order to extract any remaining sugars into the wort. The rich wort from grain

SPRUCE BEER

Beer either flavored with spruce or, more rarely, 'brewed' from spruce twigs, leaves, water, sugar or molasses. A traditional drink in Colonial America, where spruce was a readily-available bittering substitute for hops. San Francisco's Anchor Brewing offered a limited-edition spruce-flavored beer in the 1980s.

STARKBIER

German for 'strong beer,' this term is used in southern Bavaria to refer to doppelbocks, which traditionally appear during Lent (the *Starkbierzeit*, or 'strong beer time'). The boisterous festivals where brewers present the season's doppelbocks are known as Starkbierfests. Munich's Paulaner brewery holds the biggest Starkbierfest, which lasts for two weeks in its beer hall on the city's Nockherberg hill, to celebrate its famous Salvator doppelbock. The chief guest on opening night usually is the Bavarian prime minister, who gets to sample the season's first stein.

'STEAM' BEER

Although now a trademark of San Francisco's Anchor Brewing, 'steam beers' were a popular style in the American west during the mid-19th to early 20th century. Lacking the easy access to ice enjoyed by eastern and midwestern breweries, western lager brewers fermented their beer at ambient

that has not been sparged, or that has been drawn off before sparging commenced, is traditionally known as the 'first runnings.'

Above: Don Barkley of California's Mendocino Brewing hoists a glass of his high-flying Black Hawk Stout.

'ale' temperatures. To compensate, they developed long, shallow fermenting vessels designed to release as much heat as possible during the process. Because they could not be cold-matured for the traditional period, these brews were racked 'young' into barrels (where they completed fermentation). The resulting lively carbonation created a 'steam-like' hissing spray upon tapping, creating the style's name.

Anchor's classic amber brew (5%) blends a lager's clean flavors with more robust ale character. Several other American specialty brewers have introduced versions (though not under the 'steam' title; sometimes the style is called 'California common'). A number of European brewers offer 'steam' beers named not for the American style, but rather to recall the early excitement of steam-powered facilities.

STEINBIER

German for 'stone beer,' which is boiled by placing white-hot rocks into the wort. The process developed in parts of northern and central Europe – particularly Austria, where the best type of rock (greywacke, a sandstone variety that can withstand intense heat) was available naturally – as a way to boil wort at a time when brew kettles were made of wood (and therefore dangerous to expose to direct fires).

The basic procedure consists of heating stones over a wood fire before dropping them into the wort. In addition to imparting a wood-smoke flavor, the rocks create an intense boil that caramelizes some of the wort. The style was produced in Austria until the early 20th century. It was reintroduced in the 1980s by the Bavarian brewer of Rauchenfels Steinbier and Steinweizen (a stone-brewed hefeweizen). Several American specialty brewers, notably Maryland's Brimstone, have experimented with variations.

STOUT

Robustly-flavored dark (often black) beer, traditionally an ale. Available most frequently in the dry 'Irish' style, but also 'Imperial,' 'foreign-style,' 'sweet,' 'oatmeal,' and 'oyster' versions (see entries). Stout originally was a kind of porter: extra-hearty examples initially were called 'stout porters' and, in time, simply 'stouts.' Brewers also began using blackened malts and roasted barley to give stouts a more roasty, 'burnt' character than porters (made with traditional 'brown' malts) – which remains largely true today. As beer strength fell in modern times, robust stouts eclipsed their parent style to the point where porter almost totally disappeared before being rediscovered as part of the beer renaissance.

SWEET STOUT

Stout with a sweetish (as opposed to dry) character. Top examples offer delicious, soft, chocolatey flavors. The best known variety is 'milk stout,' so named because it is sweetened with lactose (unfermentable milk sugar). Milk stouts became popular in Britain during the early to mid-20th century, when they were promoted as being extra-nutritious – a concept enhanced by the fact that they usually were low in alcohol. The most famous English version, Whitbread's Mackeson, today comes in domestic (3%) and export (5%, for the Americas, Africa, etc.) versions. Several brewers offer stouts that achieve a similar creamy sweetness without actually containing lactose. These often are called 'cream stouts,' and usually approach conventional strengths. America's Sam Adams Cream Stout and England's Watney's Cream Stout are well-known. 'Oatmeal,' 'oyster,' and some 'foreign-style' stouts (see entries) also tend to have a sweetish character.

TOP FERMENTATION

Somewhat outdated term for fermentation with ale yeast, which traditionally rises to the top of beer (where it forms a dense 'yeast head') after completing its 'work.' Also appears, variously, as an adjective (top-fermenting) and noun (a top fermenter). Because many breweries now employ tall conical fermenters – where even ale yeasts settle towards the bottom – a more accurate term to denote standard ale production is 'warm fermentation.'

TRAPPIST ALE

Designation for, and strictly *only* for, the ales brewed by six Trappist monasteries in Europe. Five of these – generally known by their 'brand' names (Chimay, Orval, Rochefort, Westmalle, and Westvleteren) – are located in Belgium; the sixth (La Trappe) is in the Netherlands.

Trappist ales, fermented with multi-strain yeasts and bottle-conditioned (sometimes with additional strains), are among the world's most complex beers. They traditionally are strong (5.5-11.5%) – although the monks make lower-alcohol versions for their own use – with a detectable sweetness that comes from the addition of Belgian 'candi' sugar to the brew kettle. The number of 'Trappist-style' or 'abbey' beers offered by commercial Belgian or Dutch brewers (as well as specialty brewers

elsewhere) testifies to the popularity of the Trappist originals.

TRIP(P)EL

Flemish for 'triple,' generally denoting a brewery's highest strength (8-10%) 'Trappist-style' (or 'abbey-style') ale with a golden to deep-amber color. 'Tripel' originally may have referred to markings on the sides of wooden barrels that revealed the strength and character of the beer within (see 'Dubbel'). The best balance complex fruitiness – a handful are spiced with coriander to enhance this characteristic – with a refreshing, somewhat dry (and occasionally toasty) pale malt flavor. Hoppier examples tend to share territory with strong golden Belgian ales (such as Duvel).

Top European versions include Belgium's Westmalle Tripel and Chimay White, as well as the Netherlands' Columbus (from the 'IJ' brewery). The style is also popular with specialty brewers elsewhere, particularly in North America (witness Colorado's New Belgium Trippel and Quebec's La Fin du Monde).

TRÜB

German-derived brewing term for sediment (from coagulated proteins, hop leavings, grain particles, etc.) created during the brewing process.

UNITED STATES

European settlers brought 'modern' brewing to America. Early American ales reflected the British-influenced Colonial era, but lager brewing arrived with Central European immigrants during the mid-19th century. A century later, after Prohibition, a handful of growing brewers began to dominate the country's beer scene with bland Pilsner-style lagers – what now are internationally-(in)famous beers such as Budweiser, Miller, and Coors. Their success has made the United States the world's biggest brewing nation, in terms of production (nearly double that of Germany).

America's first modern microbrewers appeared during the late 1970s. By 1995, the country hosted more than 800 specialty breweries making beers in the broadest variety of styles available anywhere in the world –

from Belgian-style lambics to German doppelbocks! Even the major brewers have introduced specialty brands. Optimistic observers expect 'craft beers' to account for up to 10 percent of the American beer market during the next decade.

UR-/URQUELL

German prefix meaning 'original.' Urquell ('original source') has been adopted as a brand name by the older of two Pilsner breweries in the Czech city of Pilsen (where the style was born).

VIENNA LAGER

Lager (5-5.5%) characterized by an amber to reddish color and sweetly malty flavor balanced by spicy European hops (Saaz, etc.). Stronger versions parallel Märzen/Oktoberfest beers. Austrian brewer Anton Dreher, who helped develop modern lager beers, pioneered the style at his Vienna brewery. Malting advances allowed him to introduce an amber-colored lager in 1841 (previously, all lagers were dark in color). The style proved extremely popular,

and was exported (and brewed) across Europe: a heartier interpretation was the toast of the 1871 Oktoberfest (see entry). The style even made it to Mexico, where versions remain in production today.

The beer renaissance has rekindled interest in Vienna-style lagers around the world, particularly in America and Canada. A few Scandinavian winter seasonals also fit the style. Ironically, while most Austrian breweries have abandoned the style in favor of paler beers, examples have been reintroduced by several new brewpubs around Vienna itself.

VIENNA MALT

Malted barley of the variety that Austrian brewer Anton Dreher used to create his pioneering amber-colored 'Vienna' lager. It is extremely similar in production and character to 'crystal malt.' Vienna malt imparts an amber-red color, sweetish character, and toasty-nutty flavor to beer.

WATER

One of beer's most important ingredients (and certainly its main constituent). Water character contributes significantly to a beer's clarity, flavor, and mouthfeel. In the past, cities became associated with specific varieties of beer precisely because their water complemented a style. London's 'soft' water (high chloride content) was perfect for porters, for example, while Burton's hard water (high gypsum content) suited pale ale production. Modern brewers adjust the character of their water by adding or removing

mineral salts. As a result, the 'natural' quality of local water no longer is as crucial a concern for today's breweries.

WEISS(E)

German for 'white.' Used in Germany to describe an unfiltered wheat beer – either a weissbier or Berliner Weisse – presumably because such brews have a cloudy-white yeast haze. Unfiltered Kölsch beers sometimes are called wiess (a Cologne-dialect variation).

WEISSBIER

German for 'white beer.' Secondary term (to the more prosaic hefeweizen) used in Bavaria for an unfiltered wheat brew. Note its similarity to the Flemish 'witbier.'

WEIZEN/WEIZENBIER

German for 'wheat.' The term weizenbier generally indicates a Bavarian-style 'wheat beer,' either in the filtered form (kristall) or yeast-hazy version (hefe-). A few German breweries cloud the issue by describing special brews for an (outdoor) festival or event as wiesen or wies'n – words that derive from the German for 'meadow.'

Above: A marketer's dream – good beer, good company, and good times!

Wheat Beer

Any beer brewed with a proportion of wheat in addition to 'standard' barley malt. Wheat tends to give beer a clean, crisp, refreshing character. Specialty brewers in the United States have developed 'American wheat beers' – wheat-brewed ales or lagers, frequently tame in flavor, that do not fit any classic wheat-beer style (Bavarian weizen, Belgian witbier, etc.).

Whirlpool

Brewing vessel designed to separate wort from trub after the boil (prior to fermentation). It employs centrifugal force created by a whirlpool-like swirling of the wort. See 'Hop Back.'

White Beer

English translation of Flemish 'witbier,' indicating a beer of that variety.

Witbier

Flemish for 'white beer,' denoting an unfiltered (cloudy white) wheat ale (4–5%) in Belgium's centuries-old style: a quenching brew made from pale barley malt and unmalted wheat, perhaps also with a small amount of wheat malt or oats (for smoothness), that is lightly hopped and traditionally spiced with coriander and dried Curaçao orange peel. Witbiers occasionally are flavored with additional 'secret' spices such as ginger or aromatic peppers. Classic examples also are dosed with a lactobacillus culture that enhances their tart complexity.

Like Bavarians and their hefeweizens, Belgian drinkers abandoned witbiers in the mid-20th century. The style was resurrected by Pierre Celis, a former milkman who began producing a revivalist witbier in, and named after, his home town of Hoegaarden during the 1960s. It proved enormously popular, spawning a new wave of witbier from other Belgian (and Dutch) brewers. Examples of the style now are produced by specialty brewers in many countries, including Britain, Canada, and America.

Wort

Term (pronounced 'wurt') for the sugary liquid created by mixing grain with hot water during a mash. Before it has been boiled with hops in the brew kettle, this liquid sometimes is known as 'sweet wort.' Afterwards, it can be called 'hopped wort.' Fermentation turns wort into beer.

Yakima Valley

Region in the American Pacific northwest, centered around the city of Yakima in central Washington state, that produces 70 percent of America's hop crop. Although both European and domestic hops are grown in the Valley, its citrusy American varieties (Cascade, Columbus, etc.) sometimes are known simply as 'Yakima hops.' The Valley also is renowned for growing wine grapes and table fruit.

Yeast

A single-celled microorganism (actually a fungus) that feeds on sugar in 'wort' (see entry) and releases, as its 'waste,' alcohol and carbon dioxide. Most modern brewers use 'ale' or 'lager' yeast of the genus *Saccharomyces*. Lambic brewers (and a few other producers of deliberately-soured beer) also rely on 'wild' airborne *Brettanomyces* yeasts, which generate intense cidery flavors.

Before the 18th century, when the microscope enabled scientists to identify it, yeast probably was the least understood element of the brewing process – medieval brewers, thinking fermentation was a divine gift, called the yeasty agent 'godisgood.' Today, brewers regularly order special yeast strains to brew specific varieties of beer. All breweries carefully monitor their main strain to ensure that it remains in top condition (most also keep samples in a safe off-site 'yeast bank,' in case of emergency).

Zoigl(bier)

Ancient term (pronounced 'zoy-gull') for a medieval method of brewing, rather than a beer 'style.' The procedure, a holdover from the time when feudal lords or the church bestowed brewing rights on private households, is local to several towns in northeast Bavaria's Oberfalz district. Small batches of Zoiglbier are brewed in a communal brewhouse, then carted away to ferment and mature in the cellar of the house that holds the brewing rights.

When the Zoiglbier is ready, its owner informs the neighborhood of an 'open house' by displaying a star-shaped sign (Zoigl is derived from *Zeichen*, German for 'sign' or 'symbol'). Some Zoiglbiers are lagers, others are ales. They often are unfiltered and only lightly carbonated. Most resemble either a kellerbier or darker Märzen-like brew.

Zymurgy

The science of fermentation. Also the name of the magazine of the American Homebrewers Association. And truly the 'last word' in brewing.

NORTH AMERICA

Britain claims the honors, thanks to its CAMRA (Campaign for Real Ale) consumer movement, for launching the modern ale renaissance. But credit for the overall specialty beer revolution rests squarely with North America. Sure, the continent's national brewers continue to roll out their infamously bland 'Pilsner' brands. But a growing group of small breweries together have done more to revitalize classic beer styles and to innovate new ones than all the world's other brewers. From Boston to British Columbia, from Toronto to Texas, creative North American brewers bear the standard of the worldwide beer revolution.

oday, American drinkers hoist hoppy pale ales (like the classic Liberty Ale from California's Anchor Brewing) with one hand, and rich, dark lagers (perhaps Saranac Chocolate Amber from New York's F.X. Matt Brewery) with the other. Calgary beer-lovers enjoy the malty McNally's Ale while their Ontario counterparts savor the smooth, complex Niagara Falls Eisbock. Bavarian weissbiers and Belgian tripels come from Colorado. Locally-made bocks and oatmeal stouts are quaffed in Quebec. And that's not even scratching the surface of North America's burgeoning beer variety.

Coming after decades of pale, fizzy neglect, this beer revolution recalls the early centuries of North American brewing – a time when waves of European settlers first brought the ales, and later the lagers, of their homelands to the shores of their New World. Indigenous Americans had their own robust 'brews,' of course (echoes of these survive in the chicha corn-brews still enjoyed by natives in Mexico and South America). But beer as we know it today arrived with the Europeans.

All of the early North American breweries made ales in the styles of the day: porters, stouts, even the then-new 'pale' varieties. When waves of German and Eastern European immigrants began arriving in the mid-1800s, the tide turned towards the bottom-fermented 'lager' beers that were captivating beer halls from Berlin to

Fritz Maytag, the genius behind Anchor Brewing.

Right: Anchor – trailblazing micro of the 1970s.

Budapest. Before long, thousands of local breweries were offering beers in either or both varieties. The result was a vibrant, thriving North American brewing scene.

And then Prohibition arrived.

The Temperance movement of the early 20th century proved particularly sobering for North America's brewers. In both the United States and Canada (with the notable exception of Quebec), laws banned the production and sale of alcoholic beverages. Some brewers survived on legal low-alcohol brews ('near beer'), while others turned to related industries. Colorado's Coors made malted milk, for instance, and Anheuser-Busch produced ice cream at several of its refrigerated plants. But the majority of North American breweries closed their doors forever.

When Prohibition ended in 1933, the North American beer industry was but a shadow of its former frothy glory. Aggressive breweries exploited the situation, expanding both their markets and marketing strategies. In Canada, for example, the post-Prohibition combine called Canadian Breweries (later Carling O'Keefe) absorbed more than 20 independent breweries across Ontario and Quebec in an effort to build its market share. America's bigger breweries focused on producing 'national brands' that were meant to appeal to the broadest possible tastes, across the broadest possible market areas.

By the 1970s, the American brewing industry was dominated by an elite circle of 'megabrewers' (Pabst,

Left: Cask ales are growing in popularity.

Anheuser-Busch, Coors, Miller, Stroh, Heileman, Schlitz, to name a few). Across the border, Carling, Molson, and Labatt controlled Canadian brewing. Molson at least had the historical distinction of being the continent's oldest operating brewery (founded in 1786). But in terms of distinctiveness, of character, things looked bleak for North American beer. And then the beery worm began to turn.

The late 1970s saw America slowly embrace a new wave of small brewers (companies so tiny, in fact, that they initially were called 'boutique' or 'micro-' breweries). New Albion, the first recognized North American microbrewery, rolled out its premier barrel from California's 'New World' wine country in 1977. At the same time, idiosyncratic brews from surviving regional producers – San Francisco's Anchor Brewing, for example, and Pennsylvania's Yuengling Brewery (the oldest operating brewery in America) – started to recapture the public's attention.

Like many trailblazers, New Albion unfortunately proved ahead of its time. But its pioneering efforts to offer flavorful ales inspired a host of followers across America and Canada. Many of these 'original' micros have prospered: early names like Sierra Nevada and Big Rock now loom large in their once-tiny industry. A few of the most prominent 'small' brewers even have headed to Wall Street! During 1995, American investors thirsted for stock from major public offerings held by the Boston Beer Co., Pete's Brewing, Redhook Breweries, and Pyramid Breweries.

Overall, the growth of small brewers has been staggering. In 1975, America hosted 60 breweries; by 1995, there were more

than 800! Things are going so well that successful small brewers have abandoned their 'micro' moniker for the more encompassing term 'craft-brewer.' And while many in the industry are wary of increasing competition, additional companies continue to open. The foamy bubble has yet to burst. Indeed, the entire 'craft-brewing' segment still only accounts for two to three percent of the greater beer industry.

The popularity of micros has not been lost on the megabrewers, despite continuing emphasis on their bland flagship brands and further industry consolidation (Anheuser-Busch, Miller, Coors, and Stroh now dominate America, while the merger of Carling into Molson has left Canada with a 'Big Two'). Eager to enter the craft-beer arena, Anheuser-Busch purchased 25 percent of Redhook. Miller bought controlling interests in Celis of Texas and Shipyard of Maine. And both large

Above: A turn-of-the-century view of the racking cellars at Yuengling, the oldest brewery in America.

brewers, along with Coors, Stroh, and Molson, also have introduced 'craft beers' of their own. While micro-enthusiasts frequently bemoan such actions, the overall result has been a greater choice of more distinctive beers for the average American and Canadian consumer.

Distinctive beers now pop up in every facet of North American society, from 'beer lists' in fine restaurants to golf-course coolers, and taps at the corner bar. The top breweries profiled in the following pages compose a colorful snapshot of the continent's dynamic 'craft beer' industry. Enthusiasts looking to supplement this detailed account should consider the *Pocket Guide To Beer* from beer authority Michael Jackson, as well as *The Great Canadian Beer Guide* from Toronto author Stephen Beaumont.

US NORTHEAST

Along with the mid-Atlantic American states, the Northeast possesses strong Colonial-based ale traditions – not surprising, perhaps, in a region known as New England. The area's beer history and local 'Yankee pride' have helped it become the country's most fertile microbrewing ground outside of the northwest. Today, the Northeast hosts the largest craft-brewer in America (the Boston Beer Company) and many of the smallest.

Brewpubs and draft-only micros abound in New England. Relative newcomers exist side-by-side with established pioneers: Vermont's Otter Creek Brewing and Catamount Brewery, for example, and Maine's Shipyard Breweries and D.L. Geary Brewing. Echoing the national pattern, veterans continue to expand production while new breweries open every year.

Overall, Northeast ales retain a more 'English' accent than their Northwest counterparts. This orientation stems, in part, from the fact that many New England brewers use equipment and an (in)famous British 'Ringwood' yeast provided by Peter Austin & Partners, a brewery-installation company originally based in Hampshire, England. But ales are not alone in the Northeast: several brewers also offer classic lager styles or hybrids such as German-inspired altbiers.

Between bowls of clam chowder and weekends at 'the shore,' thirsty New Englanders keep tabs on the region's beer scene by reading Yankee Brew News (P.O. Box 520250, Winthrop, Massachusetts 02152-0005).

Right: Atlantic Coast's Jeff Biegert takes a sample from the fermenter to test its specific gravity. Tremont uses British hops in its acclaimed 'American-made' English-style ales.

ATLANTIC COAST BREWING

ESTABLISHED 1994

The Tremont Brewery, 50 Terminal Street
Boston, Massachusetts 02129

RECOMMENDED

Tremont Ale (4.8%),
at its best when cask-conditioned
Tremont India Pale Ale (6.4%),
complex, fruity, with citrus hop notes
Old Scratch Barley Wine (9%),
notes of chocolate, cherry, and roasted malt

This is a relatively new micro operating under its Tremont Brewery banner, which reflects the three-hill area of Boston where it is located. It is dedicated to producing English-style ales, including the use of imported barley malt, East Kent Golding and Fuggles hops, and a British ale yeast (Ringwood, but mellow for the strain) in open fermenters. Tremont's stainless steel brewing vessels, imported from England, produce fewer than 7,000 barrels (8,200hl) per year. Originally draft-only, the company began bottling in 1996.

The flagship Tremont Ale, which displays a pleasant 'Burtonized' character, reaches its peak of flavor when cask-conditioned – the brewery imported actual British casks for this purpose! A handful of Boston-area accounts, including a characterful city pub called Cornwall's,

carry the beer in this form (look for tell-tale pumps mounted on the bar). Tremont occasionally cask-conditions small amounts of its other beers, including the holiday season's excellent Old Scratch. In keeping with English barley wine tradition, sugar is added to the brew kettle to enhance this brew's original gravity (1.095 in 1995, 1.096 in 1996, etc.). Tremont IPA, available from May through August, is brewed to the style's appropriate strength and aggressively hopped with Fuggles, Styrian Goldings, and Cascades. The result is a full-bodied, complex ale with a tremendous citrusy, aromatic hop character. Other seasonal releases include a dry, roasty Porter (early spring) and nutty ESB (fall).

BOSTON BEER COMPANY

ESTABLISHED 1985

The Brewery, 30 Germania Street
Boston, Massachusetts 02130

RECOMMENDED
Samuel Adams Cream Stout (5%),
mellow 'cappuccino' of stout
Samuel Adams Scotch Ale (6%),
lots of rich malt and smoky notes
Samuel Adams Double Bock (8.5%),
richly malty with chocolate hints

The brainchild of Harvard-educated marketer Jim Koch (pronounced 'Cook'), Boston Beer's family of Samuel Adams ales and lagers are the best-known in the nation. At the same time, Koch's 'major league' marketing techniques (radio, billboards, television) and the fact that the vast majority of his beer is brewed under contract – at megaplants such as Pittsburgh Brewing, Genesee Brewing, Stroh Brewing, and Blitz-Weinhard Brewing – have vilified the company in the minds of many smaller craft-brewers. Distribution is national (indeed, international), with annual production near 1 million barrels (1,173,000hl). Boston Beer went public in 1995.

The company's original Samuel Adams Boston Lager, named after the Colonial American brewer and patriot, remains its flagship: a well-made amber brew seasoned with German Hallertau and Tettnanger hops (particularly notable when fresh). In addition, the year-round Sam Adams beers include a smooth Cream Stout, robust Scotch Ale (brewed with a notable percentage of peat-smoked malt), 'old style' Boston

Stock Ale, and gentle Golden Pilsner. Seasonals encompass spring's lush Double Bock (among the absolute best of its kind in America), a traditional Oktoberfest, and annually-changing Winter Lager. A faintly-spiced Summer Ale was introduced in 1996. The company also offers a supremely potent (17.5%), top-fermented 'Triple Bock.'

Boston Beer runs its own small brewery – the former Haeffenreffer plant – in Boston. It has a stake in Philadelphia's Samuel Adams Brew-House brewpub, and also backs a west coast contract-brewing operation called Oregon Ale & Beer Company.

A line of homebrewer-created beers was introduced in 1996 under the 'Longshot' label.

CATAMOUNT BREWING

ESTABLISHED 1986

58 South Main Street, White River Junction, Vermont 05001

RECOMMENDED
Catamount Amber Ale (4.8%),
sweetly nutty-malty with spicy hops
Catamount Porter (5.3%),
extremely soft, quaffable, chocolatey, and fruity
Catamount Christmas Ale (5.3%),
superbly fruity-citrusy pale ale

Located in a small town close to the Ivy League's Dartmouth University, Catamount was Vermont's first commercial brewery since 1893. Named

after the state's indigenous 'catamount' mountain lions, the company was founded by a homebrewing physical education teacher, Steve Mason, at a time when micros just were reaching the east coast. Growth and expansion have been steady, with production topping 20,000 barrels (23,500hl) in 1996. Catamount hopes to expand into a new facility soon. Distribution includes most of the northeast and mid-Atlantic states.

In addition to the balanced Amber and particularly drinkable Porter, Catamount offers two other year-round beers: its original Gold, clean-tasting and tangy-hoppy, and a relatively new English-inspired Pale Ale, hopped with Kent Goldings and Fuggles. All are well made examples of their respective styles. Seasonals include an Oktoberfest lager, an extremely nutty-malty spring Bock, and summer's filtered American Wheat. An annual Christmas Ale, while perhaps not quite the IPA it claims, balances a rich toasty malt character with loads of citrusy Cascade hops.

Catamount also offers a limited-edition draft series in Vermont only. Brews in 1995-96 included a double bock, dry-hopped ESB, and silky oatmeal stout.

ELM CITY BREWING

ESTABLISHED 1989

458 Grand Avenue
New Haven, Connecticut 06513

RECOMMENDED
Connecticut Ale (5%),
soft, malty, slightly nutty flavor
Draft specialties at pub and select accounts

Elm City was formerly called 'New Haven Brewing,' an underwhelming name abandoned in favor of one honoring the city's local trees. The original owner-brewer Blair Potts left the company but remains active in the region's beer scene. During 1996, the brewhouse was run by Ron Page, previously of New England Brewing. The always-creative Page introduced many new Elm City draft beers under a bi-monthly 'pub program' series. These are available on tap around the region, as well as at the brewery's expansive 350-seat restaurant. Concurrent with its new draft emphasis, Elm City has ceased bottling (with the exception of limited runs of its flagship Connecticut Ale, actually produced under contract by

F.X. Matt in New York). Total production for 1996 was expected to top 4,500 barrels (5,300hl).

In addition to Elm City's smooth, soft Connecticut Ale – best enjoyed in the clubby ambiance of Richter's saloon on New Haven Green, near Yale University – long-time fans still can enjoy its coffeelike Blackwell Stout year-round. Newer brews include Broken English Ale (a Goldings dry-hopped ESB with the slogan 'Thassa gooda beer!') and a decadent holiday-season Chocolate Cherry Porter, made by mixing pure cocoa powder and Italian cherry liqueur into a robust dark brew after fermentation! Other seasonals for 1996 included early spring's Uptown Charlie Brown Ale, a robust English style example, and late spring's smooth, creamy-sweet Mae's Bock.

D.L. GEARY BREWING

ESTABLISHED 1986

38 Evergreen Drive, Portland, Maine 04103

RECOMMENDED
Hampshire Special Ale (7%),
assertively hopped, richly fruity, toasty-malty

This pioneering micro is in the 'other' Portland. Assisted by late Traquair House laird Peter Maxwell Stuart, former medical-equipment salesman David Geary apprenticed at several small British breweries. After two years of planning, he opened his own small plant – one of the earliest in America built with the help of Peter Austin & Partners. It was the first commercial brewery in Maine for over a century.

Geary's flagship Pale Ale is copper-colored and dry, with four hop varieties (Cascade, Mt Hood, Tettnang, and Fuggles) balancing its fruity character. A relatively new London Porter would partner better with the Maine lobster depicted on both its and the Pale's label. The limited-season Hampshire Special Ale is, according to the brewery, 'only available while the weather sucks' (which in Maine means October through April). This classic wintertime strong ale has a powerful fruity character – that Ringwood yeast at work! – balanced with substantial helpings of English hops. Bottle-ageing will emphasize its rich, warming character.

Unlike many other eastern craft-brewers, Geary's remains tightly focused on its three core beers. The company has grown substantially, despite a slow start, and now sells in 15 states (mainly northeast and mid-Atlantic). Production stood at 11,050 barrels (13,000hl) in 1995.

Above: Despite the pugnacious Maine lobster logo on Geary's Pale Ale and Porter, Hampshire Special Ale is the brewery's most potent.

MASS. BAY BREWING

ESTABLISHED 1987

Harpoon Brewery, 306 Northern Avenue
Boston, Massachusetts 02210

RECOMMENDED

Harpoon India Pale Ale (5%),
refreshing Cascade-hopped brew

Mass. Bay was founded by three business school graduates who had studied the prospects for a new beer company as part of their course – making it the 'textbook' micro start-up, perhaps? All draft beer comes from the Boston brewery, but bottles are made under contract at upstate New York's F.X. Matt Brewing (see page 47). The company's Boston brewhouse has been expanded steadily to cope with expanded production (40,000 barrels /47,000hl in 1995, with nearly double that amount expected in 1996).

Mass. Bay's original Harpoon Ale has been supplemented by a much broader year-round range that includes the India Pale Ale, a German-themed Alt, and a Pilsner. Both the IPA and Alt began life as summer seasonals before entering the standard range. Current limited-season Harpoon brews include spring's notably roasty Stout, summertime's Snakebite (a cidery blend), a traditional Oktoberfest lager, and spiced Winter Warmer (nutmeg, cinnamon).

Although its beers now are available throughout the northeast and mid-Atlantic (and even Florida), the company remains locally focused. It attracts Boston beer fans, for example, by hosting brewery parties on Oktoberfest and St Patrick's Day. It also offers a free-ride shuttle service in downtown Boston that emphasizes responsible drinking (i.e., not driving). The result of these activities is something of a city-wide loyalty to Mass. Bay's beers. Then again, given the town's whaling history, any sensible Bostonian would rather stick with a Harpoon than be stuck by one.

OTTER CREEK BREWING

ESTABLISHED 1991

85 Exchange Street
Middlebury, Vermont 05753

RECOMMENDED

Copper Ale (5.85%),
well-balanced toasty malt flavor

Founded by a former homebrewer who attended college in Portland, Oregon, the microbrewing capital of America, Otter Creek actually began production with equipment purchased from Portland's Widmer Brothers Brewing! Middlebury was chosen as the brewery site because of its relaxed quality of life atmosphere and excellent quality brewing water. Expansion has been rapid and mainly locally-driven – especially when the brewery, at its start, offered only kegs of its flagship Copper Ale. Bottling commenced in 1993, pushing production even higher. In 1995, the company completed construction of a new purpose-built brewery with a capacity of 40,000 barrels (47,000hl) per year. Otter Creek distributes around the northeast.

Otter Creek Copper Ale, inspired by German altbiers, is brewed with five malts, roasted barley, and American-grown Hallertau and Tettnang hops. It has a solid copper color with smooth toasty-malt flavors and a pleasant background bitterness. It is offered year-round along with the brewery's Helles

Alt Beer, an alt-style (fermented with ale yeast, but cold conditioned) interpretation of a Munich Helles lager. Four seasonals include a sweetish, chocolatey Mud Bock Spring Ale, effervescent Summer Wheat Ale, and deep, dark Stovepipe Porter for the cooler months. Fall's Hickory Switch Smoked Amber Ale is not quite as much of a mouthful as its name suggests! Draft-only specialties have included the potent, spiced (and Shakespearean) A Winter's Ale and popular Oktoberfest (first bottled in 1996).

Above: Otter Creek Brewing's owner, Lawrence Miller.

Maibock still make appearances at the Camden pub. But Sea Dog's main focus for distribution – across the eastern seaboard – is its core range of year-round ales. In addition to Windjammer, one of the most characterful American golden ales, the company offers an Old Gollywobbler Brown Ale and Old East India Pale Ale. The Brown drinks toasty and pleasantly hoppy, while the IPA (packing a hefty 7.5% punch, and reportedly conditioned in oak barrels) is strongly fruity and seriously peppery-hoppy to match.

A Hazelnut Porter, actually flavored with hazelnuts, also is produced, along with seasonal blueberry- and cherry-flavored wheat beers.

SEA DOG BREWING

ESTABLISHED 1993

26 Front Street, Bangor, Maine 04401

RECOMMENDED

Windjammer Blonde Ale (5%),
surprisingly hoppy and firmly fruity
Oktoberfest (5.2%),
a deserving gold-medal winner
Jubilator Dopplebock (7.4%),
lusciously malty, rich

Another brewpub that grew up. The Sea Dog first barked from a brewery pub on the western shore of Penobscot Bay in the historic shipbuilding town of Camden, Maine (43 Mechanic Street, Maine 04843). It later took a bigger bite of the craft-beer market by building a larger production brewery (and adjoining pub) in Bangor. Both facilities operate simultaneously: Bangor handles English-inspired ales exclusively, while Camden still offers Sea Dog's German-style lagers. Unfortunately, at least at this time of writing, the latter were available only in kegs. Sea Dog's traditional Oktoberfest captured top honors in its category at the 1994 Great American Beer Festival.

Specialty lagers like its Jubilator Dopplebock and exuberant, spicy

SHIPYARD BREWERIES

ESTABLISHED 1992

86 Newbury Street, Portland, Maine 04101

RECOMMENDED

Longfellow Winter Ale (5.5%),
distinct roasted barley character
Old Thumper (5.6%),
huge, complex fruit with balancing bitterness

This enterprise was established in 1992 as a brewery (Kennebunkport Brewing, #8 Western Avenue, 04043) in Kennebunk, Maine. A second 'Shipyard Brewery,' which stands near the birthplace of famous poet Henry Wadsworth Longfellow in Portland, Maine, opened in 1994 close to – surprise! – the city's historic shipyard. To help fund its rapid growth, the company entered an alliance with Miller Brewing in 1995. Miller purchased 50 percent of Shipyard Breweries, providing its marketing expertise while allowing the founding team to retain control over all brewing activities.

To love Shipyard's beers is to love the Ringwood yeast strain. Alan Pugsley, wandering brewmaster for Peter Austin & Partners, not only helped set up Shipyard's facilities, but also became part-owner in 1994. The flagship Shipyard Export Ale (something of a Canadian-styled brew) clearly displays the signature Ringwood fruitiness. So does the company's pitch-black Blue Fin Stout and Mystic Seaport Pale Ale – although both, perhaps, are better balanced. Old Thumper, brewed to an 'original' recipe from England's Ringwood Brewery, offers the best blend of complex fruit, toasty malt, and firm hop character.

Shipyard also offers specialties such as winter's Longfellow and a hearty holiday-season Prelude Ale. Relatively new introductions include Longfellow's IPA, pleasantly hoppy with Fuggles and Goldings, and Chamberlain Pale Ale, named for a famous Maine governor. With so many choices, drinkers are likely to find at least one Ship(yard) they enjoy sinking.

Above: A pint for sailors in port? Maritime imagery abounds on Shipyard's labels and collateral.

ALSO WORTH TRYING

The Northeast bursts with small brewers. Check to see what's available locally when travelling in the region. Vermont hosts perhaps the most colorful Northeast micro, **McNeill's Brewery** of Brattleboro (love those tie-dye T-shirts!). McNeill's offers their beers throughout Vermont and Massachusetts (on draft and in 22oz bottles): look particularly for McNeill's IPA, which has a fresh-hop aroma and balanced toasty-malt flavor. Burlington's **Vermont Pub & Brewery** – run by industry luminary Greg Noonan, who also operates the **Seven Barrel Brewery** in Lebanon, Vermont – offers specialties such as Smoked Porter and a smooth Vermont Maple Ale. Hikers are rumored to find Bridgewater's Long Trail Ales suitably refreshing.

Neighboring New Hampshire hosts its share of brewers, including an Anheuser-Busch plant in Merrimack that produces many of that company's specialty beers. **Nutfield Brewing** of Derry attracted attention in 1995 when elder American statesman Bob Dole sampled its golden Old Man Ale. **Martha's Exchange**, in historic downtown Nashua, offers a wide range of traditional styles: try the German-inspired HefeWeiss or its potent Untouchable Scotch Ale (silver medallist at the 1994 Great American Beer Festival). Portsmouth's **Smuttynose Brewing** has gained a following for a 'rough,' unfiltered, American-hoppy Shoals Pale Ale.

Massachusetts provides many stops for the beer lover. If you can't drink your fill at the popular Boston Brewers Festival (held during May each year), head for one of the city's several brewpubs – **Commonwealth Brewery** and **Boston Beer Works** (opposite Fenway Park) are the best. In nearby Cambridge, you can 'pahk youah cahr by Hahvahd Yahd' and visit the original **John Harvard's Brewhouse**, which now operates outposts in Atlanta and other eastern cities. Newburyport's **Ould Newbury Brewing** offers unfiltered, keg-conditioned ales, including flagship Yankee amber and fresh-tasting Haystack IPA. The roof-deck beer garden at **Northampton**'s eponymous brewery – operated by the same team behind Smuttynose – offers a top spot to sample flagship Northampton Pale Ale and Black Cat Stout. **Ipswich Brewing** has secured a solid reputation on the basis of its hoppy Ipswich Ale and massive but balanced Oatmeal Stout. **Dornbush Brewing** (contracting production at Ipswich) also gets good reviews for its traditional Alt.

To the south, Rhode Island runs on brewpubs: capital Providence offers both the tiny **Union Station Brewery** (start with the clean, balanced Golden Spike Pale Ale) and newer **Trinity Brewhouse** (ask for India Point IPA, powerful and dry-hopped). In Connecticut, the **Hartford Brewery** brewpub is expanding on the strength of beers like flagship Arch Amber and Bacchus Old Ale. Norwalk's **New England Brewing** already offers bottles and kegs throughout the region. Its 'steam-style' Atlantic Amber and generously-hopped (Perle, Northern Brewer, Cascade, Saaz) Gold Stock Ale roll out of a new showcase brewery and pub, featuring a Bavarian-built brewhouse, in the city's historic south end. Production was expected to top 15,000 barrels (17,600hl) in 1996.

Finally, far northeastern Maine holds nearly 20 brewers. In addition to Geary's and Shipyard, Portland offers the famous **Gritty McDuff's** brewpub, **Stone Coast Brewing**, and **Casco Bay Brewing**. The latter's range of Katahdin Ales includes seasonals such as a winter brew spiced with honey, ginger, cinnamon, and orange. (Visit Portland's Great Lost Bear pub for the top selection of draft northeast brews). Bar Harbor offers two brewpubs – **Atlantic Brewing**, with its acclaimed Coal Porter, and **Maine Coast Brewing** – as well as micro **Bar Harbor Brewing** (try the Thunder Hole Ale and Cadillac Mountain Stout). **Sunday River Brewing** of Bethel, whose owners also operate Portland's Stone Coast, greets patrons at the bottom of one of the east coast's premier ski areas with its Redstone Ale. Bi-coastal travellers should try blending Sunday River's Black Bear Porter with California's Golden Bear Lager for an ursine (if slightly ersatz) Black & Tan!

Right: A mass-ive (but well-balanced) stout from Mass-achusetts' Ipswich Brewing. The company's beers became available in 12oz bottles during 1996.

NORTH AMERICAN WHEAT & FRUIT BEERS

Reflecting a culture that prides itself on assimilating immigrants from many different countries, perhaps it is not surprising that America has developed few beer styles that it truly can call its own. There's steam beer, of course (page 32), and 'West Coast pale ales' (pages 64–65). But what other styles have arisen from America's craft-brewing revolution? Three words give the answer: wheat and fruit.

Granted, wheat beers and fruit beers have been around for centuries in Europe. But American craft-brewers (and their Canadian counterparts) have developed interpretations of both that differ enough from the European originals to stand as distinct styles. Whether these new brews are as distinctive as the beers that inspire them, however, is another issue. In general, North American wheats and fruit beers are more straightforward in their production and finished character than traditional Bavarian or Belgian versions (excepting, of course, those brewed to replicate Bavarian or Belgian versions). They also happen to be among the top-selling craft beer styles, especially in America.

'American wheats' are, in part, a style born of expediency. America's early microbrewers lacked the capabilities (at least at their initial stages) to make traditional versions of Europe's wheat beers. They also may have wondered whether something as alien as an unfiltered Bavarian-style weizenbier or tart Berliner weisse would discourage their potential customers. As a result, pioneering micros produced 'hybrid' wheats: beers that were brewed with some wheat malt, but perhaps not as much as European examples, and fermented with the brewery's standard yeast.

Washington state's Pyramid Ales, which launched its filtered Wheaten Ale in 1985, claims credit for the first year-round, draft wheat beer brewed in America since Prohibition. The 'year round' part is a tip of the mash tun to San Francisco's

Anchor Brewing, which introduced Anchor Wheat Beer – brewed with a whopping 70 percent wheat malt! – as a small-batch summer seasonal in 1984. (Anchor's version now is available on draft throughout the year). Both beers ferment with each brewery's normal yeast, and both get a bright, refreshing 'crispness' from the wheat malt.

Today, many North American breweries offer similar filtered, golden wheat beers made with their standard yeast. These brews frequently appear as warm weather seasonals, a positioning that reflects their quenching character. Maryland's Wild Goose Brewing presents a Spring Wheat, for example, while Vermont's Catamount (American Wheat) and Michigan-headquartered Stroh (Augsburger Weiss) offer summertime versions. All tend to be relatively mellow and 'accessible' in flavor, which probably explains their popularity.

Not too long after Pyramid Wheaten debuted, another northwest micro went wheat. Widmer Brewing of Portland, Oregon, developed a filtered Weizen made with its standard altbier ale yeast and hopped with the northwest's aromatic Cascades. It later began to keg unfiltered Weizen for a local publican

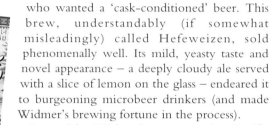

who wanted a 'cask-conditioned' beer. This brew, understandably (if somewhat misleadingly) called Hefeweizen, sold phenomenally well. Its mild, yeasty taste and novel appearance − a deeply cloudy ale served with a slice of lemon on the glass − endeared it to burgeoning microbeer drinkers (and made Widmer's brewing fortune in the process).

Spurred by Widmer's success, other Pacific northwest craft-brewers introduced their own unfiltered wheats. Popular examples today come from Redhook, Nor'Wester, and Pyramid. Several of these newer 'hefeweizens' possess a notable clean-tasting wheat character that is created by an authentic Bavarian amount of wheat malt (at least 50 percent of the grist). The region's Thomas Kemper Brewing actually tried to launch a true Bavarian-style hefeweizen, but switched to fermentation with its standard lager yeast after drinkers rejected the original's complex fruitiness!

Sales of the American hefeweizen style have grown so dramatically that even mainstream producers such as Stroh's Blitz Weinhard brewery and Anheuser-Busch/Michelob are offering examples. A handful of brewers sell unfiltered wheats without resorting to the 'hefeweizen' name (witness both Easy Street Wheat from Odell's of Colorado and Sierra Nevada's simply-named Wheat Beer).

Inspired by the Belgians, many North American craft-brewers have started using wheats, most frequently in unfiltered form, as the basis for fruit beers. Compared to the unique lambic wheat-brews that traditionally provide the beery base for Belgium's fruit beers, of course, domestic American and Canadian wheat beers taste fairly bland. But their crisp wheat flavors still help balance the sweetness of the fruit − or, rather, of the fruit concentrates and natural 'essences' favored by North American breweries. Flavors can range from the expected (raspberry, cherry, apple) to the 'exotic' (apricot, passion fruit, lemon).

At their best, such fruity suds can be supremely refreshing. They are exceedingly popular among novice craft-brew drinkers and women who 'don't like beer.' They are almost equally unpopular, along with filtered and unfiltered American wheats, among craft-beer aficionados and traditionally-minded brewers (who consider them, at best, bland).

But there can be no question that these fruit and wheat beers have helped broaden the audience for craft-brews. And they certainly qualify as distinct beer varieties developed in (North) America.

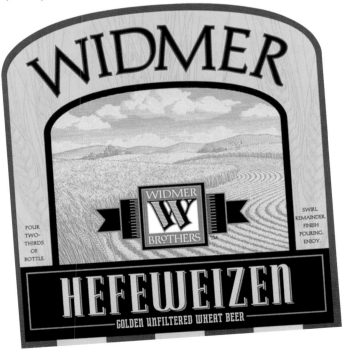

US MID-ATLANTIC

The 'mid-Atlantic' states, from New York down to northern Virginia, have a proud brewing tradition that stretches back into the earliest Colonial times. Unfortunately, even once-mighty brewing capitals such as Philadelphia (home to more than 100 breweries in the late 1800s) and New York City (host of Schaeffer, Rheingold, and other legendary brands) fell prey to post-Prohibition consolidation.

The first micros moved in during the 1980s, inspired by west coast pioneers, and many more recently have arrived. In general, mid-Atlantic craft brews divide evenly between ales and lagers. The former tend to have English accents that may reflect the region's early history. The latter testify to its life as a destination for European immigrants

Bi-monthly 'brewspapers' keep tabs on the mid-Atlantic's dynamic brewpub and beer scene. BarleyCorn (P.O. Box 549, Frederick, Maryland 21705) offers in-depth regional coverage, while Ale Street News (P.O. Box 1125, Maywood, New Jersey 07607) also reports on the northeast. The Malt Advocate, offering a classy take on beer and whisky, is distributed from Emmaus, PA (3416 Oak Hill Rd., 18049).

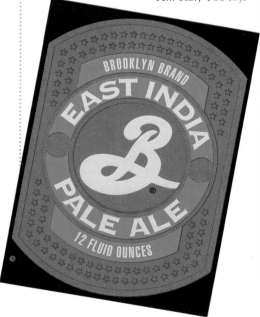

BROOKLYN BREWERY

ESTABLISHED 1988

118 N 11th Street, Brooklyn, New York 11211

〜⌘〜

RECOMMENDED
Brooklyn Lager (5.2%),
refreshing, hoppy amber brew
Black Chocolate Stout (8.2%),
smooth, rich, seductive Imperial

Brooklyn was founded by a banker and an Associated Press correspondent (who discovered that brewing was more enjoyable than dodging bullets on his Middle East assignment). Their original Brooklyn Lager was designed in the style of a 'pre-Prohibition beer' by a retired east coast brewmaster who once worked for Rheingold. Brooklyn later brought aboard its highly-regarded current brewmaster, Garrett Oliver.

Under Oliver's guidance, Brooklyn reformulated its chocolatey Brown Ale and also introduced two seasonals, Black Chocolate Stout (winter) and a powerfully hoppy East India Pale Ale (now year-round). While the majority of Brooklyn's production is contract-brewed at F.X. Matt, the company opened a small pub and brewery (to supply specialties, like a new 'Brooklyner Weisse,' for New York) in its home borough in May 1995. This new Brooklyn Brewery stands across the street from the company's offices, from

where it also runs New York's best specialty-beer distributorship.

CLIPPER CITY BREWING

ESTABLISHED 1995

4615 Hollins Ferry Road, Suite B
Baltimore, Maryland 21227

〜⌘〜

RECOMMENDED
Classic Pale Ale (4.8%),
aromatic and mellow in English style

Baltimore's 'biggest microbrewery' opened to the great anticipation of craft-

brew lovers in late 1995. Founder Hugh Sisson is famous around the city's beer scene, having lobbied the state to legalize brewpubs before promptly opening the first, Sisson's, in 1989. His new brewery's name echoes Baltimore's status as a major seaport, once known for the tall clipper ships that plied the waters of nearby Chesapeake Bay.

In addition to its English-inspired Pale Ale, excellent for washing down Maryland crabs, Clipper City also offers a straightforward Premium Lager. The latter reflects the city's German heritage – in the early 1900s around 25 percent of Baltimore's population was German – and also plays to a city-wide taste for mainstream beers. It is to be hoped that Clipper City will steer itself and the region's consumers on a course towards more distinctive beers.

DOCK STREET BREWING

ESTABLISHED 1986

225 City Line Avenue, Suite 110
Bala Cynwyd, Pennsylvania 19004

RECOMMENDED
Bohemian Pilsner (5.3%),
aromatically hoppy when fresh
Illuminator Double Bock (7.5%),
light in name alone
Beers from Brewery & Restaurant

One of the region's earliest craft brewers, established by a former chef, Dock Street takes its name from a Philadelphia avenue close to the Delaware River. Its three contract-brewed flagship brands – the original Amber Beer (a malty ale), Pilsner, and Bock (seasonal) – are available throughout the east and a few farther-flung states. The company offers more interesting ales and lagers at its flagship brewpub, Philadelphia's Dock Street Brewery & Restaurant (downtown at 2 Logan Square), which opened in 1990.

Above: No cheesesteaks here! Philadelphia's Dock Street brewpub offers gourmet fare to match its rotating range of distinctive draft ales and lagers.

Sadly, plans for a second, high-profile brewpub in Washington DC fell through in 1996.

The Philadelphia location offers attractive upscale surroundings, top-quality cuisine (as opposed to typical brewpub fare), and a rotating range of more than 60 ales and lagers. Under the guidance of its former head brewer Nicholas Funnell, Dock Street created excellent examples of classic beer styles, including a quenching Mexican Oscura (dark lager), a decidedly drinkable 'cask' dark mild, a smooth Imperial Stout, and a ripe-fruity Barley Wine.

The brewpub beers occasionally are found on draft at area restaurants (such as Philadelphia's Copa Too). Despite the DC setback, Dock Street still hopes to open similar brewery-restaurants across the mid-Atlantic – which bodes well for beer fans and 'foodies' alike.

F.X. MATT BREWING

ESTABLISHED 1888

811 Edward Street, Utica, New York 13502

RECOMMENDED
Saranac Golden (5.25%),
refreshing, dry-hopped lager
Saranac Pale Ale (5.5%),
balanced and pleasantly hoppy
Saranac Chocolate Amber (5.8%),
robust Munich-style dunkel

With its attractive brick buildings, huge copper kettles, and Victorian-style visitors' center, the F.X. Matt brewery would be right at home in the English countryside. Its origins, however, are totally Teutonic. After leaving his brewery in Germany's Black Forest region in 1878, Francis Xavier Matt plied his craft in upstate Utica (at the foothills of New York's Adirondack Mountains). There he offered both the region's traditional ales and his homeland's lagers. The brewery survived Prohibition by producing soft drinks, only to see sales decline as drinkers abandoned its Utica Club beers for new national brands.

During the 1980s, Matt began offering its services, experience, and excess capacity to the new generation of contract brewers. Their successes finally inspired brewery-head F.X. Matt II to launch his own craft-beer line under the Saranac label (named after an Adirondack lake). As sales have grown, the Saranac range has expanded from its initial Amber lager to include more adventurous beers such as an English-inspired Pale Ale (hopped with Kent Goldings). Notable seasonals include fall's Stout, usually only blended into a popular Black & Tan, and spring's complex Chocolate Amber. Overall, Matt has re-invented itself more successfully than most other older American regionals. Francis Xavier would be proud.

FREDERICK BREWING

ESTABLISHED 1993

103 South Carroll Street
Frederick, Maryland 21701

RECOMMENDED

Blue Ridge HopFest (varies),
annual early fall seasonal
Blue Ridge Steeple Stout (6%),
deeply roasted, smooth, intense
Blue Ridge Subliminator (7%),
rich doppelbock with chocolate, cherry notes

From the start, Frederick Brewing exclusively has used American ingredients for its ales and lagers. Interest in the beers was so great that, in only its first eight months of operation, Frederick increased its capacity from 2,500 to 12,000 barrels (2,900 to 14,000hl) per year. The company held a (relatively small) public stock offering in early 1996 to help raise money for a new brewery, located about five miles (8km) south of the city of Frederick, scheduled to open in 1996 with an annual capacity of 50,000 barrels (58,500hl). Frederick Brewing's original brewery will continue to operate, as well, at least through 1997.

Frederick offers six year-round beers under its Blue Ridge brand-name. These include a soft, clean Wheat Beer and the rich, big-bodied Steeple Stout (brewed with a portion of flaked rye). Frederick's seasonals arguably are more rewarding. Spring's Subliminator, brewed with over 90 pounds (41kg) of grain per bottle, is lagered for two months before release. Early fall's HopFest uses one specific hop variety (which changes every year) to highlight an unfiltered American brown ale base. Everything about 1995's version, brewed with new Ultra hops, proved popular except its small 250-barrel (290hl) production run! Unable to secure their share, many of the beer's admirers were left . . . hopping mad.

OLD DOMINION BREWING

ESTABLISHED 1990

44633 Guilford Drive, Ashburn
Virginia 22011

RECOMMENDED

Dominion Stout (4.7%),
creamy, complex, and quaffable
Tupper's Hop Pocket Ale (6%),
pale, fruity, and 'extravagantly hopped'
Dominion Millennium (10.4%),
deliciously chewy, fruity, and hoppy

Located outside of Washington DC, about three miles (5km) north of the capital's Dulles International Airport, Dominion quickly has become one of the country's most significant craft-brewers (producing 20,000 barrels/ 23,500hl in 1996). At the same time, its market remains relatively local (Virginia, DC, and parts of Maryland) – 'steep and deep,' as the saying goes. More than 15 different ales and lagers are brewed, some exclusively for restaurants and pubs in the region. Dominion also produces a root beer to an old recipe that founder Jerry Bailey (who formerly worked in the Federal Government's 'foreign aid' office) researched at the Library of Congress. Demand for root beer is so great that Bailey has considered opening a separate facility for its production.

While flagship beers such as Dominion Ale and Lager are pleasant, the brewery's abilities shine in Tupper's Hop Pocket Ale (dry hopped with whole Mt Hoods and Cascades) – actually a contract brew produced for a family associated with DC's famous Brickskeller bar. Dominion's seasonal beers, especially the rich Spring Brew bock, also are rewarding.

Most complex is Millennium, a now-annual barley wine – brewed to 100 bitterness units, dry hopped with English Kent Goldings (half a pound per barrel), and bottle conditioned – first brewed to celebrate the company's

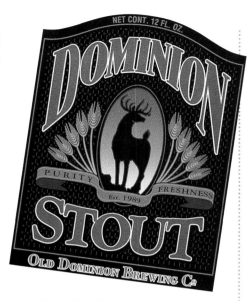

1,000th batch of beer in 1993. DC beer lovers await its yearly February release with the kind of anticipation usually reserved for Presidential elections.

PENN BREWERY

ESTABLISHED 1986

800 Vinial Street
Pittsburgh, Pennsylvania 15212

RECOMMENDED

Penn Dark (5%),
lots of caramel notes, smooth
Penn Märzen/Oktoberfest (5.6%),
rich malt in aroma and flavor
Penn St Nikolaus Bock (8.4%),
chewy, chocolatey, with rich caramel flavor

This German-inspired brewery was founded by Tom Pastorius, who spent 12 years working in Germany and is descended directly from the founder of America's first German settlement (Philadelphia's 'Germantown'). The flagship Penn Pilsner was Pennsylvania's first craft beer (albeit produced under contract). Pastorius opened his Penn Brewery brewpub in 1989. Its German-built, copper-vessel brewhouse and horizontal lagering tanks have been expanded to true micro status (18,000 barrels/21,100hl in 1996). All Penn Brewery beers now come from this facility, which stands in a renovated section of Pittsburgh's old Eberhardt & Ober Brewery.

Penn Pilsner is joined in year-round bottles and kegs by the smooth Munich dunkel-style Penn Dark, as well as an award-wining Munich-style Helles Gold. Bottled seasonals include the highly-regarded Oktoberfest and winter's potent St Nikolaus Bock. Draft specialties include a Bavarian-style Weizen, a Weizen Bock, a Maibock (soft, smooth), a hoppy Kaiser Pils, and a top-fermented Altbier.

STOUDT'S BREWING

ESTABLISHED 1987

Route 272, P.O. Box 880
Adamstown, Pennsylvania 19501

RECOMMENDED
Gold (5%),
the cleanly malty flagship
Honey Double Mai Bock (7.5%),
big body, creamy and finessed flavor

Stoudt's brews seem to increase in flavor the closer one gets to the brewery in tiny Adamstown. The one place this beery theory doesn't hold true is Denver, Colorado, where the beers have collected close to 20 total gold, silver, and bronze medals at the Great American Beer Festival. Still, there's no question that the brewery's on-site 'Gemütlichkeit' (German for good times) – Stoudt's hosts many Bavarian-themed festivals and events – brings out the best in its brews.

Situated in Pennsylvania Dutch (a corruption of 'Deutsch') country, the brewery began as a natural outgrowth of the beer garden and restaurant operated by Carol and Ed Stoudt. All their original brews were lagers, a fact that distinguished Stoudt's from other early east coast micros (most of whom made

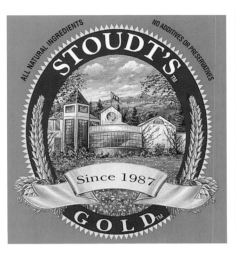

ales). Although the Dortmunder Export-style Gold, with its firmly malty character, remains the brewery flagship, bock beers have become a Stoudt's trademark: three medal-winning variations are offered. The brewery's range also now encompasses a few specialty ales, including a banana-fruity 'abbey' tripel.

VICTORY BREWING

ESTABLISHED 1996

420 Acorn Lane
Downingtown, Pennsylvania 19335

RECOMMENDED
HopDevil IPA (6.3%),
nutty malt, lots of tangy hop
St Victorious Doppelbock (7.4%),
lightly smoky and velvety smooth

Bready aromas have yielded to the fragrance of fermenting beer at this

former Pepperidge Farm bakery. Mid-Atlantic beer lovers watched with great expectation as Weihenstephan-trained Ron Barchet, former head brewer at Old Dominion, and Bill Covaleski, ex-assistant at Baltimore Brewing, opened their new micro and attached pub.

The advanced 25-barrel brewing system features integrated German designs for decoction-mashed lagers, a hopback (where the flagship HopDevil India Pale Ale gets a final helping of whole-cone Cascades), and open fermenters for ales. In addition to the IPA, Victory's main range includes a Bavarian-style Festbier and firmly malty Dortmunder (named after the surrounding Brandywine Valley).

Within weeks of opening, Covaleski and Barchet already were offering specialties as diverse as spring's St Victorious Doppelbock and hand-pumped Milltown Mild ale (3.8%). Victory is self-distributing both these special brews and its year-round brands throughout the surrounding area. 'No one is better equipped to represent us than us,' explains Covaleski. While initial reports have been positive, only time will tell if he's right to be confident of Victory.

Above: 'A Victory For Your Taste' is the confident boast of Downington-based Victory Brewing.

WILD GOOSE BREWING

ESTABLISHED 1989

20 Washington Street
Cambridge, Maryland 21613

RECOMMENDED

Porter (4.8%),
dry and full of dark fruit
Snow Goose (6.2%),
fruity, complex, warming

One of the mid-Atlantic's original micros, Wild Goose is now also among the region's most sizable (13,000 barrels/15,250hl per year). A new 50-barrel brewhouse installed in 1996 increased capacity to 38,000 barrels (44,600hl). The brewery's name comes from the signature waterfowl of Maryland's eastern shore, where Cambridge – what president Jim Lutz calls 'a quaint little town' – is located.

Since opening, Wild Goose slowly has supplemented its original Amber Ale with a chocolatey Porter, rich India Pale Ale, noble-hopped (Saaz, Hallertau) Spring Wheat, and fall's tasty Oatmeal Stout. The brewery also has successfully expanded distribution of its ales, which now are available from Maine to Miami – a total of 16 states.

Snow Goose, the hearty winter seasonal, is an annual favorite of regional fans. Styled after a traditional English old ale, it has a full body that best incorporates the fruity flavors generated by the brewery's Ringwood yeast strain (Peter Austin & Partners at work again!). The yeast shows to lesser advantage, perhaps, in Wild Goose's crisp Spring Wheat.

Overall, despite increased competition in its home market from several new and established craft-brewers, Wild Goose continues to fly high.

YUENGLING BREWERY

ESTABLISHED 1829

5th & Manhantongo Streets
Pottsville, Pennsylvania 17901

RECOMMENDED

Yuengling Porter (4.7%),
actually a balanced dark lager

The oldest operating brewery in America, founded by German immigrant David Yuengling (pronounced 'yingling') in the mining town of Pottsville (108 miles/174km northeast of Philadelphia, along the Schuykill Canal). The current brewery buildings, raised in 1831, stand on a steep hillside where tunnels were bored into the rock to take advantage of natural cool temperatures for fermentation and lagering.

By the late 1800s, Yuengling's beers had won such a following that the company constructed two additional breweries in New York state to meet demand. But Prohibition brought expansion to a halt. Like many old regionals, Yuengling survived (by producing low-alcohol 'near beer') only to see even its loyal local market – where customers refer to the beer as 'Vitamin Y' – eroded by national brands.

The brewery has reclaimed its successful position under the leadership of fifth-generation Dick Yuengling Jr. His approach involved both introducing

Above: Yuengling, America's oldest operating brewery, has been reclaiming its heritage. This picture shows its workers in 1914, only a few years before Prohibition brought production in Pottsville to a temporary close.

new brews, like a popular Black & Tan, and repositioning old ones (Lord Chesterfield Ale, Yuengling Premium Beer) to emphasize their history and tradition. Regional demand rebounded so substantially that Yuengling had to abandon out-of-state markets and expand its brewery. During 1996, the otherwise traditional company began contract-brewing in order to keep up with increasing demand.

Yuengling originally produced both lagers and ales: signs in its on-site museum tout a 'Brilliant Ale' and 'Brown Stout.' Today's beers, despite their names, are all lagers. Each offers a taste of American brewing history, but the chocolatey Porter (effectively a Munich-style dark) is the most distinctive.

D.G. **Yuengling** *& Son*

P.O. Box 539 · 5th & Mahantongo Streets · Pottsville, Pennsylvania 17901
Phone: 717-622-4141 · Fax: 717-622-4011

ZIP CITY BREWING

ESTABLISHED 1991

3 West 18th Street
New York, New York 10011

RECOMMENDED
Weizen (4%),
soft and balanced but wholly German
Rauchbier (4.25%),
traditionally smoky but smoothly drinkable
Eisbock (7.5%),
a style rarely brewed in America

Housed in the 1897 headquarters of the National Temperance Society, this handsome brewpub specializes in

German and Czech styles. Its urbane name, which fits perfectly with Manhattan's manic pace, comes from the novel *Babbit* by Sinclair Lewis ('good old Zip City' is the protagonist's home town). An Austrian brewhouse, custom designed for decoction-mashed lagers, stands exposed in the center of the pub's sleek oval bar.

Zip City has a roster of some 20 beer styles, ranging from its trademark Vienna lager and soft Weizen to specialties like a traditional Rauchbier and Belgian-style abbey dubbel. All have been so well received that Zip City began bottling and kegging for sales around the city in 1995. The flagship bottled Altbier is

supplemented with limited-season brews such as Zip City's annual Eisbock, one of the only American examples of this classic German style.

Owner Kirby Shyer hopes to build another Zip City, joining a restaurant and full-production micro (as opposed to brewpub), in a New York suburb. The expansion would be good news for beer lovers outside Manhattan, who could enjoy a Zip without the downtown trip.

ALSO WORTH TRYING

After a decade of cold-shouldering micros, New York now is awash. High-profile spots like d.b.a. (41 First Avenue) feature rarities such as the splendid Big Indian Porter from upstate's **Woodstock Brewing**. Among the brewpubs, which are opening faster than the city's cabbies drive, Manhattan's **Heartland Brewery** and Brooklyn's **Park Slope Brewing** get top reviews. In neighboring New Jersey, New Brunswick's Old Bay Restaurant (61 Church Street) is one of

the country's premier beer spots. And Princeton's **Triumph Brewing** offers an education in well-made ales and lagers for a fraction of tuition at the famous nearby university.

Savvy Philadelphia drinkers enjoy a fruity 'Extra Special Ale' and high-strength, high-flavor Imperial Stout (rarely released) from small **Yards Brewing**. Also watch taps for the complex Maple Wheat Ale from **Whitetail Brewing** (located farther west in York). Draft Belgian beers are showcased alongside micros at center city's Copa Too (263 S 15th Street). About an hour's drive south in Delaware, Wilmington has welcomed **Rockford Brewing**'s local India Pale Ale.

Baltimore beer-lovers flock to bars on Fells Point for **Oxford Brewing**'s Special Old Bitter or wintertime Santa Class ale. Watch for German-style 'DeGroen's' brews from the **Baltimore Brewing** brewpub, as well as draft specialties from local **Brimstone Brewing**. Around DC, Gaithersburg's suburban **Olde Towne Tavern** and Arlington's funked-up

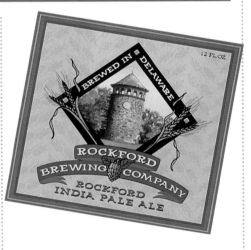

Bardo Rodeo offer completely different brewpub experiences. For a selection of local suds, head to the capital's Big Hunt (1345 Connecticut Avenue NW) or famous Brickskeller (1523 22nd Street NW), arguably the best bottled-beer bar in America.

In Virginia, look for **Potomac River Brewing**'s fruity-hoppy Rappahannock Red Ale (named after DC's other river). There's also a growing host of smaller producers such as Richmond's **Richbrau**.

U S   S O U T H E A S T

Maybe it's the hot, humid weather. Maybe it's the Bible belt's more strident religious beliefs and 'dry counties' (where no alcoholic beverages can be sold). Maybe it's obscure liquor laws, like the statute mandating that either 'Florida' or 'FL' be printed on the bottle-caps of all beers sold in that state. Whatever the reason, America's southeast – that curved swath of states from North Carolina through Louisiana – has been slow to embrace craft-brewing.

The movement largely has been carried by brewpubs (even though these remained illegal until recently in some areas). Unfortunately, their best-selling beers tend to be those closest to 'mainstream' American standards. Their proliferation nonetheless is an encouraging sign that southern tastes are turning to craft beer. So is the success of micros such as Louisiana's Abita Brewing and North Carolina's Wilmington Brewing. Southerners may yet begin to appreciate the same distinctiveness in beer that they enjoy in much of their region's food and drink, from Louisiana's spicy crayfish-boils to Kentucky's single-batch bourbons.

Southern Draft *(120 Wood Gate Drive, Canton, Georgia 30115)* is the region's colorful brewspaper. The national All About Beer *magazine is headquartered in North Carolina (1627 Marion Avenue, Durham, North Carolina).*

Above: Abita's new brewpub offers an excellent setting in which to 'take the waters.'

ABITA BREWING

ESTABLISHED 1986

P.O. Box 762, Abita Springs, Louisiana 70420

RECOMMENDED
Abita Bock (6.1%),
smooth, sweet spring seasonal
Abita Turbodog (6.1%),
deep chocolate-brown ale

Fresh brew from the Bayou? Close enough. Abita Springs stands in the piney woods across Lake Pontchartrain from New Orleans. Since its early days as a Choctaw Indian settlement, visitors have come to sample the town's 'restorative' artesian spring water. This untreated water, drawn from a 2,000-foot (610m) well, today provides the soul of Abita Brewing's lagers and ales. Despite some rough going in its early days, Abita now ranks among the country's larger craft-brewers.

The flagship Abita Amber and Golden, both clean-tasting lagers, sell well in the humid south – as does the draft-only Purple Haze, a raspberry wheat beer. Turbodog, produced year-round with Amber and Golden, is more complex and rewarding. Same goes for limited-season beers such as Abita Bock, Fallfest, and the punningly-named XXX-Mas Ale (brewed to a different recipe each year). Both Abita's year-round and seasonal brews are available throughout the southeast (and into New England).

As part of its ongoing expansion, Abita recently opened a brewpub (72011 Holly Street) to showcase its brands. It's at least as worthy of a pilgrimage as the famous springs.

BIRMINGHAM BREWING

ESTABLISHED 1992

3118 3rd Avenue S
Birmingham, Alabama 35233

RECOMMENDED
Red Mountain Red Ale (5%),
notable nutty-malt flavor

Prohibition came early to Alabama in 1908, forcing the original Birmingham Brewing Company to dump 300 barrels of fresh beer into the streets. Thankfully, no such misfortune has befallen the brewery's new incarnation. Its advanced brewhouse and bottling line produce several beers under the Red Mountain label, including a summer-season Wheat Beer and the flagship Red Ale (which picked up a medal for 'English-style brown ales' at the 1995 Great American Beer Festival).

The brewery also offers a Golden Ale and Golden Lager, as well as a pale 'Red Mountain Light' – beers that reveal where local tastes fall on the craft-brew learning curve.

OLDENBERG BREWING

ESTABLISHED 1987

400 Buttermilk Pike
Fort Mitchell, Kentucky 41017

RECOMMENDED
Outrageous Bock (5%),
pleasant American-style example

Despite the Kentucky address, only a few miles and the Ohio River separate Oldenberg from Cincinnati. Although Oldenberg's beers always have seemed slightly ahead of its local market, there are encouraging signs of change: new brewpubs have raised Cincinnati awareness of craft beer, for example. Confident of the brewery's future, more than 2,000 investors subscribed to Oldenberg's Initial Public Offering of stock in fall 1995. Distribution now includes several southern states.

Post-IPO developments include new packaging and new recipes (the smooth Holy Grail Nut Brown Ale and popular Raspberry Wheat), although Oldenberg continues to brew with local tastes in mind. The brewery flexes its muscles more in a rotating draft-only program that has offered a Pale Ale, Stout, Hefeweiss, and other traditional styles. Outside of brewing, Oldenberg is famous for 'Beer Camp,' a three-day extravaganza (held every March and September) of seminars, discussions, and activities that draws attendees from across America and Canada. Talk about happy campers . . .

WILMINGTON BREWING

ESTABLISHED 1994

111 Bryan Road
Wilmington, North Carolina 28412

RECOMMENDED
Dergy's Porter (4.8%),
lots of smooth coffee flavor

After decades in the hosiery business, Thomas Dergay abandoned socks for beer. He set up shop in coastal Wilmington, a small town best known for the eponymous Navy battleship (retired) in its harbor. The brewery actually stands a few miles out of downtown. Its new stainless-steel brewhouse, high-tech bottling line, and fermenters gleam in an otherwise un-impressive warehouse.

Dergay dropped the 'a' when it came to naming his ales. Although Dergy's Golden and Dergy's Amber were expected to appeal to local palates, it is

the coffeeish Porter which has become the brewery flagship. The character of all three beers was enhanced under the guidance of a former brewer who previously worked at Portland's Nor'Wester. Wilmington's beers can be found throughout the Carolinas and parts of Georgia.

ALSO WORTH TRYING

North Carolina is hopping on the microbrew bandwagon. Dan Thomasson, ex-brewmaster at England's Eldridge Pope (makers of Thomas Hardy's Ale), helped start up the state's new **Tomcat Brewing**. A smoky Black Radish lager comes from the coast's **Weeping Radish Brewing**. The **Carolina Brewery** offers a supremely hoppy IPA and roasty Old North State Stout, while **Carolina Brewing** presents a Pale Ale with lots of fresh hop flavor. The new **Top of the Hill** brewpub has the backing of *All About Beer*'s publisher, Daniel Bradford.

In Florida, **Miami Brewing**'s vice is not making more Hurricane Reef Amber Ale. Lager-lovers in New Orleans – where resurrected regional **Dixie Brewing** promotes the craft-beer spirit with its Blackened Voodoo lager – should visit the **Crescent City Brewhouse**. Louisiana's **Rikenjacks** beers also are well-received. Back in Birmingham, the **Magic City** brewpub offers a solid selection of ales. Tennessee's **Big River** brewpubs attract attention in Chattanooga and Nashville, while the latter city additionally hosts **Bohannon Brewing** and its Market Street Pilsner.

US MIDWEST

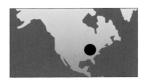

America's 'heartland' is also the center of its brewing industry. With Anheuser-Busch in St Louis, Miller in Milwaukee, and Stroh in Detroit, the nation's first-, second-, and fourth-largest brewers all are headquartered in the Midwest. And although they have introduced a few specialties, the Big Boys still churn out millions of barrels of mainstream lagers.

The Midwest's taste for lager beer originated in the waves of central and northern European immigration that flooded the region during the 1800s. German and Scandinavian settlers demanded the beers of their homelands – bocks, dunkels, weizenbiers, and more. Even as bland industrial beers claimed greater market shares, these classic styles were not forgotten. Nor were all the regional breweries that once produced them. Today, the Midwest remains a bastion of imported German brews, from rich doppelbocks to classic wheat beers *mit hefe*.

As a result, the region offers both great opportunity and challenge for microbrewers. Education is needed to overcome decades of devotion to American megabrands, but the Midwest's thirst for traditional German beer styles allows the introduction of brews (such as hefeweizens) that elsewhere are a harder sell. Micros finally appear to be reaching critical mass – even in Chicago, where a wheeler-dealer beer trade still favors the nationals. Read *Midwest Beer Notes* (339 - 6th Avenue, Clayton, Wisconsin 54004) to keep abreast.

AUGUST SCHELL BREWING

ESTABLISHED 1860

Schell's Park, P.O. Box 128
New Ulm, Minnesota 56073

❧

RECOMMENDED
Pils (5.6%),
refreshingly hoppy from imported Hallertau
Maifest (6.9%),
smoothly drinkable spring bock

A regional that battled back from the brink of collapse through new emphasis on specialty beers (both its own and brands it makes under contract). The company is still owned by descendants of German immigrant August Schell, who have maintained close ties with the surrounding area for over a century. Known regionally for mainstream lagers, the brewery first attracted national notice with its long-produced Bock (perhaps the best example of the old 'American' style).

An alliance with beer pioneer Charles Finkel (see page 73) prompted the introduction of Schell's hoppy German-style Pils and filtered Bavarian-style Weizen in 1985. The success of these brands spawned others, such as spring's balanced, refreshing Maifest (a 'blonde double bock'). A candyish DoppelBock also is offered. The German-themed company even has ventured into ales – first with its chocolatey Schmaltz's Alt (an 'alt-

porter'?), then with an English-styled Anniversary Ale brewed to mark its 135th year. Where better to celebrate than Schell's five-acre gardens and deer park (also populated by several peacocks), which adjoin the original brick brewery buildings?

CAPITAL BREWERY

ESTABLISHED 1986

7734 Terrace Avenue
Middleton, Wisconsin 53562

❧

RECOMMENDED
Garten Bräu Special (4.9%),
hoppy German-styled Pilsner
Garten Bräu Doppelbock (7.5%),
big, sweetish, chocolatey

Capital is a craft-brewer dedicated to making the midwest's favored German beers. Much of its equipment, including twin copper brewing vessels, came from Germany's Hoxter Brewery. The Garten Bräu name comes, appropriately, from an on-site beer garden whose fencing is covered with hops and grape vines.

The top-selling Special testifies to the region's taste for both classic German imports and mainstream golden lagers. Its well-made character is echoed by Garten Bräu Dark, a balanced example in the Munich style. The year-round range also includes a Bavarian-style (hefe)Weizen, English-inspired

Above: Wisconsin's Capital Brewery is a relatively new micro based in Middleton making 'Authentic German Beer,' long a favorite throughout the Midwest.

Brown Ale, and purely-American raspberry wheat ('The Razz'). Seasonals, including Capital's potent Doppelbock, are perhaps more interesting. Both a springtime Maibock and autumn Oktoberfest are worthy of celebration. Garten Bräu Wild Rice is made with Wisconsin-grown 'grain' (actually a grass) which imparts a complex, spicy character to the finished beer.

GOOSE ISLAND BEER COMPANY

ESTABLISHED 1988

1800 West Fulton, Chicago, Illinois 60612

RECOMMENDED

Kölsch (4.5%),
refreshing, well-made, with subtle complexity
Demolition Ale (8%),
dangerously drinkable Belgian-style golden
Bourbon County Stout (11.5%),
truly unique and deliciously whiskyish

A famous 'Second City' beer-maker, named after an island in the Chicago River. The original large, comfortable brewpub (1800 North Clybourn) was supplemented in 1995 with a full production craft-brewery (funded in part through ties with the Beer Across America microbrew-of-the-month club). The brewpub still offers more than 30 well-crafted, rotating styles — everything from a 'starter' Blonde Ale to a Dunkelweizenbock and Finnish-inspired Sahti.

Goose Island's flagship Honkers Ale, a balanced pale ale hopped with Styrian Goldings, is now available in bottles and barrels from the new facility. So is a Kilgubbin Red Ale — 'Kilgubbin' is Gaelic for Goose Island, once home to Irish settlers — and seasonals such as summer's Kölsch and winter's annually-changed Christmas Ale. A draft specialty series includes May's Demolition Ale (a potent Duvel-styled brew introduced when the brewpub's surrounding building was torn down in 1994) and January's Bourbon Stout. The latter is made by ageing a powerful stout for a minimum of 100 days in ex-Jim Beam Bourbon barrels. Extremely complex and surprisingly drinkable, it fortifies well against Chicago's winter weather.

GREAT LAKES BREWING

ESTABLISHED 1988

2516 Market Street, Cleveland, Ohio 44113

RECOMMENDED

Burning River Pale Ale (6%),
bags of refreshing citric hop character
The Eliot Ness (6.2%),
malty, spicy, well-made Vienna lager
Conway's Irish Ale (6.8%),
big, sweetish, deep with balancing hop

Great Lakes opened as a brewpub in an 1860s' building where industrialist John D. Rockefeller once worked.

Subsequent expansions include an outdoor beer garden and a full-production micro in an adjacent building. Between this new brewery and the original (which still makes specialties like 'Loch Erie' Scotch Ale), production topped 10,000 barrels (11,700hl) in 1995. Distribution is strongest in the midwest and south, including Tennessee and Kentucky.

Brewery flagship Dortmunder Gold is a medal-winning example of that lager style. Burning River Pale Ale — named for an infamous incident when Cleveland's then-polluted river caught on fire — is deliciously fruity and fresh-tasting. Eliot Ness, brewed with Hallertau and Tettnang hops, is well-made (if not untouchable) in the Vienna style. Seasonals include a chocolatey-malty Rockefeller Bock ('as rich as its name'), a thoroughly hoppy Commodore Perry IPA, and Christmas Ale flavored with honey, cinnamon, and ginger.

Spring's Irish Ale, named after the grandfather of owners Pat and Daniel Conway, has a strongly malty aroma and rich toasty-malt flavor balanced by peppery Kent Golding hops. Its deep character illustrates why many aficionados consider Great Lakes to be the midwest's greatest micro.

KALAMAZOO BREWING

ESTABLISHED 1985

315 E Kalamazoo Avenue
Kalamazoo, Michigan 49007

RECOMMENDED
Bell's Amber Ale (5.5%),
softly fruity and hoppy
Bell's Kalamazoo Stout (6.5%),
roasty, rich with molasses hints
Bell's Third Coast Old Ale (10.2%),
thick, chewy barley wine

The personality of Kalamazoo founder Larry Bell is best described by the name of his brewery's on-site Eccentric Cafe. Bell vacillates between shunning publicity and staging colorful stunts to get it: for example, he once produced a provocative television commercial for the brewery that showed a German-themed accordionist deliberately shattering his instrument and setting it ablaze! Brewing occurs on several now-supplementary systems, including the company's original 15-gallon (57l) soup kettle. Production was expected to top 24,000 barrels (28,200hl) in 1996. Distribution encompasses the upper midwest and greater Chicago.

The flagship Bell's Amber is joined year-round by a firm Pale Ale, a lightly-roasted Porter, a gentle Third Coast Beer, and a robust Kalamazoo Stout. The year splits between two 'seasonals' – Oberon Ale (an American wheat) in summer and Best Brown Ale in winter. But it is specialty brews, offered in limited quantities throughout the year, that draw the most attention. These include an intensely rich Expedition Stout (11.5%), über-hopped Two Hearted Ale, and warming Third Coast Old Ale. Additional specialties are brewed only for the brewery cafe.

Right: Based in Wisconsin's 'Northwoods' at Chippewa Falls since 1867, Leinenkugel recently has been making a national name for itself with specialty-style brews.

LAKEFRONT BREWERY

ESTABLISHED 1987

818 East Chambers Street
Milwaukee, Wisconsin 53212

RECOMMENDED
Riverwest Stein Beer (6%),
nutty amber lager with 'crisp' hops
Holiday Spice (9%),
billowy-spicy and extremely well balanced

Another new brewery which again joins grain and yeast in a former bakery building. The founding Klisch brothers (one is a police detective) built much of their plant from used equipment. 'I call it my Frankenstein,' jokes Russ Klisch about the jumbled facility, 'because almost every piece previously has lived, died, and been resurrected here.' For aesthetics, three horizontal fermenting tanks are painted with the heads of Larry, Curly, and Moe of television's Three Stooges.

Despite its piecemeal appearance, Lakefront produces seriously distinctive beers. The flagship Riverwest Stein Beer – not a Rauchenfels-type stone beer, but rather named for a drinking 'stein' – is clean, quaffable, and crisply hoppy

thanks to American Mt Hoods and Cascades. Other year-round brews include Lakefront Cream City Pale Ale (fruity, drinkable), East Side Dark (a strong dunkel), and Klisch Pilsner (generously hopped with Mt Hoods). The honey-fortified Winter Spice – which matures well in the bottle – caps off a range of rotating seasonals such as fall's famous Lakefront Pumpkin Beer, a late-winter Cherry Beer, spring Bock, and sweetish summertime Weiss (Bavarian style).

NEW GLARUS BREWING

ESTABLISHED 1993

P.O. Box 759, New Glarus, Wisconsin 53574

RECOMMENDED
Apple Ale (4.8%),
deliciously cider-like in character
Belgian Red (5%),
fantastically flavorful Belgian-style kriek
Snowshoe Ale (5.7%),
hoppy, fruity, darkly malty

This small micro makes two of the best fruit beers in America, if not the world. It was founded by Daniel and Deborah

Carey in a Swiss-settled town near Wisconsin capital Madison. Daniel previously worked for brewery-installation company J.V. Northwest, and ultimately rose to the role of production supervisor at Anheuser-Busch's Fort Collins plant.

New Glarus offers three year-round beers: the soft Edel Pils, a darkly chocolatey Uff-Da Bock, and a truly fruity Apple Ale. The latter, a wheat-based brown ale blended with Cortland, MacIntosh, and Jonathon apples (squeezed at a nearby orchard), has a fresh 'farm cider' flavor.

A range of six limited-season beers includes early spring's sweetish Coffee Stout, late spring's honey-brewed Norski Maibock, and summer's Solstice Weiss. But the best are winter's Snowshoe and the holiday season's exceptional Belgian Red. Brewed with aged Willamette hops and more than a pound of whole local Wisconsin cherries per 750ml bottle, Belgian Red is based on a Flanders-style sour brown ale (think Liefmans Kriek). Picking up a few bottles surely ranks among the best reasons to visit Wisconsin!

SUMMIT BREWING

ESTABLISHED 1986

2264 University Avenue
St Paul, Minnesota 55114

RECOMMENDED
Hefe Weizen (4.2%),
fruity and refreshing in Bavarian style
Great Northern Porter (5.4%),
dry, chocolatey, and roasty

One of America's 'first wave' micros, and the classic ale-brewer in the Twin Cities (St Paul and adjoining Minneapolis). Founder Mark Stutrud worked as a chemical dependency counselor before choosing craft-brewing as an 'honest' living. Summit's small

copper brewhouse – purchased from the Hirschbrau brewery in Heimertingen, Bavaria – produced approximately 29,000 barrels (34,000hl) in 1996, close to its maximum. The company expects to open a new brewery (along West Seventh Street in Crosby Lake Business Park) in 1997 that will more than triple its capacity.

Summit offers two year-round beers: the flagship Extra Pale Ale and distinctive Great Northern Porter (which captured a First Place award at the early 1987 Great American Beer Festival). These are supported with several rotating seasonal beers, including summer's pleasantly banana-fruity Hefe Weizen. There also is an autumn Alt Bier, a medium-bodied Winter Ale, an early springtime Maibock, and a late springtime India Pale Ale (dry-hopped!). The IPA was expected to become available year-round in 1996.

The company's brews have a strong local following. You might even say, given Stutrud's previous career, that the Twin Cities are 'hooked' on Summit's fresh, flavorful beers.

ALSO WORTH TRYING

In Minnesota, Minnetonka's highly-regarded **Sherlock's Home** brewpub makes excellent (true) cask-conditioned ales, while **James Page Brewing** of Minneapolis produces a smooth Amber and its pioneering Boundary Waters Wild Rice beer. To the east in Wisconsin, Milwaukee's **Sprecher Brewing** offers an excellent year-round Black Bavarian lager and special seasonals such as an Imperial Stout. **Gray Brewing** of Janesville lets you wash down the state's trademark cheese curds with a deliciously hoppy American Pale Ale, quaffable Oatmeal Stout, and spiced wintertime Wassail. Old regional **Leinenkugel Brewing** (now owned by Miller) rolls out accessible 'specialties' like an Auburn Ale and Winter Lager from both its Chippewa Falls headquarters and Milwaukee' ex-Val Blatz Brewery.

South in Chicago, the 'City of Big Shoulders,' drinkers can lift a chocolatey Big Shoulders Porter or toasty Legacy Red Ale from local **Chicago Brewing**. Also watch for a refreshing Honey Ginger Ale from the city's tiny **Golden Prairie Brewing**. In Michigan's touristy 'German theme town' of

Frankenmuth, the **Frankenmuth Brewery** (another creative name) made Bavarian-style beers before being severely damaged by a tornado in 1996: its smooth, chocolatey Frankenmuth Dark and medal-winning Bock both were worth seeking out.

Finally, in Missouri, Kansas City's **Boulevard Brewing** offers well-made specialties such as its buttery-malt Irish Ale and roasty Bully! Porter. And in Iowa, old regional **Dubuque Brewing** craft-brews under its own name and its Wild Boar brand.

Above: Frankenmuth's rich, Bavarian-style Dark uses black malt to achieve its deep, chocolatey color.

US SOUTHWEST

A sense of rugged individuality isn't the only thing Southwesterners share with their northwest counterparts: both regions are becoming rich in craft-breweries and brewpubs! Even Colorado-headquartered Coors – the largest single-site brewery in the world – crafts Imperial stouts and raspberry ales at its brewpub in Denver's new baseball stadium. Meanwhile, in Texas, Belgium's Pierre Celis creates classic ales in Austin that would be equally at home in Ostend.

This is not to imply that the southwest has stopped quaffing its share of main-stream American beer. Bland industrial brews such as Lone Star still hold a place deep in the hearts of Texans. There's also a simple reason (beyond a desire to irritate Coors) that Anheuser-Busch runs a megabrewery in Colorado's Fort Collins. But with brown ales in Boulder, hand-pumped 'cask ale' in Houston, and new micros in New Mexico, there's no question that craft beer – like everything else in the southwest – is hot.

Following the region's dynamic beer scene can be more difficult than selling sand to a scorpion. Let Southwest Brewing News *(1505 Lupine Ln, Austin, Texas 78741) do the reporting. The Association of Brewers (P.O. Box 1679, Boulder, Colorado 80306) tracks craft-brewing across the country and also organizes Denver's annual Great American Beer Festival.*

CELIS BREWERY

ESTABLISHED 1991

2431 Forbes Drive, Austin, Texas 78754

RECOMMENDED

Celis White (4.8%),
many consider it the classic witbier
Celis Golden (4.9%),
refreshing, clean, Saaz-accented Pilsner
Celis Grand Cru (8.7%),
deliciously finessed and flavorful

Founded by veteran Belgian brewer Pierre Celis, who is famous for rescuing Belgium's nearly-lost 'white beer' (witbier) style. After Belgian beer-giant Interbrew acquired his successful revivalist brewery in Hoegaarden, Belgium, Celis decided to start afresh in America. Attracted to Austin by its soft limestone water (similar to Hoegaarden's), he began brewing new versions of his famous beers.

The Celis Brewery, which features a classic copper brewhouse made in Belgium during the 1930s, stands several miles outside downtown Austin. In 1994, a need for capital prompted the Celis team to sell a majority interest to Miller Brewing. While this move worried purists, jokes about 'Miller White' have proved unjustified so far. If anything, Miller's influence (largely confined to marketing expertise) has helped Celis refocus its efforts. The megabrewer seems to want to polish Celis as the jewel in its crown of small producers.

Celis White is brewed from 50 percent barley malt and 50 percent raw winter wheat grown in Luckenbach, Texas. A traditional period of lactic fermentation leaves it tart and tangy with lots of wheaty flavor (the original Hoegaarden White seems somewhat 'softer'). Curaçao and other spices give Grand Cru, a strong golden ale, lots of aromatic character and complexity. Celis Golden gets its balanced body from six-weeks' lagering, while generous amounts of Saaz hops create its zesty floral aroma and herbal-bitter flavors. A candy-sweet Raspberry wheat beer and nutty 'Pale Bock' (actually a Belgian-styled pale ale) also are offered.

Celis introduced a strong dark ale in the 'abbey dubbel' style, much like Hoegaarden's lush Forbidden Fruit, during 1996. Such a line extension no longer seems risky at a time when Americans are starting to embrace a wide range of Belgian ales. Indeed, the future of domestic Belgian-style beers seems quite rosy. And Celis' future, in particular, seems White.

NEW BELGIUM

ESTABLISHED 1991

500 Linden Street
Fort Collins, Colorado 80524

RECOMMENDED
Abbey (6.5%),
outstanding spicy-fruity, dark malt character
Trippel (7.8%),
fresh-tasting hops balance honeyed malt
Abbey Grand Cru (8%),
America's answer to Rochefort 8°

New Belgium's is a classic tale: homebrewer Jeff Lebesch and his wife decided to take their hobby commercial. The twist was their inspiration, the great ales of Belgium. Within their first year, demand forced the founders to move the brewery out of their home and into a purpose-built location. Production more than tripled – make that 'trippeled' – between 1993 and 1994. To cope with the region's still-growing thirst, New Belgium moved into a $5-million new facility, complete with an advanced German-built Steinecker brewhouse, in 1995. The company expected to produce at least 80,000

Above: New Belgium's new brewery weds modern technology to ancient 'abbey' beers.

barrels (93,900hl) in 1996, with sales still confined to Colorado and part of Wyoming. Pretty good for a brewery that began in the owners' basement.

New Belgium's success rides on a fat tire – Fat Tire Amber Ale, to be precise. The popularity of this easy-drinking amber has grown to the point where it is Colorado's top-selling ale. A year-round Old Cherry Ale is supplemented in late fall by a brown-ale-based Frambozen. Belgian aficionados will be more interested by the Abbey (dubbel) and Trippel, which the brewery says are fermented 'with an authentic Belgian Trappist yeast strain.' The Abbey Grand Cru, introduced to mark the company's 1,000th brew, now makes occasional reappearances whenever something needs celebrating.

ODELL BREWING

ESTABLISHED 1989

800 E Lincoln, Fort Collins, Colorado 80524

RECOMMENDED
90 Shilling (5.5%),
pleasantly malty with chocolate notes
India Pale Ale (6%),
dry-hopped winter seasonal

Until April of 1996, this family-run micro made only draft beers. Doug, Wynne, and Corkie Odell founded their namesake brewery at a relatively early time (at least for Colorado). Subsequent growth has been fuelled by their malty, balanced 90 Shilling ale, which dominates taps across Fort Collins and the surrounding region (Odell's now claims some 300 tap handles across the state). Odell's moved from its original site, a historic grain elevator, to a new facility in 1994. The new brewery was expanded in early 1996 to cope with increased production.

Odell's expected to brew well over 30,000 barrels (35,200hl) in 1996, with

sales – like those of nearby New Belgium Brewing – confined to Colorado and Wyoming. In addition to the 90 Shilling, billed as a cross between a Scottish 'heavy' and an English pale ale, Odell's Ales feature an unfiltered Easy Street Wheat (American-style), a 'light' golden ale called Levity, and Cutthroat Porter (brewed with English Kent Goldings). With the exception of the porter, all now are available in bottles. There also are seasonals such as the India Pale Ale (October to March), full of hop character, and an annual 'Christmas' brew, flavored with red currants and both sweet and sour cherries.

ROCKIES BREWING/
BOULDER BEERS

ESTABLISHED 1979

2880 Wilderness Place
Boulder, Colorado 80301

RECOMMENDED

Boulder Cliffhanger Ale (4.2%),
lots of fresh hop flavor
Boulder Porter (5.2%),
pleasantly smooth and sweetish
Boulder Stout (5.8%),
sweet, complex, and mouth-filling

This sizable company has the distinction of being the oldest operating craft-brewery in America. Two homebrewers founded the original Boulder Brewing Company on a farm outside the city. The current purpose-built brewery and pub was raised in 1984. Six years later, however, management troubles and quality-control problems sent Boulder into foreclosure. The brewery has been substantially revitalized under the guidance of buyer Gina Day, a former medical technologist. (Day's husband is a restaurant pioneer behind the Rock Bottom brewpub chain and Boulder's own Walnut Brewery).

With the help of experienced Pacific northwest brewmaster David Zuckerman, Day put Boulder back on track: all recipes were reformulated, and the company name was changed (to Rockies) better to reflect its regional focus.

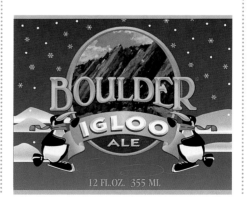

Today, Rockies offers seven year-round Boulder Ales and five seasonal brews (such as February's Cliffhanger, a lightly-fruity ale generously dry-hopped with Hallertau). The clean-tasting Boulder Extra Pale Ale and gutsy Amber Ale sell best throughout the year, although the Stout and Porter are more complex. With production expected to exceed 42,000 barrels (49,300hl) in 1996, the brewery's future – despite its name and previous troubles – seems anything but rocky.

TABERNASH BREWING

ESTABLISHED 1993

205 Denargo Market
Denver, Colorado 80216

RECOMMENDED

Tabernash Weiss (5.7%),
arguably America's best Bavarian-style wheat
Tabernash Munich (4.9%),
a smooth and nutty dunkel
Tabernash Oktoberfest (6%),
sweet, toasty malt and spicy hop

Named after an old stagecoach station in the Colorado mountains, Tabernash has a distinguished pedigree: brewmaster Eric Warner earned a diploma from Germany's famous Weihenstephan brewing school, while founder Jeff Mendel previously directed America's micro-watching Institute for Brewing Studies. Warner literally 'wrote the book' on weizens (his *German Wheat Beer*, from Brewers Publications, is an industry reference). Tabernash's crisp, tangy, unfiltered Weiss, considered by many to be the country's best Bavarian example, illustrates his skill.

Excepting the Weiss, all Tabernash beers are lagers. The founders chose this path in light of Warner's background and their desire to distinguish the company from Colorado's several ale brewers. Respectable lagering time makes Tabernash's year-round beers –

the malty, reddish Munich and Saaz-scented Golden Pilsner (both decoction-mashed) – smooth and subtle. Seasonals such as September's Oktoberfest and February's Doppelbock are appropriately richer in character. Tabernash Amber, added to the range in 1996, is an interpretation of a 'steam beer' (once a style common throughout the west). To expand both its market and marketability, Tabernash began bottling its formerly draft-only beers in mid-1996. Early reports say six-packs of Weiss are especially nice!

Above: Tabernash established its reputation with a range of draft beers. Bottles were launched in 1996.

WYNKOOP BREWING

ESTABLISHED 1988

1634 Eighteenth Street
Denver, Colorado 80202

RECOMMENDED

Sagebrush Stout (5%),
hearty, extra-smooth (from oatmeal)
India Pale Ale (5.5%),
especially refreshing on hand-pump

Above: Wynkoop Brewing produced Bach Bock to commemorate the composer's 311th birthday. Would he have been amused by the slogan, 'Music to our Beers?'

Pioneering Colorado brewpub, the oldest in the state, named after Denver mayor Edward Wynkoop (1836-1891). Located two blocks away from Coors Field in Denver's now-trendy (renovated) 'Lo(wer) Do(wntown)' area. Wynkoop was founded by former geologist John Hickenlooper, who subsequently helped open several other brewpubs and breweries across Colorado. If there is a 'godfather' of American brewpubs, Hickenlooper is he.

Wynkoop says it sold more beer in 1995 than any other brewpub in the world, including Prague's famous U Fleků (which, at 4,250 barrels/5,000hl, lost by 758 barrels). The flagship Wynkoop brew is Railyard Ale, billed as a union of English Pale Ale and German Oktoberfest lager. Other year-round beers include the IPA, and Stout. These are supplemented by a wide rotating range. Railyard and occasional other beers are brewed separately for bottles by nearby Broadway Brewing, established jointly by Wynkoop and Aspen's Flying Dog Brewery as a commercial brewing and bottling facility.

YELLOW ROSE BREWING

ESTABLISHED 1994

17201 San Pedro Avenue
San Antonio, Texas 78232

RECOMMENDED
Honcho Grande (5.1%),
smooth but hearty brown ale
Yellow Rose Pale Ale (5.1%),
the brewery flagship

This enthusiastic micro was founded by a former oral surgeon who now can claim to be 'repairing' Texan palates with his robust English-style ales. It is based in a converted ice-house in the same city as the former Lone Star brewery. The home-made brewhouse (a 10-barrel system) produces six year-round ales, available on draft throughout San Antonio and other Texas metro areas. The beers also are packaged in pint bottles with wrap-around labels that offer lessons in regional history.

In addition to its signature Pale Ale and 'Big Guy' brown ale, inspired by Mexico's legendary Pancho Villa, Yellow Rose offers a moderately dry Vigilante Porter and semi-sweet Stout. The range also includes an American-style 'Bubba Dog' wheat and Cactus Queen IPA. As its beer names suggest, Yellow Rose makes every effort to enjoy itself. Microbrewing is a tough job, reports the company's newsletter, but 'it beats canning fish!' No argument there.

ALSO WORTH TRYING

Texas has a tradition of American 'bocks' – caramel-accented versions of mainstream lagers – best represented by Shiner Bock from old regional **Spoetzl Brewing**. The state's many brewpubs (Austin's **Bitter End** and **Two-Rows** in Dallas, for example) offer more interesting beers. Houston's **St Arnold Brewing** occasionally cask-conditions its Amber Ale; look for it on hand-pump at the city's excellent GingerMan pub (5607 Morningside Drive). The GingerMan's Austin branch usually serves the fruity Balcones ESB from nearby **Hill Country Brewing**.

Arizona, already awash in brewpubs, is developing a taste for beer from new micro **McFarlane Brewing**. Neighboring New Mexico also has its share of brewpubs. On the micro front, Santa Fe's **Russell Brewing** offers several specialties in 22oz bottles, while Galisteo's **Santa Fe Brewing** (which changed ownership during 1996) supplements bottles of its soft Pale Ale with several additional kegged brews.

Colorado's more than 60 breweries make it the southwest's most developed craft-beer market. Popular brewpubs include Boulder's **Walnut**, Denver's **Champion**, Fort Collins' **Coopersmiths**, and Colorado Springs' **Phantom Canyon** (famous for a lightly-smoky Peated Porter). Denver's **Great Divide Brewing** gets good reviews for its Arapahoe Amber and St Brigid's Porter. **Irons Brewing** of Lakewood offers ales (like IronHeart Red) and lagers to 'put a little irons in your diet,' while **Left Hand Brewing** of Longmont seasons its pleasant Juju Ginger Ale with fresh-ground ginger root.

Left: Denver's Great Divide Brewery shipped approximately 8,000 barrels (9,400hl) in 1996 to quench Colorado's growing thirst for craft beer.

US CALIFORNIA

California is famous for movements both seismic and cultural. From San Francisco's 'Beat poets' to San Diego's surf-speak to L.A.'s latest batch of snappy sitcom phrases, plenty of social trends originate in the Golden State. So it went with craft-brewing. California not only hosts Anchor Brewing, the resuscitated regional that pioneered modern specialty beers, but it also gave birth to America's first 'official' microbrewery, New Albion, in the late 1970s.

Although New Albion proved ahead of its time, its philosophy has been carried forward by a wave of California craft-breweries that includes everyone from sizable Sierra Nevada to bite-size Bison Brewing. (Craft beer even has spread west to Hawaii, where islanders say 'aloha!' to Kona Brewing's ales). Lots of thirsty California consumers support the movement's growth. The San Francisco Bay Area alone contains more than twice Washington state's total population (which may explain why Seattle's Pyramid Breweries opened a sizable plant in Berkeley).

Like many of the more successful California brewers, the excellent Celebrator Beer News (P.O. Box 375, Hayward, California 94545) covers the state while also addressing the overall country.

ANCHOR BREWING

ESTABLISHED 1896

1705 Mariposa Street
San Francisco, California 94107

RECOMMENDED

Anchor Steam Beer (5%),
malty-nutty, dry, and hoppy
Liberty Ale (6%),
supremely hoppy, aromatic pale ale
Old Foghorn (8.7%),
beautifully balanced, richly complex barley wine

A San Francisco legend now so famous for its Steam Beer that fans frequently

Above: Gleaming copper in Anchor's fine brewhouse.

call the whole brewery 'Anchor Steam.' In the 1960s, however, Anchor was sinking fast before Fritz Maytag (heir to the washing-machine family), a recent graduate from nearby Stanford University, learned of its imminent demise while enjoying a glass of Steam. His initial offer to help turned into an outright purchase in 1965.

Over the next decade, Maytag tirelessly worked to revive both the brewery and its beers. Ultimately, Anchor brews became so popular that Maytag could afford to move out of the company's old, rundown facility. He built a new showplace brewery – with a hand-made copper brewhouse – in a restored coffee factory. To Maytag's eternal credit, he shared his brewery experiences with the new generation of micros in the late 1970s.

Anchor's flagship Steam Beer defines that indigenous American style (see page

32). It is joined year-round by Liberty Ale, Old Foghorn, a stout-like Porter, and draft-only Wheat Beer (American style). The golden Liberty shows an incredible Cascade-hop aroma and flavor. Foghorn, whose name resonates with San Francisco character, offers a seamless blend of rich malt, estery (see page 19) fruit, and herbal hop. Many aficionados 'lay down' Old Foghorn bottles to mature. The same goes for Anchor's annual, vintage-dated Christmas Ale. Technically called 'Our Special Ale,' it is brewed to a different recipe each year.

With the possible exception of the wheat, all of Maytag's beers have helped inspire countless new microbrewers. Anchor's pioneering significance cannot be overstated.

Above: Critics' praise runneth over for Anchor's beers.

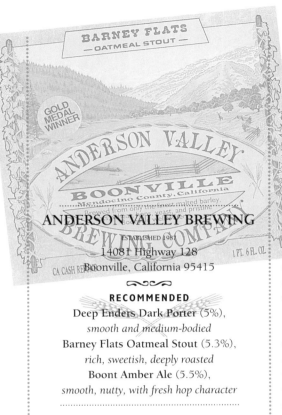

ANDERSON VALLEY BREWING
ESTABLISHED 1987
14081 Highway 128
Boonville, California 95415

RECOMMENDED
Deep Enders Dark Porter (5%),
smooth and medium-bodied
Barney Flats Oatmeal Stout (5.3%),
rich, sweetish, deeply roasted
Boont Amber Ale (5.5%),
smooth, nutty, with fresh hop character

An individualistic micro in Mendocino County's Anderson Valley. In 1996, the company supplemented its 10-barrel brewhouse – serving the on-premises Buckhorn Saloon – with a 'temporary' 30-barrel system. The latter will increase production until 1997, when a purpose-built, all-copper, German-made brewhouse (capable of 100-barrel/117hl batches) comes on-line. Anderson Valley also plans to expand its distribution, currently the strongest in California.

Anderson Valley offers six year-round ales, all named in the region's 'Boontling' dialect. The complex (dry hopped?) Boont Amber, extremely well-balanced Porter, and slightly oily (in a good way) Oatmeal Stout have the best reputations. There also is a clean, refreshing High Rollers Wheat, soft and bitter Poleeko Gold Pale Ale, and malty-sweetish Belks ESB. Occasional special brews include a rare Barley Wine and the annual Winter Solstice, seasoned with 'secret' spices.

BISON BREWING
ESTABLISHED 1988
2598 Telegraph Avenue
Berkeley, California 94704

RECOMMENDED
Virtually all beers are worth trying

This is a funky brewpub in perhaps America's most eccentric, alternative, creative town. Although it brews 'standard' styles such as an IPA and ESB, Bison excels at cutting-edge recipes. An ongoing series of ales are offered on roughly a seasonal basis. Once per month, a batch is bottled-conditioned (in 22oz bottles).

Worthy attempts have included a sour-mashed Lemongrass Wheat (lightly citric and refreshing), and summer's well-balanced Honey Basil Ale (smooth, tangy, clean-tasting). Rauchbier fans should watch for Bison's Juniper Smoked Ale, made with juniper-smoked malt, which is pleasantly tangy-fruity. An Alder Smoked Scotch Ale is soft, rich, and mellow with a bacon-smoky character. Berkeley's dynamism may be receding in the conservative 1990s, but Bison's creative pints continue to runneth over.

GORDON BIERSCH
ESTABLISHED 1988
2 Harrison Street
San Francisco, California 94105

RECOMMENDED
Weizen (4.5%),
soft and aromatic in Bavarian style

A pioneering brewpub chain founded by restauranteur Dean Biersch and brewer Dan Gordon, who studied his craft in Germany. Sites in San Jose (33 E San Fernando Street), Pasadena (41 Hugus Alley), Honolulu (1 Aloha Tower Drive, #1123), and flagship San Francisco now supplement their original Palo Alto location (640 Emerson).

Attracted by the chain's success, a large Las Vegas-based entertainment group purchased a controlling interest in the company at the end of 1995. Gordon Biersch is using this infusion of capital to construct a full-production brewery and headquarters (with a  50,000-barrel/58,700hl annual capacity) in San Jose, as well as to build additional brewpubs around the country.

Gordon Biersch specializes in classic German lagers. One notable exception is the unfiltered Weizen, introduced at the Hawaii location but now available seasonally throughout the chain.

The company's smooth Export (Dortmunder), balanced Märzen, and caramel-accented Dunkles are available year-round at the brewpubs. (Since October 1996, these also have been available in bottles).

Additionally, the brewpubs offer specialties such as spring's Maibock and fall's Dunkel-weizen.

WEST COAST PALE ALES

What color is a standard English-style pale ale? Copper?
Bronze? Perhaps even red? Hardly hues that are considered 'pale.' But
look at America's new golden-amber interpretations of style – suddenly
'pale' doesn't seem such a poor description! Factor in a liberal use of
domestic American hops such as Cascade, and you've got the distinctive
variety known throughout the country as 'West Coast pale ales.'

English pale ales skyrocketed to popularity during the 18th century. Advances in malting techniques allowed England's brewers to produce copper-red ales that, compared to the brown porters and black stouts of the time, certainly appeared 'pale.' Modern English brewers still use a lightly toasty 'pale malt' that gives their beers the appropriate copper color and a corresponding biscuit-like flavor.

Not so in America. As mainstream Pilsners captured the country's attention after the repeal of Prohibition, domestic maltsters concentrated on providing malts appropriate for that golden style. As a result, today's standard American-made 'pale malt' is both lighter in color and character than the British kind. Ales brewed entirely from this malt, without the addition of any caramel or crystal malts to give them a more 'English' color, will appear golden-amber. But that's only half of the equation.

The other half is provided by hops. Particularly the domestic American varieties today grown in the Pacific Northwest (pages 76-77) that have pungent, citric aromas and flavors. The most (in)famous American hop is Cascade, a mildew-resistant strain introduced in 1972 by the U.S. Department of Agriculture. Cascade was crossbred from English Fuggles and the Russian Serebrianka variety, with a percentage of less identifiable stock added for good measure. The result? Hugely characterful cones full of citrusy (lemons, grapefruit), piney (pine resin) aromas and flavors. Other patently 'American' varieties such as Centennial, Columbus, and Chinook display similar characteristics.

San Francisco's Anchor Brewing (page 62) was the first company that generously seasoned a golden-amber ale with these aggressive American hop varieties. During the early 1970s, Anchor owner Fritz Maytag toured famous English pale ale breweries such as Young's of London, Marston's of Burton, and Taylor's of Yorkshire. Taylor's Landlord bitter, made from 100 percent Golden Promise pale malt and late-hopped with aromatic Styrian Goldings, particularly impressed him. He returned home eager to produce a distinctly 'American' pale ale.

Above: The brewhouse at San Francisco's famous Anchor Brewing Company. Anchor pioneered the use of aggressively aromatic American hops in truly 'pale' ales.

Above: A specific gravity reading is taken in one of the open fermenters at Anchor Brewing. Anchor's Liberty Ale is a benchmark West Coast pale ale.

Pale Ale loaded with citrusy hops). Thanks to their geographic origin, beers in this style became known as 'West Coast' pale ales. Most have a gold to pale-amber color, dry but full malt body, and crisp 'American' hop character. Alcohol content is moderate (5-5.5%).

Nowadays, excellent versions come from many California breweries: North Coast (Red Seal Ale), Mad River (Steelhead Extra Pale), St Stan's (Whistle Stop Pale), etc.. Popular northwest examples include Mirror Pond Pale from Oregon's Deschutes Brewery and Fish Tale Pale Ale from Washington's Fish Brewing. (Other northwest brewers such as Hale's, Pyramid, and Elysian offer a sub-style that features the same liberal use of aggressive American hops, but possesses a richer malt character and color similar to British examples). The style has been adopted by numerous other craft-brewers and brewpubs around the country. Versions even are produced occasionally by Canadian craft-brewers and, rarely, English specialty brewers.

Overall, the 'West Coast' pale ale style surely ranks as one of America's most distinctive and characterful contributions to the world brewing renaissance.

On April 18, 1975, Anchor brewed a small run of a special ale in celebration of the 200th anniversary of Colonial American patriot Paul Revere's horseback ride to warn his rebelling countrymen that British troops were coming for them. This historic brew was made only from domestic pale malt and hopped entirely with Cascades (including a pioneering period, at least for modern American beers, of dry hopping in the maturation tank prior to bottling). The result? A pale golden ale bursting with citric Cascade character.

Variations appeared annually as Anchor's special Christmas ale until it entered the brewery's year-round line in 1983 under the thoroughly American name of Liberty Ale.

Around that time, California's then-tiny Sierra Nevada Brewing (page 68) already was creating a buzz among beer lovers with its flagship Pale Ale. This distinctive beer is made predominantly from pale malt (with small amounts of caramel and dextrin malts) and aggressively aroma-hopped (including aromatic 'late hopping') with whole Cascades. Despite Anchor's aforementioned efforts, the brewery says that Sierra Pale developed from the homebrewing experiences of founders Ken Grossman and Paul Camusi – perhaps inspired to a small degree by the highly aromatic Zinfandels and other 'New World' wines popular around Sierra Nevada's California home.

This new variety of golden, highly 'American hopped' ale caught on with both consumers and other brewers throughout California and the Pacific northwest, America's other early microbrewing region. (In fact, one of the first beers from northwest microbrewer Bert Grant was a deep-golden India

Below: Ken Grossman, co-founder of Sierra Nevada Brewing.

HUMBOLDT BREWING

ESTABLISHED 1987

856 10th Street, Arcata, California 95221

RECOMMENDED
Red Nectar (5.3%),
a fruity-hoppy 'American amber ale'

Situated in northern California's Humboldt County, approximately half-way between San Diego and Seattle, the company has expanded substantially since Mario Celotto, a former Oakland Raiders football player (and Super Bowl winner), first founded it as a brewpub: production jumped from 1,200 barrels (1,400hl) in 1992 to more than 19,000 (22,300hl) in 1995! Distribution encompasses all of California and pockets of Oregon, Nevada, and Hawaii.

What's driving this sweet growth? Humboldt's flagship Red Nectar, which balances a notable hop profile (Chinook, Willamette, Mt Hood, Cascade) with malty, fruity depth. It is available year-round along with Gold Nectar, a hoppy American pale ale. At the Arcata pub, English brewmaster Steve Parkes also offers specialties such as an Oatmeal Stout (gold medal at the 1988 Great American Beer Festival) and Cheshire Cat barley wine. Overall, Humboldt's Celotto looks set to replicate his football success in the (on the?) brewing field.

Left: Bah, Humboldt? Steve Parkes and his brews.

KONA BREWING

ESTABLISHED 1994

75-5629 Kuakini Highway
Kailua-Kona, Hawaii 96740

RECOMMENDED
Fire Rock Pale Ale (4.5%),
big nutty-malt flavor balanced with hops

The best micro in the land of luaus was founded on the actual 'Big Island' of Hawaii. As with many Hawaiian operations, the largest challenge is the cost of importing raw materials – after all, Kona is renowned for growing coffee, not hops. The cost of exports to California (which begun in 1996) is equally steep.

Kona's original brewmaster previously worked at both Oregon's BridgePort and Deschutes Brewing. The northwest's popular unfiltered wheat-brews inspired his uniquely Hawaiian version, Lilikoi Wheat Ale, flavored with island-grown passion fruit (lilikoi). Pacific Golden Ale, brewed from pale and honey malts, is the 'entry level' beer. Purists will prefer Kona's complex and satisfying flagship, Fire Rock Pale Ale, which has a rich Munich malt character and strong hop flavor (Cascades, Mt Hood).

Despite a climate that favors mainstream beers, Kona's ales slowly are catching on at trendy Hawaiian spots. There's no word, however, on whether drinking them helps you get lei'd.

LIND BREWING

ESTABLISHED 1989

1933 Davis Street
San Leandro, California 94577

RECOMMENDED
Drake's Ale (5%),
dry-hopped English-style bitter
Sir Francis Stout (5.5%),
long lingering finish
Jolly Roger's Holiday Ale (9%),
the Bay Area's most robust seasonal

A draft-only micro situated on the eastern side of San Francisco Bay. Founder Roger Lind worked previously at the defunct Devil Mountain Brewery and Berkeley's cozy Triple Rock brewpub. Lind's Berkeley attitudes remain intact: he reportedly encourages his yeast by blasting Grateful Dead tunes during fermentation.

Lind offers some 16 beers throughout the year, many under the noted Drake's Ales label. Four are available year-round: the flagship Drake's Amber, Sir Francis Stout, deliciously hoppy Drake's Gold, and Lind Raspberry Wheat.

In addition to the wintertime Jolly Roger's – known to keelhaul the unwary – seasonals include spring's Baccus Ale (a 'doppelbock') and summer's crisp Zatec Ale (seriously hopped with Saaz). Lind also offers special brews like Drake's Nog, a spiced brown ale, and Drake's IPA, made with 'extreme amounts of hops'. Such a combination of colorful attitude and creative beer is wining fans for Lind all around the Bay Area.

MAD RIVER BREWING

ESTABLISHED 1989

P.O. Box 767, Blue Lake, California 95525

RECOMMENDED

Jamaica Red Ale (4.8%),
aggressively hoppy and fruity

The company is named after a river (full of Steelhead salmon) in Humboldt County. Brewery founder Steve Smith brews with Sierra Nevada's original 17-barrel system and open square fermenters. Distribution encompasses the west and a few mid-Atlantic markets.

Mad River's beers are naturally carbonated and minimally filtered – a process that works best for the pleasantly 'rough hewn' Jamaica Red, with its richly fruity, hoppy, and darkly-malty character. While minimal filtration also favors the creamy Steelhead Extra Stout, brewery flagship Steelhead Extra Pale Ale might benefit from a clearer perspective. Mad River also offers a winter seasonal, John Barleycorn barley wine. The 1995 bottling (made with sage and local Humboldt honey) reached more than nine percent alcohol by volume! Anyone able to work through a six-pack truly has a 'steel head.'

MENDOCINO BREWING

ESTABLISHED 1983

13351 Highway 101 South
Hopland, California 95449

RECOMMENDED

Black Hawk Stout (5.8%),
roasty, fruity, and extremely quaffable
Red Tail Ale (6.4%),
toasty-malt balances fruity character
Eye of the Hawk (7.7%),
potent, limited-release amber ale

This pioneering brewer in California's wine country is located in a town that (as its name suggests) once cultivated hops. Mendocino offers a taste of microbrewing history: two of the founders worked for micro-pioneer New Albion. In fact, Mendocino began brewing with New Albion's equipment and fruity yeast (still used today).

Like many early start-ups, the original brewpub quickly expanded to meet demand. Mendocino held a direct public stock offering in 1995 (raising approximately $3.6 million) to fund construction of a second, larger brewery. This new facility, based 12 miles (19km) away in Ukiah, California, opened in fall 1996.

Mendocino flies high on bird-named beers: Red Tail Ale, Blue Heron Pale Ale, and Black Hawk Stout. The flagship Red Tail is dry and quaffable; Black Hawk offers a similar drinkability. Blue Heron is styled as fruity-bitter IPA. The Hopland brewpub also pours draft specialties such as the year-round Peregrine Pale Ale and winter's Yuletide Porter. Eye of the Hawk ('The Eye') is brewed and bottled in limited quantities three times each year. Despite its name, this mellow strong ale is no featherweight.

NORTH COAST BREWING

ESTABLISHED 1987

455 N Main Street
Fort Bragg, California 95437

RECOMMENDED

Old No. 38 Stout (5.2%),
deliciously smooth and roasty
Red Seal Ale (5.4%),
cleanly fruity and extremely hoppy
Old Rasputin Russian Imperial Stout (9.2%),
well-made interpretation of style

This brewery and pub is found in northern California's coastal Fort Bragg. Despite its location, a former mortuary, interest in North Coast's beers is extremely 'lively' – so much so that during 1995 the company built a new, bigger brewhouse to supplement its original. Red Seal Ale and the two stouts are available throughout the year, along with a Blue Star Wheat (American style) and Scrimshaw Beer (a cream ale). Seasonals include an Oktoberfest and smooth Traditional Bock (both ales), as well as the Düsseldorf-inspired Alt Nouveau.

Purists sometimes see North Coast's beers as imitations of Sierra Nevada's; the description is not fair to either brewery. Toasty-malty Red Seal bursts with bright, citric American hop character. Old No. 38, named for a retired steam-engine on Fort Bragg's railroad, is mellow but full of roasty-malt flavor. Old Rasputin offers the requisite intense notes of complex ripe fruit, warming alcohol, and 'burnt' flavors. With widespread distribution from California to North Carolina, there's no question that North Coast is giving its hometown something to Bragg about.

Left: Mendocino Brewing's Hopland brewpub.

PETE'S BREWING

ESTABLISHED 1986

514 High Street, Palo Alto, California 94301

RECOMMENDED

Pete's Wicked Amber Ale (4.8%),
smooth with balanced American hop character
Pete's Wicked Ale (5.2%),
caramel-accented, dry-hopped brown ale

Although Pete's beers are contract-brewed by Stroh, the company has retained a positive reputation among other craft brewers. This 'good will' is created largely by founder and spokesman Pete Slosberg, who began homebrewing in 1979. He went commercial seven years later with Wicked Ale ('wicked' meaning 'extremely good'). This well-made brew may be the defining American Brown Ale (it has won two medals at the Great American Beer Festival).

Subsequent beers include Wicked Lager (a credible European-style Pilsner) and Wicked Amber (well-balanced between caramel malt character and American hop flavor). Pete's has experienced greater success, however, with its more mainstream Wicked Honey Wheat, Wicked Summer Brew,

and Wicked Winter Brew. The latter, lightly seasoned with raspberry and nutmeg, is based on the 'grand champion' recipe from 1993's National Homebrew Competition. Several new brands, including a Maple Porter, were introduced in 1996.

To its credit, Pete's devotes a substantial amount of resources towards educating consumers and retailers about all specialty beers. The company went public during 1995.

SIERRA NEVADA BREWING

ESTABLISHED 1981

1075 E 20th Street, Chico, California 95928

RECOMMENDED

Pale Ale (5.5%),
a delightfully hoppy and complex classic
Porter (5.8%),
fruity, hoppy, coffeeish, and drinkable
Bigfoot Ale (10.1%),
hugely malty-rich and exceedingly hoppy

If Anchor Brewing is the 'father' of American micros, Sierra Nevada is the big brother that everyone worships. Founders Ken Grossman and Paul Camusi must be amazed at how their hoppy, complex ales have captivated the country. Sierra's purpose-built, showplace brewery opened in 1989 (replacing the converted dairy-equipment original). The attached pub offers draft specialties and once-seasonal beers (like spring's Pale Bock) that have fallen from production to leave room for expanding the production of the year-round Pale Ale, Porter, and Stout.

Sierra's medal-after-medal-winning Pale Ale, deeply complex and refreshing, defines the American 'west coast' style. The Porter remains one of the country's, if not the world's, best. Sierra's satisfying Stout, also powerfully hopped, is big, dry, and extremely roasty. Late fall sees Sierra release its

eagerly-awaited Celebration Ale, a deep-copper brew that can be startlingly hoppy. Late winter brings (in smaller quantities each year, it sadly seems) Bigfoot, an almost overpoweringly malty and hoppy barley wine which can benefit from at least a year's maturation.

Despite explosive growth – the company sold over 200,000 barrels (234,700hl) in 1995 – Sierra Nevada has not compromised either the quality or the distinctive character of its outstanding beers.

Above: Sierra Nevada draft from the brewery tap.

ST STAN'S BREWING

ESTABLISHED 1984

821 L Street, Modesto, California 95354

RECOMMENDED

Whistle Stop Pale Ale (4.6%),
crisp, refreshing and thoroughly hoppy
Amber Alt (5.8%),
clean-tasting with fresh hop character
Red Sky Ale (6%),
smooth, nutty malt and strong hops

St Stan's is the largest altbier producer in America. Around ten years after travel in

Germany inspired founder Garith Helm and his wife to take up homebrewing, they built a small brewery next to their house to producing a commercial version of their favorite alt style. In 1990, rising demand prompted the opening of St Stan's current brewery (which incorporates a pub and restaurant). The company distributes widely in California, as well as several farther flung markets.

Altbier remains a focus: alongside the flagship Amber, St Stan's offers a chocolatey Dark Alt and wintertime 'Fest' version. The brewery also has expanded its styles in recent years with Red Sky Ale and Whistle Stop Pale Ale, two beers in California's hoppy micro tradition (although they are brewed from traditional English hops in addition to aggressive American ones). Visitors to the Modesto brewery are likely to find additional draft-only brews and, perhaps, the annual Graffiti Wheat beer (a tribute to the locally-staged George Lucas movie 'American Graffiti').

Right: Shades of German brewing in Hübsch's beer.

SUDWERK PRIVATBRAUEREI HÜBSCH

ESTABLISHED 1990

2001 Second Street, Davis, California 95616

RECOMMENDED
Hübsch Pilsner (5%),
perhaps the best in America
Hübsch Märzen (5.3%),
rich, creamy, layered malt character

Another lager brewer in a sea of ales. Ron Broward founded the Hübsch brewpub (named after his mother's maiden name) to recapture the spirit of both the beers and friendly taverns of her German homeland. For authenticity, Broward installed a specially-made German brewhouse (or 'sudhaus' in German) and employed a highly-experienced German brewmaster. Resulting demand for Hübsch's excellent German-style beers has had dual results: during 1996, the company opened both a new, fully-automated Steinecker brewery (approximately 20,000-barrel/23,500hl capacity) in Davis, as well as a second brewpub in California capital Sacramento (1375 Exposition Boulevard).

Five malts help give brewery flagship Hübsch Märzen a big body and complex character. Hübsch Pilsner is elegant and refined with an outstanding floral aroma and bitterness (from Hallertau and Tettnang hops). The brewery also offers a chocolatey Dunkel and Bavarian-style Hefeweizen. Broward's German brewmaster departed in 1995.

ALSO WORTH TRYING

Northern California remains the 'craft-beer cradle.' Bay Area beer-hunters should visit **Golden Pacific Brewing**'s new facility in Berkeley (close to the also-new **Pyramid Brewery**). Golden Pacific – which merged with Berkeley's first craft-brewer, Thousand Oaks, in 1990 – offers its clean, honeyish Golden Bear Lager and nutty, hoppy Golden Gate Original Ale throughout the state. Berkeley also hosts several other breweries in its limits. Nearby, Oakland's **Pacific Coast** brewpub makes perhaps the finest malt-extract beers in the country. Reports about **El Toro Brewing** in Morgan Hill are justifiably bullish. Eclectic drafts from Santa Rosa's **Moonlight Brewing** also have been gaining a Bay Area following (although it could be just a phase!).

Microbrewers are rising more slowly in the rest of the state. Sacramento's **Rubicon** brewpub serves well-respected beers that won't make you cross. **Carmel Brewing** of Salinas, which opened in 1995, offers a clean-tasting (if a touch heavy) American-style 'Hefeweissen' and smooth, malty Holiday Ale. Hollister's **San Andreas Brewing** makes pleasant (if not earth-shaking) ales, while Mt Aukum's **El Dorado Brewing** earns praise for its Mountain Red Ale. **Murphys Creek Brewing** – of, you guessed it, Murphys Creek – also is collecting accolades.

In southern Irvine, **Steelhead Brewery** (a brewpub like its eponymous Oregon parent) pours distinctive beers, while **Bayhawk Ales** (a well-funded micro) is more mainstream. **Blind Pig Brewing** of Temecula, on the other hand, offers extremely interesting brews – 'swig a Pig' today! Way down in San Diego, two brewpubs named for German brewmaster **Karl Strauss** serve the best-known local suds.

US NORTHWEST

California may have started the craft-brewing movement, but the Northwest perfected it. Early micros such as Redhook, BridgePort, Hale's, and Pyramid (who all continue to thrive today) have been joined by many smaller producers. Portland, Oregon, hosts more breweries than any other North American city. The overall craft-beer market share in Oregon and Washington is nearly five times the national average!

The success of craft beer in the region means local competition is fierce. As a result, several of the region's biggest specialty brewers are looking farther afield, shifting their focus from northwest to national. Will Washington DC embrace the beers of Washington state? The jury's still out. Meanwhile, northwest drinkers continue to frequent the many 'alehouses' (multi-tap pubs) serving their favorite brews.

Published out of Seattle, the Pint Post (12345 Lake City Way NE #159, 98125) covers the northwest beer scene.

ALASKAN BREWING

ESTABLISHED 1986

5429 Shaune Drive, Juneau, Alaska 99801

RECOMMENDED

Alaskan Frontier Amber (4.5%),
big bodied but balanced

Alaskan Smoked Porter (6.2%),
delicious, if intense, blend of flavors

Alaska's oldest operating brewery, which has skyrocketed to success with its top-selling Alaskan Amber Ale (an 'alt' style beer reportedly based on a turn-of-the-century recipe). Three brews are offered year-round: the Amber, a notably fruity Pale Ale, and the new Alaskan Frontier amber. Production reached 34,000 barrels (40,000hl) in 1996 with distribution limited to the brewery's home state and western Washington.

Alaskan Amber is the popular flagship, found in stores and bars throughout the region. The brewery has received greater critical acclaim, however, for its Smoked Porter and Alaskan Frontier. The former, brewed with grain cold-smoked over alder wood at a local Juneau fish smoker, has received five back-to-back gold medals at the Great American Beer Festival (in the 'rauchbier' category). Frontier, previously a seasonal called Autumn Ale,

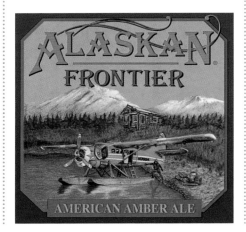

has been similarly rewarded in the Festival's 'amber ale' category. The year-round roll-out of Frontier – more distinctive than the brewery's regular Amber – may mark an effort by Alaskan to 'upgrade' its supporters' tastes. Fans already are applauding . . . .

BRIDGEPORT BREWING

ESTABLISHED 1984

1313 NW Marshall Street
Portland, Oregon 97209

RECOMMENDED

India Pale Ale (5.5%),
super-hoppy and fruity

Porter (5.5%),
smooth and well-balanced

Old Knucklehead (9%),
winter's annual barleywine

Oregon's oldest craft-brewery, BridgePort is based, along with its comfortable pub, in a century-old brick building (covered with climbing hop vines) that stands in industrial Portland. BridgePort's founders sold out to the Gambrinus Company of San Antonio, Texas, in 1995. Gambrinus, importer of Mexico's Corona beer for the western US, previously had purchased (and dramatically expanded) the Spoetzl Brewery, an old Texas regional famous for its Shiner Bock.

Above: New for 1996, BridgePort's hoppy and fruity, bottle-conditioned India Pale Ale.

The new owners put BridgePort through a $3.5 million overhaul and expansion program during 1996. A new range of naturally-conditioned ales, with a limited amount hand-pumped from small metal casks (what the British call firkins), was introduced to supplement the brewery's well-known Blue Heron Pale Ale, Coho Pacific Extra Pale Ale, and Pintail ESB. The first examples of this 'authentic Firkin beer,' an India Pale Ale and Porter, were released in early 1996. Bottle-conditioned counterparts also were introduced.

The fate of lesser-known BridgePort brews such as the enjoyable XX Stout, deeply fruity Old Knucklehead, and original BridgePort Ale (a Scottish 80-shilling confusingly renamed 'Nut Brown') remains uncertain. Expect to hear and see more as Gambrinus gives BridgePort the full benefit of its marketing muscle.

DESCHUTES BREWERY

ESTABLISHED 1988

901 SW Simpson Avenue
Bend, Oregon 97702

RECOMMENDED
Bachelor Bitter (5%),
dry-hopped with Kent Goldings
Black Butte Porter (5.6%),
sweet, smooth, and worth seeking out
Obsidian Stout (6.7%),
richly chewy and sweetish

Deschutes is a regional favorite, viewed by many as the northwest's finest brewery. Whatever your opinion, there's no question that Deschutes has advanced the cause of 'dark beer' more than any other area craft-brewer: its flagship Black Butte Porter, at once creamy and complex, is a mainstay on taps and shelves across the area. Obsidian Stout, a powerful brew in the 'foreign' style, has joined Bachelor Bitter, cleanly fruity and hoppy, in year-round bottles (as has the once-seasonal Mirror Pond Pale Ale). Winter's Jubelale also deservedly attracts attention.

Originally founded as a brewpub, Deschutes' production shot well over 40,000 barrels (47,000hl) in 1996. The original Brewery & Public House still stands in Bend (1044 NW Bond Street); its location even provides the name for the brewery's seasonal (draft-only) Bond Street Brown Ale. The separate facility listed above handles the majority of production.

Right: Not just for jaded single men, Deschutes' Bachelor Bitter is one of the northwest's finest.

FULL SAIL BREWING

ESTABLISHED 1987

506 Columbia, Hood River, Oregon 97031

RECOMMENDED
Equinox ESB (5.6%),
rich malt, tangy zesty hop
Oktoberfest (5.7%),
rare and worthwhile lager
Amber Ale (5.8%),
the king of its category

Full Sail is located at the end of a truly 'gorgeous' drive from Portland, along the scenic Columbia River Gorge. Hood River's main claim to fame is its suitability for windsurfing – sail-boarders take full advantage of gusty winds swooping down where the Hood River meets the Columbia. Their activity inspired the name of the brewery, which was founded by a former wine salesman. The current facility, with a pub overlooking the Gorge, is housed in an old fruit-packing plant. Its impressive new brewhouse, capable of expansion up to 250,000 barrels (293,000hl), is supplemented by a smaller 'brewpub' facility in Portland (The Riverplace Brewery, part of downtown's Riverplace Marina).

Year-round brews include a fruity Golden Ale and chocolatey Nut Brown Ale, in addition to the classic Amber (big-bodied, malty, and deep). These are supplemented by several limited-season brews – spring's ESB bursts with fresh hop character from English Target and Saaz varieties – and a hearty winter warmer called WasSail (get it?). There also is a series of special drafts, including the true-to-style Oktoberfest. Full Sail's beers are widely available throughout the western United States.

HAIR OF THE DOG BREWING

ESTABLISHED 1994

4509 SE 23rd, Portland, Oregon 97202

RECOMMENDED
Golden Rose (7.5%),
fruity, warming, with subtle hop profile
Adam beer (10%),
rich, complex, almost whiskey-ish

This small, upstart micro has an amusing name and slogan – 'Faithful, Loyal, Pure, Wet Nose' – but its beers are incredibly serious. Hair of the Dog produces bottle-conditioned ales designed to improve with age. Each 12oz bottle is labelled with the brew's batch-number, for easy reference. Distribution includes the west coast and a few eastern regions.

Golden Rose, made with special honey-malt and 'candi' sugar, is styled after a Belgian Tripel. Adam beer, the original brew, is an attempt to revive a well-aged strong ale reportedly once popular in Dortmund, Germany. A two-year-old bottle from Batch No. 1 was hugely complex – notes of rich malt, tropical fruits, peat smoke, chocolate, and coffee – and satisfying. Adventurous drinkers should get hold of a case, store it properly, and wait.

HALE'S ALES

ESTABLISHED 1983

4301 Leary Way NW
Seattle, Washington 98107

RECOMMENDED
Moss Bay Extra (4.6%),
rich nutty malt meets northwest hops
O'Brien's Harvest Ale (4.8%),
hoppy copper-colored seasonal
Moss Bay Stout (5.4%),
served 'Dublin style' with nitrogen

In the early 1980s, Mike Hale's passion for British beer led him to work at Gale's brewery in Hampshire, England. Armed with his experience and some Gale's yeast, he returned to Washington and built a brewery out of used dairy equipment near the city of Spokane. Driven by the slogan 'Give 'em Hale's,' his beers benefited from early interest in craft-brews. Production shifted to Spokane proper (E 5634 Commerce Street, Washington 99212) before Hale's opened a second facility near Seattle. The current Seattle headquarters opened in 1995. It features a new brewhouse – complete with English-inspired open fermenters – and an integrated pub.

Hale's success sounds pretty straightforward – until you realize that the company only sells draft beer. Wholly dependent on the northwest's active 'alehouse' scene, the brewery offers a wide range to satisfy tavern-owners' tastes. Originals such as Hale's Pale American Ale are supplemented by the Moss Bay beers, named after the location of the company's first Seattle-area brewery.

Limited specialties such as O'Brien's Harvest and a wintertime Wee Heavy (spiced with cinnamon) ensure that Hale's drafts never are out of season.

PYRAMID ALES

ESTABLISHED 1984

91 S Royal Brougham Way
Seattle, Washington 98134

RECOMMENDED★
Pyramid Pale Ale (4.9%),
'high hoppiness, a splendid thing'
Pyramid Espresso Stout (5.6%),
'among the best . . . in America'
Pyramid Snow Cap Ale (6.9%),
'rich and joyfully bold' winter seasonal

Pyramid began as 'Hart Brewing' in Kalama, a small logging town off the main Portland-Seattle highway in southwest Washington. Founder Beth Hartwell's name inspired the company's; the Pyramid brand may refer to Pyramid Peak in Washington's Cascade mountains. A small investor group purchased the company in 1989 and, three years later, also acquired Washington's Thomas Kemper Brewery (see entry below). The Pyramid and Kemper brands together make the parent company, Pyramid Breweries, one of the country's largest craft brewers.

Kalama still houses the Pyramid Ales Brewery (110 W Marine Drive, Washington 98625). The company's Seattle brewery-headquarters (address above) has supplemented production since 1995. Pyramid Breweries (as Hart Brewing) went public the same year, and is using the proceeds of its initial stock offering to build additional regional breweries around America. The first, California's Pyramid Brewery & Alehouse (901 Gilman, Berkeley, California 94710), opened in 1997.

In addition to Pale Ale and Espresso Stout, coffeeish but caffeine-free, Pyramid's range includes several wheat-brews like the popular Apricot Ale and Hefeweizen. There also are three

seasonal beers and the draft-specialty Pyramid Sphinx Series. Pyramid Ales are available throughout the west and many other American markets.

*Beer descriptions from, in order, *Atlantic Monthly* (William Least Heat Moon); *Real Beer and Good Eats* (Bruce Aidells & Denis Kelley); the *Malt Advocate*.

PIKE BREWING

ESTABLISHED 1989

140 Lakeside Avenue, Suite 300
Seattle, Washington 98122

RECOMMENDED

Pale Ale (4.5%),
rich nutty malt, balancing earthy hops
XXXXX Stout (6%),
dark roast, rich chocolate, assertive hops
India Pale Ale (6.2%),
seriously hoppy, bitter, and deep

An English-inspired brewery founded by Charles Finkel, whose Merchant du Vin company imports Samuel Smith's ales and other classic European beers. Its tiny original facility (with a four-and-a-half barrel brew kettle) stood six floors below

Seattle's Pike Place Market. This plant has been replaced by the nearby Pike Pub and Brewery (1415 First Avenue), which opened in 1996. With its dramatically increased capacity (25,000 barrels/29,300hl), the new brewery comes as a relief to thirsty regional fans.

Despite its small size, the original Pike Place Brewery had a hugely positive reputation – the result of Finkel's creative marketing and brewer Fal Allen's excellent British-style ales. Floor-malted Maris Otter barley, imported from England, imparts a wonderfully rich flavor to Pike's Pale Ale and IPA (conditioned over oak chips to simulate 'wooden cask' character). These two beers and the 'five X' Stout are available year-round.

Seattle's Pike Brewery supplies the northwest with mainly draft beer, including specialties such as winter's spiced Auld Acquaintance and the hearty Old Bawdy barleywine (a reference to the original brewery's location, the site of a former brothel). For distribution outside the region, Pike's bottles and kegs are produced under contract at Minnesota Brewing.

PORTLAND BREWING

ESTABLISHED 1986

2730 NW 31st Avenue
Portland, Oregon 97210

RECOMMENDED

Weizen (4.9%),
filtered but – finally! – Bavarian wheat
MacTarnahan's Ale (5%),
toasty, toffeeish, hoppy

Portland Brewing's original brewpub (1339 NW Flanders, Oregon 97209) still produces draft specialties in the shadow of

the city's large Blitz-Weinhard Brewery – in fact, its space recently was expanded. But most standard production now comes from the showplace facility on industrial NW 31st Avenue. Inside, the brewery's tap room adjoins a classic copper brewhouse purchased from the Sixenbräu Brewery in Bavaria. Its gleaming vessels provide a fitting birthplace for Portland's Weizen, one of the region's few versions in the Bavarian style.

Portland's annual capacity now tops 100,000 barrels (117,350hl); growth has been funded through a series of stock offerings. Among its core brands, MacTarnahan's Amber Ale, malt accented in the 'Scottish style,' has replaced (sadly) original flagship Portland Ale in the top spot. The Weizen and a sweetly coffeeish Haystack Black porter are relatively recent introductions.

The brewery's year-round range also includes Wheat BerryBrew (flavored with Oregon marionberries, a blackberry hybrid) and the sweetish, clean-tasting Oregon Honey Beer. Three seasonals are offered: winter's Icicle Creek (warming and sweetish again) is perhaps best known. Portland's ales are available across the west and in a handful of eastern markets. To support additional growth, the company began contract brewing some beer at Stroh's Minnesota plant during 1996.

REDHOOK ALE BREWERIES

ESTABLISHED 1982

3400 Phinney Avenue N
Seattle, Washington 98103

RECOMMENDED
Redhook Rye (5%),
unfiltered and refreshingly tangy
Ballard Bitter IPA (5.5%),
pleasantly hoppy with fruity, buttery malt
'Blue Line' Series of specialty beers

The powerhouse of Northwest craft-brewing, Redhook moved from its original location in Seattle's Ballard district to its current premises, an old brick 'trolley barn' in the city's Fremont area, in 1987. The company also operates sizable new breweries (with attached pubs) in Woodinville, Washington (14300 NE 145th Street, 98072) and Portsmouth, New Hampshire (35 Corporate Drive, Pease International Tradeport, 03801).

Redhook is best known for its Extra Special Bitter, a smooth amber ale with toffee, butterscotch flavors that seem to have increased in recent years. Other year-round brews include Redhook Rye, Hefeweizen (in the northwest style), and Double Black Stout (brewed with Seattle's famous Starbucks coffee). Ballard Bitter, one of the original beers, has been 'hopped up' and relabelled as an IPA. Special draft-only brews, such as a pineapple-fruity Barley Wine, are rolled out under the 'Blue Line' series.

Redhook went public in 1995. The company also has entered a far-reaching distribution deal with Anheuser-Busch (which holds 25 percent equity in Redhook). Critics' cries of 'Budhook' notwithstanding, Redhook ESB may become the first craft-beer marketed nationally with the full might of the world's biggest brewer.

ROGUE ALES

ESTABLISHED 1988

2320 OSU Drive, Newport, Oregon 97365

RECOMMENDED
Mogul Ale (6.5%),
chewy, chocolatey, powerfully hoppy
Old Crustacean (11.3%),
hugely fruity-hoppy barley wine
Imperial Stout (11%),
deep and deceptively smooth

A small fishing town on the Oregon coast seems an unlikely home for this aggressive craft-brewer. The company is named after Oregon's Rogue River, but its moniker also encapsulates both the brewery's philosophy and the colorful personality of its founder Jack Joyce. A broad range of traditional and exotic-nouveau ales is offered; almost every one illustrates head brewer John Maier's passion for citric northwest hops. The top-selling St Rogue Red Ale is even dry-hopped in its kegs!

Rogue's take-no-prisoners attitude comes off best in its bigger beers. Old Crustacean, legendarily hoppy when fresh, turns mellow and finessed with a few years' age. A portion of rolled oats makes the rich Imperial Stout (and complex Shakespeare Stout) deceptively drinkable. Both 'Old Crusty' and the Imperial are sold in 7oz bottles as part of Rogue's XS Series. Mogul Ale, the winter seasonal, shines on draft.

Left: Redhook's own taproom in funky Fremont, Seattle.

Opinions divide on several of the brewery's other ales – a hazelnut-flavored brown, for example, and spring's punny Maierbock – as well as its practice of selling the same beer under many different labels. But, then again, Rogue really doesn't care about other people's opinions. Rogue Ales are available in more than 30 states.

THOMAS KEMPER LAGERS

ESTABLISHED 1985

1201 1st Avenue South
Seattle, Washington 98134

RECOMMENDED★
Thomas Kemper Belgian White (4.4%),
'bright, refreshing' in witbier style
Thomas Kemper WinterBräu (6.1%),
'lusty, gutsy . . . bittersweet, robust'
Thomas Kemper Mai-bock (6.6%),
'a classic beer . . . balances itself well'

One of the country's few specialist lager producers, an orientation that continues to distinguish it in the ale-loving northwest. The name comes from

founders Andy Thomas and Will Kemper, who no longer are with the company. Originally located on Bainbridge Island, across Puget Sound from Seattle, Thomas Kemper soon moved north to the coastal town of Poulsbo (on Washington's scenic Kitsap Peninsula). The beers there benefited from the experience of brewmaster Rande Reed, who was brought aboard to correct early problems.

The brewery was acquired by Washington's Pyramid Breweries (see entry) in 1992, which saw a natural fit between its ales and Thomas Kemper's lagers. Thomas Kemper lagers are now brewed primarily at the company's Seattle brewery. The Poulsbo facility, along with its associated pub, was closed in 1996. Kemper continues to specialize in Bavarian-style lagers – the same German yeast ferments everything from spring's Mai-bock to the year-round Hefeweizen, Amber Lager, and popular WeizenBerry (raspberry wheat). Only the brewery's Belgian White is made with a special ale strain. Distribution is widespread in the west and in select other areas.

*Beer descriptions from, in order, the *San Diego Union-Tribune*; *The Seattle Times* (Tom Stockley); *All About Beer* (Darryl Richman).

WILD RIVER BREWING

ESTABLISHED 1990

595 NE 'E' Street, Grants Pass, Oregon 97526

~~~

RECOMMENDED

Hefe Weizen (5%),
restrained but pleasant Bavarian style
ESB (5.5%),
rich caramel character
Russian Imperial Stout (7.2%),
richly malty yet drinkable

Located in southwest Oregon, close to the California border, the company

operates two small brewery-restaurants: Grants Pass is newer and its brewery is about double the size of the original location in nearby Cave Junction. Driven by demand, Wild River is giving greater emphasis to off-premise sales throughout the region and north into Portland.

Former head brewer Hubert Smith was a devoted fan of England's Brakspear Brewery. His big, bold ales have received several medals at the Great American Beer Festival. Wild River's ESB, brewed with both traditional Fuggles and new-world Willamettes hops, is perhaps the northwest's best bottled version. The balanced, 'lower octane' Imperial

Russian Stout is based on a Whitbread Triple Stout recipe from the 1880s. Several additional ales, from a traditional German-style Kölsch to a potent barley wine, are offered.

ALSO WORTH TRYING

Washington hosts several other craft-brewers making interesting beers. Salmon Bay Bitter from Seattle's **Maritime Pacific** is a satisfying example of the traditional British style. **Elysian Brewing** opened to great expectation in the city during 1996. Serious drinkers watch for a powerfully dry-hopped IPA and crisp, quenching Bavarian Hefeweizen from Mukilteo's tiny **Diamond Knot Brewery**. Carved cowboy tap-handles denote ales from northern **Winthrop Brewing**, including the punny Hop-Along Red. Savvy drinkers in capital city Olympia catch fresh **Fish Tale Ales** at the local Fishbowl brewpub. Heading east, German-themed **Leavenworth** hosts an eponymous micro making aggressive ales and lagers. Yakima, famous for its surrounding hop fields, also is home to the widely-distributed **Grant's Ales**. Around Spokane and northern Idaho, the best regional brews come all the way from Montana's **Kessler Brewing**.

In Oregon, thirsty Portlanders go to the dogs at the **Lucky Labrador**

brewpub and wet their whistle with the hoppy-fruity Red Thistle from McMinnville's **Golden Valley Brewery**. **Widmer Brewing**, whose murky Hefeweizen pioneered the restrained northwest style, operates a 'Gasthaus' pub at its Portland headquarters: stop in to sample the far more rewarding Widmer Altbier and occasional seasonal specialties. At the end of every July, Portland's outdoor Oregon Brewers Festival packs in the crowds. To the south, Eugene's **Steelhead** brewpub offers a range of adventurous beers. Farther west, in the prosaic town of Government Camp on the south slope of Mt Hood, well-hopped ales are crafted by **Mt Hood Brewing**. Even non-climbers will enjoy the Ice Axe IPA, Pinnacle ESB, and rich Hogsback Oatmeal Stout (made with molasses and licorice).

HOP GROWING IN THE NORTHWEST

Head east from Seattle, over the Cascade mountains, towards the center of Washington state. Here you will find North America's top (in terms of both quality and quantity) hop-growing region. It doesn't look like much at first: compared to the maritime feel of the western Puget Sound area, land east of the Cascades has a sparse desert-like quality – especially when the summer sun beats down from a cloudless sky onto dry canyons and brown foothills. But thanks to irrigation both natural and man-made, parts of the region offer fertile soil and benign farming conditions that rank among the country's best.

Washington's central Yakima Valley, in particular, is famous for growing table fruit and wine grapes. It also happens to produce the most hops in North America. Yakima hops today account for around 70 percent of America's total hop crop. Oregon (the Willamette Valley) and Idaho (the Snake River Valley), respectively, produce 20 and 10 percent. Hops also are grown north of the Canadian-American border in British Columbia.

Together, these four Pacific northwest regions constitute the continent's 'hop basket.' Locally-developed varieties such as Cascade and Centennial, with their pungent and powerful character, have become something of a signature in North American craft beers.

Hops have been an important crop in North America since 1612, when Dutch settlers constructed a commercial brewery on Manhattan Island. Cultivation moved westward along with American expansion – pioneers always had a thirst for beer in addition to adventure!

Hops were first grown in the western United States during the 1850s: northern California was a substantial producer before shifting its attention to grapes, as the name of Hopland, a city in the heart of today's wine country, attests. (In recent years, Hopland-headquartered Mendocino Brewing has brought the bitter blossoms back to town).

Hops arrived in the Yakima Valley in 1868. In addition to the excellent growing conditions, cultivation was aided by an abundant supply of indigenous American ('American Indian') labor at harvest-time that rivalled the flocks of 'vacationing' Londoners that used to pick England's hop fields. Over the course of the past century, the Valley has become the world's second-largest hop producing area (behind Germany). Visit Yakima or other Pacific northwest hop fields in late summer and you will see areas literally bursting with blossom-covered vines. Dangling down from networks of 18-foot (5.5m) tall trellises, the hops form aromatic green walls.

All kinds of hops are grown in the Pacific northwest: classic European types (Hallertau, Saaz), traditional English ones (Goldings), and unquestionably North American crops such as Cluster, Columbus, and Chinook. It is the latter that have put northwest hops on the brewing map. In general, domestic North American hops display an aggressive 'citric' character. They offer 'bright' aromas and flavors reminiscent of citrus fruits like lemons, oranges, and even grapefruit. They also can show 'piney' or resinous notes.

European brewers tend to dislike such characteristics, which they describe as tasting 'rough' or smelling similar to 'cat's pee' (an unappetizing thought, indeed, for thirsty beer lovers). But it

Above: Blossom-covered hop vines trail in aromatic swathes from their tall trellises.

Above: In fall, workers in the Yakima Valley bring in the harvest from the hop fields.

Above: In the kilns, blasts of hot air dry freshly-harvested hops, dramatically reducing their moisture content. The thick, fragrant atmosphere is like a 'lupulin sauna.'

Above: After drying, the hops are packed into 200-pound (91kg) bales. These are taken away for processing into pellets or stored at near-freezing temperatures until needed.

is precisely the powerful notes of Pacific northwest hops that make them attractive to new-wave brewers in America and (to a lesser degree) Canada. Many microbrewers have embraced domestic hops as a way to give their beers an unmistakable North American stamp. Take a recipe for a classic British pale ale or German altbier, substitute Cascade hops, and *voilà*! The result is a beer that, despite its stylistic origins, stands firmly in the New World.

Considering the distinctive character of Pacific northwest hops, it is ironic that the region's ideal climate (coupled with modern farming techniques) allow domestically-raised versions of European hops – Yakima-grown Tettnang, for example – to approximate their Continental progenitors with extreme accuracy. Anheuser-Busch, a company exceedingly picky about its hops (despite what the character of its beers suggests), actually supplements its Czech Saaz with Idaho-raised Saaz. America also offers domestic hops that closely replicate

Europe's best. Oregon's Willamettes are near relatives of England's famous Fuggles, for instance, while Mt Hood's are styled after German Hallertau. Displaying a typical northwest turn, both North American varieties tend to be slightly 'brighter' in character than their cousins across the pond. But they remain fairly true to their origins, providing a definite taste of the 'Old World' in local beers.

At the same time, aggressively flavorful North American hops are finding new audiences outside their homeland. Small brewers throughout Britain, in particular, have started to boil with the flavorful blossoms. (The Roosters microbrewery in north Yorkshire packs plenty of Pacific northwest personality into its appropriately named Yankee ale). German brewers, on the other hand, still approach Pacific northwest hops with suspicion. When the first batch of a Bavarian Pilsner is seasoned with Liberty – another Yakima-grown Hallertau derivative – the North American hop revolution clearly will have arrived!

CANADA WEST

The phrase 'Canada West' conjures up images of Vancouver and other Pacific coastal cities, or perhaps of all British Columbia itself. But in specialty beer terms, Canada West encompasses British Columbia eastward through Manitoba. Both the Pacific and Prairie craft-brews of Canada share a broadly similar character — malt-accented, 'soft' — that separates them from more aggressively-flavorful ales and lagers found in the eastern regions.

The best example of this 'western' character is McNally's Ale, a supremely malty Irish-styled ale produced by Alberta's Big Rock Brewery. Even in Vancouver, only three hours' drive from super-hoppy Seattle, the majority of microbrews — from Shaftebury Cream Ale to Granville Island's soft Pale Ale — remain malt-accented. Nevertheless, there are exceptions: Sailor Hägar's Brewery in North Vancouver, for example, offers a seasonal India Pale Ale that seems to come straight from the Yakima hop-fields of Washington state.

It is mainly western brewers who gather each November at the Great Canadian Beer Festival in Victoria, British Columbia. Sponsored by the Canadian branch of Britain's Campaign for Real Ale, it offers a convenient way to get a taste of Canada's westerly craft-brewing industry.

BIG ROCK BREWERY

ESTABLISHED 1985

6403 - 35 Street SE, Calgary, Alberta T2C 1N2

RECOMMENDED
Warthog Ale (5%),
nutty, toffee flavors with balancing hop
Cold Cock Winter Porter (6%),
pleasantly rich, smooth and complex
McNally's Ale (7%),
deeply complex and thoroughly rewarding

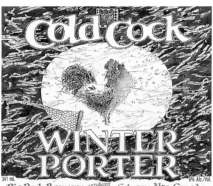

The largest ale-making craft brewer in Canada, Big Rock was founded by former lawyer Edward McNally, who became interested in brewing after retiring to a farm and serving as director of a Canadian barley growers' association. Sales grew steadily (if slowly) at first, but were aided by the 1987 introduction of McNally's Ale and the foothold it gave the company in the American micro market. In 1996, Big Rock announced plans to replace all of its existing brewing facilities — including two expanded-site buildings named Bigger Rock and Big Big Big Rock, respectively — with a completely new plant in Calgary (ultimately capable of producing 383,500 barrels/450,000hl per year). Distribution is widespread throughout the United States and Canada. The company trades publicly on Canada's Alberta Stock Exchange and America's Nasdaq.

Big Rock brews several year-round beers, including the pleasantly malty Traditional Ale, the soft and golden Classical Ale, the pioneering (for Canada) Magpie Rye Ale, the more complex Warthog, and Grasshöpper Wheat (the best thing about it is the umlaut). Observers remain amazed that Cold Cock Winter Porter (only sold in the United States) was able to make it successfully past America's label authorities, despite its rooster-in-a-snowstorm illustration. This is an above-average winter brew, stylistically less a porter than a British-style strong ale. The star of the Big Rock show, however, is McNally's Ale, brewed in the 'Irish style.' Orange-amber in color, with a mouthfilling, smooth, deep malt character and balancing toasty-bitter flavor, it ranks among the most rewarding beers brewed in North America.

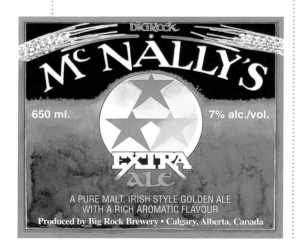

BOWEN ISLAND BREWING

ESTABLISHED 1994

595 Artisan Lane, P.O. Box 68
Bowen Island, British Columbia V0N 1G0

RECOMMENDED
Special Bitter (4.5%),
dark malt character with notable hops
Harvest Ale (4.5%),
brewed with fresh-harvested Mt Hood hops

This is a small 'cottage brewery' accessible from the British Columbia mainland via Horseshoe Bay ferry. It is now distributed around the province in bottles and kegs, with its strongest representation in Vancouver. Three year-round beers are offered, including the flagship Bowen Ale (a sweetish pale ale lightly balanced by American hops) and Blonde Ale (brewed with 25 percent wheat malt). Brewed in the mild 'Canadian ale' style, Bowen Blonde may be British Columbia's best cross-over beer: it will 'make a lager drinker swoon,' according to the slick *Vancouver Magazine.*

Bowen's third always-available beer is Special Bitter. Brewed with crystal, chocolate, and Vienna malts for a deep red color, it is richer, maltier, and hoppier – thanks to Cascades, Goldings, and Mt Hoods – than the standard Canadian craft-brewed 'British ale.' The seasonal Harvest Ale, malty-toasty and smooth, is followed by an adventurous Winter Ale. This edgy brew (for British Columbia, anyway) actually is a dry 'cherry stout' brewed with 200 pounds (91kg) of dark cherry puree per every 634 gallons (2,400l). Overall, tiny Bowen Island brews pleasant, flavorful ales that stand a cut above many of the region's more established micros.

GRANVILLE ISLAND BREWING

ESTABLISHED 1984

1441 Cartwright Street
Vancouver, British Columbia V6H 3R7

RECOMMENDED
Island Bock (6.5%),
smooth, rich, cherryish malt character

Canada's 'original' micro – actually the first free-standing microbrewery to open in the country. The name came from its location, Granville Island, a thriving creative community located in the heart of Vancouver. The Island's waterfront markets bustle with artisans, craftspeople, and the tourists that come to admire them. Founder Mitchell Taylor chose the site for its colorful character and proximity to the yuppie-touristy Vancouver market.

Despite its pride of place in Canadian micro mythology, the brewery has a checkered business history: it merged with an energy company in 1985, then was purchased in 1989 by a distillery company that also owned older regional Pacific Western Brewing. The distillery group, now known as Cascadia Brands, retains control of Granville Island Brewing. It has upgraded the brewing facilities and introduced an aggressive marketing campaign (including exports to Seattle and other American areas).

Today, Granville Island offers six year-round beers. These encompass the original, flagship Island Lager (a balanced Bavarian-style Helles), soft Lord Granville Pale Ale, and fuller-bodied Anniversary Amber Ale. Island Bock, introduced in 1987, is the most distinctive, with a smooth, rich (chocolatey?) flavor and softly warming finish. It is to be hoped that the company's new 'Taste The Art' marketing slogan can help to win a broader audience for Granville's Bock and, perhaps, allow the launch of similarly flavorful beers.

Below: A 'family portrait' of Granville Island's beer range, marketed aggressively with the slogan 'Taste The Art.'

OKANAGAN SPRING BREWERY

ESTABLISHED 1985

2801 - 27A Avenue, Vernon
British Columbia V1T 1T5

RECOMMENDED
Old English Porter (8.5%),
ripe fruit and mellow chocolate notes

The Okanagan Valley is one of the most picturesque, pristine regions of the British Columbia heartland. Its fertile farmland grows some of Canada's best wheat, barley, peaches, grapes, pears, and cherries. In Bavaria, such bucolic settings support many small 'town breweries.' And, indeed, this concept provided the inspiration for the Okanagan Spring Brewery. Founded by two German immigrants and a visiting brewmaster friend, the company originally envisioned serving only its surrounding Okanagan area (within a 30-mile/50km radius). By 1986, however, the brewery had expanded distribution to Vancouver. Its beers now sell widely throughout the province. In fact, Okanagan is British Columbia's biggest craft-brewer: 1996 production capacity reached 149,000 barrels (175,000hl).

Okanagan's original Premium Lager now leads a more diverse range: Pilsner, Pale Ale, Brown Ale, Spring Wheat (filtered), St Patrick's Stout, and Old English Porter. The clean-tasting Pale, Okanagan's flagship, is copper in color and (in keeping with something of a Canadian brewing tradition) apparently fermented with a lager yeast. A highly-regarded, dark 'Old Munich Wheat' seems to have fallen by the wayside. Thankfully, Okanagan's potent Porter continues to thrive. This mellow, mahogany-colored brew (bottle-conditioned) is smooth, and chocolatey

with lots of banana fruit. The balanced Stout is similarly smooth, if slightly more roasty. The brewery recently introduced cans of Pale, Brown, Lager, and Stout in order to – get this – make them 'easier and safer to transport for West Coast outdoor enthusiasts.'

Okanagan merged with eastern Canada's Sleeman Brewing in 1995, with the latter's shareholders retaining the majority of the new company's ownership.

SAILOR HÄGAR'S BREWERY

ESTABLISHED 1994

86 Semisch Avenue, North Vancouver,
British Columbia V7M 3H8

RECOMMENDED
Lohin's ESB (5.6%),
toasty malt, caramel hints, hoppy finish
India Pale Ale (6.5%),
probably BC's best hop-head beer

A pub that became a brewpub that became a microbrewery, Sailor Hägar's is accessible via 'sea bus' ferry across Burrard Inlet from downtown Vancouver. It is worth the trip for the pub alone, which provides an enjoyable English-style setting – and a spectacular view of the Vancouver skyline. The brewery itself is a compact, stainless steel affair tucked in a small building up the road (talk about long beer lines). Between the two is Sailor Hägar's Beer & Wine Shop, which offers PET-bottle six-packs of the company's beers in addition to a wide range of west coast craft-brands (from America and Canada).

Sailor Hägar's brewmaster Gary Lohin makes respectable lagers, including a vaguely Märzen-styled 'Scandinavian Amber.' But Lohin's adventurous skills show best in ales such as his extremely drinkable ESB: served through a hand-pump, it has a smooth, creamy mouthfeel with toasty malt

notes, a solidly hoppy character, and a dry, hoppy finish. A seasonal (late fall) IPA bursts with citric American hop notes and would be perfectly at home at any Seattle alehouse.

Other occasional specialties have included a lightly-peated Wee Heavy and Northwest-hoppy Columbus Pale Ale. As a result, Sailor Hägar's probably is the best spot in Vancouver to visit for distinctive, locally-brewed beers.

VANCOUVER ISLAND BREWERY

ESTABLISHED 1985

2330 Government Street
Victoria, British Columbia V8T 5G5

RECOMMENDED

Hermann's Dark Lager (5.5%),
light, pleasant chocolate and caramel notes
Hermannator (varies),
*eagerly-awaited, supremely hearty
winter seasonal*

Another early Canadian micro. Founded on Vancouver Island in an industrial location lacking aesthetic appeal, the brewery originally operated as 'Island Pacific.' Its subsequent change of name and site – to new digs downtown in Victoria – were instituted to help overcome what Canadian beer expert Stephen Beaumont calls its status as 'the forgotten player' in the country's craft-brewing history.

If Vancouver Island has suffered from a low profile, the fault does not lie with its beers. Respected German brewer Hermann Hoerterer developed many of the main brands. Although Herr Hermann has moved on, the beers (by their very names) still testify to his influence.

Vancouver Island Premium Lager, the company flagship, heads a small family that includes the sweetly fruity Piper's Pale Ale and alliteratively named (at least if you're German) Victoria Weizen. The latter, although filtered, delivers plenty of Bavarian character with its big 'banana' aroma and fruity-wheaty flavors. Hermann's Dark Lager, surely one of the best German-inspired dunkels brewed in Canada, offers smooth, chocolatey flavors before a balanced, bittersweet finish. Hermannator, a hugely characterful winter brew, has alternated between doppelbock and eisbock status over the years.

ALSO WORTH TRYING

British Columbia capital Victoria hosts two of western Canada's best brewpubs. **Spinnakers**, the first modern brewpub (as we understand the term) in Canada, opened in 1984. A wide rotating selection features several truly cask-conditioned ales. Standards include Doc Hadfield's Pale Ale (with an excellent 'fresh hop' character), while more exotic offerings have included a well-made Tsarist Imperial Stout and deliberately-soured 'lambic.'

Victoria's other famous brewpub is **Buckerfield's Brewery**, informally known as Swan's because it is part of the attractive, lively Swan Hotel complex. Both its darkly-malty Scotch Ale and exceptionally smooth Oatmeal Stout, pleasantly roasty and bitter, are far more characterful than the easily quaffable Buckerfield's Bitter. For a broad selection of regional micros, head to downtown Victoria's Sticky Wicket pub (919 Douglas Street, in the Strathcona Hotel).

Vancouver hop-heads rejoice over the fruity-hoppy, sweetish Red Sky Alt Bier from the city's **Storm Brewing**, a tiny operation that opened in 1995. The city's most popular craft beers come from sizable area micro **Shaftebury Brewing**: its RainForest Amber Ale is

richer and bigger in character than the brown-aleish 'Cream Ale' (perhaps the name refers to smoothness?). Young trendies pack the slick **Yaletown** brewpub more for the prospects of picking up a date than one of the standard brews: across town, the **Steam Works** brewpub offers equivalent bodies and a more attractive selection of beers. Outposts of the Fogg n' Suds pub chain, based in the city, serve a decent selection of nearby Canadian micros with beers on tap.

North of Vancouver, open fermenters at **Horseshoe Bay Brewing** produce barrels and bottle-conditioned versions of its flagship Bay Ale, Pale Ale, Nut Brown Ale, and potent (7%) Triple Frambozen. Also worthy of an appreciative sip in British Columbia are the beers of **Whistler Brewing**, including the 'artistic' Whistler Mother's Pale Ale.

In Edmonton, Alberta, **Alley Kat Brewing** offers a pale ale, Alley Kat Amber, seasonal specials, and a popular apricot-flavored beer called Aprikat. Meanwhile, Alberta's **Banff Brewery** bucks the micro trend with German-style lagers, including White Horn Pilsner and Storm Mountain Bavarian Dark. Calgary's Buzzards Cafe has its own Buzzard's Breath Ale (brewed by Big Rock) and a solid selection of micros on tap.

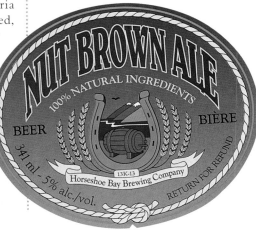

CANADA EAST

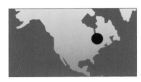

Eastern Canada's history swims in ale. After all, it was the beer style du jour of early settlers and the French Regime of the 17th century. During the next 200 years, the influence of English, Scottish, and Irish brewers only enhanced this ale tradition. Even as lager became Canada's national style, the eastern regions retained a taste for top-fermented brews that made the area fertile territory for imports and the most flavorful offerings of big Canadian brewers.

Today, Ontario and Quebec host the most dynamic segments of Canada's craft-brewing industry. Micros abound, although the 'Maritimes' (Newfoundland, Prince Edward Island, Nova Scotia, etc.) mainly make do with brewpubs like the excellent Granite Brewery in Halifax. And with a few notable exceptions – Brasal's rich Bock and Creemore Springs eponymous Lager, for example – ales remain the favored style.

Tastes embrace everything from the hoppy (McAuslan's St Ambroise Pale) to the malty (Hart's Festive Brown) to the cutting-edge creative (Niagara Falls Apple Ale, Unibroue's Belgian-styled range). Jean Talon, an early Quebec governor who built a brewery in order to reduce the province's dependence on imported drink, would be proud.

BRASAL BREWERY (BRASSERIE BRASAL)

ESTABLISHED 1989

8477, Rue Cordner, Lasalle, Montreal
Quebec M8N 2X2

RECOMMENDED
Special Amber (6.1%),
'über Vienna,' or nut-brown lager?
Brasal Bock (7.8%),
seamlessly smooth, outstandingly flavorful

A 'culturally challenging' micro: located in French Canada, founded by two Austrians, producing Bavarian-inspired

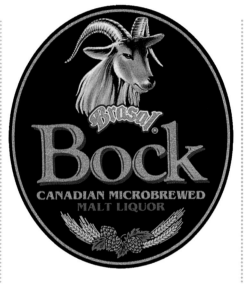

lagers. The name is a contraction of Brasserie Allemande ('German Brewery'). Despite Quebec's taste for ale, or perhaps because of it, the owners saw a niche market for fresh, locally-brewed lager beers like those of their homeland. Today, Brasal claims a craft-beer market share in the province of nearly 30 percent! Exports to neighboring Ontario, Alberta, and, more importantly, America also are growing.

A distribution agreement with Holsten Imports has established Brasal's beers in key United States markets from Washington DC to Seattle. The brewery expected 1996 production to be well over 8,500 barrels (10,000hl).

Brasal takes pains to note that all of its beers are made according to the

Reinheitsgebot (the Bavarian purity law). Drinkers will be more impressed by the character of Brasal's brews, which is uniformly good. The flagship Hopps Bräu, a fresh-tasting (and slightly 'muscular') Pilsner, clearly illustrates the brewery's founding purpose. Brasal's big-bodied Special boasts a Vienna lager's spiciness, the nutty flavors of a brown ale, and a potency greater than either. Best is the rich ruby-colored Bock – lagered for three months – with its coffee, caramel, and lightly fruity notes. A top example of the dunkelbock style, it should help Quebec ale-o-philes learn to love lagers. All of Brasal's beers, including a low-alcohol/low-calorie 'Light,' are available year-round.

CREEMORE SPRINGS BREWERY

ESTABLISHED 1987

139 Mill Street, Creemore, Ontario L0M 1G0

RECOMMENDED
Premium Lager (5%),
exceptionally well-rounded and fresh-tasting

Creemore, a rural town around two hours north of Toronto, isn't quite as bucolic as it first appears: many of the sleepy houses belong to big-city escapees or vacationers. Operating out of the town's converted 1890's May Hardware

Store,' Creemore Springs Brewery is a thriving example of doing only one thing extremely well. Unlike almost every other craft-brewer in North America, Creemore specializes in only one beer: Creemore Springs Premium Lager.

Reportedly inspired by the Czech Republic's Pilsner Urquell, Creemore Springs Lager is deeper and fuller bodied – less a Pilsner than an extremely fresh-tasting amber lager. Its soft, full flavor (a balance between sweetish, faintly nutty malt, and floral, spicy hops) is best appreciated on draft. To this end, Creemore Springs sold only kegs for more than a year after opening. When 500ml bottles were introduced, fans were grateful enough to overlook the 'malt liquor' screw-caps. Production in 1996 was expected to surpass 12,800 barrels (15,000hl): significant barrelage for any micro.

1996 also saw Creemore introduce its first-ever limited edition brew, urBock, as a Christmas-time seasonal.

HART BREWING

ESTABLISHED 1991

175 Industrial Avenue
Carleton Place, Ontario

RECOMMENDED

Dragon's Breath Pale Ale (4.5%),
fresh hop aroma and character
Hart Amber Ale (5%),
complex fruit and toasty malt
Hart Festive Brown Ale (6%),
nutty, spicy, lots of smooth depth

This is the premier Ottawa Valley micro. Founder Lorne Hart, a retired engineer, and his partners established the brewery after a market analysis showed that the Ottawa area could support such a project. Despite a few lean early years

– the Ottawa region was not as thirsty as Hart's analysis had suggested! – the company's bottom line has been buoyed recently by both expansion into Toronto and greater distribution through Canadian beer stores. In short, Ontario finally appears to be following the brewery's advice to 'Have a Hart.' Production capacity for 1996 stood at 10,200 barrels (12,000hl).

Hart's flagship Amber Ale and several other beers were formulated by peripatetic brewmaster Alan Pugsley (in his pre-Shipyard days). The Amber offers plenty of depth, strong balancing hops, and subdued (for the Pugsley/Ringwood yeast) complex fruit. Both the winey (cherryish?) Finnigan's Irish Red Ale and smooth, rich, deeply drinkable Festive Brown head in a thoroughly malty direction. Hart also brews a crisp, blonde Valley Gold beer and fruity Cream Ale. Winter brings a vinous Hardy Stout, while a 'slightly hopped' Hart Wheat greets Ottawa summers. Kegs and bottles of the brightly hoppy Dragon's Breath Pale are produced under license from the local Kingston Brewing brewpub.

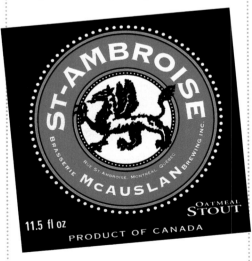

Above: McAuslan wants you to drink your oatmeal.

McAUSLAN BREWING (BRASSERIE McAUSLAN)

ESTABLISHED 1989

4850, Rue St Ambroise
Montreal, Quebec H4C 3N8

RECOMMENDED

Griffon Extra Pale Ale (5.0%),
softly fruity, clean honeyed malt character
St Ambroise Pale Ale (5.0%),
pleasantly (somewhat aggressively) hoppy
St Ambroise Oatmeal Stout (5.5%),
excellent dry example of style

McAuslan is one of the best known names in Canadian craft brewing. Founder Peter McAuslan homebrewed for years before making the leap from college administrator to professional microbrewer. Itinerant brewer Alan Pugsley helped McAuslan build his plant and develop the recipe for St Ambroise Pale, the original brew. Today, brewing is supervised by Ellen Bounsall, a trained biologist who happens to be McAuslan's wife. McAuslan's beers now are available widely in Quebec, as well as the United States. The brewery expected to produce more than 17,000 barrels (20,000hl) in 1996.

All of McAuslan's beers have a more restrained character than others brewed with the Ringwood yeast and Peter Austin equipment (the Pugsley connection). The St Ambroise beers are the most distinctive: the Pale bursts with citric hop character over lightly toasty malt and complex fruit; the flagship Oatmeal Stout, drier and more coffeeish than many examples, balances its smooth character with strong roasted notes. McAuslan's Griffon line, purposely designed to be 'more accessible,' includes the soft, quaffable Extra Pale and a caramel-accented, medium-bodied Brown Ale. In addition, McAuslan makes an 'extra special pale ale' (ESP?) called Frontenac for its local market.

NIAGARA FALLS BREWING

ESTABLISHED 1989

6863 Lundy's Lane
Niagara Falls, Ontario L2G 1V7

RECOMMENDED

Brock's Extra Stout (5.8%),
deliciously coffeeish, incredibly roasty
Eisbock (8%),
an annual brew well worth seeking
Maple Wheat (8.5%),
subtle, finessed with balanced maple flavor

This colorful micro is not too far east of the famous Falls (so far, no one has gone over in one of the brewery's barrels!). It was founded by two brothers who previously operated a brewery in Addis Ababa, Ethiopia, along with a few partners with a background in the region's wine industry.

While a mainstream-oriented Trapper Premium Canadian Lager once was Niagara's top seller, the brewery also produces a wide range of more distinctive beers. These are becoming widely available in Ontario and, since 1995, America. Production for 1996 approached 17,000 barrels (20,000hl).

Brock's Extra Stout tastes powerfully of roasted grain, with hints of licorice. Although potent, Maple Wheat – brewed with Ontario-harvested maple syrup – is almost 'refined' in its delicate

balance. A strong ale called Olde Jock is similarly smooth, if sweetish, while Gritstone Premium Ale has a spicy-nutty character and notable orange/apricot fruitiness. Niagara also offers two actual fruit beers, a cherry-sweet Kriek and crisp, aromatic, well-balanced Apple Ale.

Enthusiasts await the annual winter arrival of Niagara Falls Eisbock with almost religious fervor. Although its character varies from vintage to vintage, this copper-colored, spicy-sweet, lightly fruity brew tends to be more drinkable than classic German examples. In 1996, the brewery released a special 'Eisbock Gold' that had been frozen to a finished alcohol content of 8.6% and lagered for 11 months.

UNIBROUE

ESTABLISHED 1990

80, Des Carrieres, Chambly, Quebec J3L 2H6

RECOMMENDED

Blanche de Chambly (5%),
fragrant, lemony, pleasantly tart Belgian 'white'
Maudite (8%),
peppery, faintly minty, richly malty-sweet
La Fin du Monde (9%),
rich, honeyed, hints of lemony flavor

An aesthetically-minded micro making Belgian-inspired ales, Unibroue was founded after the owner reached an arrangement with Belgium's Riva brewery to produce their Dentergems Witbier recipe in Canada.

After a few years' operation on used equipment, Unibroue opened a purpose-built modern brewery in 1993. The company has expanded both production and distribution aggressively, creating subsidiary importers in both America (Unibrew USA) and France (Unibroue France).

All of Unibroue's ales are bottle-conditioned. The flagship Blanche de Chambly ('White of Chambly') is

deliciously dry, 'wheaty,' and citrus-tart with vanilla notes – neither as soft as Hoegaarden, nor as firm as Celis. Maudite ('Damned') takes its name from a French Canadian legend about a 'flying canoe' full of trappers who sold their souls in order to make it home in time for a party: amber-bronze in color, it is smooth and malty-rich with spicy accents. La Fin du Monde ('The End of the World'), which falls between a strong golden ale (think Duvel) and a Belgian tripel, offers a more finessed, honeyish malt character.

Both Maudite and La Fin benefit from several months (at least) bottle ageing. Unibroue also brews a faintly smoky 'whiskey malt' beer called Raftman, as well as the cleanly malty, sweetish La Galliarde (a spiced ale in the 'medieval style').

In 1995, the company introduced an acclaimed strong, spiced cherry ale called Quelque Chose as a winter seasonal.

WELLINGTON COUNTY BREWERY

ESTABLISHED 1985

950 Woodlawn Road W
Guelph, Ontario N1K 1B8

∼∾∽

RECOMMENDED
Arkell Best Bitter (4%),
at its best when cask-conditioned
County Ale (5%),
fruity but well-balanced amber
Iron Duke (6.5%),
strong, malty, nutty complexity

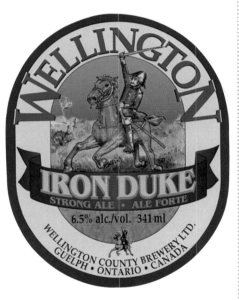

This early Ontario micro was established by a group of British ale enthusiasts to provide locally-brewed, authentic cask-conditioned ales – a noble plan that hit a major snag after the first casks of Best Bitter and County Ale rolled out the door. The majority of area publicans, it seemed, were either unable or unwilling to provide the extra effort needed to serve true 'real ale.' Wellington quickly (and successfully) began offering filtered ales in standard kegs and bottles. Production neared 6,000 barrels (7,000hl) in 1996, with distribution throughout southern Ontario.

A handful of accounts still serve Wellington's original Best Bitter (a dry, hoppy session brew) and County Ale in cask-conditioned form. A Special Pale Ale (SPA) splits the difference between the two, in terms of character and strength. Iron Duke, a robust reddish ale with layers of malt flavor, now stands as the flagship beer (to the point where Wellington describes itself as 'The Iron Duke Brewery'). The company also offers a well made Premium Lager in the Vienna style, a new 'Honey Lager,' and a rich Imperial Stout.

All of Wellington's ales are unified by characteristically English-favored ingredients like East Kent (and Styrian) Golding hops.

ALSO WORTH TRYING

Quebec drinkers say *oui* to French-accented breweries such as **Brasserie Seigneuriale** and **Les Brasseurs GMT** (and its golden Belle Gueule lager). The aleish Boréale brews (soft Blonde, malty Rousse, and stout-like Noire) from **Les Brasseurs du Nord** also are favorite local beers. Montreal micro-lovers drain the taps and bottles at Le Petit Moulinsart (1239 St Paul Street, W Montreal).

Ontario offers several additional suds of note, such as the deep, satisfying Rebellion Lager from **Upper Canada Brewing** (one of the region's earliest micros). British traditionalists may prefer the Best Bitter from Toronto's **Granite Brewery**, the second outpost of this Halifax-headquartered brewpub. **Conners Brewery** originally of St Catharines also offers a balanced Best Bitter, along with a complex, coffeeish 'Imperial' Stout. Conners was acquired at the end of 1996 by Waterloo's **Brick Brewing** (try Brick's complex seasonal Anniversary Bock and crisp Kaiser Pilsner). In Elora, **Taylor & Bate Brewery** has achieved a 'jolly good' reputation for its English-inspired ales.

Toronto's C'est What beer bar (67 Front Street E) and Ottawa's Solstice Pub (75 University Avenue) both feature regional micros.

Below: Beers from Toronto's Upper Canada Brewing.

THE BEERS OF MEXICO AND THE CARIBBEAN

Unlike their northern North American neighbors, Mexico and the Caribbean islands have yet to embrace microbreweries. But finding distinctive beers in these regions is not quite as difficult as suggested by the prevalent images of golden lagers on sun-drenched beaches. Both areas have retained notable specialty-brewing traditions: Mexico's come from the golden age of central European lagers, while the Caribbean's stem from the stout-hearted era of British Empire.

By the time Spanish conquistadors introduced European brewing to Mexico during the 16th century, natives throughout the country (and Central/South America) had been making rough indigenous beers for centuries. The most common were porridge-like brews created from local ingredients, frequently featuring corn as the base grain – the variety called chicha probably is best known. Like most early beers, these fermented 'spontaneously' with wild yeasts (occasionally getting a 'starter' from yeast introduced via the brewer's saliva). All were consumed relatively quickly, sometimes during special drinking ceremonies. A few still are produced today in extremely rural districts.

Mexico's hot climate, which disrupted fermentation and encouraged spoilage, relegated beer to a secondary position behind stable distilled spirits such as tequila until the introduction of commercial ice-making and refrigeration during the 1800s. The arrival of these technologies coincided with the glory days of European lager brewing, leading Mexico to adopt this newer beer variety instead of old-world ales. Immigrant brewmasters from central Europe – perhaps encouraged by the short period when Mexico was part of the Austrian Empire – introduced the styles of their homelands: Munich's dunkels, Vienna's ambers, and golden Pilsners.

Today, it is golden beers that have made Mexico's brewing fortune. A number of high-adjunct, lightly-hopped pale lagers (Corona, Sol, Chihuahua, Pacifico, etc.), originally developed as cheap quenchers for Mexican workers, have rocketed to international success on the strength of sunshine-and-suds imagery. But while the country's brewers – now split into the two main groups of Modelo and Moctezuma-Cuauhtémoc – market these brands with all their might, they also still offer more interesting beers. Cuauhtémoc's Saaz-hopped Bohemia (5.4%), for example, pays homage in both name and character to classic Pilsners.

Mexico even offers darker brews whose genesis falls somewhere between Vienna, Munich, and the country's early attempts at brewing with sun-dried (reddish) malts. Viennese

influence is obvious in Modelo's Victoria, a rich amber-colored lager introduced in 1865 and now Mexico's oldest brand (and the brewery's third-best seller). Unfortunately, it is only available in the country's central and southeast regions. Moctezuma's similar Dos Equis amber lager (4.8%), on the other hand, is broadly exported.

Modelo also makes two negra ('black' in Spanish) lagers, deep red-brown in color, that stylistically owe more to Bavaria's capital: the kräusened Negra Modelo (5.3%), widely available in export markets, is smooth and chocolatey; Leon Negra, a regional brand from the company's Yucatan brewery, has a greater hop character. These beers and others in their style – darker than a Vienna lager, but not as full-bodied or rich-tasting as a Munich dunkel – sometimes are known as *oscura* (Spanish for 'dark'). Moctezuma sadly has discontinued its Tres Equis Oscura. The Mexican brewers also have been abandoning a tradition of still-darker, richer Christmas beers like Moctezuma's Noche Buena.

As in Mexico, the hot climate of the Caribbean has helped make golden Pilsner-style lagers the region's most popular beers. Jamaica's clean-tasting Red Stripe lager (4.7%), originally launched as a light-colored ale, is the most famous version: the enthusiastic support of tourists and Jamaican emigrants has helped it achieve broad popularity outside its homeland. Red Stripe is the flagship of Jamaica's Desnoes & Geddes brewery, founded in 1918 as a soft-drink company.

Golden lagers aside, the Caribbean's most distinctive beers reflect an earlier ale-brewing tradition that stems from the period when much of the region was under British rule. As early as the 1800s, Guinness shipped a potent West Indies Porter to the Caribbean that, despite its dark color and strength, was refreshing thanks to its naturally sour character. This evolved into the deliberately-soured Foreign Extra Stout (7.5%) still made by Guinness today. A version is produced locally for the Caribbean by Jamaica's Desnoes & Geddes. D&G also offers its own sweeter,

more chocolatey Dragon Stout (7%), nowadays brewed with the company's lager yeast. Similar foreign-style stouts, also lagers, have been brewed in Barbados (Banks) and Haiti (Prestige Stout). An equally-potent Porter (8%) from Brazil's Brahma brewing group is available on the region's western periphery.

Why do such brews stay popular around the Caribbean? In part because, thanks to their potency, they have become associated with enhancing male virility. D&G is notorious for advertising its own brand in Jamaica with suggestive slogans such as 'Dragon Puts It Back.' Guinness purchased 51 percent of D&G in 1993, ensuring that at least the brewery itself will remain well-endowed for the foreseeable future.

EUROPE

*Clear evidence exists that the sophisticated Sumerian civilization,
in what is now Iraq, brewed a kind of beer from various grains including
barley as long as 5,000 years ago. Ancient Celtic and Germanic tribes
produced similarly intoxicating delights but we shall probably never know
whether the early Europeans stumbled on brewing accidently, nor when
they did so, nor if they had received the wisdom from nomadic tribes.*

We have to wait until the 1st century AD for the first written record of European brewing when the Roman historian Tacitus noted in his work entitled *Germania* that the 'barbarians' east and north of the Rhine and Danube got drunk on a brew made from fermented grains. As far as archeologists can tell, the Celts and Teutons used methods very similar to those of the Sumerians to obtain their favored tipple: soaking grain and then leaving it to ferment by reaction with wild yeasts in the air. It would probably have been a porridge-like concoction with various herbs or spices added for flavoring.

It must have been enjoyable though, because more than 200 years after Tacitus, when the Roman empire was under pressure from the untamed Teutonic farmer-warriors, we know that their drinking habits had not changed; Emperor Julian referred to them as 'the sons of malt.'

The term 'beer' (or *bier, bière, birra*) has its origins in earlier languages of northern Europe – Norse and Saxon – as does 'ale' which is similar to the modern words used in Scandinavian countries for beer – öl and øl (pronounced awl).

Recorded history in Europe for the period from the collapse of the Roman Empire until the Middle Ages reveals little apart from invasion, pillage, and plunder. Monasteries were the chief founts of knowledge in the Dark Ages, and brewing was among their activities.

Some older beer styles and seasonal specialties – Bavaria's doppelbock, for example – can be traced back to the monasteries or events in the religious calendar.

It is not clear when hops first became an ingredient in beer, but monastic records reveal that hops were cultivated in parts of Charlemagne's empire – notably in what

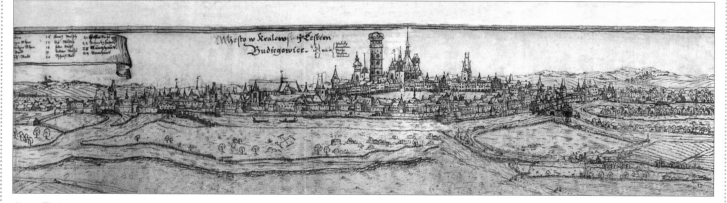

Above: The history of brewing in Ceské Budejovice, the home of Budweiser Budvar, dates back to 1265. This drawing of the city by Jan Willenberg dates from 1602.

is today's Bavaria – in the 9th century, and that Bohemian hops were traded across Europe early in the 10th century.

Brewing rights granted to selected burghers in medieval towns marked the first phase in the serious organization of brewing in Europe. And this event still has some powerful echoes today. In Plzeň, the Czech home of the world's first golden-colored beer, descendants of 260 families granted brewing rights in 1295 by King Wenceslas II were in 1994 given a collective share of almost 10 percent in the large Pilsner Urquell Corporation when it was re-privatized after 40 years of communist state control.

In Bavaria, beer was the subject of the world's first consumer protection law, the Reinheitsgebot of 1516, which stipulated that beer could be made only from barley, hops, and water.

European brewing's second phase was marked by the 19th century scientific industrialization of the craft, triggered by the thirsts of rising urban populations. In central Europe it led to regular bottom fermentation, adding the German word lager to beer's vocabulary. This era ushered in a degree of standardization in brewing and, apart from in Britain and isolated pockets in Germany and Belgium, the decline of ale brewing.

Above: Mo Rolfe of England's Hog's Back Brewery typifies the new generation of brewer.

Above: Zum Uerige is one of the few German brewpubs still committed to ale-brewing

Brewing's third phase is still being played out as monolithic national and international combines gobble up rival breweries and reduce consumer choice to a few mass-produced and heavily advertised brands. Although this phase has done much damage to the diversity and richness of brewing – in Europe and elsewhere – it has, ironically, stimulated a brewing renaissance triggered by a consumer backlash against this homogenization of taste and product.

The new 'sons of malt' emerged in Britain in the 1970s in the shape of the Campaign for Real Ale (CAMRA). Their simple objective was to prevent the disappearance of Britain's rich, localized ale-brewing heritage and its replacement with ersatz national products which were great achievements of packaging and marketing and little else. The result of CAMRA's long and, at times, vitriolic campaign against the big 'bad' brewers – or rather the boardroom directors and their economies-of-scale logic – was a re-awakening of public interest in beer.

CAMRA's success inspired similar consumer movements in Belgium and the Netherlands and has led to the European Beer Consumers Union. Across Europe, from Finland to Switzerland and Ireland to the Ukraine, hundreds of microbreweries and brewpubs have sprung up in response to the brewing giants. And beyond Europe, especially in the United States, a microbrewing revolution is under way to challenge brewing juggernauts such as Anheuser-Busch, begetter of Budweiser.

At a time when the business of brewing is being concentrated into fewer hands, more beer drinkers than ever before are becoming aware of what's on offer, and what's at risk.

The multitude of beer styles to be found today in Europe, many of which have spawned copies good, bad, or even better around the world, are the result of centuries of evolution. They range from the dark stouts and fruity ales of Britain to the golden Pilsners of central Europe. And in between there are tart, champagne-like wheat beers and strong pale and dark bocks in Germany, and sour wild yeast lambics and fruit beers in Belgium. The range and variety is enormous, belying the superficial impression that European beer equals fizzy cold lager.

Right: Drie Ringen sells its beers in its own brewery bar.

ENGLAND
LONDON AND SOUTHEAST

London is awash with traditional ale these days, but there is precious little brewing done in the capital. The big players, who expended so much energy creating their national corporations, have departed. Once great London brewing names – Charrington, Courage, Truman (founded in 1666), Watney, and even Whitbread – have been killed off or are brewed elsewhere.

The two survivors, with brewing roots dating from the 17th century, are Fuller's and Young's. Happily, new London brewing in pubs or micros has sprung up with the appearance of the Greyhound Brewery (Streatham Common), O'Hanlon's (Vauxhall, brewing stout), Orange Brewery (brewpub, Pimlico), Yorkshire Grey (brewpub, Bloomsbury), and the Freedom brewery in Parsons Green which specializes in Bavarian-style bottom-fermenting beer.

FULLER'S

ESTABLISHED LATE 1600s

Griffin Brewery, Chiswick Lane South
London W4 2QB

RECOMMENDED
Chiswick Bitter (3.5%),
amber, dry, fruity with the smack of hops
London Pride (4.1%),
copper, intense malt and fruit flavors, bitter-dry
ESB (5.5%),
copper-red, rich melody of flavors

An indication of how things have changed in the last 20 years is the fact that ESB used to be the strongest regular draft ale available in Britain. Without legal pressures of the kind which cursed Scandinavian brewing, most British brewers had quietly weaned drinkers on to 3.5% beers; anything over 4% was considered strong; ESB's 5.5% was for the daring, or reckless. Nowadays, ESB (Extra Special Bitter) is a slightly above average strength.

There has been brewing on the same River Thames location near Hammersmith since the days of the 17th century diarist Samuel Pepys, who might well have supped in the Dove, a Fuller's pub gem which nestles on the waterfront near the brewery.

A variety of barley malts, but primarily Alexis, plus a little flaked maize are used. Hops vary according to the brew but include Northdown, Challenger, Goldings, and Target.

Fuller's now produces several seasonal specialties, including Hock, a 3.2% fruity dark mild for spring; IPA, a 4.8% hoppy and very bitter early summer offering; and a full-bodied, dry porter.

The Fuller family, associated with the brewery since 1829, are still involved today.

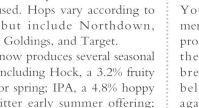

Right: In the brewhouse at Young's in Wandsworth. Young's cherishes its traditions – beer is still delivered locally by horse-drawn drays.

YOUNG'S

ESTABLISHED 1675

The Ram Brewery, High Street, Wandsworth
London SW18 4JD

RECOMMENDED
Bitter (termed Ordinary) (3.7%),
pale, gentle malt and hoppiness, finally dry
Special (4.6%),
amber, malty, full-bodied, bittersweet
Winter Warmer (5%),
ruby, rich, and fruity-dry

Young's holds a special place in the memories of those who campaigned for proper English ale as it ebbed away in the 1970s. Young's was the only brewery in the capital which still believed in itself and held the line against bland pasteurized and CO_2-injected imitations. Brewery boss John Young vowed to keep producing real ale, and did so. Of that time, he said recently: 'CAMRA came along and we had the most tremendous boost. It was a very rare example of the clock being totally turned back...'

Maris Otter is the main barley malt, plus Fuggles and Goldings hops. Young's have introduced a range of seasonal brews for adventurous palates: the spicy, Belgium-style Wheat Beer (4%) made with coriander and ground orange peel is the latest, reflecting the fact that the brewery's deputy chairman James Young is half Belgian; Oatmeal Stout (4.5%), a dark fruity mild (3.2%); and Ram Rod (4.8%, strong bitter).

The brewery still delivers by horse-drawn dray to its closest pubs in Wandsworth. In central London, the Guinea, a Young's pub in a mews off Berkeley Square, is worth hunting out.

BRAKSPEAR

ESTABLISHED 1799

WH Brakspear & Sons, The Brewery
Henley-on-Thames, Oxon RG9 2BU

~~~

RECOMMENDED

Bitter (3.4%),
*amber, big malt aroma and flavor, hop
bitterness and dry finish*
Special (4%),
copper, maltiness balanced by fruity flavors
OBJ (5%),
*red-brown, rich full-bodied fruit-malt before
a big hoppy finale*

Beer has been brewed on this spot since the 1600s but the Brakspear family can trace their involvement 'only' to 1799.

The brewery still uses a two-story fermentation process which is unusual nowadays. Fermenting beer 'drops' from one set of open vessels to another beneath as a way of filtering solids and excess yeast. This gives the green beer more chance to breathe and reactivates slumbering yeast cells.

Brakspear favors the older barley variety Maris Otter, which is more costly than newer varieties but arguably is more flavorsome. Pipkin black malt goes into all the beers too. A

cocktail of hops is used, from Fuggles to Goldings, and all the beers are dry hopped. Brakspear's beers have high bitterness levels.

HARVEY'S

ESTABLISHED 1790

Bridge Wharf Brewery, 6 Cliffe High Street,
Lewes, Sussex BN7 2AH

~~~

RECOMMENDED

Sussex Best Bitter (4%),
amber, malt and fruit flavors, hoppy-dry finish
Armada Ale (4.5%),
golden, fruitiness gives way to dry bitterness
1859 Porter (4.8%),
black, strong hop aroma, dry roasty, bitter taste
Tom Paine (5.5%),
pale ale, strong hop nose and hoppy, dry taste

Head brewer Miles Jenner poetically defines his day's work in the brewhouse as an event producing 'the heavenly smell which lingers over Lewes...' Harvey's brewery is a classic piece of towering Victorian Gothic, a centerpiece in this picturesque ancient castle town. The brewery uses timeless traditional methods and equipment, whole hops from the surrounding Kent and Sussex fields, and water from a well which was sunk in 1875. They favor Maris Otter and Pipkin barley malt.

There are four permanent ales plus a colorful collection of seasonal brews. Most notable is the 1859 Porter, named after the year the recipe was written in Henry Harvey's diary. It is made with three malts, including black, and sold on draft only in March, but in bottle (unfiltered) year-round. It came second in CAMRA's

1995 Champion Beer of Britain competition. Tom Paine honors the radical English philosopher who lived in Lewes for six years before departing for America in 1774 to support the cause of Independence. Christmas Ale (8.1%) resembles the former dark ecclesiastical Stock Ales. It is matured for several weeks in tanks to which freshly harvested local whole hops are added.

Harveys' owns 33 pubs. One of them – The Dorset Arms in Lewes – dates from 1670.

ALSO WORTH TRYING

Shepherd Neame, one of Britain's oldest breweries, in Faversham, Kent, offers Master Brew (3.7%, amber, very malty-dry and hoppy) and Original Porter which contains licorice (5.2%, fruity and bitter). The micro **Pilgrim** of Reigate, Surrey, has Saracen Stout (4.5%, malty-dry and bitter) and Springbok wheat beer (5.2%, pale, citric fruitiness), also in Surrey at Tongham, the **Hog's Back** micro has Hop Garden Gold (4.6%, golden, dry, and A over T (9%, dark, fruity rich), Old Speckled Hen (5.2%, amber, malty and dry) from **Morland's** of Abingdon near Oxford has a national following; and in Oxford, **Morrell's** naturally has Varsity (4.3%, bittersweet).

THE MIDLANDS

The creation of pale malt in the early 19th century coincided with a demand from British colonists in hot climes for beer that was more refreshing than traditional heavy porters. Burton upon Trent discovered that its sulfur-and-calcium-rich water was ideal for India Pale Ales. And the Burton brewers invented an intricate fermentation system called Union Sets which cleansed their beers of excess yeast adding clarity to produce dry, bitter, clear beers – just what the British Empire ordered.

The West Midlands, which had a more frontline role in the industrial revolution at home, developed a taste for sweeter, dark mild ales which better refreshed factory and mine workers.

This very English beer style remains strongest here, with Highgate of Walsall and Banks's of Wolverhampton producing large quantities of such brews. Distinctive dark milds also come from Batham's (Brierley Hill), Holden's (Woodsetton, Dudley), and in Nottingham from Hardy's & Hanson's.

BASS

ESTABLISHED 1777

137 High Street, Burton upon Trent
Staffs DE14 1JZ

RECOMMENDED

Bass Draught (4.4%),
dark amber, fruity with firm malt flavors and some gentle hoppiness in the background. Full-bodied with a fruity-dry finish and aftertaste

Historically Bass is Britain's most famous brewer. William Bass's fortunes rose with the export of India Pale Ale to the British colonies. The familiar red triangle became the world's first registered trademark.

Bass's merger with other great British brewing companies – Worthington (Burton), Charrington (London), and Tennents (Scotland) – created Britain's biggest brewing conglomerate, a title lost only in 1995 to the new amalgamation of Scottish-Courage.

Draught Bass remains one of Britain's biggest real ales, but critics say that it lost character with the end of its Union fermentation system in the 1980s. Today, Bass is fermented in open squares with Halcyon barley malt and Northdown and Challenger hops. Bass remains exceptional when it has been allowed to mature in the pub cellar, but it is often served 'green' and also appears in pasteurized forms.

The bottle-conditioned Worthington White Shield (5.6%), believed to be similar to the India Pale Ales of the 19th century, is now made at the group's Mitchells & Butlers brewery, Birmingham. White Shield today is more hop-spicy since being revamped in 1992, and it is now sold in supermarkets as well as pubs.

MARSTON'S

ESTABLISHED 1834

Marston, Thompson & Evershed
Albion Brewery, Shobnall Road
Burton upon Trent, Staffs DE14 2BW

RECOMMENDED

Bitter (3.7%),
amber, subtle creamy malt taste, fruity-dry finish
Pedigree (4.5%)
red-brown, powerful taste with sulfury, fruity-dryness dominating
Owd Rodger (7.6%),
ruby, powerful malty and fruity strong ale

Marston was the dominant and oldest established of several local brewing families who joined forces in 1898. It is the only brewery still using the intricate, messy but flavor-influencing fermentation system known as the Burton Unions (see above).

The company's commitment to the Unions was demonstrated by a £1 million refurbishment scheme in 1992. Not every Marston beer is 'unionized' – only Pedigree and the new Burton Old Ale (6.2%), which won a silver medal in 1996 – but all use the same yeast. Marston's uses Fuggles and Goldings hops and mostly pale malt, plus some caramel in the darker brews. Glucose is used in all beers – 15 percent of Pedigree's fermentables.

Marston's owns more than 850 pubs and its most popular beer, Pedigree, is virtually a national brand. Limited edition draft beers, dubbed Head Brewer's Choice, appear monthly.

HIGHGATE

ESTABLISHED 1893

Highgate Brewery, Sandymount Road
Walsall WS1 3AP

RECOMMENDED

Highgate Dark Mild (3.2%),
dark brown, malty aroma, full-bodied dry, nutty
Highgate Old Ale (5.1%),
ruby, rich fruit and bitter malt taste

This classic Victorian tower brewery is a protected building and the only one left in Britain whose mainstream product remains a mild ale, catering to the unchanging tastebuds of England's West Midlands region where for decades it was the local coalminers' favorite sweat-replacing sustenance.

Highgate clings to life as well as tradition. It has changed owners numerous times and bizarrely owes its survival to the strict wartime rationing of raw materials imposed in the 1940s. Highgate was bought by local rival Mitchells and Butlers in 1939 for its pub estate, but the onset of World War II encouraged M&B to keep the brewery ticking over so that it could claim its full share of rationed grain and hops.

M&B was later taken over by Bass and again seemed destined to die under business rationalization, but in 1995 Highgate (capacity 50,000 barrels, 82,000hl) left the Bass stable in a management buyout led by Steve Nuttall. He encourages visits to Highgate to see beer made by equipment that was first used by founder James Fletcher in the 1890s. Brewer Neil Bain uses Challenger and Progress whole hops, three malts including roasted black malt, and some caramel.

HANBY ALES

ESTABLISHED 1989

New Brewer, Aston Park, Wem
Shropshire SY4 5SD

RECOMMENDED

Drawwell Bitter (3.9%),
amber, hoppy throughout with fruity tones
Shropshire Stout (4.4%),
black, firm roast malt flavor, some fruitiness
Nutcracker (6%),
pale, rich, and fruity-dry

In remarkable acts of defiance, redundant brewers offloaded by the destructive English company Greenall Whitley have made something of a habit

of opening up their own little breweries where Greenall closed perfectly good, viable ones. It happened in Warrington in northwest England (see Coach House), and it happened in the picturesque Shropshire market town of Wem, once a great malting center.

Former Greenalls head brewer Jack Hanby was determined to keep brewing alive in Wem when his ex-employers closed the 200-year-old brewery there. Today he produces a much more colorful range of beer than Greenalls ever did, including ginger- and maraschino cherry-flavored editions of Nutcracker.

The Hanby micro has expanded twice to meet demand and now produces more than 1,000 barrels (1,650hl) a year. Greenalls maintains a grip on pubs in Wem, so Hanby's own pub The Star – offering the full range – is in nearby Market Drayton.

ALSO WORTH TRYING

Banks's Ale (3.5%, mild, fruity and dry) is widely available: **Batham** Mild (3.6%, hoppy and nutty-dry); Bridge Bitter (4.2%, fruity-dry) from Burton on Trent micro **Burton Bridge**: Kimberley Mild (3.1%, mellow maltiness) from **Hardy & Hanson; Holden's** Black Country Mild (3.6%, hoppy); **Ind Coope's** Burton Ale (4.8%, rich maltiness, fruity aftertaste) and **Allsopps'** seasonal Devil's Kiss made with treacle and ginger (5.2%, spicy-dry); Mansfield's **Deakins** seasonal range, notably Wild Boar (6%, dark fruit richness); at rural Shropshire's **Craven Arms** village micro, Wood's Special Bitter (4%, malty-dry, hoppy); at Oakham, east of Leicester, **Oakham Ales** has Jeffrey Hudson (3.8%, very pale, very dry hoppy bitter).

THE LIFE AND TIMES
OF THE BRITISH PUB

The perfect British pub does not exist. It has always meant different things to different people, although it is often imagined to be a quaint weathered stone edifice harboring a fat, jolly landlord and a roaring log fire. Perhaps this popular image has lurked in the national subconscious ever since the Roman invaders arrived two millennia ago and set up their tabernae, the roadside inns which provided shelter, warmth, and sustenance for travellers.

The tavern, inn, or pub – public house – has been evolving ever since; consequently there is no such thing as a typical one. For some, the ideal pub is a tiny and basic, nicotine-stained back street 'boozer' in a grimy industrial suburb, like the Eagle in Salford, Manchester; for others it's a more gentrified history-laden hostelry, like the Dove by the River Thames in Hammersmith, London. Pubs proliferated most during the long Victorian age as industrialization brought great urban growth and an even greater thirst for beer. But at the end of the 20th century fewer people than ever are visiting pubs – a quarter of Britain's adult population never venture inside one.

The decline of the pub was signalled a quarter of a century ago by writer, and subsequently pub owner, Christopher Hutt in his angry book *The Death of the English Pub*, which reported how convivial hostelries across the country were being tranformed into quick profit-taking 'retail outlets.' He blamed it on a trend to standardization embraced by a brewing industry which was contracting into fewer hands as six giant brewing combines emerged from a fever of takeovers and mergers to control 80 percent of the beer market and most of the country's pubs. 'Standardization means elimination of choice and is the enemy of the distinctive but infinitely variable atmosphere that is the hallmark of the really good pub,' Hutt said then. But the pub is still with us. Although thousands have died in the last two decades, the bulk of British beer is still drunk in them.

The social scientists offer a long list of reasons for the declining importance of the pub as a national social institution: better alternative leisure activities, more income, less income, more TV channels, an ageing population. Simon Lang of the Henley Centre for Forecasting thinks the pub was only ever a 'default activity' – somewhere to go because there was nowhere else and nothing else better to do.

But the inescapable fact is that many pubs, in town, village, and rural idyll, have been closed because they didn't conform to the economies-of-scale logic of the brewing giants, as Hutt foretold. And many surviving pubs are a far cry from the ideal image, real or imagined. They are brasher and less convivial, often with deafening canned music or corny cheap entertainment like karaoke, or flashing and burping electronic gaming machines filling up every spare space to maximize company profits.

Above: The pub on the corner – the Grapes is a monument to Victorian traditions.

Left: Chris Holmes (right), one of a new breed of innovative owners who are striving to reverse the decline in pub popularity.

Since the early 20th century most pubs have been owned by breweries in order to provide them with guaranteed markets for their beer; that was why the big six combines of the 1970s ended up with as many as 10,000 apiece. Today, those big six have contracted to four even bigger groups which control 84 percent of the beer market. But the law has changed too, curbing the number of pubs which one company can own to a maximun of 2,000. And a proposed European Union fair competition law might bar brewers from owning pubs at all.

The legal change has encouraged more entrepreneurial outsiders to become pub owners. One of these is Chris Holmes who has built up a small chain of what he believes are ideal pubs, combining his skills as a former business management lecturer and an enthusiasm for drinking real ale in pleasant surroundings and company. He is a past-chairman of CAMRA, and takes some small pleasure from the fact that most of his bustling pubs – dotted through the east Midlands towns of Derby, Nottingham, Loughborough, Kegworth, and Chesterfield – were previously owned by large brewing companies.

Holmes has his own theory about the decline of the pub: 'Too many have gone over to mono culture, that means their

owners deliberately make them attractive only to narrow segments of the population, usually teenagers and early twenties groups. The result is that older people are driven away. It's part of a misplaced conception that youngsters have the most disposable income. When we bought and re-opened the Victoria at Beeston (near Nottingham) it was instantly popular with local people. Yet previously it had been deserted. When we talked to these new customers and asked where they went before in the area, it was fascinating to discover that quite a lot of them – in their 30s, 40, 50s, and 60s – had stopped going to pubs because what was on offer didn't appeal to them.'

When Holmes bought his first pub his philosophy was to refashion it and run it the way he liked pubs, and hope that enough people felt the same way. That philosophy runs

Above: Beautifully ornate 19th century bars like this one are a relatively rare sight today.

through all nine pubs in his Tynemill chain. 'Our aim is for any decent member of the population, be they young, middle-aged, or elderly, to feel comfortable and happy. We don't want anyone to feel that they are in an environment which is alien.'

The ingredients are a changing selection of traditional draft ales – 'we offer lager, but if sales went above 20 percent we would know there was something wrong with our ale quality' – a variety of rooms, no gaming machines, no music (except for the Swan in the Rushes at Loughborough, which has an old blues and jazz jukebox), and traditional food. He feels strongly about maintaining the traditional socializing influence of pubs within a community. Tynemill's Red Lion at Kegworth has both teenagers and nonagenarians among its regular customers. 'As soon as you stick a load of teenagers in a pub with no older people around them, the social constraints go.'

There are still about 60,000 pubs left in Britain, although another 5,000 may have vanished by the time we toast the new millennium. But people like Holmes believe the pub has a future 'as long as there are sensible policies and stewardship by those in the industry.' Let's hope so, otherwise – in the damning words of the French-born writer Hilaire Belloc, who so loved pubs he became a British citizen – 'When you have lost your inns, drown your empty selves, for you will have lost the last of England.'

Right: Chris Holmes has revitalized the Victoria.

NORTHWEST ENGLAND

Manchester has a vibrant local brewing industry with roots that reach back to the cotton-spinning industrial revolution of the 19th century. There are still five traditional real ale breweries in the city, and four of them – Hyde's, Holt, Robinson, and Lees – remain family owned. The fifth, Boddingtons, is now drunk nationally following its purchase in 1989 by national giant Whitbread.

Beyond Manchester a string of solidly traditional ale breweries stretches from Cains of Liverpool to Jennings of Cockermouth in the scenic Lake District.

Northwest beers tend to be dry. The northwest is one of the last bastions of the English mild ale style, with both pale and dark varieties being produced.

JOSEPH HOLT

ESTABLISHED 1849

Derby Brewery, Empire Street
Manchester M3 1JD

RECOMMENDED
Dark Mild (3.2%),
fruity with a fullsome dry, roast malt body
Bitter (4%),
reddish-brown, very hoppy, bitter and dry; classic of the style
Sixex (6%),
fruity, rich, strong dark ale, November-March

Eccentric but lovable Holt shuns publicity and advertising and operates behind high Victorian redbrick walls, making it almost as inaccessible as the top security prison nearby. But such is the popularity of Holt's low-priced beers, they are delivered to many of the firm's 120 pubs in giant hogsheads – 54-gallon (245l) casks which have become a rarity elsewhere. A blend of four malts goes into the Bitter, which registers 40 units

of bitterness (IBUs). It is made with Goldings and Northdown English hops.

Holt is reluctant to sell outside a tightly controlled trading area in case the beer is mistreated, and also declines to exhibit because the brewery's philosophy is to 'brew beer for our pubs, not to win prizes.' Some Holt's pubs have classic Edwardian interiors featuring red mahogany and etched glass, notably the Lamb in Eccles and the Grapes in Peel Green. In central Manchester, Holt's is at the Old Monkey on Portland Street.

HYDE'S

ESTABLISHED 1863

Anvil Brewery, Moss Lane West
Manchester M15 5PH

RECOMMENDED
Pale Mild (3.5%),
fruity with a malt background
Bitter (3.8%),
a balance of malt and hop flavors before a slightly citric-dry finish
Fourex (6.5%),
dark ruby, fruity-dry strong ale, November-February

Hyde's is the smallest of Manchester's family brewers, but in recent years has become the most innovative by producing a changing portfolio of seasonal beers to supplement the regulars. Head brewer

Allan Mackie says Hyde's wants to 'make it attractive for people to come to us rather than anyone else.'

Maris Otter is the main barley malt and whole Fuggles the main hop; a little torrefied (or dried) wheat goes into some beers. All Hyde's beers are dry hopped with Fuggles. From late 1996, the brewery converted 100 percent to using its own soft well-water. Seasonal beers have included a pale, wheaten Summer Ale (3.2%), an IPA (4.2%) and Forge (4.2%), a mellow ruby-colored autumn ale.

The Hyde family story is one of female doggedness – the brewery was run by Annie Hyde for 50 years, and she steered it through turbulent times from the 1880s, when aged 21, until the mid-1930s. Today, six members of the Hyde family are actively involved. Hyde's beers are at the Grey Horse, Portland Street, central Manchester.

COACH HOUSE BREWING CO

ESTABLISHED 1991

Wharf Street, Howley, Warrington
Cheshire WA1 2DQ

RECOMMENDED

Coachman's Best Bitter (3.7%),
hoppy and malty
Gunpowder Strong Mild (3.8%),
very dark, firm roasted dry-malt flavor
Innkeeper's Special Reserve (4.5%),
copper-dark, fruity, but finally very bitter
Post Horn Premium Ale (5%),
big hoppy aroma, deep fruity taste

Coach House was founded by four of the hundreds of people sacked when Britain's then biggest regional brewer, Greenall Whitley, blithely shut down its classic redbrick tower brewery in Warrington in 1991 after 228 years brewing to become instead the country's biggest pub-owning real estate company. Peter Booth and Neil Chancellor, both Greenall brewers, teamed up with two ex-Greenall managers.

Coach House aims at innovation with a portfolio of more than 10 beers ranging from strong dark mild and a porter to pale ales. Recipes are sometimes created from old brewing books. In only its second year, Coach House won prizes at the Great British Beer Festival (page 11). Blunderbus Old Porter (5.5%) came first in 1993 and 1994 in the Porter and Stout Class and was runner up to the 1994 Champion Beer of Britain. Other award winners are Gunpowder Mild and Post Horn. The beers are on tap in the Lower Angel, Warrington, and Wetherspoon pubs in London and Manchester.

JENNINGS

ESTABLISHED 1828

Castle Brewery, Cockermouth
Cumbria CA13 9NE

RECOMMENDED

Dark Mild (3.1%),
mellow and malty
Bitter (3.5%),
red-brown, malt-fruit flavors with a mellow dry finish
Cockahoop (4.5%),
deep copper hue, fruity taste, malty finish
Sneck Lifter (5.1%),
dark complex blend of malt and hops

For many years one of England's quiet mild & bitter brewers in the pretty home town of both poet William Wordsworth and the *Bounty* mutineer Fletcher Christian, Jennings today produces a much broader range of ales.

The family brewery uses its own well-water drawn from the surrounding Lakeland hills, a fact that contributes to Jennings' distinctive character. Sneck Lifter is local beer terminology meaning someone short of cash and seeking one memorable pint. Seasonal beers include a dark ruby, rich Christmas 'old' ale of 6.5%.

The full range is on tap in the 18th century Bush Hotel, Cockermouth; some are at the City Arms, Kennedy Street, central Manchester.

Above: Lees's red-brick Victorian tower brewery.

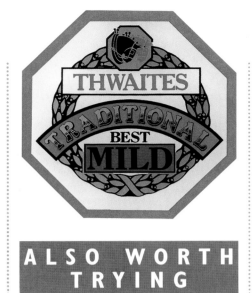

ALSO WORTH TRYING

Robinson's pale malty Mild (3.3%) and dark, rich, winey Old Tom strong ale (8.5%) in pubs near the Stockport brewery; **Lees's** dry, clean, pale Bitter (4.2%) from northeast Manchester. In Heywood near Bury, north Manchester, the micro **Oak** has Old Oak Ale (4.5%, dark, hop fruit, and bitter); Forshaw Bitter (4%) is a richly hoppy brew from the **Burtonwood** brewery near Warrington which also has an excellent seasonal range including Almond's Stout (4.2%, black, creamy, malty-dry). In Lancaster try **Mitchell's** Lancaster Bomber (4.4%), a golden all-grain brew with a gently malty background and dry, bitter finish. Also recommended are **Thwaites'** classic malty, slightly bitter Dark Mild in Blackburn, north of Manchester; **Cain's** spicy-dry Bitter (4.1%) in Liverpool; micro **Moorhouse's** malty-dry coal black Black Cat Mild (3.4%) in Burnley. In northern Cumbria around Keswick the **Yates** micro has a very pale, very dry Bitter (3.7%); **Boddingtons** Bitter (3.8%), a very pale, citric-dry ale, less mouth-tinglingly bitter than previously,

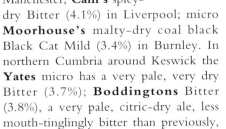

THE NORTHEAST

There is England and then there is Yorkshire, a county which forms a large part of the English northeast region. Yorkshire folk can be as stubborn and individualistic as the type of brewing yeast which has evolved here. It needs a lot of prodding and stirring to finish the job. The result is a firm, creamy beer.

Some of Britain's most famous old brewing names reside here – Newcastle Brown, Samuel Smith, Tetley, Timothy Taylor, Theakston, plus more than 20 microbreweries. The Tetley brewery in Leeds – part of the Carlsberg-Tetley giant – is Britain's biggest single producer of traditional cask-conditioned ale. The modernized brewery still ferments in traditional-style squares and dry hops the nationally available Bitter.

BLACK SHEEP BREWERY

ESTABLISHED 1992

Wellgarth, Masham
North Yorkshire HG4 4EN

RECOMMENDED

Black Sheep Best Bitter (3.8%),
golden, hoppy tasting with a dry finish
Black Sheep Special (4.4%),
pale brown, pungent malty aroma and bittersweet taste
Riggwelter (5.9%),
dark brown, roasted coffee-bitterness

Subtle English humor led to the inspirational name of Black Sheep for the new brewery in this tiny two-brewery farming town where beer has been produced by the Theakston family since 1827. Black Sheep was established by Paul Theakston after his own family brewery in Masham, T&R Theakston, was taken over by

British giant Scottish & Newcastle (now Scottish Courage) in 1987. Paul had worked in the Theakston brewery since he was a teenager in the 1960s and he could not face being part of a corporate conglomerate.

Black Sheep is housed ironically in the remains of a brewery taken over by Theakston's in 1919. Traditional Yorkshire open fermenting squares of slate are used along with Yorkshire malt and dales water. The sheep theme carries through to Riggwelter, local dialect for an overweight sheep which has rolled on its back and cannot get back on its feet.

Maris Otter is the main malt used, along with Fuggles, Goldings, and Progress hops. Black Sheep beers can be drunk in a brewery visitor center and in York at the Maltings pub, Lendal Bridge. There are 'shepherded' brewery tours daily.

CASTLE EDEN

ESTABLISHED IN 1826 AS NIMMO'S BREWERY

PO Box 13, Castle Eden, Cleveland TS27 4SX

RECOMMENDED

Castle Eden Ale (4.2%),
amber, hoppy background and bittersweet
Fuggles IPA (5.5%),
pale ale, rich fruitiness before a long, hoppy, dry finish
Whitbread Porter (4.6%)
black, rich in coffee-like flavors, hoppy

This comparatively small brewery in the large Whitbread group seems to have emerged from a long night of uncertainty to become a key player in Whitbread's new-found taste for traditional beers. Sadly this comes after a period in which the company closed many breweries.

Castle Eden is brewing up some innovative specialties for Whitbread's Classic Ales revolving portfolio, often using unusual ingredients such as ginger, licorice, and nutmeg, and a single hop variety (as with the beers Green Bullet and Fuggles IPA). The series began in 1994. Most are brewed only for a limited season, but Whitbread put Fuggles IPA into regular production by public demand which included delivery of a petition to Castle Eden. Castle Eden Classics have included a ginger ale and a Christmas ale made with myrrh. Classics are widely distributed in Whitbread pubs, especially those in the Hogsheads chain.

MALTON BREWERY COMPANY

ESTABLISHED 1985

Crown Hotel, Wheelgate, Malton
North Yorkshire YO17 0HP

RECOMMENDED

Double Chance (4%),
*pale, very hoppy, some fruitiness before dry,
refreshing finish*
Pickwick Porter (4.2%),
*black, roasted malt aroma and taste,
full-bodied and dry*
Crown Bitter (4.4%),
*pale amber, fruity rich, dry and slightly
bitter aftertaste*
Owd Bob (5.9%),
dark brown, rich hop and fruit flavors

The horseshoe emblem of this thriving micro illustrates a connection with the world of horse racing. The brewery is in converted stables at the rear of the Crown, a onetime coaching inn in this picturesque north Yorkshire market town. The stables once housed the British Grand National race winner Double Chance, and this is also the name of the brewery's most noted beer.

Brewer Anna Barlett uses several malts and mostly Challenger hops; Malton's beers have a fruity complexity, finishing dry. Pickwick Porter was a finalist in the 1993 Champion Beer of Britain competition organized by CAMRA, as was the winter season strong ale Owd Bob (owd is Yorkshire dialect for old).

TIMOTHY TAYLOR

ESTABLISHED 1858

Knowle Spring Brewery, Keighley
North Yorkshire BD21 1AW

RECOMMENDED

Golden Best (3.5%),
pale mild beer, soft malty, slightly sweet flavor
Best Bitter (4%),
golden, a fruit-malt aroma before a bitter taste
Ram Tam (4.3%),
dark chestnut, fruity, and bittersweet
Landlord (4.3%),
*pale ale, firm flowery aroma, fruit and malt
flavors, dry aftertaste*

Above: The Taylor brewery in Keighley.

Landlord – the most noted beer from this small family brewery on the east side of the Pennine hills – is now sought after in pubs across the country after being voted Champion Beer of Britain three times by CAMRA. But before its sudden rise to consumer fame, Landlord had been quietly collecting prizes in brewing industry competitions since 1955. Since then, Landlord has collected 40 awards.

But Taylor's entire beer range are prize winners, a feat attributed by brewers Allan Hey and Peter Eells to their combination of natural spring water, best barley malt, hop blends, and 'our own unique strain of yeast.' For Landlord, only Golden Promise pale malt is used and a mix of Fuggles and Goldings hops.

Landlord is a guest beer in many pubs and a resident in the brewery's own 29 pubs, mainly in and around Keighley. Landlord's creator, Allan Hey, drinks it at the Grouse Inn, Oakworth.

ALSO WORTH TRYING

In Tadcaster, **Sam Smith's** Old Brewery Bitter (4%, sweet fruit, woody flavors), and separate but once related **John Smith's** Imperial Russian Stout (10%, dark-brown, rich fruit dryness in bottle-conditioned form); **Tetley** Bitter (3.6%, creaminess balanced by tart fruity dryness); **Theakston** Old Peculier (5.6%, dark, rich fruit, bittersweet). Farther north in Hartlepool is **Cameron's** Strongarm (4%, red-brown, malty-dry); **Vaux** of Sunderland's Samson (4.2%, copper, fruity) and Double Maxim (4.2%, malty, bittersweet brown ale) are also good. **Newcastle Breweries** (part of Scottish-Courage) is most renowned for its bottled Newcastle Brown Ale (4%, amber-red, malty-sweet); also in Newcastle the micro **Big Lamp** has a popular Bitter (3.9%, red-brown, citric fruitiness, hoppy dry).

Tyneside is home to the last worker-cooperative brewery, **Northern Clubs Federation**, established in 1919 to maintain low-priced beer supplies to working men's clubs at a time of shortages and rising prices. Its beers, including a brown ale, tend to be sweet.

Right: The cooper's art is alive and well at Samuel Smith's Tadcaster brewery, which also maintains traditional brewing methods. Old Brewery Bitter is particularly recomended.

THE SOUTHWEST

A region of Britain which 25 years ago was what some enthusiasts termed a 'beer desert' because of its domination by bland national brands. Today it is richly endowed, with almost 60 thriving microbreweries.

Some are 1990s era, like tiny Cottage Brewing Co which won the CAMRA 1995 Champion Beer of Britain award; others, such as Butcombe, Smiles, and Ringwood, have been brewing since the renaissance of the late 1970s.

A few old established independent family brewers who survived the industry's severe contractions still exist, including Donnington, Eldridge Pope, Gales, and Morland. And Britain's oldest brewpub, the Blue Anchor, is in deepest Cornwall at Helston.

BUTCOMBE

ESTABLISHED 1978

Butcombe Brewery, Butcombe
Bristol, Avon BS18 6XQ

RECOMMENDED
Butcombe Bitter (4.1%),
amber, mix of malt and fruitiness before a clean, dry finish

Butcombe was not only one of the first microbreweries spawned by the beer renaissance in Britain, it has also been one of the most successful. Founder Simon Whitmore's first brewery, sited in farm buildings on the doorstep of Bristol, had an annual capacity of just over 500 barrels (820hl), but it has been extended three times to achieve its current capacity of 18,000 barrels (29,500hl) and a workforce of 14. Until late 1996 the brewery pursued a

one-beer policy – because of demand for the Bitter and lack of capacity – but a new 4.8% ale was due on the market.

The award-winning Butcombe Bitter is made with Maris Otter barley malt, a mix of English and German hops and water from the limestone Mendip Hills. About 70 percent of Butcombe Bitter is sold in pubs within 50 miles (80km) of the brewery.

Success is especially sweet for Whitmore: he paid for the first brewhouse with his redundancy payoff from brewing giant Courage (now Scottish-Courage).

WADWORTH

ESTABLISHED 1885

Northgate Brewery, Devizes
Wiltshire SN10 1JW

RECOMMENDED
Henry's IPA (3.8%),
light brown, quite malty with a dryish finish
6X (4.3%),
copper, full-bodied, bittersweet
Harvest Ale (or Malt & Hops) (4.5%),
golden, hop fruitiness, quenchingly dry

'Waddies' is one of the tough family brewers who stood up to the bullying takeover tactics common in the 1960s and 1970s which saw a large slice of Britain's brewing fraternity disappear as six rival national combines fought to control the market through pub ownership.

But this redbrick tower brewery,

which still prefers to send out beer in wooden casks, ignored the pressures and carried on brewing its flagship brand 6X for a small tied estate. Today, that beer is so popular it is widely distributed as a 'guest' beer in pubs far beyond Devizes.

Wadworth, still managed by descendants of the original Henry Wadworth, is one of the last employers of a brewery cooper to keep the oak casks maintained. The brewer's staple ingredients are Pipkin pale malt and Fuggles whole hops, but he believes that the local water plays a crucial role in Wadworth's fuller, rounded beer quality. A wider range of hops have been employed recently, including Czech varieties, to help create an expanding portfolio of seasonal brews.

ELDRIDGE POPE

ESTABLISHED 1837

Dorchester Brewery, Weymouth Avenue
Dorchester, Dorset DT1 1QT

RECOMMENDED
Blackdown Porter (4%),
black, roasted bitter malt, background fruitiness
Hardy Country Bitter (4.2%),
amber, quenching fruity dry ale
Royal Oak (5%),
dark amber, very fruity and finally bittersweet
Thomas Hardy's Ale (12%),
russet, sweetish when new, dries with ageing

The Eldridges started it, Victorian novelist Thomas Hardy praised it, and

the Popes have carried it on – paying tribute in turn to Hardy. This old established traditional brewery has found new fame as the producer of the world's strongest bottle-conditioned beer. Thomas Hardy's Ale, originally a one-off for a local festival to commemorate the famous son of the town, is now brewed permanently in limited batches and matured for three months in the brewery before being bottled and vintage stamped.

The brewery has its own well-water, which is hardened, and uses primarily Pipkin pale malt and mainly Challenger and Northdown hops; Goldings are used for dry hopping all the beers. Old Spiced Ale (6%), drawing on pre-19th century practices, is a lightly hopped winter season brew made with a mix of nutmeg, cloves, and cinnamon added to the casks instead of dry hopping.

....

HOP BACK

ESTABLISHED 1987

Hop Back Brewery, Unit 21 Batten Road Industrial Estate, Downton, Salisbury Wiltshire SP5 3HU

~~~

RECOMMENDED

GFB (3.5%),
pale very hoppy and dry bitter ale
Entire Stout (4.8%),
black, dry roasted malt flavor, finally bitter
Summer Lightning (5%),
pale golden, firm hop and fruit flavors and dry
Thunderstorm (5%),
pale clear wheat beer, light, slightly spicy

....

A clutch of awards has given this micro one of the biggest beer profiles in Britain; its summer beer is now on tap year round. In 1996, Lightning also became a nationally distributed bottle-conditioned beer. GFB was named

Above: Award-winning ale from Hop Back.

champion of its class at the Brewing Industry International Awards in Burton on Trent in 1996.

Hop Back began life in the cellar of the Wyndham Arms, Salisbury, in 1987 when John and Julie Gilbert decided to brew beer for their pub. Today, the operation has expanded into a separate brewery producing 7,500 barrels (12,250hl) a year. The original Wyndham brewpub equipment has been transferred to one of four Hop Back pubs, the Hopleaf in Southampton Street, Reading, where it turns out exotic brews such as ginger-flavored stout and rye beer.

Hop Back primarily uses Pipkin pale malt and Challenger and Goldings hops, but in a 1996 National Hop Association competition for single variety beers, the brewery's Thunderstorm wheat beer won using Progress hops.

One of Hop Back's four pubs is in London: the Sultan, Norman Road, Wimbledon.

Right: A strong Cottage brew from Somerset.

ALSO WORTH TRYING

At Burnham-on-Sea, Somerset, **RCH's** Wheat Beer (4.4.%, amber, sharp and spicy); Wiveliscombe, also in Somerset, has two micros: **Cotleigh** with Barn Owl Bitter (4.5%, copper, malty) and **Exmoor** with Exmoor Gold (4.5%, golden, very dry). At West Lydford, still in Somerset, the **Cottage** brewery's award-winning Norman Conquest (7%, fruity, winey); in the Bristol area, **Smiles** Best Bitter (4.1%, pale brown, malty-dry) and Bristol Stout (4.7%, black, creamy, bittersweet – January–April). Salisbury also has **Gibbs Mew** brewery noted for Bishop's Tipple (6.5%, dark brown, malty, fruity, dry). Ringwood in Hampshire has **Ringwood's** Old Thumper (5.8%, pale amber, fruity, bittersweet); in Gloucestershire at Stow-in-the-Wold **Donnington** has SBA (4%, copper, fruity, malty-dry) and is one of Britain's most photogenic old breweries. **Gales** of Portsmouth produces the bottle-conditioned Prize Old Ale (9%, mahogany, very fruity and dry when matured); and Cheltenham is **Whitbread Flowers** home, noted for its Classic series of exotic seasonal beers.

ANGLIA AND EASTERN ENGLAND

The area of eastern England from Chelmsford, east of London, north to the Wash remains largely rural – Britain's granary for brewers' malt. It is home to several distinguished old family brewers – Adnams at Southwold, Ridley of Hartford End near Chelmsford, Elgood's of Wisbech in Cambridgeshire, the much larger Greene King of Bury St Edmunds (with which the writer Graham Greene was associated), and Bateman of Wainfleet.

The late, unlamented Watney Mann bought and closed two Norwich breweries in the 1970s and set about property asset-stripping. But since then Anglia has spawned a clutch of microbreweries, the most enduring and successful of which are Crouch Vale at South Woodham Ferrers in Essex; Mauldons of Sudbury in Suffolk – run by a former Watney's brewer; Nethergate of Clare near Sudbury, which uses spices and herbs in some of its beers, and Woodforde's of Woodbastwick in Norfolk. And now Norwich has a brewery again – the micro Reindeer.

One of Britain's oldest breweries, Tolly Cobbold of Ipswich which was founded in 1723, is again flourishing after ownership changes threatened its survival.

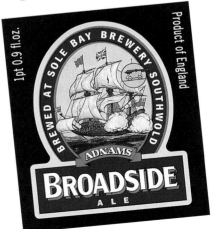

ADNAMS

ESTABLISHED 1890

Sole Bay Brewery, Southwold
Suffolk IP18 6JW

∿∿∿

RECOMMENDED
Mild (3.2%),
dark, malty with gentle hop background
Old (4.1%),
dark, malty and soft in the mouth
Extra (4.3%),
dark amber, malty, spicy, and very dry
Broadside (4.7%),
amber, rich mix of maltiness and fruit flavors

Few English beer drinkers nowadays haven't heard of Adnams, and many will have tasted the award-winning Extra. But ask them where the Adnams brewery is and the response will be as vaguely distant as the little Victorian museum-piece of a seaside 'resort' that is home to the Sole Bay Brewery. As if to underline Southwold's remoteness on a windswept stretch of empy, flat Suffolk coastline, Adnams delivers to the local pubs by horse-drawn dray.

But if Southwold is a pretty place which time nearly forgot, the brewery's expanding portfolio certainly isn't. Since

its centenary, Adnams has increasingly reached out beyond the fen country and into the cities.

There are several short seasonal specialties including May Day (5%, spring), Barley Mow (5%, autumn), and Tally Ho (7%, Christmas).

Several malts including Maris Otter pale are used and Fuggles, Goldings, and Challenger whole hops. Some beers are additionally dry hopped.

A visit to Southwold should be part of every beer tourist's itinerary, including a stop at the Lord Nelson in East Street.

Above: Seaside Southwold seen from Adnams brewery.

WOODFORDE'S

ESTABLISHED 1980

Broadland Brewery, Woodbastwick
Norfolk NR13 6SW

RECOMMENDED
Mardler's Mild (3.5%),
dark brown, roasted malt flavor, fruity finish
Emerald Ale (4.2%),
black stout, dry maltiness with solid bitter end
Norfolk Nog (4.5%),
red-brown, malty aroma, full-bodied malt and fruit flavors
Headcracker (7%),
pale ale, hop and fruit flavors and rich fruity-dry finish

A long list of excellent beers have flowed from this award-winning expanded micro which began life in the city of Norwich and then moved up country in 1989 to find more brewing space in a rural setting, where spring water is also plentiful.

Halcyon is the brewer's preferred barley malt, while the hops are mostly Fuggles and Goldings. Norfolk Nog was 1992 Champion Beer of Britain in the CAMRA-sponsored national tasting competition. Mardler's and Headcracker were 1993 finalists. There is also a bottle-conditioned strong ale, Norfolk Nip (8.6%).

Woodforde's caters for brewery visitors and has a reception center together with a 'brewery tap' – the thatched and wood-beamed Fur & Feather pub, between Salhouse and Woodbastwick.

CROUCH VALE

ESTABLISHED 1981

Crouch Vale Brewery, 12 Redhills Road
South Woodham Ferrers, Essex CM3 5UP

RECOMMENDED
Millennium Gold (4.2%),
gold colored, firm hoppiness, fruity and bitter
Essex Porter (5%),
dark, roast-malt aroma, fruity and bittersweet
Strong Anglian Special (5%),
chestnut brown, fruity aroma, bitter flavor, dry

This enterprising village micro, located between Southend and Chelmsford, produces a big menu of beers, often contract-brewing to order for pubs in addition to producing its own portfolio of eight or more beers, some of them seasonal such as Santa's Revenge, an amber 5.8% Christmas brew. Owner-brewer Colin Bocking's style is fruity and dry. He uses several English malts, including Maris Otter, and mostly Challenger and East Kent Goldings hops. Some of his beers are dry hopped for added bite.

Crouch Vale owns the 15th century Cap & Feathers inn at Tillingham near the Essex coast, which is noted for its home-oak-smoked sea fish.

T.D. RIDLEY

ESTABLISHED 1842

Hartford End Brewery, Chelmsford
Essex CM3 1JZ

RECOMMENDED
IPA Bitter (3.6%),
amber, fruity, almost tart, bitter-dry
Witchfinder Porter (4.3%),
rich maltiness, hop bitterness
Spectacular (4.6%),
very pale, slightly malty, dry

This classic tower-style Victorian redbrick brewery looms suprisingly out of the surrounding countryside like a thirsty traveller's mirage. T.D. Ridley & Sons is one of Britain's slowly dwindling band of traditional country family brewers, quietly but enthusiastically serving its 60 or so pubs in the surrounding towns and villages. Its 150th anniversary a few years ago triggered a rethink and an expansion of the brewhouse's offerings.

Today there are six regular and seasonal beers where previously Ridley was a 'bread and butter' mild and bitter operation. The dark winter months are warmed locally with a fruity, rich, ruby Winter Ale (5%). IPA Bitter is a noteworthy example of the style and came first in its class in the 1992 CAMRA national beer competitions. Ridley's dry-hopped, nutty, ruby Mild (3.5%) was first in its class in the 1995 competitions.

ALSO WORTH TRYING

Black Adder (5.3%), beautifully balanced dry stout and 1991 Champion Beer of Britain, from **Mauldons**; coriander-spiced Umbel Ale (3.8%), from **Nethergate**; **Greene King's** Abbot Ale (5%), a rich, fruity, bittersweet, amber brew, and the blended old winter ale Suffolk Strong (6.4%); **Tolly Cobbold's** hoppy and dry India Pale Ale (IPA, 4.2%). Also look out for **Elgood's** Barleymead (4.8%), a fruity, dry, autumn pale ale made with barley and hops from latest harvest; Fargo Strong (5%), a malty, rich, slightly tart offering from **Charles Wells** of Bedford; from another Suffolk micro – **Reepham Brewery** of Reepham – Velvet (4.3%), a smooth, malty-sweet stout; and last but not least **Bateman's** XXXB (5%), hoppy and fruity bitter, and Salem Porter (5%), dark, nutty, and dry.

SCOTLAND

Scotland's romantic image is reflected in its brewing. At Traquair, near Peebles, an ancient brewery sits in Scotland's oldest inhabited castle where Bonnie Prince Charlie hid from English soldiers after the Battle of Culloden Moor in 1746. Another brewery shares its birthplace with novelist John Buchan, author of that most-filmed romantic thriller **The Thirty-Nine Steps.** *Less romantic, however, was the decimation of Scottish brewing in the 1960s and 1970s in takeovers and closures led by Edinburgh-based Scottish & Newcastle, now Scottish Courage.*

A microbrewing renaissance which began in the 1980s is now blossoming. Scotland has a taste for lager beer which long predates the trend in England, but all the new developments are in ale brewing. Traditionally, Scottish ale is maltier, sweeter, darker than England's, but some breweries now produce drier, paler varieties. The Scots often use the terms Light and Heavy, or an old currency system (60/- to 90/- in ascending ABV order), to denote alcoholic strength.

BROUGHTON ALES

ESTABLISHED 1979

Broughton, Biggar
Peeblesshire ML12 6HQ

RECOMMENDED
Oatmeal Stout (3.8%),
dark with a sweeter, creamier finish imparted by the oats
Greenmantle Ale (4%),
reddish brown, fruity and bittersweet
Merlin's Ale (4.2%),
unusually pale, well hopped and dry for Scotland
Old Jock (6.7%),
dark, malty, strong ale

David Younger, of an old Scottish brewing family, founded this small

brewery after leaving an executive job with Edinburgh brewing giant S&N. It expanded and thrived until a typical small business cashflow crisis in 1995 led to financial rescue by Englishman Giles Litchfield, who plans to distribute Broughton ales to a wider market. The brewery nestles in the gentle hill border country from where it draws naturally soft waters. Greenmantle Ale is named after the sequel to local novelist John Buchan's *The Thirty-Nine Steps* thriller.

Above: Horse-drawn beer from Caledonian.

CALEDONIAN BREWING

ESTABLISHED 1869

Slateford Road, Edinburgh,
Lothian EH11 1PH

RECOMMENDED
Deuchar's IPA (3.8%),
very pale, very hoppy, quenching bitterness
80/- (4.1%),
reddish-copper color, malty-dry
Caledonian Porter (4.1%),
dark, roasted malt flavors and hoppy-dry
Merman XXX (4.8%),
ruby-colored IPA, richly malty and full-bodied
Edinburgh Strong Ale (6.4%),
generous hopping counterbalances a heavy malt accent

It's hard to contemplate that this brewing powerhouse – producing 13 draft ales plus several bottled specialties – was saved from extinction in 1987 by a group of managers appalled that the owners intended to close it. The managers bought the 'Caley' and it has since become an award-winning and innovative driving force in Scotland's brewing renaissance. Because of Edinburgh's hard, mineral-rich water, the city was once one of Britain's leading brewing centers. It boasted 30 breweries in the late 19th

century, which led to its nickname 'Auld Reekie' (old smelly). Some of the most revered of those vanished breweries are recollected in Caledonian's beer names – Deuchar's, Campbell, Hope & King, and Murray's. Despite a severe fire several years ago, 'Caley' remains a mostly unchanged Victorian redbrick structure. Its brewing coppers are the last of their kind – open, cauldron-shaped, and heated by direct gas flame. The distinctive hop flavors of Caledonian beers come from liberal use of Goldings and Fuggles varieties.

This was the first British brewery to produce organic beer – Golden Promise, named after the pale malt variety. Merman is named after a mythical man-fish which legend says protected Edinburgh shipping. The full beer range is available at the Caledonian Sample Room, on Slateford Road, next to the brewery.

MACLAY

ESTABLISHED 1830

Thistle Brewery, Alloa
Clackmannanshire FK10 1ED

RECOMMENDED
Broadsword (3.8%),
pale golden, firm-bodied with a fruity finish
Oat Malt Stout (4.5%),
dark ruby, rich, and creamy. An 1890s' recipe
Wallace India Pale Ale (4.5%),
hoppy with a long, dry taste
Scotch Ale (5%),
golden in color but full of fruity, malty flavors

The natural, mineral-rich, hard well-waters have long given this very traditional tower-style brewery an advantageous ingredient in its brewing. The water is drawn from more than 500

feet (150m) below ground where it collects after seeping slowly through the Ochil Hills. Locally-grown grain from the River Forth's flood plain is also used. The present Maclay brewery in this seaside, coalmining town dates from 1869, and the family owners take pride in the fact that methods of production have changed little since then – except that gas has replaced coal for energy.

Maclay beers tend to be drier and hoppier than the Scottish average – a reflection, perhaps, of the water source? Nowadays, Maclay has an ever-changing and expanding portfolio; its seasonal Summer Ale (3.6%) is particularly hoppy and refreshing.

TRAQUAIR

Traquair House Brewery, Innerleithen
Peeblesshire EH44 6PW

RECOMMENDED
Bear Ale (5%),
deep copper, with a woody taste and dryish finish
Traquair House Ale (7%),
bottled specialty, dark, rich, and port-like

The gates of this ancient manor have been firmly shut since the last Scottish attempt to take the English throne in

1745. Like the vanquished 'Bonnie' Prince Charlie, who hid here, the owners are Stuarts who have vowed only to reopen the gates when a Stuart regains the throne. Fortunately, no such oath hangs over Traquair's medieval brewhouse, which was rediscovered in the 1960s and cranked back into life after 100 years of cobwebs were removed.

Traquair now maintains an aristocratic brewing tradition which was commonplace across the estates of Europe from the Middle Ages until the Industrial Revolution ushered in large-scale brewing. Its beers are available locally, although the bottled variety – sometimes unfiltered – has become a collectors' prize worldwide. There's a House beer festival in late May.

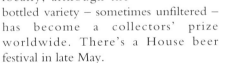

ALSO WORTH TRYING

Sandy Hunter's Ale (3.6%), a hoppy and finally very fruity pale beer from the **Belhaven** east coast brewery at Dunbar; Borve Extra Strong (10%), a malty, slightly smoky heavyweight from the tiny **Borve House** brewery at Ruthven, north of Aberdeen; Arrol's 80/- (4.4%), a new, fruity-malty ale from **Carlsberg-Tetley's** brewery at Alloa. From the most northerly brewery in Britain, the **Orkney Brewery** at Quoyloo on the main island, northwest of Kirkwall, comes the mysterious-sounding Dark Island (4.6), rich, bittersweet, and, naturally, dark; while Younger No 3 (4.5%), dark and fruity, is from the giant **Scottish Courage** Fountain Brewery (formerly McEwan) in Edinburgh.

WALES

The 19th century temperance movement exerted a stern and debilitating grip on Welsh drinking habits, leaving in its wake a taste for weak insipid beers. The main breweries are in the south — Brain's, Felinfoel, Crown Buckley and Bass's Welsh Brewers.

A handful of microbreweries — Plassey of Wrexham, Dyffryn of Denbigh, Snowdonia of Blaenau Ffestiniog — inhabit the north with Border-Wrexham, one of the first lager breweries in Britain now owned by Marston's. The Principality's top-selling brew is a pasteurized 3.3% ale with a name like a washing powder — Allbright.

BRAIN'S

ESTABLISHED 1882

The Old Brewery, 49 St Mary Street
Cardiff CF1 1SP

RECOMMENDED

Dark (3.5%),
ruby-red mild, malty with gentle hop dryness
SA Bitter (4.2%),
dark amber, malt and fruit flavors, bittersweet

It's inevitable that a brewery with this name would come up with the advertising slogan: It's Brain's You Want. Equally catchy has been the customers' sharp rejoinder 'Skull Attack' to describe Brain's strongest brew — SA (the initials actually stand for Special Ale). Brain's is the most traditional of Wales' breweries, still family owned and offering real ales throughout its estate of 115 pubs

in Cardiff and the old mining valleys. The company stayed with real ale brewing when many rivals in the 1960s and 1970s turned to emasculated pasteurized forms.

The brewers use a mix of pale and crystal malts, with some dark malt for the Mild, and glucose. Fuggles and Goldings whole hops go in all the beers. In Cardiff, Brain's range is best sampled at the Albert pub next to the brewery in St Mary Street and near the railway station.

DYFFRYN

ESTABLISHED 1993

Dyffryn Clwyd Brewery, Chapel Place
Denbigh, Clwyd LL16 3TJ

RECOMMENDED

Castle Bitter (4.2%),
dark amber, malty-dry, long rich aftertaste
Jack Tar Porter (4.5%),
black, bitter roast-malt taste, fullsome
Four Thumbs (4.8%),
amber, fruity, slight tart-spiciness, dry finish

Publican Ioan Evans has come to the rescue of a region where beer choice

was otherwise limited with a mini-brewery in Denbigh's old Butter Market building producing a colorful range of ales, some of which are seasonal.

Dyffryn uses interesting combinations of pale and dark barley malts and wheat malt, plus Goldings and Challenger hops. The brewery's most popular beer is Four Thumbs. At Christmas, look out for De Laceys (6.2%), a dark amber, fruity-rich ale. In Denbigh, the beers are at the Brook House Mill pub. Further afield the range is in the Glan Aber Hotel, in scenic Betws-y-coed.

ALSO WORTH TRYING

Dinas Draught (3.6%, hoppy pale ale) from **Aberystwyth Ales**; James Buckley Ale (3.9%, malty and dryish) from **Crown Buckley** of Llanelli; Double Dragon (4.2%, pale and dry), from **Felinfoel**, also Llanelli; Tudno (5%, heavily hopped beer for Wales) from **Plassey** in Wrexham with a visitor center (tel: 01978-780922); and Rejoice Stout (6%, dry maltiness and bitter) from the newest and zaniest micro, **Reckless Eric's Brewing Company** at Cilfynydd between Merthyr Tydfil and Cardiff.

IRELAND

Ireland is synonymous with coal-black stout. Guinness in Dublin is the giant, but Beamish and Murphy's – both in Cork – are sizeable rivals, especially now they are foreign-owned (Scottish-Courage has Beamish, Heineken has Murphy's). Guinness owns Smithwicks, Cherry's, and Macardle's, undistinguished ale breweries all.

Ireland is the last great pub culture: 90 percent of all beer is drunk in pubs, and an annual per capita consumption of 216 pints (123 liters) places Ireland fourth in the world drinking league.

The microbrewing revolution arrived in Ireland only in 1995 with Biddy Early (see below), followed in 1996 by the Porter House stout brewpub in Parliament Street, Dublin.

ARTHUR GUINNESS

ESTABLISHED 1759

St James's Gate, Dublin 8

❧

RECOMMENDED

Draught Stout (4.1 %),
smooth, roasted malt, bitter
Original or Extra Stout (bottled, 4.1%),
fruity with a coarse bitterness
Foreign Extra (bottled, 7.5%),
tart fruitiness mingles with intense bitterness

Guinness comes in 19 varieties, brewed in 45 countries and mostly using a

Above: A corner of Ireland that is forever Guinness.

concentrate produced in Dublin. Another 27 countries receive finished draft Guinness – at varying strengths – direct from Dublin.

Arthur popularized the term stout when in the 18th century he brewed a stronger porter which he introduced to compete with imported fashionable English porter; it took on a more bitter flavor when his son, also called Arthur, used unmalted roasted barley to avoid tax.

In Ireland, bottled Guinness is unpasteurized and continues to condition with a very fine yeast content, but since 1992 it has been pasteurized in Britain. Foreign Extra is blended the way 18th century London porter was: it is a mix of young and old beer, some of which has been matured in wood and acquired a slightly sour character.

BIDDY EARLY

ESTABLISHED 1995

Biddy Early Brewery, Inagh, Co Clare

❧

RECOMMENDED

Black Biddy Stout (4.4%),
black, very fruity aroma, malty and dry

A touch of Irish blarney comes with Biddy Early – a lass who was entrusted by fairies with a cure-all magic bottle. A disbelieving priest threw it into the river at Inagh where, years later, brewer Peadar Garvey stumbled across it.

Peadar, a chemist, uses three malts including some wheat, Pride and American Ganena hops, soft spring water from his brother's nearby farm, local carigeen moss for body and clarity, and, of course, the bottle's secrets.

'These days one million tourists pass my front door every summer and I wanted to give them a reason to stop,' explains Peadar.

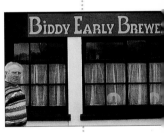

Right: Peadar outside Ireland's first stout brewpub.

ALSO WORTH TRYING

Beamish Stout (4.3%, creamy-sweet); **Murphy's** Stout (4.3%, malty-dry); and in Ulster **Hilden** Great Northern Porter (4%, fruity-dry). In 1996, **Whitbread** – UK brewers of Murphy's under licence – produced an unfiltered, unpasteurized Murphy's Oyster Stout (5%) in Cheltenham, using crushed oysters. And **Guinness's** London brewery brewed Harwood's Porter (4.8%), named after the 18th century brewer credited with inventing the style.

LAMBIC BEERS

A succulent T-bone steak. A farmhouse cheese as delicious as it is stinky. A classic Belgian lambic. The three are linked by one simple fact: all are spoiled. Or, to use a more euphemistic term, 'well matured.' The side of beef hangs in a cool, dry locker until the decay of its cellular structure makes it 'tender.' The cheese ages until it sports blue, moldy veins. And the lambic — well, lambics are a tribute to the art of controlled spoilage.

First and foremost, of course, lambics are a tribute to tradition. They are a style of beer, local to the Senne Valley around Brussels, that has been brewed in Belgium for centuries. The 16th-century paintings of Pieter Bruegel (the Elder) actually portray Flemish peasants partying with jugs of lambic, their native brew. So what exactly is a lambic? Think of it as 'wheat beer gone bad.' Not in the sense of being raised on the wrong side of the tracks; rather, as noted above, in the sense of being spoiled.

Lambics are produced entirely by spontaneous fermentation using airborne wild yeasts – a practice as ancient as it is natural. In fact, most of the practices and procedures surrounding the production of lambic are somewhat antiquated. All lambics are brewed from a mash of pale barley malt and raw (unmalted) wheat, for example, a blend which recalls older days when farmer-brewers harvested mixed grain fields. According to current Belgian

regulations, 'lambics' must be brewed from at least 30 percent raw wheat. Modern Belgian brewer Frank Boon makes his famous versions from a grist that includes 43 percent unmalted wheat. His venerable cast-iron mash tun, like those of several other traditional lambic brewers, is fitted with a revolving rake to stir the resulting thickly-gummy grain mixture.

Lambic mashes create a cloudy, off-white wort which brewers boil with generous amounts of 'aged' hops – hops that deliberately have been allowed to grow old and thereby to lose their herbal aromas and bitter flavors. All that remains, and all that lambic brewers want, are the preservative compounds which hops impart to beer. It is not uncommon to find two- or three-year old sacks of hops in lambic breweries. After so much time, the aged hops themselves begin to display something of a 'stinky cheese' aroma.

Up to this point, the lambic brewing process merely is intriguing. The excitement really begins during fermentation. Whereas most modern beers are fermented carefully with select cultured yeast strains, lambic fermentation is left literally to the winds. Hot wort is pumped up to a wide, shallow 'cool ship' beneath a vented roof at the top of the brewery. The vents are opened, and wild yeasts descend from the sky to have their way with the sugary wort.

Following an overnight period of inoculation, the wort is run into unlined, untreated wooden casks where it experiences a series of progressive fermentations and reactions sparked by the wild yeasts and microorganisms resident in the wood (acetobacters, lactobacilli, etc.). To avoid disturbing the microbiological activity that creates their beer's character,

Above: Belle Vue's cooper is a busy man – the brewery uses some 10,000 barrels annually.

lambic brewers do not clean their cellars. Walk past the rows of casks and you'll find large blotches of mold growing around bung-holes, not to mention cobwebs hanging from dusty corners!

Lambic generally matures in casks between one and five years (sometimes longer if a batch is particularly 'rough'). Producers occasionally offer unblended lambic on draft or in a bottle. Much more frequently, the beer is blended for bottling as gueuze or refermented with fruit to create the tangy-sweet beers known as kriek ('cherry' in Flemish) or frambozen/framboise ('raspberry'). Blending is where the top producers demonstrate their skill: an artfully-made gueuze or fruit beer offers a range of complex, challenging, and ultimately satisfying flavors that show just how apt a comparison with characterful 'ripe' cheese can be.

In fact, a few of today's outstanding lambic-based beers come not from brewers but rather professional blenders. These operations purchase wort from lambic breweries, mature it in their own cellars and oak barrels, and create their own finished beers. Lambic blending once was a widespread activity among Belgian taverns and restaurants that wanted to serve a 'house'

Above: An employee of the Cantillon Brewery in Brussels draws a sample of maturing two-year-old lambic from its wooden cask.

beer. Today, sadly, only two blenders survive: Drie Fonteinen (a cafe in the Brussels suburb of Beersel) and Hanssens (a free-standing operation in Dworp, south of Brussels). Both make traditional gueuze and kriek that rank among the absolute best in Belgium (and therefore the world).

Other top producers, in terms of aggressive traditional character, include the aforementioned Boon (the Mariage Parfait range), Cantillon, Oud Beersel, Lindemans (Cuvée René gueuze), and Interbrew-owned Belle Vue (Séléction Lambic). The latter two brewers, along with several others, also offer blander, sweetened lambic-based beers – illustrating the extent to which blending can influence finished character. As a result of the beer renaissance, it is to be hoped that such 'mainstream' producers will refocus at least part of their efforts towards crafting traditional lambic brews that testify to the challenging and rewarding art behind this classic style.

BELGIUM

Belgium is the world's most exotic beer country. More styles and flavors are created here than anywhere else. Although Pilsner-style beers dominate, Belgium is the greatest ale producer after Britain. Sales of standard pale lagers have slipped as more Belgians rediscover the myriad specialties – from the unique wild-fermentation lambics of the Brussels area to the spiced wheat beers and red and brown soured ales.

Growing interest in more characterful beers has also turned Belgium into a big beer exporter – about 25 percent of production now goes abroad. The choice comes from 118 breweries, more today than a decade ago.

Some are tiny, like Kerkom; some are part of the huge conglomerate Interbrew; others are run by monks. Together they quench one of the world's biggest thirsts: Belgians drink on average 112 liters (197 UK pints) a year, making them sixth in the world consumption league.

BELLE VUE

ESTABLISHED 1913

Rue Delaunoystraat 58, Sint Jans Molenbeek
1080 Brussels

RECOMMENDED
Gueuze (5%),
yellow-amber, candy aroma, sugared almond flavor, dryish aftertaste
Kriek (5.2%),
dark red, almond aroma, tart fruit, slightly bitter flavor, crisp dry finish
Framboise (5.2%),
pink-red, fruity aroma, light tartness
Séléction Lambic (5.3%),
unfiltered, almond aroma, tart-sour, very dry

The biggest of the lambic producers houses more than 10,000 wooden barrels, mostly old oak, in which the wild yeast-

fermented beer matures for six months to three years (see pages 108-109).

Many of the 700-liter (185-US gallon, 154-UK gallon) barrels – replete with their own taste-influencing micro-organisms – are over 80 years old and several coopers work full time on them. New wood is never employed.

A ratio of 64-36 percent of barley malt to unmalted wheat is used, while hops are two years old. Whole Belgian cherries, including the stones which add an almond flavor, are added to the casks to make kriek. Juice is used for framboise.

Molenbeek – as Belle Vue is commonly known – is one of three lambic breweries now owned by Interbrew. Confusingly, two of them are called Belle Vue (the other one is in Zuun on the southwest edge of the city, the third is De Neve at Schepdaal, near Zuun). All the blending takes place at Molenbeek.

Some products are sweetened, filtered, and pasteurized but not the 1993-introduced Séléction Lambic, which is really a gueuze made with blends which are at least two years old. Molenbeek has daily tours and its own pub.

Above: Cantillon's plain facade hides an exotic interior.

CANTILLON

ESTABLISHED 1900

Rue Gheude 56, Anderlecht 1, 070 Brussels

RECOMMENDED
Grand Cru (5.5%, 4-year-old),
very pale, mellow, cidery and very dry
Gueuze (5%, 7-month-old bottle),
sharp-sour aroma, very tart, dry and quite bitter
Framboise (5%, '93 lambic, '95 fruit),
light red, very fruity aroma, very tart and dry

Cleanliness is the watchword in most breweries, but Cantillon's owner-brewer John Pierre Van Roy gleefully tells visitors: 'Here we like the dirt. We need it to make our special beer.' Visitors can wander in any time during the working day to explore the 19th century pulley- and lever-driven machinery, the dark cobwebbed corridors lined with wooden casks or re-used champagne bottles... and hope to stumble on Van Roy for an impromptu lecture on his 'working beer museum.'

Brewing takes place between October and April when the wild yeasts of Brussels are most active; blending and the addition of fruit proceeds during summer. Cantillon uses a 65-35 percent barley to wheat mix and Belgian Brewer's Gold hops which are at least three years old. The lambic matures for up to three years in the cask; none is blended under one year old. Blends are rough filtered, bottled, and left to referment for six to nine months.

Cantillon beers are drier and sharper than their rivals. Whole cherries (de-stoned) and raspberries are used to make kriek and framboise.

DE KLUIS

ESTABLISHED 1965

Stoopkenstraat 46, 3320 Hoegaarden

༄

RECOMMENDED

Hoegaarden Witbier/White (4.8%),
pale cloudy yellow, orange aroma, dry
Das (5%),
dark amber, malty and bittersweet
Spéciale (5.6%),
golden, seasonal wheat beer, fruity and dry
Grand Cru (8.6%),
hazy peach color, very fruity aroma and taste
Forbidden Fruit (8.8%),
dark red, fruity aroma, spicy and bittersweet

The dominant feature in Hoegaarden is a tall, towered church, the best Belgian example of ecclesiastical rococo. Anyone gazing for more than a few seconds at the triple-onioned dome atop the tower will notice that it leans slightly, like a drunk. Legend says this reflects the mood of Hoegaarden when the church was built – there were 30 breweries and a population of 2,000. The dominant beer style then was white, or wheat, beer, but by the late 1950s the last local wheat beer brewery had closed.

De Kluis was the idea of milkman Pieter Celis, who was inspired by the laments of old men in the town. He triggered a revival of wheat beer brewing across Belgium. Celis has gone but De Kluis, now owned by the giant Interbrew group, has grown from a single barrel experiment to a company producing 800,000hl (627,000 US barrels, 450,000 UK barrels) a year. Three quarters of production is Hoegaarden Witbier. Crushed coriander spice and bitter orange peel is used in the witbier and several of the other De Kluis beers. Tours of the brewery, which has a pub restaurant, take place daily.

PALM

ESTABLISHED 1747

Steenhuffeldorp 3, 1840 Steenhuffel

༄

RECOMMENDED

Palm Spéciale (5%),
dark amber, malty, slightly burnt taste
Steendonk (4.6%),
very pale, cloudy, lightly fruity-dry
John Martin's Pale Ale (5.8%),
pale, very hoppy aroma and flavor, dry

Palm is one of Belgium's largest independent family breweries. The main beer is the top-fermenting Palm Spéciale.

Above: Brabant draft horses learning their trade.

Soft, untreated well-water is used with a mixture of barley malts and some maize. Styrian and Kent Goldings hops are favored, with the less bitter Saaz for the Steendonk wheat beer which uses a ratio of 50-50 barley malt to unmalted wheat, plus ground coriander and orange peel.

The John Martin's Pale Ale is dry hopped during a secondary (tank) fermentation by an ingenious method of periodically flushing the green beer over a bed of whole Styrian Goldings.

Disappointingly the beers are pasteurized – although this policy is being reviewed for the wheat beer because of a recognition that it masks the delicate spicy flavors. Brewery tours include visiting the stables where Brabant workhorses are reared in the grounds of a restored manor, and a House of Beer Culture serving numerous beers.

ALSO WORTH TRYING

Brussels has numerous specialist bars that are worth visiting. Among the best are: Bier Circus, Rue de l'Enseignement 89, notable for lambic and gueuze; and In't Spinnekopke, Place du Jardin aux Fleurs 1, which serves several beers on draft, and which is also good for food. Try Vander Linden Lambic (6%, dry) and Faro (4%, fruity); and Frank Boon's Mariage Parfait gueuze (6%, fruity-dry). The home of the Confederation of Belgian Brewers at Grand'Place 10 has a small museum – and a bar!

Above: The home of an ale that thinks it's a Pilsner.

MOORTGAT

ESTABLISHED 1871

Brouwerij Moortgat, Breendonkdorp 58
2870 Breendonk

RECOMMENDED
Godefroy (6%),
amber, smooth soft body and fruity
Duvel (8.5%),
*golden, pronounced hop aroma, fruity and
finally bitter*
Maredsous 10 (9.5%),
dark brown, fruity before a rich malty-dryness

The Moortgats were originally farmer-brewers. Jan-Leonard Moortgat turned an ancient farm practice destined for the family table into a commercial business by personally delivering his beer by horse and cart to the wealthier folk of late 19th century Brussels 30km (20 miles) to the south. Today, the brewery produces 250,000hl (213,000 US barrels, 153,000 UK barrels) a year.

Moortgat has always been an ale brewery but it was Jan-Leonard's son Albert who created the family's most successful and famous brew – Duvel. Originally it was dark and based on strong Scotch ales which have been popular in Belgium since World War I when Scottish soldiers introduced the style. Albert first called the beer Victory Ale, but a friend who tasted it said it was a 'devil of a beer' – *duvel* is Flemish for devil. Moortgat developed today's Pilsner color of Duvel to counteract the trend to pale lager, and it now accounts for 75 percent of brewery production.

Duvel enjoys a slow and complicated warm and cold fermentation and maturation. It is three months old when it leaves the brewery, having spent at least four weeks conditioning in the bottle. Delicate pale barley malt from the Belgian fields and Bohemian and Slovenian hops are the ingredients, together with a little glucose. It has a shelf life of three years and becomes more fruity with age.

Godefroy and the Maredsous series of four so-called Abbey beers (named after the Maredsous Benedictine monastery at Denee in the southern Namur province) are also bottle-conditioned beers. Duvel is widely available and exported to Britain, the US, Japan, and southern Europe. Moortgat, which welcome visits to the brewery, also make a quality hoppy Pilsner, Bel Pils, and has worked on developing a wheat beer – Steendonk – with Palm Brewery (page 111).

DE KONINCK

ESTABLISHED 1833

Brouwerij de Koninck, Mechelsesteenweg 291
2018 Antwerpen 1

RECOMMENDED
De Koninck (5%),
*amber-red, maltiness and fruitiness balanced by
final hop dryness*
Cuvée (8%),
red-brown, soft, rich, and spicy

De Koninck is noteworthy for concentrating on one classic of Belgian ale brewing. The large-scale switch to lager beers at the end of the 19th century swept past this family brewery without stopping.

De Koninck is a 100 percent barley beer using pale Pilsner malt and some Vienna malt to give the distinctive reddish-copper color. Bohemian Saaz and Belgian whole hops are used. An unhurried fermentation lasts eight days before it is cold-conditioned for two weeks. In winter, De Koninck is only rough-filtered before bottling, but pasteurized in hot summers.

The beer is traditionally served in Antwerp slightly chilled in a distinctive stem glass known as a bolleke.

Some Antwerp pubs serve De Koninck on draft, notably the Pelgrim opposite the brewery, which also has the curious practice of serving liquid yeast from the brewery in tiny glasses. Some customers like to add this bitter tonic to their De Koninck.

Cuvée Antwerpen was originally brewed in 1993 to celebrate the city's year as Europe's Cultural Capital, but is now a regular.

Left: Classic ale in a bolleke.

STELLA ARTOIS

ESTABLISHED 1366

Vaartstraat 94, 3000 Leuven

RECOMMENDED

Stella Pils (5%),
pale golden, hoppy with a malty background and dryish finish
Leffe Blonde (6.6%),
pale ale, hoppy aroma, fruit-malt flavors, dryish
Leffe Brune/Bruin (6.5%),
dark ruby, dark chocolatey taste, malty-dry
Leffe Triple (8.4%),
deep golden, fruity, crisp, and clean-tasting, bottle-conditioned

Two breweries straddle both sides of the motorway which skirts the edge of this old beer and student town in central Belgium. They are the center of the giant Interbrew company which, despite the anonymous hybrid name, is largely owned by two Belgian families.

Leuven No. 1 houses large traditional floor maltings and will concentrate on the company's ale portfolio, particularly the Leffe Abbey range, plus experimental brewing. Leuven No. 2 is a lager plant, one of a new breed of almost people-less, automated, monster breweries. But its brewhouse has a cathedral-like quality: towering, majestic, silent, and very aesthetic. Pink tiles clothe the ceiling

and floor and arty lighting bathes the 15 giant stainless steel kettles in a warm, golden hue.

Opened in 1992 and with an annual capacity of four million hectolitres (3.4 million US barrels, 2.4 million UK barrels), No. 2 is a far cry from Artois's origins in Den Hoorn (The Horn), a Leuven brewpub in the 1300s. The Artois family can trace their ownership of The Horn back to Sebastien Artois in 1717. Their most famous Pilsner-style brand dates from 1926 when it began life as a Christmas season beer: it was called Stella, or star, and is now the main brew at No. 2. Pale barley malt from Holland, France, and Germany, a little maize, Saaz hops, and water from deep wells are used.

ALKEN-MAES

ESTABLISHED 1988

Waarloosveld 10, 2550 Waarloos

RECOMMENDED

Maes Pils (5.1%),
light-bodied with a gentle malty-dry quality
Cristal Pils (4.8%),
full-bodied with firm hoppiness and dryish
Mort Subite Gueuze, (4%),
sour-sweet fruit character, dryish finish
Grimbergen Dubbel (6.2%),
dark red-brown, full-bodied, bittersweet

Alken-Maes is Belgium's second largest brewing company, behind Interbrew. Its core consists of two old established breweries – Alken (1881), and Maes (1880). Along the way it has acquired smaller breweries, and, after a period of British (Watney) ownership, is now part of the mushrooming French food and drinks group Danone (Kronenbourg).

The company is based at Waarloos,

near Antwerp, in the old Maes Brewery which still boasts a fine set of gleaming copper brewing kettles. Maes Pils is brewed here, while Cristal Pils comes out of the Alken brewery, to the southeast. Both are well lagered and are not pasteurized.

There is some interchange of brewing lambic at Kobbegem and Schepdaal, where Interbrew has a separate brewery, while the sweet Grimbergen and Ciney Abbey-style ales are brewed at the Union Brewery in Jumet in Hainaut province.

The company is reshaping itself and there was industrial unrest at Waarloos over plans to concentrate more at Alken from 1998.

Alken-Maes claims to have seen the future with the establishment of Ambiorix, a Ghent bar where customers serve themselves from beer fonts which are activated by a credit card.

Incidentally, Mort Subite is named after a card game once played in the Art Deco café-bar of the same name in old town Brussels near the Grand Square.

ALSO WORTH TRYING

In Leuven the brewpub **Domus**, Tiensestraat 8, has Dubbel Domus (7%, dark amber lager, honeyed) and Leuvens Witbier (5%, unfiltered); **Het Anker** of Michelen has Gouden Carolus (7.8%, red-brown, tart-sweet, spicy); Tarwebier wheat (5%, dry) from **Haacht Brewery** in Boortmeerbeek; and the tiny **Kerkom Brewery**, northeast of Hoegaarden, offers Bink (5.5%, pale ale, hoppy).

Above: Cathedral-like beauty in one of Europe's monster breweries. The stainless steel brewing kettles are illuminated like objects of devotion.

TIMMERMANS

ESTABLISHED 1888

Kerkstraat 11, 1711 Itterbeek

RECOMMENDED

Gueuze (5%),
*dry with some tartness and bitter background,
short finish*
Bourgogne des Flandres (5%),
burgundy, fruity, soft-bodied, slightly tart, dry
Kriek (5%),
*acidic fruitiness, dry and clean, slightly woody
aftertaste*
Pêche (4%),
*pale golden, peach aroma, sharp, peach-fruity,
bittersweet aftertaste*
Lambic Blanche Wit (3.5%),
very pale wheat beer, cloudy, tart, spicy, and dry

Timmermans is one of Belgium's traditional lambic brewers of the Senne Valley just southwest of Brussels (see Lambic feature, pages 108–109), which has also begun producing other beer styles and hybrids. The brewery, which still numbers Timmerman family members among its workforce although outside shareholders now control it, has also expanded its range of lambic-fruit beer blends by introducing peach and blackcurrant.

Timmermans lambic is matured for between one and three years in oak barrels. Little of it is now sold in pure form; it is mostly blended to form gueuze beer or as the base for traditional kriek (cherry) and framboise (raspberry), and the newer cassis (blackcurrant) and pêche (peach). Whole cherries are fermented with lambic for several months in barrels to produce kriek, but syrup essences may be used for the other fruit beers.

Timmermans created the country's first lambic-based wheat beer, Blanche Wit, whose ingredients include coriander and dried orange peel. It has a lower ABV than wheat beers brewed with cultured yeasts. Only young lambic is used.

Bourgogne des Flandres is a hybrid red ale style, prepared by Timmermans – blending lambic and a conventionally fermented ale from another brewery – for a Belgian wholesaler who owns the brand name. Historically, the brand is associated with Bruges.

LEFÈBVRE

ESTABLISHED 1876

Rue de Croly 52, 1430 Quenast

RECOMMENDED

Student Witbier (4.5%),
pale wheat beer, spicy, fruity, and light-bodied
Saison 1900 (5%),
*pale amber, fruity-sharp, gingery spiciness,
refreshingly dry*
Floreffe Tripel (7.5%),
*amber, rich fruit and hoppy spiciness, bitter
finish*
Floreffe Meilleure (8%),
dark copper, spicy, malty ale hinting of mint

A wide variety of beers – mostly top-fermenting ale – is produced by this small brewery which still uses coal to heat its brew kettles. Lefèbvre's annual production is only about 15,000hl (12,800 US barrels, 9,200 UK barrels), small change for Interbrew and Alken-Maes, but they range from a Pilsner to brown ale, with Abbey brands and a Saison style in between.

The family brewery began life catering for quarry workers with dry, quenching acidic beer of the saison style. Lefèbvre's version is well hopped, spiced with ginger, and is bottle-conditioned to encourage a mellowing maturity. The name Saison 1900 recalls the heyday of quarrying in and around Quenast, which is a dozen miles southwest of Brussels.

Lefèbvre produces several strong, bottled-conditioned ales under the name of Floreffe Abbey to the southeast near Namur. The Abbey has a café where visitors can drink its own-label beers – including an 8% mint-flavored edition, Floreffe Meilleure – as well as sample the Norbertine monks' homemade bread and cheese.

TRAPPIST ORVAL

ESTABLISHED 1931

Brasserie d'Orval, Abbaye Notre Dame
6823 Villers-devant-Orval

RECOMMENDED

Orval (6-7.1%),
*golden, very hoppy and orange fruity; drier,
more mellow when older*

Monks brewed here in the 18th century, but the old monastery was destroyed by cannon fire from French revolutionaries who thought the French king was hiding there. The present brewery was established to help pay for the beautiful 1920s monastery.

Left: Trappist tranquillity at Orval.

achieve an astonishingly high attenuation of 96 percent to 99 percent.

The brewery, set in peaceful, dense woodlands near Florenville, close to the French border, can be visited by appointment. Orval is exported to Britain and the USA.

Orval is third largest of the Belgian Trappist breweries after Westmalle and Chimay, with an annual output of 38,000hl (32,000 US barrels, 23,000 UK barrels). It produces just one beer – in a distinctively shaped bottle designed by the monastery's architect, Henry Vaes.

Orval's triple fermentation process lasts 10-12 weeks. A week-long primary open fermentation is followed by a secondary process for three weeks in dry hopped closed tanks and using different yeast. The beer is then bottled unfiltered and primed with another yeast and candy sugar. The bottles are kept for a further six to eight weeks before dispatch. The brewery gives its beer a five-year shelf life.

Very hard, untreated water comes from a spring, the hops are whole Bavarian Hallertau and Styrian Goldings, the pale and caramel barley malt blend is French, Dutch, and German. 'Our aim is to produce a hoppy, yeasty beer so we prefer barley malt with a discreet taste,' explains director François de Harenne. But much of the beer's great character is also attributable to the several yeast strains, including local 'wild' ones developed in the monastery's own laboratory, says de Harenne. These

WESTMALLE

ESTABLISHED 1836

Abdij Trappisten van Westmalle, 2149 Malle

~∞~

RECOMMENDED

Dubbel (6.5%),
chestnut brown, rich maltiness, dry fruitiness
Trippel (9%),
very pale golden, hoppy, fruity and dry

The flat geography and Flemish culture around Westmalle contrasts sharply with the southern monasteries of Chimay, Rochefort, and Orval in their wooded French-speaking valleys. It is the biggest of Belgium's five Trappist breweries. Westmalle's brewing monks are credited with creating the Dubbel and Tripel designations, since copied by Belgian and Dutch secular breweries.

Barley malt usually comes from southern Germany and France, while combinations of English, German, and Czech whole hops are used. The beers undergo two fermentations and are warm-conditioned for several weeks after bottling so that they are between six and eight weeks old before

they leave the brewery. But they have a comfortably drinkable life of five years.

Nearby Turnhout, one of the architectural jewels of Belgium, has several bars serving Westmalle beers, notably Den Spytighen Duvel which means The Spiteful Devil.

ALSO WORTH TRYING

Belgium has three other Trappist ale breweries. Two are in the southeast – at **Forges-les-Chimay** (Notre Dame de Scourmont) in Hainaut province, and **Rochefort** (Notre Dame de St Rémy) in south Namur province. **Westvleteren** (Sint Sixtus) is in the northwest.

The beers are: Chimay Rouge (7%, red-brown, fruity), Chimay Blanche (8%, pale amber, hoppy), Chimay Bleu (9%, dark, spicy), Rochefort 6 (7.5%, brown, fruity), Rochefort 8 (9.2%, dark amber, bittersweet), Rochefort 10 (11.3%, dark, winey), Westvleteren Special 6 (6.2%, dark, malty), Extra 8 (8%, dark, fruity), Abt 12 (11.5%, dark, fruity, and malty).

The La Malle Poste in Rochefort serves the monks' beers and has accommodation. A monastery-owned café-restaurant at Orval serves the beer and excellent food. Visit Café de Vrede in Westvleteren. Chimay is widely available.

Left: Monks at the Chimay Trappist Monastery have been brewing their distinctive beers since the 1860s.

RODENBACH

ESTABLISHED 1836

Spanjestraat 133, 8800 Roeselare

RECOMMENDED

Rodenbach (5%),
reddish brown, light-bodied, slightly sour, very quenching quality
Grand Cru (6.5%),
dark red, fuller bodied and richer than Rodenbach, but also tart
Alexander (6.5%),
kriek-like, fruity aroma, sweet and sour flavors, tart finish

Rodenbach's three beers are ales, loosely defined as Belgian Reds. Each one is created with a slightly different process, making them especially indigenous to western Flanders. Brewery spring water and conventional ingredients are used for the Rodenbach and Grand Cru; cherry essence is added to the Alexander.

What makes the Rodenbach beers unusual and different is the method of maturing and blending. After normal open fermentation of about one week, using several barley malts and low bittering hops, the beer is transferred to tanks for a six-week secondary fermentation. At this stage it is still defined as 'young.' Some of this beer is transferred to large oak vats – the brewery has almost 300 of them. Here, in direct contact with the untreated wood, the beer acquires its sour oaky character interacting with house micro-bacteria. Beer which spends time in the vats is deemed 'old' after a further 20 months. This ageing is similar to the methods traditionally used by English brewers before 19th century industrialization.

Rodenbach is young and old beer blended. Grand Cru is 100 percent old beer. Alexander – named after the brewery's founder – is old beer mixed with cherry juice.

Disappointingly, all three beers are pasteurized before bottling. Descendants of Alexander are still involved in the brewery, which also has a small museum.

LIEFMANS

ESTABLISHED 1679

Aalstraat 200, 9700 Oudenaarde

RECOMMENDED

Oud Bruin (5%),
brown ale, lighter bodied than Goudenband, bittersweet
Goudenband (6%),
dark brown, malty tinged sweet and sour, smooth and creamy
Kriek (6%),
dark red, dark sour fruit flavor, fruity-dry finish

Between Brussels and the French border towards Lille is traditionally sourish, brown-ale-brewing country. The acknowledged classic of the style is considered to be Goudenband. Using methods not unlike Rodenbach's, Liefmans blends old and young brews to achieve the desired flavors.

To obtain its color the beer has a blend of colored and roasted dark barley malts. A young brown – which is confusingly sold separately as Oud Bruin (Old Brown) – is mixed with a stronger version matured in tanks for at least six months. The blend is then bottled with a fresh dose of yeast to re-ferment for up to three months before leaving the brewery.

Liefmans is one of the oldest breweries in the area, so old that when it was bought by the Riva group of Dentergem in 1990, the brewhouse was considered too decrepit for further use. Using water which has been treated to resemble that in Oudenaarde, the brew mash is boiled a few miles away at Riva's Dentergem brewery and then taken by road tanker to Liefmans for the rest of the process.

The Liefmans brewery also makes cherry and raspberry fruit beers, using Oud Bruin as the base. These re-ferment and are matured for two months. Brewery visits are possible.

DUPONT

ESTABLISHED 1850

Rue Basse 5, 7904 Tourpes

RECOMMENDED

Vieille Provision Saison (6.5%),
coppery, pronounced hoppiness, dry
Moinette Brune (8.5%),
*brown, sweet fruitiness balanced by hops,
bittersweet*
Bons Voeux (9.5%),
*dark amber, bottle-conditioned Xmas ale, fruity
rich, dryish*

Originally a saison brewer, the family-run business has branched out into a variety of styles and pursued the 'green' market by producing beers made only with organically grown (chemical-free) ingredients, under the tag Biologique.

Dupont beers – named after the family that acquired the brewery early this century – tend to be dryish with hoppiness to the fore; hops from Kent and Slovenia are favored, with pale and colored barley malt from the domestic market and France. The brewery produces a variety of beers under the Moinette name, which has ancient monastic associations.

For a small brewery of under 10,000hl (8,500 US barrels, 6,000 UK barrels) capacity, Dupont is a prolific provider of confusingly named similar beers. The full name for Bons Voeux is: Avec les Bons Voeux de la Brasserie ('With the best wishes of the brewery').

Dupont beers are increasingly available outside the area of Tourpes, which is between Silly and Tournai in the French border district of western Hainaut province. There's a café-bar next to the brewery,

which can be visited only by appointment. In Tournai, the Cave à Bières café-bar, on Quai Taille Pierres, offers Dupont beers among a good selection of regional specialties.

SILLY

ESTABLISHED 1850

Brasserie de Silly, Ville basse 141, 7830 Silly

RECOMMENDED

Blanche Titje (5%),
*pale cloudy wheat beer, spicy, tart fruitiness,
and finally dry*
Saison de Silly (5%),
*reddish-amber, fruity and soft, slight tartness
to finish*
Brug (5%),
pale ale, good hop aroma and character

A small, rural ale brewery with its origins in the traditional farmer-brewer culture in this region that straddles the French-Belgian border, Silly is still owned and managed by descendants of founder farmer Nicholas Meynsbrughen. Innocently, the family adopted the name of the village – so called after the River Sil – for their brewing. A trifle silly in the light of subsequent exports to the English-speaking world.

The brewery produces a broad range of beers, most recently a wheat beer. But its roots lie in the saison style, and perfectionists believe the Meynsbrughen's practices remain closest to the old methods associated with seasonal brewing before the advent of refrigeration.

Saison de Silly is produced by blending two brews, one of which has been aged in tanks for up to 12 months. Both beers have unusually long primary open fermentations, which may help modify the acidic tendency of such beers.

De Silly's range includes several pale ales, a coppery Scotch Ale (8%) and a powerful bronze strong ale called Divine (9.5%) which, despite its strength, has a

quite hoppy character. The brewer prefers Goldings whole hops and a mix of Belgian barley malts. There's a pub next door to the brewery, Café de la Brasserie, which serves Silly beers.

ALSO WORTH TRYING

The **Claryse Brewery**, also in Oudenaarde, has several brown ales including Felix Oudenaards (5.5%, fruity-sweet); in nearby Mater the **Roman Brewery** of 16th century origin offers its versions of brown ale: Roman Oudenaards (5%, malty, bittersweet) and Dobbelen Bruinen (8%, dark, rich and slightly bitter); at Zottegem, south of Ghent, the very small **Crombe Brewery** has Zottegems Bruin (5%, malty-dry).

Ghent has several specialist beer cafés, notably Hopduvel, Rokerelstraat 10, and Het Waterhuis, Groentelmarkt 9.

FRANCE

Beer was once an everyday drink throughout much of France. In 1900 there were 3,000 breweries, many of them farm-based. Today there are just 28 left, and 80 percent of the market is controlled by two companies — pasta giant Danone, which includes the German-sounding Kronenbourg and Kanterbrau brands, and Dutch Heineken, which recently bought France's last large independent brewer, Fischer.

But France has not remained impervious to the beer renaissance. Brewpubs are springing up across the country: for example, in Angers (Loire Valley), Limoges, Lille, Paris, Mulhouse, Morlaix, Strasbourg, and Tours. And a surviving handful of traditional ale breweries in the northern Pas-de-Calais area are back in vogue with a bière de garde style.

France rates seventh in the European beer production league, but much of the output is bland, low-priced lager for export — especially via the Channel ports to visiting Britons looking for cut-price bargains. French annual per capita beer consumption is 39 liters (69 UK pints) — compared with Britain's 102 (180).

DUYCK

ESTABLISHED 1922

Brasserie Duyck, Rue Nationale 113
59144 Jenlain

RECOMMENDED

Jenlain (6.5%),
amber, yeasty aroma, malty and bittersweet, usually unfiltered in bottle
Sebourg (6%),
pale ale, fruity-dry with a hoppy background
Bière de Noël (6.8%),
rich, sweet-malt flavors, soft finish
Printemps (6.5%),
March (Mars) red-brown beer, malty, spicy, full-bodied

Family-owned Duyck began life as a farmhouse brewery but has since expanded to become a successful commercial brewer. All Duyck beers are top-fermented ales in bière de garde style. Duyck is credited with leading the revival in interest in this style through its biggest selling beer Jenlain, named after the brewery's home village south of Valenciennes. Jenlain is now exported to nine countries, and expansion has broadened Duyck's portfolio with seasonal specialties. Bière de Noël celebrates Christmas, its malty overtones tempered with hops from Alsace. Printemps is brewed in December with three malts and drunk in February–March.

The name Sebourg revives a pale ale style produces by brewers in the village of that name until the 1930s. All Duyck beers are matured for a minimum of one month. The brewery produces 85,000hl (72,500 US barrels, 52,000 UK barrels) a year, using well-water drawn from beneath the village. Duyck has its own beer café in Lille at 43 Place Rihour serving the full range plus an unfiltered house draft bière de garde.

LA CHOULETTE

ESTABLISHED 1885

16 Rue des Ecoles, 59111 Hordain

RECOMMENDED

Ambrée (7.5%),
amber, firm malty-sweet flavors, bittersweet
Blonde (7.5%),
pale, clean hop taste, dryish
Abbaye de Vaucelles (7.5%),
amber, sweet fruit balanced by spicy dryness
Robespierre (8%),
golden, yeasty aroma, full-bodied maltiness and bittersweet

La Choulette takes its name from the oval ball which is used in an anarchic form of golf still played in northern France. The brewery began life as a farmhouse operation and changed hands — and names — a number of times before Alain Dhaussy's arrival in the late 1970s.

Dhaussy switched from brewing the pale lager favored by the previous owner back to the traditional top-fermenting styles of the region. His beers are rich and full-bodied, using French barley malt and Bavarian hops. They are filtered but not pasteurized and mostly packaged in bottles, some of which have cork and wire seals.

The Abbaye is linked with the monks of Vaucelles at Cambrai and includes herbs in the recipe. A version of Ambrée has raspberries added in the Belgian framboise style. Christmas is celebrated with a Bière de Noël.

La Choulette's beers are distributed mainly in the small towns and villages around Hordain, which is near Valenciennes and the Belgian border, but specialist stockists in Britain also carry them. The brewery, which also has a small museum, can be visited.

ST MARTIAL

ESTABLISHED 1985

Brasserie St Martial, 8 Place Denis-Dussoubs
87000 Limoges

RECOMMENDED

Blanche-Weiss (4.4%),
amber, tart fruitiness, bittersweet finish
Bitter (5.5%),
pale ale, some malt sweetness, hoppy
Stout (6.2%),
black, mild dry-roast maltiness

In a region of France where brewing beer is as rare as haggis hunting, Jean Michard is a *cause célèbre* with his small

ale brewery located in the porcelain-manufacturing town of Limoges. His enthusiasm is infectious and his beers – ranging from a Bavarian-style wheat beer to an Irish stout – are popular in several bars and restaurants.

Michard uses only malted barley or wheat, a mix of Czech and Kent Golding hops, and his own yeast culture which he has nurtured for more than five years. He already had a passion for beer when he opened a café-bar offering a variety of beer styles and when he discovered that the Limoges area once boasted 49 breweries, he 'decided it would be more interesting for my customers and for me to brew it myself.' St Martial is the patron saint of Limoges.

Jean Michard's beer range includes a Belgium Abbaye-style strong golden ale of 8% which goes through a bottle refermentation process siumilar to some Trappist beers. Most of St Martial beers can be drunk unfiltered on draft in Le Paris Café-Bar next door to the brewery – or if you are in Paris itself, you'll find some of them in La Butte en Vigne on Rue Poulbot, Montmartre.

KRONENBOURG

ESTABLISHED 1664

Brasserie Kronenbourg, 86 Route
d'Oberhausbergen, 67067 Strasbourg

RECOMMENDED

Kronenbourg 1664 (5.9%),
deep golden, malt and hop flavors, bittersweet
1664 Brune (6%),
dark brown, full-bodied, malty and dryish
Bière de Noël (6.5%),
deep golden, malty and bittersweet

It may be owned by Europe's second largest pasta manufacturer and sport a rather Germanic name, but Kronenbourg is still solidly French with brewing roots which stretch back over 300 years to a riverside brewpub in Strasbourg. The

brewery, part of the Danone group produces 10 million hl (8.5 million US barrels, 6.1 million UK barrels) a year.

The Kronenbourg name derives from the suburb of Strasbourg – Cronenbourg – whither the descendants of original brewer Jerome Hatt moved their expanding enterprise. Early this century the brewery produced a popular German-style bock, but today the red-and-white-labelled Kronenbourg pale lager is France's most familiar beer, with 30 percent of the market.

Kronenbourg's main brewery remains in Strasbourg, and a second one is sited at Obernai. Others in the group are at Champigneulles in Lorraine and Rennes in Britanny; they operate under the label Kanterbrau.

ALSO WORTH TRYING

In the north, the unfiltered wheat beer Blanche (5.5%, fruity-dry) at **Les Brasseurs** brewpub in central Lille; rich fruit wheat beer L'Angelus (7% pale) from the **Annoeullin** brewery, near Lille; Colvert (7%, pale, fruity-sweet bière de garde) from **Peronne**; the powerful bière de garde 3 Monts (8%, amber, slightly tart) from **St Sylvestre**, French Flanders. To the east, the dark smoky-flavored Adelscott (6.6%) from **Fischer** in Schiltigheim; **Schutzenberger**, also in Schiltigheim, imitates the German doppelbock with Jubilator (7%, very pale and hoppy) and Patriator (7%, brown and malty); **Meteor** at Hochfelden has Mortimer (8%, amber, very malty, slightly smoky) and a quite hoppy dry Pils (4.9%).

A Glass For Every Season

Drinking beer from glass is not just a matter of cheap convenience. Glass is a psychological necessity because we all drink with our eyes in a subconscious act of wary inspecton which has its origins in beer's murky past. Why else do we hold a glass of beer up to the light to examine its color and clarity? It reassures us before we embrace the aroma and then the taste. Before glass was mass-produced cheaply to provide see-through drinking vessels, our ancestors had to trust to luck when they supped. Luck that the contents were wholesome; luck that they were not being sold short.

Before the 19th century most beer was muddy brown or black in color. Brewers hid its unsavory appearance – and sometimes dubious contents – behind earthenware or pewter or tin. It might explain the origin of the phrase 'pot luck.'

Over time glass has been shaped to suit different beer styles. The Belgians and the Germans are the greatest enthusiasts for different styles of beer glass. A great German Pilsner beer, such as König of Duisburg on the River Rhine, deserves a tulip glass to trap the perfumed aroma of the hop; an effervescent wheat beer, like Munich's Franziskaner, needs a tall flower vase shape to cope with the great rush of foam when a bottle is opened. A Belgian Trappist beer like Rochefort wouldn't feel comfortable if it wasn't poured into a chunky stemmed, wide-mouthed glass goblet. And you have to drink in Belgium to be served a Scotch ale in a glass the shape of a thistle – the national emblem of Scotland.

Germans still fit pewter lids to some beer glasses, and it's not just for show. Sitting under chestnut trees in a south Bavarian beer garden can result in all sorts of unwanted objects dropping into your beer – wasps, leaves, flower petals, and even pretzel crumbs. The sturdiness of some Bavarian beer glasses has to match the robustness of Germanic drinking habits. The heavy, quarter-inch-thick Masskrug – often misnamed a stein by foreigners – is favored when friends gather in a beer hall, or a beer garden, or at the Oktoberfest. They raise their Masskrugs before drinking and crash them together with cries of 'Prost!' – Cheers.

In Australia, beer glasses have been influenced more by the climate than anything else. The macho Australian male image promoted abroad is not matched by their often Thumbelina-sized beer glasses.

Swig-sized glasses stem from drinking habits in the days before air conditioning. Aussies prefer beer colder than a mountain stream in Spring – as low as 36°F (2°C) – so they didn't want it sitting around for long in a big glass getting warm in their steamy summer climate.

Sizes range up from puny four ounces to a rare pint, and to confuse an outsider, glass names mean different things in different states. In Sydney a 'Middy' is ten ounces, while across the country in Perth it's only seven ounces. In Adelaide, a

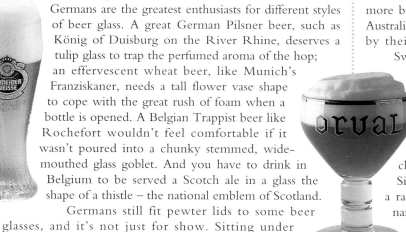

'Schooner' of beer measures nine ounces; in Sydney the same name will get you 15oz of beer. Other glass measures are called Pony, Butcher, and Pot. In Tasmania, the island state off the southeast coast of Australia noted for its Cascade and Boag beers, glasses are known simply by the fluid ounces they hold: a Four, a Six, an Eight, and a Ten.

Glass also enables drinkers to see how much beer they are getting. When the earthenware pot was the norm, short measures were rife. To discourage this, impoverished Germans in the 19th century smeared bacon rind on the inside of their mugs before they were filled. The grease smear ensured that the foam quickly dispersed to reveal the beer level before the purchaser began drinking. But a greasy glass is ruinous for drinkers who judge the quality of their beer by the so-called Brussels lace pattern of foam left behind on the inside as the beer level goes down. A pils drinker is particularly fond of the 'lace' effect, as are ale drinkers in northern England who imbibe through a dense, creamy collar created by the beer being drawn into the glass via a pump with a narrow aperture known as a sparkler.

In Britain, the pint glass measure for beer has been preserved in pubs even though the country has gone otherwise metric to harmonize with its European Union neighbors. But, unlike most other countries, a 20oz pint of beer in Britain can legally include the head, often leaving the customer with only 18oz of beer. Drinkers can insist on the glass being filled with liquid to the brim, but then they lose their 'collar' of foam which laces the glass as the beer is drunk.

The most impractical beer glass shape is the English yard of ale — a three feet (one metre) long, narrow tube with a bulbous base. It holds two and a half pints of beer (1.42l) and is used for drinking competitions. Its size and shape make it very difficult to drink out of without choking or being drenched with beer. Englishman Peter Dowdeswell holds the record for emptying the contents of a yard of ale down his throat in five seconds. A previous record-holder was former Australian prime minister Bob Hawke, who took 12 seconds while a student at Oxford. Thankfully, most of us have found easier ways of enjoying our beer.

Left: A good beer appeals to eye just as it does to the nose and palate. This glass, with its reassuringly solid handle and raised lid, seems to send out the invitation 'Drink Me.'

THE NETHERLANDS

Although 90 percent of the Dutch beer market is still golden lager, the trend is encouragingly towards darker top- as well as bottom-fermenting beers. Beer drinkers under the age of 30 are showing the greatest interest in new-old styles like 'boks,' wheat beers, stouts, and ales.

Heineken dominates about 55 percent of the national market but as the number of old independent breweries dwindles, so too does the number of new microbreweries grow. Today there are about 50, mostly tiny, breweries in existence. In the 1970s there were less than 20.

The Dutch fall just short of being in the world's top ten beer-drinking nations with an annual per capita intake of 91 liters (160 UK pints).

HEINEKEN

ESTABLISHED 1863

Tweede Weteringplantsoen 21

1017 Amsterdam

RECOMMENDED

Heineken (5%),
very pale, gentle hoppiness and dryish finish
Kylian (6.5%),
copper-red, malty-dry and smooth
Van Vollenhoven's Stout (6.5%),
fullsome, fruity but less bitter than most stouts
Tarwebok (6.5%),
dark brown, fruit and malt sweetness balanced by wheat content

Market limitations in the Netherlands, combined with easy access to the sea, long ago encouraged Heineken to become an international company. Today, it is the world's second largest brewing group – linked with more than 100 breweries and producing 64.3 million hectoliters (54.8 million US barrels, 39.3 million UK barrels) a year.

Its principal brand is called simply Heineken, although there are many variations of it in the 170 countries where it sells 17 million hl (14.5 million US barrels, 10.4 million UK barrels) a year. There are two Heineken breweries in the Netherlands, but neither is located in the Amsterdam home base. One is at 's Hertogenbosch, the other at Zoeterwoude. Heineken also now owns Brand's of Wiljre near Maastricht.

The company is dabbling in ale styles, although the Stout is curiously bottom-fermented. There are two versions of top-fermented Kylian: George Killian, named after a defunct brewery in Ireland, is brewed at Heineken's French brewery near Lille; cousin Kylian is 100 percent Dutch.

Heineken is reluctant to talk about the type of malt and hops it uses – 'You might call it the chef's little secret,' said a spokesman – but in recent years it has become pro-German Purity Law with its lager beers. Sugar and caramel go into some of the other beers. Tarwebok is 17 percent wheat. Amstel, the country's other top-selling pale lager, is named after a defunct Amsterdam brewery.

IJ

ESTABLISHED 1984

Brouwerij 't IJ, Funenkade 7, 1018 Amsterdam

RECOMMENDED

Mug Bitter (5%),
pale, hoppy, and finally slightly bitter
Natte (6%),
brown, malty, fruity, and dry
Bock (6.5%),
red-brown, malt-rich, and fruity
Columbus (9%),
amber, full-bodied, strong pale ale, very fruity

Above: IJ's brewery has a working windmill attached.

There's an element of eccentricity about the Netherlands' oldest microbrewery. It's built in a former public bath house and part of the building is a still functioning windmill. The name IJ is a roundabout way of saying 'egg' in Dutch – an egg is part of the brewery's emblem.

It's no longer the only source of ale in Amsterdam but all the brewing, guided by owner Kaspar Peterson, is top-fermenting; some of it mimics Belgian styles, some German, and there's an English-style bitter.

The beers are increasingly available in special Amsterdam café-bars and most are served on draft in the simple bar adjoining the IJ brewery in the city's harbor dockland district. However, this keeps eccentric hours: 3–8pm.

ALSO WORTH TRYING

In Amsterdam look out for Bethanien (4.5%, hoppy pale ale) and Tarwebier (5%, pale wheat) at the brewpub **Maximiliaans** in the old town on Kloveniers Burgwal street; and the Wildeman bar on Kolksteeg in front of the main railway station has a wide selection of Dutch beers.

GROLSCH

ESTABLISHED 1898

Grolsche Bierbrouwerij, Brouwerijstraat 1
7523 Enschede

RECOMMENDED
Zomergoud (4.5%),
very pale, light-bodied and citric dry
Pilsner/Premium Lager (4.8%),
golden, malty flavors, gentle hoppiness to finish
Amber (5%),
light maltiness, some fruit character, hoppy
Wintervorst (7.5%),
chestnut brown, full-bodied, slightly spicy

Grolsch is known internationally for its Premium Lager – sold in the Netherlands as a Pilsner. But in recent years the company has been brewing up some new and more exotic tastes in both top- and bottom-fermenting beer styles.

Its seasonal specialties includes Zomergoud (Summer Blond), a quenching ale brewed with pale Pilsner

malt, lemon peel, and dried lime tree and elderberry tree blossoms. The other seasons are heralded with bock styles, culminating in mid-winter's Wintervorst, an ale spiced with orange peel and clover honey. The top-fermenting Amber uses three barley malts and a little wheat malt.

These are inspiring beers from a large two-brewery (Groenlo and Enchede) business (1.9 million hl, 1.6 million US barrels, 1.16 million UK barrels) which could have stuck to simply brewing pale lagers in competition with Heineken. Grolsch's beers enjoy slow, traditional fermentation and generous maturation times – the Pilsner is matured for six to eight weeks in traditional horizontal lagering tanks. And the company refuses to pasteurize any of its beers, even for the export market, on the grounds that it damages the delicate flavor characteristics which the brewers have strived to obtain. Bavarian and Bohemian hops and several malts are used.

Grolsch owns the English ale brewery Ruddles.

DRIE RINGEN

ESTABLISHED 1989

Amersfoortsche Brouwerij, Kleine Spui 18
3811 Amersfoort

RECOMMENDED
Hopfenbier (5%),
pale ale, fruity with a hoppy finish
Amersfoort Wit (5%),
amber, fullsome, sweet-sour wheat beer
Tripel (7.5%),
amber, richly fruity, heavy bittersweet finish

A small but industrious brewery which has specialized in top-fermenting styles since opening and so rekindling a local craft which was once a dominant feature of this ancient and picturesque town.

Drie Ringen lays great store by its yeast and boasts its own laboratory, something which much bigger breweries sometimes lack. Beers tend to be fruity but the use of German and Belgian hops is generous. Beers are filtered but not pasteurized. Seasonal beers produced include a spring bock (Meibok) and an English-like winter warmer called Winterbier (8%).

A small café-bar at the brewery sells the Ringen beers on draft; it is open from noon to 6pm only.

ALSO WORTH TRYING

In old Utrecht, a small house brewery in the cavernous café **Ouden** at Oude Gracht 99 brews several wheat beers, notably Ouwe Daen (5%, unfiltered, coarse, malty and smooth). The specialist beer café Belgie which offers a wide selection of Dutch beers is on the same street at No. 196. And the Jan Primus on Jan van Scorelstraat also has a big selection.

Left: Drie Ringen has rekindled local interest in ale.

KONINGSHOEVEN

ESTABLISHED 1884

Trappistenbierbrouwerij de Schaapskooi
Eindhovenseweg 3, 5056 RP Berkel-Enschot

RECOMMENDED

(all are prefixed La Trappe)
Enkel (5.5%),
amber, yeasty, honey-sweetness, hop spicy
Dubbel (6.5%),
ruby, fruity, rich, and smoothly bittersweet
Tripel (8%),
amber, hop aroma gives way to a spicy-dry taste
Quadrupel (10%),
red-brown, rich, full-bodied, bittersweet

This is usually referred to as the sixth Trappist monastery brewery, although the other five are all in Belgium. Numerous other monastery breweries exist, mostly in Germany and Austria, but the world can only muster six owned by the Trappist order. Koningshoeven produces only top-fermenting ales and despite its limited output – about 25,000hl (21,300 US barrels, 15,300 UK barrels) a year – it is very commercially minded. At different times it has had contracts with the Belgian giant Stella Artois (Interbrew) and the British Allied-Carlsberg group.

The classic range are prefixed La Trappe and are all bottle-conditioned and mature with age. Similar varieties are marketed with different names, sometimes for supermarket chains, and some of these are filtered. Originally there was just a Dubbel, then came a Tripel, a Quadrupel and finally, in 1995, the one you would have thought they'd have produced first – the single (Enkel).

Koningshoeven has its own well-water supply and its

De Paters Trappisten, Abdij O.L.V. Koningshoeven

La Trappe
TRAPPISTENBIER

own developed house yeast. A mix of barley malts are used, plus small quanties of candy sugar, and primarily Hallertau bittering and Goldings aroma hops.

The brewery sometimes engages in contract-brewing for others. The monks' keen commercial sense probably stems from Koningshoeven's origins: the founding monks built a brewery first in order to earn money to build their church and home. And despite their serious purpose in life, the monks have a sense of humor which is also very practical. A brewhouse inscription says: 'There is no beer in heaven, so we drink it here.'

ST CHRISTOFFEL

ESTABLISHED 1986

Bredeweg 14, 6042 Roermond

RECOMMENDED

Christoffel Blond (5%), *very pale, very hoppy*
Robertus (6%),
red-amber, full-bodied, malty and dry

The name of this tiny brewery commemorates the local patron saint who once metaphorically guarded over the district's now redundant coalminers; it's much better work standing guard over a brewhouse. Founder Leon Brand is of the old Brand brewing family whose own brewery in Wiljre near Maastricht has been taken over by Heineken. But Leon is anyway more

interested in the German way of brewing, as his extremely hoppy Pilsner testifies.

He is a graduate of Germany's premier brewing school at Weihenstephan near Munich and brews according to the German beer purity law. German hops are responsible for the big bite of Christoffel beers which are conditioned for up to eight weeks and are not pasteurized.

There's no brewery pub, but St Christoffel beers can be found in numerous specialty Dutch bars in bottled form, and usually on draft in the Belgique Café in central Amsterdam on Gravenstraat.

ALSO WORTH TRYING

De Kroon at Oirschot between Eindhoven and Tilburg has Briljant (6.5%, pale, full-bodied, malty lager), a pale Meibok (May bock, 6.5%) and a new wheat beer; at Budel, south of Eindhoven, the **Budelse** brewery offers a Düsseldorf-style, top-fermenting Alt (5.5%, golden and quite bitter) and Capucijn (6.5%, amber ale, fruity and spicy). Nearby Valkenswaard has the Café Bolleke offering 150 different beers.

GULPENER
RIJK AAN SMAAK · RIJK AAN TRADITIE
ANNO 1825
LIMBURGS BIER
MEIBOCK
B.V. GULPENER BIERBROUWERIJ GULPEN

GULPENER

ESTABLISHED 1825

Gulpener Bierbrouwerij, Rijksweg 16
6271 AE Gulpen

RECOMMENDED

Mestreechs Aajt (3.5%),
almost black, very fruity, dry, lightly tart
Korenwolf Witbier (5%),
hazy-lemon color, light-bodied, spicy
Witte Kerst (6.5%),
deep amber, fruity, long hoppy finish
Château Neubourg (5.5%),
pale Pilsner, rich hop-malt aroma, full-bodied
Dort (6.5%),
pale brown, malty, bitter-sweet
Meibock (6.5%),
pale, malty-dry with some hoppiness

Medium-sized family brewer Gulpener (130,000hl, 111,000 US barrels, 80,000 UK barrels) has one of the most colorful beer portfolios in the country. Since 1996 all ingredients are produced locally. 'It took time, but now we have someone in Limbourg province also growing hops for us and that was the last thing we had to organize,' explained marketing manager Desiree Hendriks. The brewery draws its own spring water from local marlstone hills.

The wheat beer Korenwolf is named after the grain-storing hamster, and the beer is made from a mix of oats, rye, wheat, and barley, plus dried elderberry blossom for a touch of fruitiness. Witte Kerst (White Christmas) is seasonal and its ingredients, which include secret spices, vary from year to year on the whim of the brewers. Each edition is year-stamped.

Another Gulpener curio is Sjoes (pronounced schuss) which means a shot or a dash. A dash of the dark malty Ould Bruin goes in the Gulpener's main Pilsner. The brewery produces a bottled blend (4.5%), but drinkers have it made up on draft in pubs.

Mestreechs Aajt (dialect for Maastricht Old) is a blend of new and aged bottom- and top-fermenting beers, one of which is exposed to wild yeasts. The process takes at least one year to complete. Recent blending has involved Pils, Ould Bruin, and Dort. Gulpener beers are widely available in Holland; in Gulpen they are all at the brewpub Herberg de Zwarte Ruiter (Black Knight).

ALFA

ESTABLISHED 1870

Bierbrouwerij Schinnen, Thull 15
6365 Schinnen

RECOMMENDED

Alfa Pils (5%),
malty but dryish
Lentebok (6.5%),
amber, full-bodied, bittersweet
Super Dortmunder (7%),
pale amber, fruity-sweet

This member of the dwindling band of old established Dutch independent family brewers has long been a voluntary supporter of the German Reinheitsgebot purity law as well as of German beer styles. Super Dortmunder is almost in a class of its own at 7%.

The medium-sized brewery (60,000hl, 51,000 US barrels, 36,500 UK barrels) has its own source of soft well-water and uses German and Bohemian whole hops. The beers have a malty accent and some are sweetish, although the pils makes full use of Bohemian Saaz hops to provide a hoppy-dryish quality.

Descendants of founder Joseph Meens are still in control of the brewery which is generally known by its slightly baffling trade name Alfa. Perhaps that's what they call the swashbuckling musketeer who appears on bottle labels.

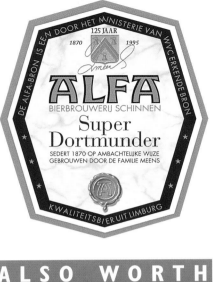

ALSO WORTH TRYING

Other Limbourg brews to look out for are Valkenburgs Witbier (4.8%, unfiltered, spicy) and Jubileeuw (5%, malty Pils) from the **Leeuws** (Lion) brewery in Valkenburg, just north of Gulpen; the **Lindeboom** (Lime Tree) brewery at Neer near Roermond has a full-bodied bock (6.5%, dark amber, malty-dry) and a very hoppy pils (5%); in Maastricht the **De Ridder** brewery offers Wieckse Wit (5%, unfiltered, spicy-sweet wheat); and at Wijlre near Maastricht the **Brand** brewery has the impressive bock Imperator (6.5%, amber and richly malty).

Above: Gleaming brewhouse coppers at Brand's brewery.

AUSTRIA

Austria is perhaps better known for Mozart and skiing holidays than for beer. But this is a quietly busy beer country, fifth in the world drinking league with an annual per capita consumption of 116 liters (204 UK pints).

Hops have been grown since the beginning of the 13th century along the Danube north of Linz, where some of Europe's oldest written brewing records date to 1229. There are still several brewery cooperatives whose ownership is rooted in medieval rights. In the 19th century, Viennese brewer Anton Dreher was at the forefront of technical developments which led to bottom-fermentation (lager) beer and his distinctive 'Vienna Red' style.

Austria today has 74 breweries with beer styles similar to Bavaria: pale and dark brown lagers, strong bocks, top-fermenting wheats. Laws prohibit chemical additives in beer; some breweries voluntarily comply with Germany's Reinheitsgebot.

Austrian brewers tend to be conservative, perhaps due to the dominance of two giants – Brau AG and Steirerbrau – who hold about 66 percent of the market.

SALMBRÄU

ESTABLISHED 1994

Rennweg 8, A-1030 Wien

❧

RECOMMENDED

Märzen (5.5%),
amber-red, malty with hint of fruitiness
Hell (5%),
pale, unfiltered, citric fruitiness, dry
Pilsner (5%),
yeasty-fruity aroma, bitter-dry
Bock (6.5%),
dark brown, malty, full-bodied, bittersweet

Vienna's smartest brewpub is in 17th century cellars which were once part of

a monastery and used for storing wine. The cellars adjoin the architectural splendors of the baroque Belevedere Palace near Schwarzenbergplatz – a mix of beer hall and restaurant, where the brewing coppers twinkle at the drinkers.

Brewer Ivan Farkas, from Slovakia, uses four malts including Munich and Vienna varieties. Czech aroma hops are mixed three to one with the bitter varieties from Bavaria's Hallertau. Salm is cultivating its own yeast, based on a supply from the Czech Budvar Brewery. All the beers are unfiltered, including the Pilsner, reflecting a trend in the German-speaking world for 'natural' products. They are matured for four to eight weeks and then served direct from the maturation tanks via bar fonts.

Owner Walter Welledits, whose family firm builds and exports mini-brewery equipment as far afield as New York, is in no doubt as to why his and other Vienna brewpubs are thriving. 'The rise of the brewpub is due to the failure of the big breweries to deliver what people want. They produce thin, fast-brewed

beers which lack individual character and flavor. We can give the customers what they want – taste and choice.'

Right: Brewer Ivan Farkas admires his Salmbräu coppers.

SIEBERNSTERNBRÄU

ESTABLISHED 1993

Siebernsterngasse 19, 1070 Wien

❧

RECOMMENDED

Wiener Märzen (5.5%),
red-brown, fruity-dry with spicy, yeasty finish
Dunkel (5%),
chestnut, malty-sweetness becomes drier
Helles (5%),
amber, bittersweet taste, hoppy, dry aftertaste

This is a fashionable cellar brewpub a five-minute, No. 49 tram ride from Vienna's famous inner ring (Burg Ring).

Siebernstern's beers are bottom-fermented, lagered for about one month, and are all unfiltered, in the Viennese microbrewing fashion. The beers are available only on draft and are dispensed directly from the lagering tanks. Customers queuing for the mature flavored beers of the 'Seven Stars' brewery tend to be under 30, which might tell Austria's big mass production brewers something.

Right: Take a tram to Vienna's 'Seven Stars' brewpub.

WIESELBURG

ESTABLISHED 1770

Brauerei Wieselburg
Josef-Riedmullerstrasse 2, 3250 Wieselburg

RECOMMENDED
Wieselburger Gold (5%),
golden, malty-sweet with late hop flavor
Kaiser Märzen (5.5%),
reddish-brown, rich malty flavors, dryish finish
Wieselburger Zwickelbier (4.8%),
amber cloudy, yeasty and fruity, bittersweet

Buried in quiet farming country through which gently flows the Danube, Wieselburg seems an unlikely location for Austria's biggest single brewery (1,300,000hl, 1,108,000 US barrels, 795,000 UK barrels). But there had been brewing here for centuries before the arrival of the Brau AG giant and its current edge-of-town brewery.

Wieselburg produces some of Austria's blandest beers – the supermarket loss-leader Schutzenbräu – and also some of the tastiest. The chief beers are the five Kaiser lagers, including a bock and the hoppy Kaiser Kurpils, but the brewery continues to produce local Wieselburger beers, including an unfiltered variety and a Märzen style.

The brewery has its own water supply. A cocktail of Czech, German, and Austrian hops is used. The stronger beers are lagered for up to two months, but all are pasteurized – save for the Zwickelbier, an unfiltered brew on tap in the former brewery, now converted into a beer hall, the Brauhof on Hauptplatz (main square).

WEITRA

ESTABLISHED 1988

Brauhotel Weitra, Rathausplatz 6
3970 Weitra

RECOMMENDED
Hausbier (5.2%),
ruby, unfiltered, yeasty aroma, bittersweet

If Niederösterreich boasts the country's biggest brewery, it also has the distinction of being home to the smallest too. North of Wieselburg and close to the Czech border, ancient Weitra also houses some of the oldest written records of Austrian brewing, dating from the early 14th century.

Today's hotel-microbrewery is in buildings which date from the 17th century when it was a brewery under the control of the lord of the manor. The Pöpperl family acquired it early this century, but moved brewing operations to a larger site. But in the late 1980s Hermann Pöpperl took up his brewing right – which was still valid from medieval times. Today he brews in the old malting cellars.

The town has a castle dating from the 12th century, and a second small brewery, also run by the Pöpperl family, in Sparkasseplatz. It produces two pale beers in the crisp, hoppy, Bohemian style. Weitra is a pleasant stopover on a journey to or from Bohemia and the home of Budweiser Budvar. The Brauhotel has excellent accommodation.

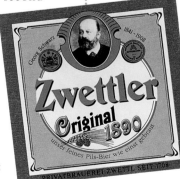

ALSO WORTH TRYING

Other beers worth seeking out in Vienna: **Medl's** Märzen (5.5%) malty-dry, and unfiltered Pilsner (4.8%) at Linzerstrasse 275 in Penzing; at the slightly eccentric **Brauhaus Nussdorf**, in the northern suburb of the same name, the top-fermented black, fruity, dry Sir Henry's Stout (5.2%); in Elizabethstrasse, Vienna's biggest beer hall, **Gösserbräu**, serves the pale, slightly fruity lager of that name; and in the pedestrianized old town, Bierhof (open 4pm) in the Haarhof alley off Naglergasse has six draft beers, including several unfiltered pale and dark lagers from Austria's **Ottakringer**

and **Kapsreiter** breweries. The main beer of Vienna's major brewer Ottakringer is Gold Fassl, a pale lager with light hoppiness and gentle fruity-dry finish.

In other parts of Niederösterreich (Lower Austria): Trojan Edelmärzen (5.5%, amber, malty-dry) in Schrems, near Weitra; a top-fermenting Altbier (4.8%, amber, malt sweetness) produced by **Brauerei Lehn** in Piesting, a village south of Vienna; a dark malty 6.5% Weihnachtsbier (Xmas bock) at Hainfeld, east of Wieselburg; and at Zwettl, 17km (10 miles) south of Weitra, an unfiltered **Zwettler** Zwickl (5.6%) plus Zwettler Original 1890, a well-hopped and slightly fruity Pilsner.

BRAUCOMMUNE

ESTABLISHED 1777

Promenade 7, 4240 Freistadt

RECOMMENDED

Ratsherrentrunk (5.5%),
*pale-amber Märzen, fruit-sweetness, hoppy,
bitter aftertaste*
Dunkles (4.8%),
brown, firm malty aroma and taste, nutty-dry
Weihnachtsbock (6.5%),
*ruby Xmas brew, rich, malt-fruitiness,
bittersweet*

It sounds like something straight out of the French revolution but the Braucommune is not quite a peoples' brewery. It's a cooperative shared by 150 townsfolk, among them local publicans, with share rights reaching back centuries.

Above: A label for Braucommune's Dunkel lager.

Central Europe has jealously guarded medieval brewing rights which were granted by lords of the manor and are handed down through families or inherited with ownership of a house or tavern. Here in Freistadt the cooperative brewery stems from an 18th century merger between two town breweries, one owned by the council, the other by the ancient brewing burghers. These burghers have also retained a taste for tradition. The brewery has its own well, uses Austrian malt and hops, lagers for at least six weeks and does not pasteurize.

The Commune produces about 50,000hl (42,500 US barrels, 30,000 UK barrels) a year and its beers are well distributed in the district, particularly the Ratsherrentrunk – which means the town councillors' drink. In Freistadt, the Goldener Hirsch, in Bohmertorgasse, has old associations with the Braucommune as well as its beers. The town is on the main route between Linz and the Czech Budweiser Budvar brewery at Ceské Budějovice.

RIED

ESTABLISHED 1432

Brauerei Ried, Brauhausgasse 24
4910 Ried im Innkreis

RECOMMENDED

Rieder Braune (4.2%),
dark brown, malty dry and keen hop bitterness
Helles Weizen (5%),
*pale amber, unfiltered, tart fruitiness balanced
by bittersweetness*
Dunkles Weizen (5%),
*dark brown, unfiltered, malty-sweetness recedes
in hop finish*

Ried is another Austrian cooperative brewery, owned among others by local publicans who have had a controlling interest since the beginning of the 20th century. The town's brewing history has been heavily influence by Bavaria which today is 15km (9 miles) away, across a frontier designated by the River Inn.

But at various periods in history Ried has been part of Bavaria and its brewers were then obliged to comply with the Bavarian beer purity law. Today they don't, and a little rice is used in some brews. The brewer favors bitter hops from Bavaria's Tettnang fields plus the aromatic Bohemian Saaz, which may help explain why Brauerei Ried's beers have a little more hop bite than some other Austrian brews. Some beers are 'green' – made with organically grown ingredients.

The town carries on a wheat beer tradition which was reduced when a small, specialist wheat beer producer closed in the early 1980s. But the town still has a second, smaller brewery, Kellerbräu. The cooperative is three times bigger than Kellerbräu with annual production of 72,000hl (61,000 US barrels, 44,000 UK barrels).

ALSO WORTH TRYING

Austria's biggest concentration of breweries is in the Bavarian border region north of Salzburg across to Freistadt. Worth seeking out: **Ritterbräu** Export (5.5%, amber, malty) at Neumarkt am Hausdruck; **Brauerei Baumgärtner** at Schärding has a spicy, malty Märzen (5.5%) and the neighboring **Brauerei Kapsreiter** offers a brown, malty-dry Landbier (5.3%); in Ried, **Kellerbräu's** Annen Pils (4.9%, firm hop bitterness); further south at Vorchdorf the **Eggenberger** brewery has an oddity called Nessie (7.5%) which has a very dry, smoky flavor from smoked malt, plus Austria's strongest beer Urbock 23 (9.5%). Northeast (Kefermarkt) and southeast (Klam bei Grein) of Linz are two small castle breweries. The latter's **Burgbrauerei Clam** produces two ales, top-fermented then cold-conditioned like Düsseldorf Alt.

STIFTSBRÄUEREI SCHLÄGL

ESTABLISHED 1580

Aigen, 4160 Schlägl

RECOMMENDED

Gold Roggen (4.9%),
golden, top-fermented rye beer, slightly tart
Märzen (5%),
reddish-amber, full-bodied and spicy
Doppelmalz (5.2%),
dark brown, Munich-style dunkel
Doppelbock (7%),
dark amber, rich malty body, dryish

Unlike many other breweries with deep roots, Austria's only monastery brewery is probably being modest about its late 16th century origins. Cistercian monks established their settlement here over 300 years earlier in 1218. But the monastery is also guardian of an ancient library and is fastidious about facts. Surviving brewhouse records start in 1580.

The small brewery maintains traditional methods, with open fermentation and long lagering in stone cellars – a minimum of six weeks for the everyday beers, while the midwinter Doppelbock matures for 12 weeks. Hops are from the surrounding Mühlviertel fields, and calcium-rich, untreated water is drawn from a well which the monks say is fed from the Bohemian Forest across the nearby border.

In the past pilgrims and beggars were given beer at the gate; today's visitors have to pay, but can enjoy an atmospheric beer cellar. Beforehand, the adjoining ornate baroque church and the library and art collections are also worth visiting.

JOSEF HUBER

ESTABLISHED 1727

Brauerei Huber, Brauweg 2, 6380 St Johann

RECOMMENDED

Edelweizen Hell (5.2%),
unfiltered, spicy with gentle citric background
Edelweizen Dunkel (5.2%),
dark brown, unfiltered, mellow malt sweetness balanced by spritzy light tart finish
Augustinus (5.6%),
brown, malt fruit flavors, dry finish

By today's standards this is a micro-brewery – 20,000hl (17,000 US barrels, 12,200 UK barrels) a year – and probably the world's oldest. But although Huber's interesting range of beers are distributed in a radius of only 30km (19 miles) from the brewery, they have been drunk by people from all over western Europe and beyond because of St Johann's position as a major winter skiing resort.

The family-run brewery has its own well, observes the German Reinheitsgebot purity law, and uses only Bavarian and Bohemian whole hops. Brewing methods are traditional, all the beers are conditioned for at least six weeks and there is no pasteurization. Huber's wheat beers are very Bavarian in style. There are filtered and unfiltered versions of the pale wheat variety.

ALSO WORTH TRYING

Western Austria – the finger of land pointing at Switzerland and a major skiing playground – has about 20 breweries, from Salzburg at the base to Dornbirn at the tip. Three of these are in Salzburg, two are in Innsbruck, and four nestle close together in the fingernail province of Vorarlberg at Egg, Bludenz, Frastanz, and Dornbirn.

Beers worth seeking include: Sigl Weizengold unfiltered pale and dark varieties in Obertrum; the monastery Märzen (5.2%, dark amber, unfiltered) of **Augustinerbräu** in Salzburg; **Bernd Tobisch's** unfiltered wheat beer (5%, lemon-gold, tart-sweet) at the Die Weisse pub next to the tiny brewery in Virgilgasse 9, Salzburg; **Ponguer** Dunkel (5.2%, dark brown, malty bittersweet) from Schwarzach in the mountains near the beauty spot Zell am See; **Branger** Märzen (5.5%, reddish-brown, malty) from the 1993-established micro in Innsbruck; Edelpils (4.8%, very hoppy and dry) from the **Egg** brewery in Vorarlberg; and in the mountains above the Inn Valley southeast of Innsbruck the small **Zillertal** brewery at Zell am Ziller – in the same family for 300 years – produces a powerful 7.5% amber May bock called Gauderbock for the local spring festival which has its roots in the 16th century.

THE CZECH REPUBLIC

The Czechs are the world's thirstiest beer drinkers, downing 161 liters (283 UK pints) per person a year. So it's hardly surprising that when Czechoslovakia split into two republics in 1993, the Czechs ended up with most of the breweries. There are 85 today, although this number seems certain to shrink as the brewing industry confronts a free-for-all market economy.

The privatization of the industry since 1990 has led to fierce competition and the entry of foreign buyers – from Austria, Britain, Germany, and the US. Britain's Bass has declared an ambition to control 25 percent of the total market and in 1996 already had 16 percent. Such developments may be good for shareholders but they are not necessarily so for consumers. On a brighter note, also since 1990, the Czechs' love of beer has led to the creation of 18 microbreweries.

STAROPRAMEN

ESTABLISHED 1869

Smíchov Brewery, Nádražní 84
154 54 Praha 5

RECOMMENDED

Staropramen pale 12 (5%),
golden, hop flower aroma, malty flavors, crisp dry finish
Staropramen dark 12 (4.6%),
dark brown, burnt malt taste, malty-dry finish

Smíchov is the largest of Prague's five breweries and part of the three-brewery company called Prazské Pivovary in which British brewer Bass has an influential share (40 percent in 1996). The group has about ten percent of the domestic beer market. Smíchov concentrates on producing Staropramen.

Smíchov (1.3 million hl, 1.1 million US barrels, 790,000 UK barrels) was created during the 19th century

industrialization of Prague alongside the River Vltava, from which a soft water supply is drawn. Against the Czech trend, and at Bass's insistence, the brewery has remained a traditional operation with 140 open fermentation squares and classical horizontal lagering tanks. A new brewhouse is due to open in 1997 but Bass adviser Steve Denny, a microbiologist, said it would continue to allow oxidization of the liquor. 'We won't change the physical and chemical processes.'

Staropramen is 100 percent barley malt, fermented for seven days. The 10 degree beer is lagered for three weeks and the 12 degree for 10 weeks.

U FLEKŮ

ESTABLISHED 1499

Kremencova 11, Nove Mesto, Prague 1

RECOMMENDED

Flekovsky dark 13 (5.5%),
black, yeasty aroma, thick, malty and spicy taste

U Fleků is unchallenged contender for the title of World's Oldest Brewpub. It is a thriving leftover of a system which flourished in Prague – where there were

Above: The entrance to Prague's historic U Fleků.

dozens of brewpubs until the early 19th century – and throughout Europe before the industrialization of brewing.

The house beer, bottom-fermented, is as earthy as the pub. Four malts are used, including Munich and roasted, plus Bohemian hops, and it is lagered for at least six weeks. U Fleků is once again privately owned but not by the family whose name it has borne since the 18th

Above: Cool beer in U Fleků's cool courtyard.

century. The small brewery was modernized in a most unobtrusive way during its communist tenure and nothing has been done to detract from the medieval-like dark, vaulted drinking rooms whose walls and ceilings are covered in ancient paintings paying tribute to God's 'gifts' to brewing. But commercialization has brought some unwelcome changes – such as an admission charge and high prices which drive away locals in favor of tourists.

PILSNER URQUELL

ESTABLISHED 1842

Plzeňský Prazdroj, U Prazdroje 1
304 97 Plzeň

RECOMMENDED
Pilsner Urquell 12 (4.4%),
pale golden, heady hop aroma, firm-bodied hoppiness, gentle malt background and bitter-dry finish

This historic brewery's uniqueness has disappeared in a splurge of modernization and expansion. The oak fermenting vessels and huge maturation barrels which performed their magical work in dank, sandstone cellars have been replaced by a forest of closed conical fermentation tanks as tall as Space Shuttle launchers. The new stainless steel operation has halved the time it takes to make Urquell 12 to about four weeks.

These changes were made in the name of progress. Ironically, an official communist handbook of 1986 sentimentally sums up what had been special: 'Since the last century beer has been produced by means of a single unchanging technological procedure.

The unimitable (sic) taste and aroma are attributed to the quality of water, the malt itself and to the microclimatic conditions of the 9km (5.5 miles) long underground corridors.'

Bohemian Žatec (Saaz) whole hops, Moravian pale malt, and the brewery's own very soft well-water are still employed. Urquell is freshest in the 500-seat beer hall in the converted old maltings inside the brewery yard. Daily brewery tours (tel: 019-706-2632, fax: 019-706-2715) are available. See also 'The Origins of Pilsner' (pages 132-133)

DOMAZLICE

ESTABLISHED 1341

Pivovar Domažlice, Komenskeho 10
334 37 Domažlice

RECOMMENDED
Prior kvasnicové (unfiltered wheat 5.0%),
deep amber, very yeasty aroma, very dry with a bitter, spicy flavor
Purkmistr tmávé 12 (4.8%)
black, malty aroma, rich coffee bitterness

Domažlice is the smallest of the four breweries in the Pilsner Urquell Corporation group – a fifth was closed in 1995 – but it seems to have found a safe niche producing specialty beers.

Purkmistr is one of the tastiest and most widely available dark beers in the Czech Republic, although it is less palatable in its 10-degree form.

Perhaps it was more than coincidence that led to this old established brewery near the Bavarian border producing a Bavarian-style wheat beer. Many Bavarians visit Domažlice which has rekindled historic links with towns just across the border. But the Prior wheat is more bitter than many Bavarian wheat beers. In Domažlice, Prior and Purkmistr can be drunk at the beer-restaurant Pivnice U Certa.

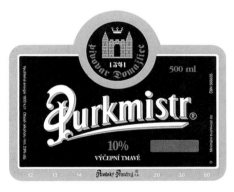

ALSO WORTH TRYING

From Prague Breweries' **Holesovice** brewery near Prague Castle, Mestan dark 11 (4.1%, brown, malty, bitter-sweet); Radegast pale 12 (5.1%, fruity and dryish) one of the first national brands, from Frydek-Mistek near the Slovak border; Bernard Dark 11 (4.9%, light brown, full-bodied, malty-dry) from a small but modernized brewery in Humpolec southeast of Prague; Pilsner Urquell's stablemate from Plzeň,

Gambrinus 12 (5.1%, very pale, slightly fruity, and hoppy); Lucan (3.6%, fruity pale lager), and Chmelar – meaning hop picker – (4.2%, golden, hoppy, dry) are brewed in Žatec; Primator Dark 12 (5.1%, brown, chocolatey, dry) from **Nachod's** municipally-owned brewery; and from Pardubice, about 100km (60 miles) east of Prague, Pardubice Porter (7%, dark ruby, licorice sweetness becomes dry).

THE ORIGINS OF PILSNER

The story of the world's most widely known beer style – Pilsner – is peppered with ironies, but it begins humiliatingly on the town square of Plzeň in Bohemia on an unusually mild day in February 1838. In a spectacle not unlike a public execution, townsfolk watched with grim satisfaction as the local authorities declared 36 barrels of beer unfit for human consumption and forced the brewers to watch as the barrels were broken open and the contents poured over the cobbles in front of the town hall.

It was not the first time that local beer had been found wanting, but the problem was not confined to Plzeň. Until the early part of the 19th century brewing everywhere was a largely unscientific practice plagued by infection due to lack of hygiene or excessively warm temperatures. In style the beer was ale. It was usually murkily dark; it was unfiltered; and in central Europe in particular, warm summers and the absence of refrigeration often made it go sour.

But that public humilation in Plzeň town square galvanized the local brewers into action. They had heard about new techniques being used across the border to the west in southern Bavaria to produce a new type of beer – what is now called lager beer. The Bavarians had recognized that some yeast – bottom-fermenting yeast – worked better in colder temperatures. It was still a largely unscientific perception, but the Bavarians knew that by storing their beer in cold places – in mountain caves or ice-filled cellars – it matured better and its taste improved.

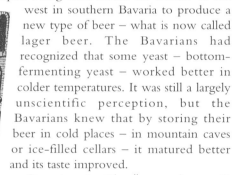

Brewing in Plzeň was then still undertaken on a very small scale, in brewpubs, by 260 families with hereditary rights granted by King Wenceslas II when he issued the town with its foundation charter in 1295. They all pooled their resources to build a large cooperative brewery which could produce the new style of beer. As it neared completion in early 1842 they dispatched one of the shareholders, Martin Stelzer, to scour Bavaria for a brewer who knew the new techniques and who would move to Plzeň and work for them. Stelzer hired Josef Groll, a 29 year-old brewer and maltster from the small Bavarian town of Vilshofen in the Bavarian Forest, near Passau.

For Groll it was a dream: a free hand in a brand new brewery equipped with labyrinthine, naturally cold cellars dug into the soft sandstone. His employers wanted him to reproduce the new style of Bavarian beer, pale brown, malty, clean, and fresh tasting. What emerged surprised everyone, not least Groll.

'He intended to brew a quite different beer but the result was not what he expected,' says the director of the Plzeň Brewery Museum, Peter Zizkovsky, who has researched into the origins of Pilsner Urquell. 'It was a kind of mistake – but a very good one.'

Groll had married his new Bavarian brewing methods – lager – with Bohemian ingredients, most importantly the local pale barley malt. The first batch of beer from the new Bürgerliches Brauhaus, or Burghers' Brewery, was ready to drink at the town's Martinmas Fair in November 1842. It caused a sensation and Groll was the toast of the town. The accidental combination of local raw materials and Groll's techniques resulted in the world's first golden-colored, hoppy beer.

It was initially called Kaiserquell in deference to the Austrian emperor whose royal household was soon regularly supplied with it, so adding to its fashionability. But inevitably, the beer was dubbed 'Pilsner' and later Pilsner Urquell, which is German meaning 'Pilsner from the primary or original source.' In Czech, it's called Prazdroj.

It is better known today by the German name because for centuries many parts of Bohemia had ethnic German as well as Czech-speaking communities, and at the time of this brewing development German was the official language as the region was ruled from Vienna. Pilsen is the German way of spelling the town; Plzeň the Czech. Nowadays, the Czechs will label their beer for export 'Pilsner,' but in Germany and many other countries it is spelt Pilsener, or abbreviated to Pils.

The brewery which was to have such a world impact nevertheless had a modest beginning, and in its first year produced less than 50 barrels a week. Today, using technology which makes traditionalists cringe, annual production is more than 1,125,000hl (969,000 US barrels, 687,000 UK barrels) and the beer is exported to 52 countries.

Its early fame was helped by the development of two spas in Bohemia near Plzeň, best known by their German names, Karlsbad and Marienbad (Karlovy Vary and Mariánské Lásně), which attracted Europe's rich and famous. They sipped the nauseating spa waters at their doctors' insistence, but heartily drank a Pilsner afterwards.

Pilsner's rapid rise in popularity was also helped by the increasing use of glass, instead of metal and earthenware mugs, which allowed the beer's unique golden sparkle to be admired. People were beginning to drink with their eyes for the first time.

Above: The way it was: abandoned methods in Plzeň. Such cellars are no longer used.

Sadly, down the decades the genuine article has spawned countless inferior pale imitations made by those seeking to benefit from the fame of the original by labelling their products Pilsner. German brewers generally come closest to copying Urquell.

Brewer Groll may have secured a place in brewing history, but his tenure in Plzeň was short. The townspeople were ecstatic about his brewing but grew to dislike him personally, according to Zizkovsky. Groll fought with many citizens of Plzeň and when his contract expired in 1845 it was not renewed. He returned to the obscurity of rural Bavaria.

However, such was now the prestige of working in Plzeň, that the brewery organized an international competition to find Groll's successor. And another Bavarian won it – Sebastian Baumgärtner. He came from Munich where he had brewed another beer which was becoming famous, the strong Salvator doppelbock. In fact, Urquell's first four brewers were all Bavarians and their reign lasted until the beginning of the 20th century. 'Their instructions were simple,' says Zizkovsky. 'Brew the beer like Groll did.'

The heirs of those citizens who were granted eternal brewing rights in 1295 continue to fare well. They were given a collective shareholding of 9.5 percent in Urquell when it was sold back into private ownership in 1994 after the communist state-owned era – a small fortune in anybody's currency. The rest of the Corporation is now owned by Czech banks and investment groups. And in a attempt to protect the Czech Republic's 'family silver,' the government has placed a five-year ban on the sale of any shareholding to foreign interests. This moratorium also prohibits, for the next few years at least, Pilsner Urquell from being brewed abroad under licence.

Above: Žatec, or Saaz, hops growing in northern Bohemia.

BUDWEISER BUDVAR

ESTABLISHED 1895

Budějovický Budvar, Karoliny Svetle 4
370 21 České Budějovice

RECOMMENDED

Budvar 12 (5%),
copper color, rich malty aroma and taste, soft bittersweet finish.
The brewery also produces a 10 degree (4.1%) version which is increasingly distributed domestically, plus an 8 degree **Budvar 'light'** (3%),
primarily for Sweden

The fame of this jewel in the Czech brewing crown is shared almost equally between its beer and its David and Goliath battles with the American giant Anheuser-Busch. A trademark dispute over the name 'Budweiser' has been in progress between the two for over 50 years, but their rivalry has intensified in the 1990s as A–B pursues a shareholding in Budvar.

During the communist era, Budvar was a rarity in its own country because most of it was exported. Since 1989 annual brewing capacity has doubled to 900,000hl (767,000 US barrels, 500,000 UK barrels), with foreign markets taking 60 percent. Budvar exports more beer than any other Czech brewery; almost half goes to the discerning Germans.

It remains largely a traditionalist producer, using open fermentation and

Above: Budweiser Budvar is proud of its long traditions.

classical slow lagering in horizontal tanks. However, the faster system of enclosed continuous fermentation looms.

The brewhouse of eight tall, gleaming coppers is perhaps the most spectacular sight in the Czech brewing industry. Budvar 12 is made from 100 percent Moravian barley malt, full flower Bohemian hops, a single yeast strain known as No. 2 (Urquell has No. 1), and naturally soft water from a vast underground lake tapped exclusively by Budvar. The beer is now pasteurized in bottle.

The Czech government has received about 50 foreign offers for Budvar, but as we went to press Budvar remained state-owned – one of the few breweries still to be so. Budvar 12 is widely available now within the Czech Republic, but in České Budějovice it is best at Masné Kramy, an atmospheric town-center beer hall which was once a meat market.

REGENT

ESTABLISHED 1379

Pivovar Regent, Trocnovske namesti 12
37914 Třeboň

RECOMMENDED

Regent tmávé 12 (Regent Black in UK, 4.2%),
coal black, licorice aroma, full-bodied, slightly burnt malt flavor and dryish finish
Bohemia Regent 12 (4.8%),
copper-colored, yeasty aroma, fruity flavor
Bohemia Regent 10 (3.5%),
noticeably thinner but a refreshing dry taste

This handsome brewery has been in the same Renaissance buildings, converted from a manorial armory, since 1698 when it moved from a nearby site which

had been a brewhouse since the 14th century. The brewery's own malt, from local barley fields, is still partially turned by hand in 16th century cellars.

The beers are fermented in open squares and lagered traditionally in horizontal tanks. There is a risk of modernizing being undertaken to expand production, although head brewer Ivan Dufek believes that 'quality is best managed in small quantities.' Třeboň's 12 degree beers are fermented for ten days. Naturally very soft water comes from two 90m (300ft) deep wells. The 12 degree beers are lagered for six to eight weeks. All the beers are flash pasteurized.

Today, the dark beer accounts for only two percent of the annual 350,000hl (298,000 US barrels, 210,000 UK barrels) annual output, but in the 19th century Třeboň's dark beers were in great demand throughout the Hapsburg empire, including the Vienna royal court. Local demand for the dark beer rises at Christmas when it is traditionally drunk with a meal of carp from surrounding lakes, cooked in dark sweet sauce.

Regent's beers are exported to Austria, Britain, Finland, Germany, Italy, and Sweden. Brewery tours can be booked in advance.

HEROLD

ESTABLISHED 1720

Pivovar Herold, Březnice

RECOMMENDED

Pale 10 (3.8%),
straw-colored, hoppy aroma, crisp, clean taste
Pale 12 (4.8%),
bronze, firm hop aroma, fuller bodied than pale 10 with clean dry finish
Herold wheat (5.2%),
bronze, lemony aroma, crisply tart and spicy
Dark 13 (5.2%),
black, coffeeish flavor, malty-dry finish

Herold was closed in 1988 during communist plans for rationalization. The dilapidated baroque buildings were due for demolition when brewer Stanislav Janostik persuaded the authorities to stay the execution. 'I don't know why really. The situation looked hopeless, but I just didn't want to see the buildings destroyed.' Janostik, one of the most innovative Czech brewers, got the brewery re-opened again in 1990 after the communist collapse, and then celebrated by brewing the first Czech wheat beer for 75 years.

Herold is a small, classical, country brewery, 70km (44 miles) south of Prague, near Příbram, producing less than 60,000hl (51,000 US barrels, 36,500 UK barrels) a year. It has its own maltings where wheat malt is also produced. Naturally soft water comes from a 100-year-old well and is untreated. Hops are from Germany, Belgium, and Žatec.

The brewery uses 16 open fermentation squares and classical lagering is in deep natural cellars dug into the rock beneath the brewery where the temperature is steady at 2°C (36°F). Beers mature for two to three months. Draft beer for the domestic market is not pasteurized. The brewery, now privately owned, has a policy of adhering to traditional methods and will not switch to closed conical fermenters, said Janostik. Herold Wheat is produced with a top-fermenting yeast from Bavaria. It is warm-conditioned for one month.

LOBKOWICZ

ESTABLISHED 1630

Lobkowiczký pivovar, 262 52 Vysoký Chlumec

RECOMMENDED

Pale 12 (5%),
pale golden, light hop aroma, clean tasting, dry
Dark 12 (4.6%),
ruby-brown, roasted malt aroma, malty flavor

Except for the 41-year communist era, this small country estate brewery has belonged to the Lobkowicz family for four centuries. Since being returned to the family in 1992, a close business link has developed with giant Austrian brewers Brau AG.

It is a classical Czech brewery using open fermentation and cellar lagering, although pasteurization of the finished product now takes place. Water comes from wells sunk beneath the estate

forests, local barley is processed in the brewery's own maltings.

Beers include an occasional pale 14 Special at 5.5% ABV. The pale 12 is exported to Britain as Lobkov Export. In return for a low-interest loan Lobkowicz now produces one of Austria's biggest brands, Kaiser, for the Czech market. Lobkowicz will eventually devote one third of its 120,000hl (102,000 US barrel, 73,000 UK barrel) capacity to Kaiser Premium (5%).

Lobkowicz beers can be drunk at U Hynku, Stupartska 6, in Prague Old Town, and Restaurace St Hospoda near the Lobkowicz family castle in Vysoký Chlumec.

ALSO WORTH TRYING

In south Bohemia, in the beautiful medieval town of Český Krumlov, **Eggenberg** pale 12 (5%, full-bodied, hoppy); České Budějovice's other brewery, **Samson**, offers a dark 10 (3.6%, tawny-brown, coffeeish) and pale 12 – marketed abroad as Crystal (5.2%, copper, slightly fruity, dry finish); in Protivín **Platan** pale 12 (5%, dry, hoppy) and Platan dark 10 (3.6%, burnt malt, dry); **Strakonice's** Nektar pale 10 (3.8%, fruity, very dry) and Dudak pale 12 (4.8%, vanilla aroma, crisply dry). New microbreweries are in **Kácov**, **Tabor** and **Zvíkovské Podhradí**, near Pisek. The one at Kácov, 50km (30 miles) south of Prague along the Prague-Brno motorway, is inside a defunct brewery dating from 1457 and has plans to open a small 'beer hotel.' Kácov unfiltered beers are at U Bergneru, Slezska 134, Prague.

PEGAS

ESTABLISHED 1992

Jabuska 4, 602 00 Brno

RECOMMENDED

(all unfiltered)

Ginger beer (4%),
red-brown, peppery aroma, soft textured, mild

Pegas pale (4%),
copper, yeasty aroma, soft full-bodied and bittersweet finish

Pegas dark (4%),
dark brown, chewy, coarse beer, fruity-dry

A wheat beer occasionally is brewed

This is probably the most successful and innovative microbrewery to open since a free market economy was reinstituted in the Czech Republic. The private owners have fashioned a modern version of an ancient town inn: food, drink, and lodging under one roof. The beer is brewed in the basement, it's drunk on the ground floor in a busy beer hall, and can be slept off in clean bedrooms above.

Bushy-bearded, shy, but enthusiastic brewer Vladimir Stejskal has produced a wheat beer and a refreshing bottom-fermented ginger beer, with ground ginger root replacing some hop content.

Vladimir does not think much of filtration: 'It deprives beer of many good qualities of taste and nutrients.' That view is clearly shared by Pegas customers. He brews about 3,000 barrels a year.

Above: Hotel Pegas – Brno's highly popular brewpub.

Some is sold to other pubs in the area, but most of it is drunk in house – about 1,150l (2,000 pints) a day. Most beer is matured for 21 days following a six-day fermentation. Pelletized Žatec hops and four different Czech malts are used.

RADEGAST

ESTABLISHED 1970

Pivovar Radegast, Frydek-Mistek
739 51 Nosovice

RECOMMENDED

Radegast pale 12 (5.1%),
golden, fruity aroma, dryish taste and finish

Radegast dark 10 (3.6%),
dark brown, malty with a slightly burnt caramel edge

To other Czech brewing companies, Radegast is as menacing as the pagan Slavonic god after which it is named. Quickly privatized when the free market was re-established because of its large and relatively modern condition, Radegast has become an aggressive company. Its takeover of a north Bohemian brewery in late 1995 took it into second place in brewing size behind the Pilsner Urquell Corporation, knocking Prague Breweries into third place.

Radegast's greenfield Moravian site close to the Slovak and Polish borders is an off-beat location on the redrawn map of central Europe, but in the late 1960s it must have seemed like good planning to site it adajcent to fraternal east European Comecon neighbors.

Radegast was the first large new Czech brewery for about 60 years. By 1995, annual production was up to 1.6 million hl (1.36 million US barrels, 1 million UK barrels) with further expansion up to 2 million hl (1.7 million US barrels, 1.2 million UK barrels) envisaged. Moravian barley malt is used with hops from several sources including some Bohemian Žatec. Fast fermenters are employed. A strong 18 degree (7% ABV) Bock has been test marketed and may become a year-round beer.

Today's 100 percent Czech ownership comprises a mix of banks, shareholding funds, and about 15,000 small investors who were allowed to take part in the country's so-called coupon privatization gold rush. The company now also has an influential 13 percent stake in the equally popular Velké Popovice brewery.

OLOMOUC

ESTABLISHED 1896

Pivovar Olomouc, Holicé, 772 11 Olomouc

RECOMMENDED

Holan 10 (3.5%),
amber, unfiltered version is fruity-dry with a yeasty aroma

Vaclav 12 (5.6%),
amber, hoppy aroma, bittersweet with a malty background

Granat 12 (5.6%),
deep burgundy, coffee aroma, rich malty flavor, long, dry finish

Nazi occupiers closed the brewery in World War II, but the communists reopened it in 1948. Such can be the political fate of brewing. The unsung hero of the brewhouse is Granat, which sadly is almost as popular in Taiwan, where some of it is exported, as in its home town. Local pungent curd cheese called Olomoucké is the perfect accompaniment to it .

Olomouc has its own maltings and produces pale malt from Moravian barley; its own well-water is medium hard and is untreated. Moravian as well as Žatec hops go in the brewhouse's five coppers, plus Bavarian Hallertau hop extract. Olomouc converted to closed computer-controlled fermentation in 1990 but has stayed with traditional lagering – 35 to 40 days for the 12.

Granat makes up ten percent of Olomouc's output but the brewery, which is part of a privatized group of six Moravian breweries, has been operating below its capacity of 200,000hl (170,000 US barrels, 122,000 UK barrels). In 1995 it contracted to brew America's infamous Texan brand, Lone Star.

VELKÉ POPOVICE

ESTABLISHED 1871

Pivovar Velké Popovice, Ringhofferova 1
251 69 Velké Popovice

RECOMMENDED

Kozel pale 12 (5%),
hoppy and dry tasting with a hint of fruitiness
Kozel dark 10 (4.3%),
dark brown, malty aroma, fullsome and fruity

This brewery is so popular that, when it was privatized in 1993, the share issue was greatly oversubscribed and more than 25,000 people acquired small shareholdings. Unfortunately, Popovice's biggest shareholder with a 13 percent stake is Radegast, the mushrooming brewing giant in Moravia.

The brewery was founded on a country estate by 19th century Prague industrialist and idealist Franz Ringhoffer. His plan was: grow the hops and barley, brew the beer, feed the spent waste to cattle. It proved highly successful.

Popovice remains a traditionalist producer – open fermentation, horizontal lagering in small scale tanks, unpasteurized beer on demand, but general manager Jiri Kozak has spoken about the 'delicate finesse of conical fermenters,' which probably heralds high-tech developments.

Popovice is expanding aggressively and has captured about five percent of the Czech market – producing 1.2 million hl (1 million US barrels, 730,000 UK barrels) a year. The dark 10 was re-introduced in 1991. Kozel means 'billy goat' – the brewery's emblem.

ALSO WORTH TRYING

Brno's **Starobrno** Premium (5.1%), is golden, full-bodied and malty, ending bittersweet (an unfiltered version is fruity and drier), while dark Drak (Dragon, 5.9%) is chocolatey-rich and malty-sweet, matured for four months for Christmas; Granat (3.5%), dark brown with a long malty taste, comes from **Černa Horá Brewery** north of Brno; Jezek pale 11 (3.8) has a lemony aroma, and fruity-dry taste from the **Jezek** (hedgehog) **Brewery** in Jihlava, now owned by Austria's Zwettl Brewery; the **Ostravar** Brewery in Ostrava (now owned by Britain's Bass) offers Ondras 12 (5.2%), golden, hoppy, crisp, and Vranik Porter (3.8%), chestnut brown, with burnt malt flavor, and long, dry finish; on the Austrian border in spectacular castle country at Znojmo the small **Hostan Brewery** has a full-bodied, dry, hoppy beer in Hostan Pale 12 (4.8%), plus Hostan Granat 10 (4%).

GERMANY
MUNICH

Munich is the center of the world's most densely breweried region. The city has 11 breweries, including several newish brewpubs, and there are 20 more brewhouses within a radius of 40km (25 miles). Beyond that, it is difficult to keep count – about 750 throughout Bavaria, although the number is dropping.

Munich's 'Big Six' are Augustiner, Hofbräu, Hacker-Pschorr, Löwenbräu, Paulaner, and Spaten. Munich is associated with the development of bottom-fermentation – lager brewing – and 'Munich Style' is still copied as far away as South America. This usually means dark amber or brown, although today the city's everyday beer is golden – called hell, or helles. Munich is also a center of seasonal strong bock beer brewing, the most noteworthy being Paulaner's Salvator, Hofbräu's Maibock, and Hacker-Pschorr's Hubertus (see pages 146-147).

HOFBRÄU

ESTABLISHED 1589

Staatliches Hofbräuhaus in München,
81829 Munich

RECOMMENDED

Münchner Kindl Weiss (5.1%),
burnished gold, yeasty, fruity sharpness
Export (5.2%),
copper, malty with hint of fruit, bittersweet
Dunkel (5.2%),
brown, tart fruitiness, malty-dry finish
Märzen (5.7%),
ruby red, rich malt aroma, malt-accented, dry
Maibock (7.2%),
copper, rich malt laced with hops to give a spicy malty-dry taste

The world's most famous beer hall is no longer home to the brewery of kings.

Hofbräu beers today are brewed in a nondescript, ultra-modern building surrounded by wheat and barley fields on the eastern edge of the city. But all the historic imagery lives on in the Hofbräuhaus in the heart of Munich's old town center.

Hofbräu – meaning 'royal court brew' – belonged to Bavaria's ruling monarchy for 330 years until the family abdicated in 1919 amid Germany's post-World War I political chaos. It was then acquired by the Bavarian state and has remained in public ownership ever since.

For a couple of centuries the royal brewery was a great wheat beer (weissbier) producer – helped by the monarch's monopoly of the wheat market. Hofbräu is also closely associated with the development of bock. A classic

pale version – Maibock – blends three Bavarian malts and Hallertau hops. It is lagered for eight weeks and tapped before the Bavarian Prime Minister, or Munich's Lord Mayor, at a typical Bavarian beer ritual. Such Hofbräuhaus ceremonies are held upstairs, while the ground floor caters for crowds who sway to the obligatory brass brand.

An historical aside: this is the only hostelry known to have given succor to both Lenin and Hitler – at different turbulent times.

ISARBRÄU

ESTABLISHED 1988

Isarbräu Gaststätte, Kreuzeck Strasse 23
80686 Munich

RECOMMENDED

Isartal Weisse (5.4%),
dark amber, tart fruitiness and dryish
Dunkles (5.2%),
black, firm hoppiness with a malty interplay

The gleaming copper works sparkle at the fashionable customers in this chic, wood-panelled, brewpub/restaurant located in a converted railway station booking hall. You can set your watch by the suburban trains which stop on the adjacent platform – bringing the early evening rush of thirsty drinkers.

Isarbräu began as a wheat-beer-only producer, recognizing the rising appeal of the beer style in the 1980s, but the brewer has since become more adventurous, producing seasonal specialties and a black lager 'brewed to a Czech recipe,' using Bohemian hops instead of the nearby Hallertau.

SPATEN

ESTABLISHED 1397

Spaten-Franziskaner-Brau, Mars-strasse 46
80335 Munich

RECOMMENDED

Ludwig Thomas Dunkel (5.5%),
dark lager, malty, fruity dryness
Franziskaner Hell Weissbier (5%),
copper, cloudy wheat, fruity with tart dryness
Pilsner (5%),
powerful hop flavor battles with a malty background, bitter-dry
Premium Bock (6.5%),
golden, maltiness tempered by hoppy background
Optimator (7.3%),
dark ruby, full-bodied malt richness, spicy

Spaten is one of Munich's oldest and most historically significant breweries although Augustiner claims an even older medieval lineage. Spaten – 'spade' in German – achieved its place at the top table of brewing history after the Sedlmayr family took over in the early 19th century.

Gabriel Sedlmayr junior made giant strides in the 1830s and 1840s in understanding the importance and action of yeast in beer-making. The Sedlmayr family is still largely in control of Spaten, which has grown significantly in recent years through acquisitions to rank tenth in size nationally, owning six breweries across southern Germany.

The Munich brewery remains in the city center, not far from the main railway station, and still draws brewing

Above: A spade logo identifies Munich's Spaten brewery.

water from its own deep wells. The brewer favors Bavarian summer barleys, and hops come from nearby Hallertau north of Munich.

The stronger beers such as Optimator are still matured traditionally in deep vaulted cellars. The best place in Munich to sample the Spaten range is the Spatenhaus, Residenz Strasse 12.

FORSCHUNGSBRAUEREI

ESTABLISHED 1936

Unterhachingstrasse 76, Perlach
Munich 81737

RECOMMENDED

Pilsissimus Export (5.4%),
deep amber, soft malty body, firm hoppiness
St Jakobus Bock (7.8%),
amber, full-bodied maltiness and spicy

On the southeast edge of Munich, flanked on one side by cornfields, this middle-aged microbrewery opens only seven months of the year. The rest of the time the Jakob family, who founded the brewery, carry out experimental work for other brewers. But when the cosy mahogany-panelled tavern and beer

garden attached to the brewery are open, beer lovers from far and near swarm to it like flies round an open jam jar. The beer is served only in liter-sized earthenware mugs, which makes drinking the bock a little dangerous as well as delightful. Sweet south Bavarian pale and colored malts, plus Hallertau hops are combined with a special Jakob house yeast.

The pub's annual re-opening in early March, and the shutdown in mid-October, are well celebrated.

ALSO WORTH TRYING

In Munich, **Augustiner's** Helles (5.2%, delicate malt sweetness); **Löwenbräu's** Weissbier (5.3%, tart dry) and Dunkel, which is becoming rare (5.3%, spicy-dry); **Hacker-Pschorr's** magnificent spring season Hubertus Bock (6.8%, copper, fruity, hoppy, dry); **Paulaner's** Salvator Doppelbock (7.5%, dark ruby, malty-dry, dangerously drinkable) and Pilsener (4.8%, very hoppy, very dry) are best tried at the Nockherberg beer hall and garden where there are usually half a dozen varieties on tap.

In the Munch region, the **Andechs Monastery**, near Ammersee Lake, has export Dunkel (5%, nutty) and Doppelbock (7%, fruity); **Kaltenberg's** König Ludwig Dunkel (5.1%, malty, bitter); **Maisacher's** Export (5.5%, pale, hoppy bitter, dry); at Au in the Hallertau hop-growing district, **Schlossbräu** serves distinctive pale and dark unfiltered beers in castle cellars; not to be missed is the pub adjoining the world's oldest brewery – **Weihenstephan** (1040) in Freising – offering a beer menu (Bierkarte) with 10 choices.

AYINGER

ESTABLISHED 1878

Brauerei Aying, 85653 Aying

RECOMMENDED

Altbairisch Dunkel (5%),
reddish brown, nutty flavor and malty aftertaste
Jahrhundert-Bier (5.5%),
pale, full-bodied, malty-dry
Bräu-Weisse (5.1%),
*pale wheat, light tartiness, bitter edge, light
dryish finish*
Ur-Weisse (5.8%),
*dark brown wheat, rich dark tart fruit, malt
sweetness*
Maibock (7.2%),
*very pale, hoppy aroma, apple-fruity flavors and
bittersweet*
Celebrator (7.5%),
*dark doppelbock, rich fruitcake, warm maltiness
and dryish finish*

Some brewers specialize in only one particular beer and style; others specialize in variety. Ayinger relishes being in the latter category. The family-owned brewery produces 12 different beers over the year, ranging from everyday pale and dark lagers to wheat beers and seasonal and festival specials. Ayinger trades successfully on its country Bavarian status and confirms the quality of its range by luring many

residents of beer-saturated Munich 25km (15 miles) away to drink at the picturesque brewery 'tap,' Liebhard's Bräustüberl, where pale and dark lagers are served unfiltered on draft. A new innovation is a spring-bottled, unfiltered pale lager (Frühlingsbier, 4.9%). The wheat (weisse) beers are unfiltered.

South Bavarian malt, Bavarian hops, and local spring water are the ingredients. Celebrator, previously called Fortunator, is made with four different barley malts and is matured for four to six months.

The relatively small, 120,000hl-a-year (102,000 US barrels, 73,500 UK barrels) brewery has made a big impression exporting its beer to North America, Italy, France, and Denmark, and winning awards in the United States. Some brands are brewed under licence in Britain by Yorkshire family brewer Samuel Smith.

REUTBERG

ESTABLISHED 1677

Brauereigenossenschaft Reutberg
Am Reutberg 3, 83679 Sachsenkam

RECOMMENDED

Dunkel (4.8%),
*dark brown, big malty-dry flavor, gently hoppy
finish*
Märzen (5.6%),
reddish-brown, fruity with a malt background
Josefibier (6.9%),
dark amber, malty and spicy, dryish
Maibock (6.9%),
*pale golden, hoppy aroma, rich malt flavor,
bittersweet*

The first brewers here were Franciscan nuns, but the present small brewery owes its existence to the fortitude of a local priest who rallied the villagers in the early 1920s when Germany's post-war economic collapse brought brewing at Reutberg to a standstill. Father Alois

Daisenberger, anxious to prevent the structures of his local community from collapsing – and clearly liking a mug of beer – organized a cooperative to keep the brewery in operation.

After some ups and downs that cooperative – Genossenschaft – is today stronger than ever. There are more than 2,000 stakeholders and no-one may hold more than 2,000DM (£800/$1,240) worth of shares. It remains a very rural enterprise – owning its own farm which grows the brewery's sweet barley. Hops used to be home-grown too, but these are now bought in from the Hallertau district north of Munich.

Above: The rustic facade of Reutberg's cooperative.

Josefi is brewed to a 100-year-old recipe and appears only during Lent. It takes its name from a beer originally produced by the nuns to sustain them during the Lenten fast. The nuns are still in the adjoining small convent, though brewer Andreas März declined to say whether they still enjoy a glass or two. The stronger beers are lagered for three months.

An oak-panelled tavern also adjoins the brewery, but most beer-drinking visitors are attracted to Reutberg to sit under chestnut trees and enjoy probably the most beautiful beer-garden view in southern Germany, overlooking a broad sweep of the Bavarian Alps.

KRONENBRÄU

ESTABLISHED 1893

Haupt Strasse, 86450 Altenmünster

RECOMMENDED

Steinbier (4.9%),
*brown, smoky, slightly burnt malt flavor, bitter
and finally very dry*
Dunkelweissbier (5%),
*dark brown, cloudy, toasted malt and tart fruit,
bitterish finish*

Brewing with red-hot stones might seem eccentric, but it was once commonplace in parts of Austria. It was done because brewers had difficulty boiling their wort without damaging the wooden cooking 'pot' with direct heat – and because they had access to a stone called greywacke. Most stone shatters at high temperature, but greywacke can withstand temperatures of 1,200°C (2,200°F). The brewers heated their greywacke stones over beechwood fires and then immersed them in the wort to bring it to the boil.

The method has been adapted by innovative Bavarian brewer Gerd Borges to obtain a smoky, slightly burnt beer flavor. In Altenmünster, pre-heated stones are placed in an open stainless steel bath and the wort is then poured over them. Some malt sugars in the wort stick to the stones, which are removed after they cool while open top-fermentation takes place. Those stones are then placed in maturation tanks – where the green beer is transferred and held for more than two months – and this triggers a secondary fermentation. Tettnang and Hallertau hops are preferred.

A dark wheat beer (Dunkelweiss) is made with the same initial technique, but after primary fermentation it is roughly filtered into bottles and then undergoes a second fermentation. This takes place over three weeks in warm, and later cold, stores.

The beers can be drunk in the Bräustuberl Kronen (closed Mondays) next to the brewery, northwest of Ausburg.

IRSEER KLOSTERBRÄU

ESTABLISHED 1389

Klosterring 1, 87660 Irsee

RECOMMENDED

Kloster Weizen (5.2%),
*pale, cloudy wheat, yeasty, quite bitter, and
tart-dry*
Kloster-Urtrunk (5.6%),
*copper, unfiltered, hoppy and fruity, bitter-dry
finish*
Abts Trunk (11.5%),
*dark, rich, thick and oily like a liqueur,
warming dryish finish*

The recipes of the some of the beers here have been drawn from monastic records, but the brewing monks who had been around since at least the 14th century were sent packing in 1803 during the Napoleonic upheavals – and they have never returned. The brewery is now privately managed along with a pub hotel boasting a stone-vaulted drinking hall and a small museum of brewing antiquities.

The Urtrunk is made with several south Bavarian barley malts and Hallertau hops and is bottom-fermented. It is conditioned traditionally in horizontal tanks in naturally cold, stone-vaulted cellars for at least eight weeks. Urtrunk is served direct from the cellars unfiltered to customers in the adjoining pub, and is also bottled unfiltered. Abts Trunk, incidentally, means the 'abbot's drink.'

During the 19th century, the mentally ill were locked up in the monastery's small, cell-like rooms. Today, its function is even worse: it is where people are trained to become government bureaucrats.

ALSO WORTH TRYING

In south Bavaria, near the Alpine village of Oberammergau famous for its Passion Play, **Ettal Monastery** brews an excellent Dunkel Export (5%, coffeeish, malty-dry) and Curator Doppelbock (7.3%, ruby-red, malty, bitter aftertaste); farther west along the hill line at Nesselwang, **Postbräu** offers Der Postillion (5.3%, dark, malty, bittersweet wheat beer) and a beer museum; beside the expansive Tegernsee lake the Brewhouse of the Bavarian Duke (**Herzoglich Bayerisches Brauhaus**) has a 17th century vaulted beer cellar serving Dunkel Bock (6.4%, malty-sweet); to the east along the River Inn at Au am Inn, **Klosterbräu** offers delicious Märzen (5.5%, brown, nutty, malty-dry) in a cosy old inn; and at Zwiesel close to the Czech border, **Jankabräu** has the Märzen-like Kupfer Spezial (5.6%, copper, fruity-rich, hoppy, dry).

Left: Hallertau hops are used in Klosterbräu's fruity, bitter-dry Urtrunk.

WHEAT BEERS

Weizenbier, Bavaria's most fashionable beer, was a brewing relic in the 1970s, kept alive by a few specialist breweries as 'a Sunday beer after church,' as one brewer put it. Then, it had a mere five percent of the thirsty Bavarian market; today its share has grown to 30 percent.

Hundreds of breweries now seek a slice of that market. In the early 1980s it was found only in bottled form, now it is widely available on draft. It is mostly cloudy because Germans perceive this as indicative of natural, unprocessed yeasty goodness. Ironically, some brewers are merely creating a protein haze to satisfy customers and their beer may be pasteurized. Bottles which are marked *Flaschengärung* are traditionally conditioned and still have living yeast, although some brewers have begun using lager yeasts at the bottling stage. This stabilizes the beer, but robs it of some fruity, tart character.

SCHNEIDER

ESTABLISHED 1850

Emil-Ott Strasse 1, 93309 Kelheim

RECOMMENDED

Schneider Weisse (5.4%),
dark amber, vanilla nose, malty, gently tart

Aventinus (8%),
dark brown, rich fruit aroma, dryish

In the mid-19th century, Georg Schneider was one of the first commoners entrusted with a licence to brew wheat beer. The monarchy and its myriad offshoots had for centuries monopolized the wheat grain market for their own wheat beer breweries. Brewing in the center of Munich, Georg

Above: Schneider Weisse satisfies the biggest thirst!

helped keep the style alive as the new lagers became more popular.

The family now brews in Kelheim in the scenic Mühltal valley. Schneider remains very traditionalist, with open fermenters and the same top-fermenting yeast at all stages. Local hops are used; wheat-barley blends vary up to 60-40 percent.

Primary fermentation of up to five days is followed by bottling, unfiltered, with more yeast and a little unfermented wort. Bottles then have a week at 20°C (68°F) to trigger refermentation and two weeks cold-conditioning before dispatch.

The best place to drink Schneider is the Weisses Bräuhaus in Tal, near Munich's Marienplatz.

HOPF

ESTABLISHED 1910

Weissbrauerei Hans Hopf
Schützenstrasse 10, 83714 Miesbach

RECOMMENDED

Weizen ale (4.7%),
red-brown, yeasty aroma, initial sweetness dries

Weisse Export (4.9%),
deep golden, yeasty aroma, tart lemon taste, bitter-dry edge

Dunkle Weisse (4.9%),
red-brown, coffeeish-malt flavor, bittersweet

Weisseisbock (7.5%),
pear-like aroma, pale, fruity, slightly tart

Hopf is a small award-winning family brewery in the foothills of the Bavarian

Alps which helped hold the wheat beer line when the style became unfashionable. Bottled versions are top-fermented in open fermenters. After four days, the green beer is filtered and mixed with fresh yeast and unfermented wort before bottling and warm-conditioning at 10°C (50°F) for two to three weeks. Draft versions (Export and Dunkles) are fermented in closed tanks with a top-fermenting yeast for ten days and then kegged directly. In 1981, Johann Hopf invented a system for dispensing unfiltered wheat beer on draft. The ratio of wheat malt to barley malt varies between 40 and 50 percent. Saaz and Hallertau hops are used.

Third generation Johann is a regular judge at the Great American Beer Festival. He enjoys innovation and his Weizen ale has an English yeast. The Weisseisbock is chilled to minus 2°C (28°F) for one week after primary fermentation. The alcohol separates from the frozen liquid, after which fresh wort and yeast are added for a secondary fermentation for three weeks.

In Miesbach, visit the Weissbier-bräustüberl on Marienplatz.

Above: Maisel's Spring festival celebrates wheat beers.

MAISEL

ESTABLISHED 1887

Brauerei Gebrüder Maisel
Hindenburger Strasse 9, 95445 Bayreuth

❧

RECOMMENDED

Maisel's Weisse (5.2%),
copper-red wheat, yeasty, apple-fruit tasting, tart-dry finish
Weizen Kristall (5%),
golden filtered wheat, spritzy and dry
Weizenbock (7%),
dark amber, richly full-bodied, spicy

Beer production at the Maisel family brewery has grown by nearly 20 percent in the last ten years to meet the rising demand for wheat beers. Maisel was one of the first to respond to the revival of the old style and today its wheat range accounts for about 70 percent of an annual output of 520,000hl (443,000 US barrels, 320,000 UK barrels), even though the brewery produces a broad range of other beer styles. Ironically,

much of Maisel's wheat beer is drunk outside Bavaria in northern Germany.

Maisel has its own spring water (which has filtered through the granite of the nearby Fichtel Hills) and uses Bavarian grains and Hallertau hops. Rapid expansion has led to closed fermentation in conicals for some beers, but Maisel's Weisse is warm bottle-conditioned for several weeks before leaving the brewery.

In addition to a Pilsner (4.8%, perfumy, dry), Maisel also produces a top-fermenting oddity called Dampfbier (4.9%), amber-red, fruity, and hoppy-dry like English bitter. Any allusion to steam (the meaning of the German word *Dampf*) is confined to Maisel's classical redbrick tower brewery, adjacent to the modern conicals, which the family has preserved as a complete working museum. There is no connection with US 'steam beers.' Tours of the brewery are available Monday to Thursday; call 0921-401-234 two days in advance to ensure an English-speaking guide. Maisel has a Spring wheat beer festival in the brewery grounds on the weekend before Ascension Day.

ANDORFER

ESTABLISHED 1919

Brauerei Andorfer, Rennweg 1, 29413 Andorf

❧

RECOMMENDED

Andorfer Weiss (5.3%),
amber, malty sweetness becomes tart-dry
Weizenbock (6.2%),
dark brown, full-bodied, chocolatey and smooth

It isn't easy to find this old brewpub wheat beer specialist in the steep hills above ancient Passau where a confluence of three rivers swells the Danube as it enters Austria. You have to

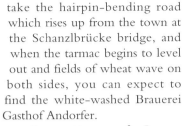

take the hairpin-bending road which rises up from the town at the Schanzlbrücke bridge, and when the tarmac begins to level out and fields of wheat wave on both sides, you can expect to find the white-washed Brauerei Gasthof Andorfer.

Generations of Passau students knew about this gem long before Bavarian wheat beer emerged from the brewing relics drawer to enjoy a renaissance. The family that has brewed here since the end of World War I maintain an unchanging atmosphere; customers come for the beer and to sit in the warren of timeless, dark, wood-panelled rooms.

ALSO WORTH TRYING

Some other Bavarian wheat beers worth sampling: **Augsburg's** Hasenbräu White Hare (Weisser Hase, 5.2%, sweet-sour); big producer **Erdinger** offers bock wheat Pikantus (7.3%, brown, fruity) and a dark style Dunkelweiss (5.6%, chocolatey) best drunk in the brewery's stone-vaulted beer hall in Erding market square, Lange Zeile; on the edge of the Bavarian Alps, **Karg Brewery** in Murnau has two noteworthy wheat beers: Hell Weiss (5%, yeasty, tart fruity, dry), and Schwarzer Woiperlinger (5.3%, dark, apple tartness, sharp  and dry); at Haag, near beautiful Wasserburg southeast of Munich, **Unertl's** Hefeweissbier is very fruity and yeasty (4.8%); and **Weihenstephan** at Freising offers a classic clear variety, Kristallweizen (5.4%, golden, sharp tart fruit, dry) as well as a fruity Hefe.

FRANCONIA

Franconia is a rural region about the size of Wales, with about 400 mostly small family breweries. Scores are run by farmers who supply beer to the village pub, along with pork to the butcher's shop. Some villages have two or three breweries. Bamberg has nine, Bayreuth seven, Amberg five and Kulmbach four. Some old brewing methods and styles have persisted too – smoked beer (Bamberg), Kellerbier (Buttenheim). Kulmbach brews Germany's strongest beer (Kulminator, 13.5%). Brewing in communal village brewhouses also continues with groups of households exercising medieval brewing rights.

Most brewing is now by bottom-fermentation, although some communal beers – known colloquially as Zoigl (pronounced zoy-gull) – are top-fermented.

Sadly, the number of breweries dwindles annually due to economic pressures and new, aggressive marketing from outside the region. Only beer drinkers can prevent Franconia's unique brewing heritage from withering away.

SCHLENKERLA

ESTABLISHED 1678

Brauerei Heller, Dominikaner Strasse 6
96049 Bamberg

RECOMMENDED

Schlenkerla Rauchbier (4.8%),
dark ruby, smoky, slightly oily, very dry
Urbock (October-Christmas, 7.5%),
richer, more full-bodied but still quite smoky

Five generations of the Trum family have brewed Rauchbier, which acquires its taste from infusing germinating barley with beechwood smoke. Originally, this was common practice in the Bamberg area to dry the malted grains for brewing because

Above: The Schlenkerla tavern is an antique jewel.

beechwood was the most abundant local heating fuel. Today it is done specifically as a flavoring agent, using a smoke 'house' in the small brewery now wedged in a tangle of narrow winding streets up the hill from the Schlenkerla tavern (Dominikaner Strasse).

Rauchbier is bottom-fermented in open vessels and lagered for six weeks, filtered but not pasteurized. The beer is served direct from wooden casks in the classic tavern, parts of which dates from the 14th century when it was a monastery. It's closed on Tuesdays.

ST GEORGEN

ESTABLISHED 1624

Marktstrasse 12, 96155 Buttenheim

RECOMMENDED

Vollbier (4.6%),
copper, fruity aroma, gentle malt taste, dry
Kellerbier (4.9%),
amber-red, unfiltered, intensely hoppy, fruity, huge hoppy dry finish
Märzen (5.6%),
dark amber, rich maltiness, apple fruitiness

Before sophisticated filtration and pasteurization were commonplace, hops had a far more prominent role as a preservative. This was especially so with a method of lager brewing which did

not stimulate a vigorous secondary fermentation in the conditioning tanks. It became known as Kellerbier, an unfiltered beer with a level of carbonation like an English ale.

The beer from St Georgen has pale and colored malts and whole hops from Hallertau, and uses soft local water. It is conditioned for about six weeks, and is invariably racked into wooden casks, and served by gravity dispense.

Next door is...another brewery. Löwen is run by a different branch of family Modschiedler which owns St Georgen. It too brews Kellerbier (4.7%, huge hoppy aroma, fruity). Between them they produce 12 different beers – all with a pronounced hoppy character. Both breweries have pubs attached with accommodation.

ALSO WORTH TRYING

In Franconia look out for: Bamberg's **Spezial** Lagerbier (4.9%, lightly smoked), on Obere König Strasse, and opposite **Fässla's** Märzen (5.3%, nutty); **Mahr's** brewery tavern, also in Bamberg, has Vollbier (5.1%, apple fruity); at Memmelsdorf the brewpub **Drei Kronen** offers Stöffla (5.2%, unfiltered, smoky, dry); Märzen is brewed in tiny Neuhaus south of Bayreuth by three families using the **Communbrauhaus** (visit Gaststube Reindl); Bayreuth's **Schinner** has Braunbier (5.1%, malty, slightly tart); Nuremburg's **Altstadhof** brewpub near the castle has Hausbier (4.8%, yeasty, dryish).

Bamberg organizes beer seminars (tel: 0951-871-161) and Bayreuth tourist office (0921-88588) has a program of brewery visits and tastings.

BLACK BEERS

Schwarzbier was commonplace in the 19th and early 20th centuries, but the swing to pale lager undermined it. Insular, rural Franconia was less keen to change, while neglect and an absence of commercial pressures in former East Germany combined to help several black beers survive. Two eastern black brews have been given a new lease of life by new brewery owners from the west (see below).

POTTENSTEIN
Brauerei Georg Mager
ESTABLISHED 1774
Gasthausbrauerei Hufeisen
ESTABLISHED 1803
Wagner Bräu
ESTABLISHED 1840

RECOMMENDED
Mager Dunkles (5.2%),
very hoppy, smooth and quite bitter
Hufeisen Urdunkel (5.4%),
unfiltered, malty with a coffee bitterness
Wagner Altfränkisch Dunkel (5.2%),
burnt malt aroma, full-bodied, malty-dry taste

Elsewhere in the world this quiet, picturesque village surrounded by phallic

Above: Black beer brewing is a Pottenstein specialty.

rock formations would be unusual because it has three High Street breweries. In brewery-rich Franconia, Pottenstein is merely of interest because these three specialize in the black lager art.

Each describes their rich, dark brew as dunkel, which can mean anything from light to dark brown. In Pottenstein, they have a black, porter-like quality although they are bottom-fermented.

The smallest of the three, a modernized brewpub where the gleaming copper sits in the drinking room, brews only black beer, with an occasional dark wheat beer, but the other two have a portfolio of beers. All three also offer accommodation.

NEUZELLE
ESTABLISHED 1589
Neuzeller Klosterbräu, Brauhausplatz 1
15898 Neuzelle

RECOMMENDED
Schwarzbier (4.1%),
toasted malt flavors, smoky, dry finish
Bibulibus (4.8%),
amber, unfiltered, hoppy and fruity

Neuzelle was too small for the big west German brewing companies to gobble up after reunification, as they did with most other East German breweries, but Bavarian Helmut Fritsche has put Neuzelle back on the brewing map and has doubled annual production to nearly 50,000hl (42,500 US barrels, 30,500 UK barrels). More than 50 percent of this is the Schwarzbier. It's claimed that the black beer and unfiltered Bibulibus (from the Latin for drink, *bibere*) are brewed to old recipes left by the Cistercian monks when their property was confiscated in the Napoleonic era. Both beers are bottom-fermented, however.

Fritsche has invested ten million Deutschmarks but has kept traditional methods which he uses to good

commercial effect. 'In the Middle Ages Schwarzbier was the daily bread of the monks, today it is for connoisseurs,' he says. There are no computer-driven operations and a 100-year-old malt mill is still in use. A cooper has been found to make oak casks for local draft beer distribution. Water comes from two brewery wells, barley is grown locally and Fritsche is looking for a farmer also to grow hops locally.

ALSO WORTH TRYING

Other notable black beers: in Franconia, Kulmbach's **Monchshof** produces Klosterschwarz, nicknamed the Black Pils (4.7%, yeasty, hoppy, dry); old farm brewpub **Will** at Schederndorf between Bamberg and Bayreuth brews an unfiltered black lagerbier matured in oak casks (5.3%, smooth, sweet malt, hoppy dry finish); northwards into Thuringia and at Bad Köstritz, near Gera, the Bitburger-owned brewery produces **Köstritzer** Schwarzbier (4.6%, fruity with chocolatey bitterness).

Outside the region, the **Moritz Fiege** brewery in Bochum, near Dortmund, introduced Black Max black beer in 1995.

MUNICH – CITY OF BEER CULTURE

Some cities boast more breweries, some brew more beer. But nowhere else manages to convey the culture of beer quite like Munich, capital of Germany's state of Bavaria. Munich – Münchenn in German – is a city of stark contrasts and contradictions, and beer always seems to flow into the reckoning. It has some of Europe's most exclusive five-star nouvelle cuisine restaurants, and yet hosts the world's most indulgent beer drinking spectacle, the annual Oktoberfest.

Munich is the home of classy BMW, Germany's computer industry, notable art galleries, the most German millionaires – and also the world's biggest pub (the Mathäser, seating 5,000 people), the world's biggest beer garden (Hirschgarten: 8,500), and the most famous beer hall (Hofbräuhaus).

It is a city of high culture: it can boast an opera company, four major orchestras, an annual international film festival, Renaissance and Baroque architecture, and two pristine palaces to remind the world of its royal past. But beer, rather than vintage wine and champagne, lubricates the social circuit – not least at the opera house which even has it own special brew, a doppelbock appropriately called Operator.

Travellers can pass through other important European brewing cities, such as Copenhagen in Denmark or Dortmund in northern Germany, without noticing that they are on an important part of the world beer map. But Munich refuses to let anyone fail to smell, taste, or – at the very least – sense its beery heritage. Even the German Post Office franks letters leaving the city: 'Bierstadt München' (Munich the Beer City).

Right: In 1987, on St Andreas Day (30 November), Munich's 'Big Six' breweries renewed their oath of allegiance to the city's 500-year-old *Reinheitsgebot* or Beer Purity Law.

Beer heralds the seasons here: the end of winter is celebrated with doppelbock; spring is welcomed with Maibock; summer is a 100 crowded beer gardens; autumn almost drowns under the staggering statistics of the Oktoberfest beer festival when ten million pints are drunk during 16 thigh-slapping, brass band-blasting days.

Munich's beery pedigree can be traced back to the early Middle Ages and is also closely associated with the Beer Purity Law, *das Reinheitsgebot*, of 1516. The strong, dark doppelbocks and paler bocks are old Munich specialities, as are wheat beers, and the everyday malty lagers which have been copied around the world under the description 'Munich Style.'

The city's brewing fame stems from the mid-19th century when it was at the forefront of technical advances which perfected the technique of bottom-fermented beer – or lager as it is known in some countries. The pioneering work centered around brewer Gabriel Sedlmayr, whose family is still linked with the city's Spaten Brewery. Today, trainee brewers flock from all corners of the globe to study at two influential brewing schools in the Munich district: Weihenstephan and Doemens.

Münchners are world leaders in beer drinking, averaging 199 liters (350 UK pints) per person per year – higher than both the German national average and the international league champions, the Czechs.

Above: The beer garden is an integral and much loved part of the social fabric in Munich.

like going to the Hofbräuhaus,' she explained, 'where good beer is enjoyed by all classes.'

The number and size of Munich's beer gardens is a city phenomenon. They have their origins in the occasions when fresh beer, which had been stored – lagered – in cool corners of the town before the invention of refrigeration, was tapped. When word got out that a store was being opened up, townsfolk turned up demanding to drink the beer on the spot, when they knew it was freshest, rather than waiting for it to turn up in the taverns. Over time, drinkers brought picnics and eventually such rituals became a family outing.

Today the gardens are an important social meeting place after work and at weekends when the cityfolk seek relief from their cramped apartments in hot weather. The most famous include: Chinesischer Turm (Löwenbräu), Am Nockherberg (Paulaner), Hirschgarten (Augustiner), Neue Schiessstätte (Kaltenberg), and Waldwirtschaft (Spaten). Drinkers are often serenaded with brass oompah bands.

In summer 1995, 15,000 angry Münchners marched through the city after a court ruled that one treasured haunt – the Waldwirtschaft – had to close early because the noise was disturbing some local residents. The Society for the Protection of Beer Garden Culture presented a protest petition of 200,000 names. It caused such a furore that the state government held a special meeting which resulted in a new regulation guaranteeing that all beer gardens could remain open until 11pm. State Premier Edmund Stoiber was obliged to appear before the demonstrators and declare: 'Your beer gardens are safe.'

Their thirst is slaked by the products of 11 breweries, some of which are centuries old, while others have been brewing for less than ten years. The six largest are Hofbräu, Hacker-Pschorr, Löwenbräu, Paulaner, Spaten, and Augustiner, which is the oldest, claiming a history reaching back to 1328. The other five are micros and brewpubs: Forschung, Isarbräu, Unionsbräu (a revived local brewery name), Fliegerbräu, and Paulaner Brauhaus.

Many beer traditions have their roots in the religious calendar and the first of Munich's beer seasons – the Starkbierzeit – is linked with Lent. Munich monks of the 17th century are credited with brewing a strong beer to fortify them while they fasted. This is acknowledged to be the forerunner of the original doppelbock, today's Paulaner Salvator, with a strength of 7.5 ABV. Most people might think it wise to treat such a strong beer with respect, but Munich folk drink it by the liter mug.

Drinking this heady dark brew in such quantities is known in Munich as the *Frühlingskur* – the 'spring cure.' Several of the city's breweries hold special strong beer festivals – *Starkbierfest* – featuring their version of the doppelbock.

Barely has everyone recovered from the spring cure – which is supposed to wipe away the ills of winter – than it's time to celebrate the arrival of summer with rich, spicy, pale Maibock, in particular the varieties produced by Hofbräu and Hacker-Pschorr (Hubertusbock). This means more singing, dancing, and sausage eating – and another excuse to don the *Lederhosen*.

Beer is an unusual social leveller in Munich, and this is not a recent phenomenon. Early this century Lenin's girlfriend Krupskaya wrote to a friend while the couple lived in exile in Munich before the 1917 Russian Revolution: 'We particularly

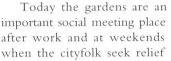

Above: Decorated drays add a splash of color to the Oktoberfest opening ceremonies.

PILSNERS

It speaks volumes that Germany is the biggest export market for Czech Pilsner Urquell. Beer-xenophobe Germans don't drink much foreign brew. But this appreciation of Urquell has not stopped German brewers from trying to surpass the Czech beer. There are hundreds of varieties of German pils or Pilsner (the German spelling for Plzeň when the town was dominated by German speakers was Pilsen), accounting for 60 percent of all beer drunk in Germany.

Many other countries insult Plzeň by stealing the style name and sticking it on thin, bland lagers whose only link with Urquell is the color. German brewers are nothing if not good Pilsner brewers and, in a diffuse market, pils brands are the only ones to have achieved anything like national eminence. Prominent varieties include Bitburger, Dinkelacker, Fürstenberg, Herforder, Jever, König, Krombacher, Maisel, Paulaner, Stauder, Veltins, and Warsteiner. In deference to Urquell, German brewers always prefix their Pilsners with the brewing place name, to avoid any suggestion that it came from Plzeň.

Above: Checking the wort at Bitburger's brewery.

done that while remaining a family-owned business. Perhaps the Simon family's success is all the more remarkable because the brewery is in a quiet rural corner of Germany's Moselle wine-producing region near the border with Luxembourg.

Today the slogan *Bitte ein Bit* – a Bit, please – is understood throughout Germany. The essential ingredients are pale barley malts from the Rhineland and Bavaria, and a mix of aroma and bittering hops from Germany's southern growing districts, plus the brewery's own Siegelhopfen variety grown around Holsthum, a few miles south of the brewery. Bitburger is almost fully fermented to leave little sugar behind; it is lagered for a generous three months and, significantly, is not pasteurized – a process which could mask the beer's delicate hop flavor. Bitburger is exported to 35 countries.

Wilhelmshaven. It is not so widely available as some of its major rivals.

Three 32m (105ft) high reflective glass towers are the centerpiece of a modern expanded brewery in the middle of the small, cobble-laned castle town of the same name. It has an annual output of 1.3 million hl (1.1 million US barrels, 795,000 UK barrels), ranking it twentieth in the German brewing league.

Jever's light but exceptionally dry, aperitif-like bitterness is partially attributable to the very soft well-water which the brewery has used since 1867. A combination of Hallertau and Tettnang hops are employed along with northern pale malts.

Jever's masters have sadly killed the noted Jever Maibock (spring bock). Instead, the real Pilsner is joined by Jever Fun, which is bizarrely described as a 'full-blooded beer but with the alcohol removed.' Shurely shome mishtake? The brewery has a museum and a September bierfest.

BITBURGER

ESTABLISHED 1817

Bitburger Brauerei, 54634 Bitburg

RECOMMENDED
Bitburger Pils (4.6%),
very pale, big hop aroma, soft, dry, bitter

Growth from a farmhouse miniature to its current status as the producer of Germany's joint second biggest-selling beer brand (with Krombacher Pils) is quite an achievement in a country packed with about one quarter of the world's breweries. Bitburger has

JEVER

ESTABLISHED 1848

Friesisches Bräuhaus zu Jever
Elisabethufer 17, 26441 Jever

RECOMMENDED
Jever Pils (4.9%),
very pale, malt and hop flavors, very dry

Jever Pils is referred to as the Friesian Tang, after the flat, windswept North Sea coastal area around the port of

DORTMUND

KRONEN

ESTABLISHED 1430

Märkische Strasse 85, 44141 Dortmund

RECOMMENDED
Export (4.8%),
deep golden, firm malty body, slightly bitter
Kronen Pils (5%),
initial maltiness overtaken by hops, clean
Classic (5.3%),
very pale, malty but firm smack of hops

Kronen is the smallest of Dortmund's three brewery groups, although small is a relative term. Family-owned Kronen

Above: Dortmund, Germany's principal brewing city.

has bought the city's two smaller independent breweries – Thier and Stiftsbräu – and some brewing is now centralized at Kronen brewery.

Kronen uses Hallertau and Tettnang hops but buys in malt from several countries after closing its own maltings in 1995 on cost grounds. Beers undergo a week-long fermentation and are then transferred to large conical lagering tanks for two to three weeks. There is no pasteurization. Pilsner (Kronen, Thier, and Stifts varieties) is the biggest product; Export is Kronen's biggest bottled beer and now the biggest of Dortmund's Export varieties.

Kronen, which also brews a top-fermenting Alt, is Dortmund's oldest brewery, dating from a 15th century brewery inn. The family link began in 1729 with Johann Wenker, who is honored today by a brewpub named after him. Kronen inherited Dortmund's other brewpub, Hövel (see below), when it acquired Thier in 1992.

Some Kronen beers, including Export, are served in Dortmund's brewing museum, adjacent to the brewery entrance.

BERLIN

LUISEN

ESTABLISHED 1989

Luisenplatz, 10585 Berlin

RECOMMENDED

Luisenbräu (4.9%),
copper, unfiltered, malty, soft-bodied

Reunification of Germany reconnected hedonistic Berlin to the delights of brewing diversity. In addition to the two dominant Schultheiss and Kindl breweries, Berlin now also has several brewpubs.

The oldest of these, which attracts a trendy student crowd, is Luisen. But it is not their exclusive preserve. The large corner pub with its brewing kettles set back behind rough and ready scrubtop tables, stands opposite the Charlottenburg Palace tourist attraction. And the airport bus, which runs every 15 minutes, very conveniently stops outside. Provided you have paid for your beer, you can sit sipping in a window seat and dash out as the bus draws up.

The beer is made with pale and colored malts and Hallertau hops, matured for several weeks, and is served on draft direct from the cellar conditioning tanks. Other beers are occasionally brewed.

ALSO WORTH TRYING

Dortmund is Germany's biggest beer-producing city. Three large groups brew 6.2 million hl (5.3 million US barrels, 3.8 million UK barrels) annually – which is equivalent to nearly half Belgium's entire production. But the city's most famous beer style, Export, is being subsumed by Pilsners. Worth seeking are: **Dortmunder Union** Original (5%, pale Export, malty, fruity, hop-spicy) and Brinkhoff's (5%, light-bodied, hoppy-dry); **DAB** Export (4.9%, light-bodied, malty-dry); several top-fermenting brews include **Stiftsbräu** Clarissen (4.6%, amber-red, fruity-dry); **Hövel's** brewpub (Hoher Wall, inner ring road) has Bitterbier (5.5%, red-brown, dry, bitter) and Perlweizen wheat beer; and the **Wenker** brewpub (Marktplatz) has Urtrüb (5%, pale, unfiltered, fruity, yeasty).

In Berlin: the city's own beer style is Berliner Weisse, a lighter, weaker, but also more tart, sourish variation of the Bavarian Weissbier. **Schultheiss** (3%, very fruity-sour) and **Kindl** (3%, sharp, less fruity, dry) are ideal summer beers, sometimes drunk with a dash of fruit essence to mellow the sourness. They are waiting to be rediscovered. Berlin's newest brewery, the **Bier Company** on Körte Strasse in the Kreuzberg district, produces everything from Pilsner to stout, and offers brewing courses for new hopefuls.

Above: Inside Berlin's cosy Luisen brewpub.

Above: This picturesque facade belongs to the Alt Köln pub-restaurant in the middle of Cologne.

ALT & KÖLSCH

Like defiant medieval fortified cities refusing to surrender to marauding armies, Düsseldorf and Cologne remain outposts of ale brewing. While the rest of Germany succumbed to lager brewing, these two neighbors today maintain distinctive top-fermenting beer styles in more than 20 breweries.

Düsseldorf calls its style Altbier – old beer – while in Cologne they have Kölsch, named after the city's German spelling – Köln. Altbier is generally coppery in color while Kölsch (brewed with small amounts of wheat) can be as pale as Pilsner.

Kölsch is protected by a kind of *appellation contrôlée* and can be so called only within Cologne, which lays claim to having more breweries than any other city in the world – 17. Some have been brewing for centuries, such as Gaffel, others are brewpub newcomers, like Hellers. A guided Kölsch pub tour is offered by Cologne Tourist Office (Unter Fettenhennen 19, 50667 Köln, fax: 221-221-3320).

SCHUMACHER

ESTABLISHED 1838

Ost Strasse 123, 40210 Düsseldorf

RECOMMENDED
Schumacher Alt (4.5%),
fruity and dry with a clean, crisp finish
Latzenbier (5.5%),
more full-bodied and hoppier than Alt

Brewer Herbert Enderlein shakes his head almost in disgust at the mere mention of Pilsner, and he has done his bit to stem the golden lager tide. Since 1985 he has teased out a 50 percent increase in production from the cramped, family-owned brewery behind its rambling beer hall-like pub.

This has been done without cutting any corners. Primary fermentation is in open vessels, preferred after the brewery dabbled with closed fermenters which Enderlein believes altered the beer's taste. This first phase at 18-22°C (64-72°F) lasts for three days, followed by a 15 to 20-day maturation period in closed tanks at 4°C (39°F) when a secondary fermentation takes place. Also eschewing speed, the brewery uses a kühlschiff – literally, a cooling ship – which is a 30cm (12in) deep tray about the size of four billiard tables in which the wort is cooled naturally after boiling and before fermentation. Schumacher uses only pale barley malt, from Germany's Mosel region, and only aromatic Hallertau Mittelfrüh whole hops. The beer is filtered but not pasteurized.

In Schumacher's quietly busy beer hall, customers empty seven 36-gallon (163l) barrels a day, seven days a week. Latzenbier is a winter beer.

Right: Zum Schlüssel is one of several brewpubs in Düsseldorf dedicated to preserving Altbier styles and offering something other than conventional lager.

ZUM UERIGE

ESTABLISHED 1847

Bergerstrasse 1, 40213 Düsseldorf

RECOMMENDED
Alt (4.5%),
deep copper, hoppy, sharp and bitter finish
Weissbier (5.2%),
amber, unfiltered, spicy, fruity and tart-dry
Sticke (5.5%),
dark amber, malty aroma, but quite hoppy

This is the most atmospheric of Düsseldorf's old brewpubs. If you discount the electric lighting, the inside could still be in the 1800s. Customers can pick from a warren of small drinking rooms linked by narrow corridors and, at the rear overlooking the gleaming copper-clad brewhouse seen through a plate glass window, there is a large hall.

Zum Uerige – the nickname of a former cantankerous landlord – uses some colored malt in the mash to give it a darker hue than, say, Schumacher, and Tettnang bittering hops, as well as Hallertau aromatic.

Like Schuhmacher, the brewery also boasts a kühlschiff for cooling the wort. The beer is served without CO_2 pressure direct from wooden casks which are rolled along the corridors at

frequent intervals, scattering customers in their way. Sticke Bier is available only in the early new year and in autumn.

Above: Inside Cologne's Malzmühle brewpub the atmosphere is warm and welcoming – the epitome of the German term *Gemütlich*.

MALZMÜHLE

ESTABLISHED 1839

Brauerei Schwarz, Heumarkt 6
50667 Cologne

∽∽∾

RECOMMENDED
Mühlen Kölsch (5%),
mild, malty, and gently spicy

Just beyond the pedestrianized section of the old town, on the edge of Heumarket but separated by a busy tram line, it's easy enough to overlook this old-established Cologne brewpub. That would be a pity because not only does the Malzmühle offer an excellent example of the local style, it is also an atmospheric place to drink Kölsch.

The little brewery jammed into the back yard still ferments in open squares and afterwards the beer enjoys a lazy three-week cold maturation. Five percent of the fermentables is wheat malt – a special dispensation granted to Kölsch brewers who would otherwise have to comply with Germany's 100 percent barley malt purity law. Hallertau bittering hops are used, although not so many as to spoil the beer's soft malty character.

HELLER

ESTABLISHED 1992

Hellers Brauhaus, Roon Strasse 33
50674 Cologne

∽∽∾

RECOMMENDED
Ur Wiess (4.8%),
hazy gold, yeasty aroma, fullsome fruitiness
Heller Kölsch (4.8%),
golden, malt and fruit flavors, less dry

You would think that 16 breweries in one city would suffice, but this is Germany. Hans Heller's hankering after his own bar developed into a resolve to have his own beer as well. So he fitted some refurbished old brewing equipment behind his capacious vaulted cellar bar.

He brews a typically pale, bright, top-fermenting version of the city's own style, and an unfiltered version which he cannot call Kölsch because Cologne has one of the world's tightest regulations governing a beer style, and cloudy is not in the specifications.

The concept of new beer in Germany is something natural and wholesome, and often carries the term Naturtrüb (meaning naturally cloudy) for good measure. To give an additional healthy attraction to his beers, Hans uses only organically grown ingredients. He uses Bavarian hops and north German pale malt.

ALSO WORTH TRYING

Also well worth seeking out in Düsseldorf: the Altbier brewpubs **Zum Schlüssel** (5%, malty-dry) on Bolkerstrasse; **Im Füchsen** (4.8%, initially malty-sweet becoming hoppy) on Ratingerstrasse. These two plus Uerige are within ten minutes walk of one another in the old town. The biggest Altbier producer, **Diebel** (4.8%, hoppy and dry), is brewed across the Rhine at Issum and is widely available.

In Cologne, a clutch of Kölsch taverns, some dating from the 14th century, some established within the last ten years, cluster round the twin spired cathedral. **Früh** (5%, fruity-dry) is closest on Am Hof; on Unter Taschenmacher at the **Sion Brauhaus**, where there was a brewery in 1318, sample Sion (4.8%, gently fruity); No. 22 Altmarkt has **Gaffel** (4.8%, very dry); **Päffgen** (5%, quite hoppy) in Frisenstrasse (Heumarkt); and the biggest brand **Küppers** is in the large Alt Köln pub-restaurant next to the cathedral.

SWITZERLAND

Closures and mergers during the 1970s and 1980s saw the number of breweries in Switzerland almost halved. The market is now dominated by the Feldschlösschen group with breweries at Rheinfelden, Fribourg, Wabern, Sion, and Basel, followed by Hürlimann in Zurich producing the world's strongest regularly brewed beer – the 14% ABV Samichlaus.

But the independent brewers are fighting back. Reduced to competing for just under 10 percent of the total market, 16 of them have founded their own mutual protection society. In a rousing speech, founding president Karl Locher asked: 'Have we arrived at the American level where from east to west, from north to south you see not only the same Kentucky fried chicken…but also the same market-controlling beer brands? We must stay true to ourselves because beer is an individual drink, as different as land and people…'

Today Switzerland has 36 breweries – a slight increase as micros open to cater for a new generation's demand for 'handcrafted' beers. The majority of Switzerland's breweries are in the German-speaking northeast. At St Gallen, where the borders of Switzerland, Austria, and Germany meet, archeologists have found evidence of a brewhouse in 9th century monastery ruins.

FRAUENFELD

ESTABLISHED 1876

Actienbrauerei Frauenfeld
Hohenzornstrasse 2, 8500 Frauenfeld

RECOMMENDED

Spezial Dunkel (4.9%),
brown, malty sweetness balanced by hop flavor
Weizenbier (5.1%),
deep golden, light fruitiness, bittersweet finish
Ittinger Klosterbräu (5.1%)
amber, full-bodied nutty flavor, hoppy

In the 1970s this small innovative family brewery was the first in Switzerland to produce bottle-conditioned wheat beer, and today it remains one of the country's tastiest contributions to the style. The brewery now has its own hop garden in the grounds of a former monastery at nearby Kartause Ittingen which once brewed its own beer. With the help of a rediscovered recipe, the Frauenfeld brewery has recreated one of those old monastic beers in the form of Ittinger Klosterbräu. Although bottom-fermented, it is brewed to the Reinheitsgebot standard with several types of malt and is matured for 14 weeks.

The most recent innovation has been the opening of a pub virtually inside the brewery with views of the brewhouse, and the production of a special unfiltered house lager. This is one of a chain of new franchised bakery-cum-brewpubs called Back und Brau, created by one of the Hürlimann brewing

family. The gardens at Kartause Ittingen are open to the public and there is a restaurant serving Ittingerbräu.

STADTBÜHLER

ESTABLISHED 1858

Brauerei Stadtbühl, Herisauerstrasse 49
9202 Gossau

RECOMMENDED

Hell Lagerbier (4.8%),
pale amber, gently hopped, bittersweet
Dunkel (4.8%),
dark brown, mild malty-dry flavor
Fürstenbräu (5.6%),
copper, richly fruity, spicy and hoppy

This brewery is one of the highest in Europe. It stands at 634m (2,080ft) above sea level on the edge of the Säntis Mountains, which must have a good brewing climate because local archives record that monks in the Middle Ages brewed a beer in the vicinity. They called it Cozesauva.

Stadtbühl is a small brewery, verging on a micro, with an annual output in the region of 10,000hl (8,500 US barrels, 6,000 UK barrels). Its traditional brewing methods would still be recognized by founder Joseph Krucker, whose fifth-generation descendants are still in charge. The brewing copper is still steam-heated. South Bavarian barley malt and hops are used.

RUGENBRÄU

ESTABLISHED 1866

3800 Matten-Interlaken

RECOMMENDED

Alpenperle (5.3%),
very pale maize beer, spritzy and bittersweet
Dunkel (5.1%),
*dark brown, sweet maltiness, touch of fruit,
finishing dry*
Festbier (5.5%),
*dark amber, sweet rich maltiness dries in a
hoppy end flourish*

Josef Hofweber, whose descendants still own this small Alpine brewery, arrived in the beautiful Berner Oberland mountains at the foot of the Jungfrau and Eiger via an impressive brewing route through Bavaria and Bohemia. His journeyman brewing took in the dramatic technical changes from ale to lager in the mid-19th century before he finally quit his native Bavaria in 1883 because of punitive beer taxes.

Josef's specialty was dark lager and the brewery still produces a good example in the south Bavarian brown style. But in recent years Rugenbräu's chief specialty has been a maize beer, the Alpenperle. Maize is used in small quantities throughout the world as a substitute for barley malt which may be hard or expensive

BRAUEREI·A·HÜRLIMANN·ZÜRICH

to obtain. In Bavaria, it's an illegal adjunct under the barley-only purity law there, but in this case the Alpenperle's fermentable content is intentionally 30 percent maize to obtain a specific taste.

ZIEGELHOF

ESTABLISHED 1850

Brauerei Ziegelhof, 4410 Liestal

RECOMMENDED

Goldbräu (4.8%),
pale golden, well-hopped Pilsner, bitter-dry
Special Dunkel (5.3%),
dark, full-bodied, hop spiciness, dryish finish
Rauacherbräu (7.2%),
*dark bock, rich maltiness, hint of dark fruit,
bittersweet*

Ziegelhof is said to be the last old-established independent family brewer in an area of northwest Switzerland where previously there had been 11 breweries, all of which – in Ziegelhof's words – 'fell victim to the industry's concentration process.' The small (40,000hl, 34,000 US barrels, 24,500 UK barrels) brewery has been in the Meyer family since 1863.

Beer-making here follows the German purity law code, and styles are similar to those found in Bavaria with the exception of Goldbräu which is closer to a Bohemian pils. All the beers are matured in traditional style – for at least ten weeks – to give more rounded flavor. Rauacherbräu is matured for considerably longer, and is named after an ancient tribe that lived in the area long before the Romans arrived. The brewery has suspended production of a Bavarian-style wheat beer. The beers are best tasted in Ziegelhof's own pub 'tap' in Liestal's Zeughausplatz.

ALSO WORTH TRYING

Willys Urbräu (4.9%, amber, unfiltered, malty) and dark bock or Starkbier (6.2%, roasted malt flavor, bittersweet) at Weinfelden, near Frauenfeld; top-fermented Anker (5.6%, brown, malty-dry) a cross between a brown ale and a Düsseldorfer Alt from **Cardinal** at Fribourg; Maisgold (5.2%, golden, fruity-sweet) a maize beer from the **Rosengarten** brewery in Einsiedeln south of Zurich; **Hürlimann's** Samichlaus (14%, brown, richly malty and vinous) brewed once a year on December 6, St Nicholas' Day – when the old central European Father Christmas appears – and matured for one

year; **Locher** brewery in Appenzell titillates with a Vollmondbier (4.8%, pale, dry lager) brewed on nights of a full moon; Hopfenperle lager (5.2%, pale golden, moderately hoppy-dry) of **Feldchlösschen**; **Lowenbräu** in Zurich imports Scottish whisky malt to produce its gimmicky Celtic Whiskybrew (5%).

Two brewpubs offer wheat beer, **Zum Frohsinn** in Romanshornerstrasse, Arbon on the banks of Lake Constance, and the **Ueli Fischerstube** in Rheingasse, Basel. There's a house brewery in **Restaurant Kreuz**, Spiez, on Lake Thuner near Interlaken, and a micro in Florhofstrasse, Wädenswil, on Lake Zurich. At St Gallen, the beer shop **Birreria** in Brühlgasse has a tiny brewery producing 'Cream Ale.' In deference to the Czechs the term Pilsner is not used in Swiss brewing. Beers in this style are sometimes labelled Premium Lager.

DENMARK

Denmark is the least temperance-minded of the Scandinavian countries – and Danes celebrate by being the world's third-biggest beer drinkers. They enjoy about 128 liters (225 UK pints) per capita annually, and mostly in bottled form. That's about 380 bottles per person, although some of this is low alcohol 'Let' beer. Under five percent of beer sold is draft.

Carlsberg occupies an historic place in the development of modern bottom-fermented beer styles (see below). Its unique spirit of philanthropy is, however, tempered by the company's crushing dominance of Danish brewing – about 80 percent of the domestic market. Small independents survive in Thisted, Skive, Kolding, Haderslev, Assens, and Maribo and Vaeggerlose on Lolland island.

CARLSBERG

ESTABLISHED 1847

Vesterfaelledvej 100, 1799 Copenhagen

RECOMMENDED

Gamle (4.2%),
dark brown, soft malty character, bittersweet finish

Carlsberg Hof or Pilsner (4.7%),
light hop aroma, malt flavor, malty-dry

Tuborg Grøn (Green, 4.7%),
golden, more pronounced hoppiness than Hof

Elephant (7.5%),
bronze, bock-like quality, malt sweetness with some hop notes

Gammel Porter (7.7%),
black, prominent roast malt bitterness, dry

Carlsberg is one of the world's ten largest brewing companies, and perhaps the most unusual. The yeast used by most brewers today is called *Saccharomyces carlsbergensis* – in honor of the brewery's yeast research in the late 19th century – and the company donates much of its large profits to science and the arts through the Carlsberg Foundation which has a controlling share.

The brewing giant traces its roots to the beginning of the 19th century and the enthusiastic farmer-turned-brewer Christian Jacobsen; the name Carlsberg was created in 1847 when the new family brewery was named after Jacobsen's grandson Carl. The brewery was built on a hill, which in Danish is *berg*. The Jacobsens played a leading role in the conversion of the world from top-fermenting ale brewing to bottom fermentation (lager) after Christian's son Jacob had studied under Munich brewing pioneer Gabriel Sedlmayr in the 1840s.

Denmark's other internationally famous brewing name, Tuborg, merged with Carlsberg in 1970 to form United

Above: Carlsberg's Elephant Gate, a suitably imposing entrance to one of the world's biggest breweries and the place where the lager yeast *Saccharomyces carlsbergensis* was first isolated in the 19th century.

Breweries, which now has financial interests in seven of Denmark's remaining 18 breweries.

Carlsberg does not follow the German all-malt purity law at home – where sugar is used – but does brew all-malt beer for export to Germany. Seasonal beers are Julebryg (5.5%) and Paskebryg (7.8%), both reddish and malty dry. Varieties of Carlsberg's pale Hof lager are produced under licence in about 25 breweries abroad.

ALBANI

ESTABLISHED 1859

Albani Bryggerierne, Tvaergade 2
5100 Odense

RECOMMENDED

Odense Pilsner (4.9%),
firm-bodied, malt-accented, dryish aftertaste

Giraf (6.9%),
deep golden, bock-like, malty-sweet, bittersweet

Original Albani Porter (7.8%),
very dark, roasted malt dryness, light hoppiness

You would think that a brewery which shares the same home town as the world-famous fairytale writer Hans Christian Andersen would have somehow contrived to name a beer after him. Instead, they chose the noble but far less distinguished giraffe in the time-honored Danish tradition of associating beers with animals. Andersen would have been in his

fifties when Albani was founded, but he lived until 1875 so it's quite possible that he supped the brewery's beer on visits home to this large central Danish island.

Albani is a sizeable independent brewery producing about one million hectoliters (850,000 US barrels, 610,000 UK barrels) a year. It has its own soft well-water and practices traditional long lagering of up to ten weeks for the strongest beers. Some maize is used with the barley malt. Two yeast strains are used, although the brewery will not elucidate further.

FAXE

ESTABLISHED 1901

Bryggerierne Faxe, Torvegad 35, 4640 Fakse

RECOMMENDED

Faxe Fad Premium (4.8%),
golden, full-bodied, malty with a dryish finish
Pils (5%),
malty-dry with only gentle hop character, like a south German variety
Bock (6.2%),
dark amber, fullsome maltiness and sweetish palate

Faxe remains a mostly family-owned brewery which developed from a small country business established by husband and wife team Conrad and Nikoline Nielsen. The brewery has always had access to the big Copenhagen market 32km (20 miles) north of Fakse, but it acquired national acclaim with its unpasteurized Faxe Fad beer. Most Danish beer is pasteurized but to signal that this brand wasn't, Faxe used the term fad which is Danish for draft – even though it is a bottled brew.

Faxe Fad became a favorite among discerning drinkers when other Danish brewers tried to put pressure on Faxe to pasteurize the beer in order not to 'taint'

beer bottles which in Denmark are a returnable standard size so that they can be recycled throughout the brewing industry.

The industry pressure backfired and Faxe Fad prospered. For a time, Faxe was a brewing renegade in Denmark, but now has trading links with Carlsberg and Ceres.

CERES

ESTABLISHED 1865

Bryggerierne Ceres, Aarhus, Jutland

RECOMMENDED

Julebryg/Christmas Beer (5.8%),
amber, full-bodied maltiness, bittersweet
Dansk Dortmunder (7.5%),
amber, fruitier than a German Dortmunder, medium-dry
Porter (7.7%),
dark brown, malt and fruit flavors, spicy-dry

Students of the university in Aarhus on the mainland east coast were fans of Red Eric when he was a full-blooded novelty from Ceres back in the 1970s. But food regulators in Brussels banned the brew because the coloring agent used by the brewery to make it red contravened European health laws.

Red Eric celebrated the Viking explorer who put the icy wastes of Greenland on the map in the 10th century. But Ceres has a penchant for producing specialty beers, and today's Aarhus students have several lusty – if less colorful – brews to choose from.

There is a portfolio of strong beers and the brewer is not frightened of using dark and roasted malts, as witnessed not only by the Porter but an almost black Stout, which has acquired the local spelling of Stowt (7.7%). A taste for these styles probably originates in the 18th century Baltic Sea trade when such British brews were exported as far as St Petersburg.

Ceres now owns the Thor brewery in Randers 32km (20 miles) north which has similar specialties, notably Buur (7.5%), an amber, malty, sweet, Bock-like beer the brewery claims has been brewed since 1500. The name is local dialect for beer, not unlike a southwest England pronunciation.

ALSO WORTH TRYING

The Carlsberg subsidiary **Wilbroe**, one of the country's oldest surviving breweries, in Elsinor has the bottom-fermented Imperial Stout (7.5%, fruity, bitter coffee); the small **Maarebaek** brewery produces a powerful Royal Viking (9.2%, copper-brown, malty rich, bittersweet) which is also exported to France where it is a favorite of the beer lovers' society Artisans de la Bière; in Copenhagen, the **Apollo** brewpub on Vesterbrogade, Tivoli, has several unfiltered and yeasty draft beers – still a novelty in Denmark.

NORWAY

In Norway, government controls on alcohol are repressive and tax on beer is the highest in Europe. The decision in 1994 to remain outside the European Union means no let up in the anti-alcohol culture.

Despite the heavy hand of restraint in a land which spawned the beer-loving Vikings, Norway still has 15 breweries, although the industry is dominated by the Ringnes group (now merged with Sweden's Pripps). Norway also maintains a beer purity law similar to Germany's, whose beer styles Norway most seeks to emulate – if not German drinking habits. Annual per capita consumption is 49 liters (86 UK pints) – about the same as Greece and barely more than half what the Finns enjoy.

AASS

ESTABLISHED 1834

Aass Bryggeri, Ole Steensgatan 10
3015 Drammen

RECOMMENDED
Bayer (4.5%),
chestnut-brown, malt accented and dryish
Aass Pilsner (4.5%),
firm Saaz hop aroma, hoppy-dry throughout
Juleøl (6.2%),
reddish-brown, malty with a hoppy finish
Bock (6.5%),
very dark, rich and full-bodied, malty-dry

Norway's oldest brewery is housed in an elegant, artistically illuminated, art deco-like waterfront brewery on the River Drammen, south of the capital Oslo. It produces 14 different beers among which

are some of the country's best, particularly the rich, dark bock which is matured for up to six months.

Jule means 'Christmas,' for which season the Juleøl is traditionally brewed. Bayer takes its name from the German for Bavaria – Bayern – whose malty, dark brown-amber style Norwegian brewers aim to copy. All Aass's beers are matured for at least two months.

MACK

ESTABLISHED 1977

Macks Ølbryggeri, 9005 Tromso

RECOMMENDED
Arctic Beer (4.5%),
very pale, light-bodied, gently hoppy, crisply dry
Bayerøl (4.5%),
dark brown, malt accented, bittersweet
Bokøl (6.5%),
copper, firm hop aroma and taste
Gull Mack (6.5%),
golden, full-bodied maltiness, hop spiciness

Mack is 300km (185 miles) inside the Arctic Circle and miles from anywhere but the North Pole. The small, newish brewery lubricates the throats of seamen based in this fishing port of 40,000 inhabitants.

Despite the isolated location, 100 percent barley malt is used, a mix of pale and colored, plus Bavarian hops. The beers are traditionally lagered – the strong editions for up to 10 weeks. If the Arctic Circle is a journey too far to

drink Arctic beer, there are several restaurant-pubs in Oslo which stock Mack brews. They include Mauds, and the Solsiden on Akershuskaia.

Above: Mack, where cold fermentation comes naturally.

ALSO WORTH TRYING

The **Ringnes** group of five breweries – the biggest of which is in Oslo – dominates the market, producing some palatable, dryish brews, notably the standard Ringnes Lager (4.5%, pale, malty, hoppy-dry); the Oslo brewpub **Mikro Brygerri** in Bogstadveien street produces several interesting top-fermented ales; the **Hansa Brewery** in Bergen produces a Bayer (5%, brown, malty, and bittersweet) and a juniper beer (8.5%, fruity, dry); a new micro called **Akershu**s, after the province adjoining Oslo, offers top-fermenting beers including wheat beer, Krystall (4.8%, pale amber, citric fruity).

SWEDEN

Swedish brewing has been much plagued by the interference of a nanny government. The number of breweries halved during the 1970s when a new law prohibited mainstream middle-strength beer.

Today there are 12 breweries left, and the industry is dominated by the Stockholm-based Pripps group, which has merged with Norway's main brewing group, Ringnes. The Swedish government has shed its shareholding in Pripps and the Volvo car company plans to sell its 50 percent stake.

Sweden's membership of the European Union in 1995 has eased alcohol restrictions and Sweden's first all-ale microbrewery opened in 1994. Joining the Union means that much stronger beers, such as bocks, can be brewed again – after a 100-year ban.

....

SPENDRUP

ESTABLISHED 1859

Eriksgatan 113, 113 43 Stockholm

~~~

RECOMMENDED

Norrlands Guld (4.5%),
golden, malty, clean-tasting, bittersweet
Old Gold (5%),
golden, full-bodied Pilsner style, dry and bitter
Fifty-Fifty (5%),
amber, nutty-dry flavor, fruity finish

....

Brewing dynasties often have unlikely origins. The Spendrup family arrived in the beer business via a trainee priest who renounced his vows and took up distilling schnapps. Perhaps Peter Mathias might have followed in Europe's great monastic brewing traditions, but his Spendrups Akvavit became the everyday toast of taverns in Copenhagen in the late 18th century.

The family moved across the Baltic Sea to Sweden in the 19th century and switched to brewing. Great-great grandson Louis Herbert studied brewing in Germany and afterwards introduced the Reinsheitsgebot purity law into Sweden; all Spendrups beers made at its two breweries – at Grängesberg in the central lakes region, and Vårby on the east coast – are still 100 percent barley malt. Spendrup brews under licence Maclay of Scotland's Scotch Ale – and Fifty-Fifty is a curious blend of the Ale and Spendrup Premium lager.

....

KÄLLEFALL

ESTABLISHED 1993

Kallefalls Brygerri, Museigatan 3
522 33 Tidaholm

~~~

RECOMMENDED

Pale Ale (4.5%),
amber, firm hoppiness, and a bitter-dry finish
Brown Ale (5%),
brown, blend of roasted malt and fruity flavors
Strong Ale (7%),
copper, warming malt taste, hint of fruitiness

....

Deep in the heart of Sweden's lakeland, near the southwestern shores of the Vättern, may seem an unlikely place to ignite Swedish tastebuds with the country's first and only ale brewery for many years. But this micro has enjoyed rapid success, pushing its beers beyond rural Tidaholm into Stockholm, Göteborg and Uppsala.

The brewery is named after the springs from which it draws water. Barley malt and hops are imported from Britain, as was the brewing equipment. Brewing advice came from the English brewers MacMullens of Hertford.

Above: Pripps Carnegie Porter can benefit from an extended period of bottle-ageing.

ALSO WORTH TRYING

Pripps-bottled Carnegie Porter (5.5%, black, top-fermented, roast maltiness and dry) is a link with Sweden's brewing past and is vintage dated – the brewers reckon it will last 10 years; Pripps also produce small quanties of a Carnegie Pale Ale, but the main brand is Pripps Blå (Blue) pale lager in four strengths: 2.3%, 3.5%, 5.2%, and, recently, 7.2%; **Falcon** in Falkenberg offers a Munich-style beer, Bayerskt (5%, brown, malty).

FINLAND

In Finnish folklore, Pekko was the pagan god of beer. But Finland's beer-drinking pleasures have been undermined by draconian restrictions for much of this century. Between 1919 and 1932 there was total alcohol prohibition.

Hartwall *(1.8 million hl, 1.53 million US barrels, 1.1 million UK barrels) is Finland's largest company with four breweries and about 50 percent of the market, followed by Sinebrychoff. But microbrewing has mushroomed in the 1990s to encompass 30 brewpubs and microbreweries.*

The new brewers mostly produce unfiltered dark and pale lagers but also some wheat beers, and a few ales and stouts. In late 1995 the Finnish Microbreweries Association (Suomen Pienpanimoliitto) was established with 13 members.

An old established brewery at Lappeenranta, as close to St Petersburg as it is to Helsinki, has been re-opened. Interest is also rekindling in Finland's ancient farmhouse beer style, sahti, made with oats, rye, and juniper berries.

Finland's annual per capita beer consumption is 86 liters (151 UK pints), similar to that of the Dutch.

Left: A streetcar named Pub – innovative Finnish brewer Sinebrychoff uses this tram, which is converted into a mobile bar-restaurant, to publicize its extensive range of beers around the streets of the capital Helsinki.

SINEBRYCHOFF

ESTABLISHED 1819

Oy Sinebrychoff AB, Alikeravantie 40
FIN-04201 Kerava

RECOMMENDED

Portteri (7.2%),
black, roasted malt aroma, full-bodied smoothness, coffee-bitter taste
Brewmaster's Brown Ale (4.5%),
chestnut brown, malty sweet and fruity
Jouluolut (5%),
reddish-brown Xmas specialty, rich, and malty

Sinebrychoff – nicknamed 'Koff' – is one of Scandinavia's most innovative brewing companies, maintaining a range of styles from brown ale to Pilsner. Koff III was 1996 champion bottled pale lager at Britain's Brewing Industry International Awards. In 1993 Koff opened Finland's first brewpub, the Kappeli Panimo (Eteläesplanadi 10, Helsinki), which has produced several specialties, including a Bavarian-style wheat beer. Interest in beer is kindled by a Koff bar-restaurant tram which plies the capital's tram line routes.

Founder Nikolai Sinebrychoff's original Helsinki brewhouse was closed in 1993 following the opening of a new greenfield site brewery at Kerava, just north of Helsinki, which added the brown ale to its portfolio in 1994. A second Koff brewery is at Pori on the southwest coast. Sinebrychoff is now part of a very large investment group, Rettig, the majority shareholder in the Vena Brewery in St Petersburg – which may explain the introduction of a lager cornily called Leningrad Cowboy.

MESTARI PANIMO

ESTABLISHED 1994

Kauppakatu 30, Jyväskylä

RECOMMENDED

Pesiaali pale (4.7%),
pale amber, yeasty nose, hoppy, sharp-bodied, dryish finish
Pesiaali dark (4.7%),
dark brown, malty, soft-bodied

This is one of the new breed of brewpubs, located in central Finland where it is particularly popular with Jyväskylä University students. The owners brew their two house lager beers according to the German purity law – continuing Finland's long love affair with Bavaria in beery matters. The pale and amber barley malt used is Finnish, but the hops are German Hallertau. Fermentation is in open vessels and is followed by cold lagering for about a month. The beers are served unfiltered.

Pesiaali means something 'new and special,' a term coined by the architect who designed the town's old labor hall in which Mestari Panimo is housed.

Above: Synebrychoff's Kappeli brewpub in Helsinki offers an interesting variety of seasonal beers.

PALVASALMI

ESTABLISHED 1995

Koulutie 1, Saarijärvi

RECOMMENDED

Best Pal (4.5%),
pale amber, fruity and quite hoppy
Bitter (4.5%),
darker than Pal, more malty but also hoppy
Tarmo Stout (4.5%),
near black, firm-bodied, roasty-nutty tasting

Four brothers and sisters who set up this newest of Scandinavian microbreweries proudly announced to the world via their own spot on the Internet that the Palvasalmi is Finland's first real ale brewery. Equipment – including bar handpumps and firkin casks – as well as barley malt, hops, and yeast have been imported from England. One of the sisters, Kirsti Ratinen, is the brewster and she is committed to the British traditional style. She has already produced five different ales; the first and most popular is Best Pal which is in the style of an English bitter. She uses Goldings and Fuggles hops and water is untreated.

The Palvasalmi ales are quite hoppy, even bitter, by Finnish standards – Best Pal has 35 units of bitterness, which puts it on a par with some of Britain's most astringent bitters. The family foursome chose real ale because they wanted to brew something out of the ordinary in Finland. The ales are in several pub-restaurants in Saarijärvi and also Kuokkala and a suitable bar is being sought in Helsinki. Some bars have filtered versions and dispense through gas pumps. One of the best places to try the brews as real ales is the Teatteri Eurooppa in Saarijärvi.

PERHO

ESTABLISHED 1994

Ravintolakoulu Perho
Mechelininkatu 7, Helsinki

RECOMMENDED

Perhon Olut (4.7%),
brown, soft, malty-sweet, gentle hop background
Kölsch (4.2%),
pale, some fruitiness with hoppy-dry finish

The 'Butterfly' brewery is part of the Helsinki Culinary School and brewing has now become part of the students' curriculum. There are ambitious plans for a wide range of beer styles.

Perhon Olut is sometimes unfiltered and curiously uses a yeast obtained from Scotland, colored malts from Finland, and Czech hops. The beer they describe as Kölsch is, however, brewed with bottom-fermenting yeast and a mixture of Czech and English Fuggles hops.

The house beers are served in a public restaurant attached to the School and customers also have a choice of 40 other bottled beers.

ALSO WORTH TRYING

In Helsinki, the **Kappeli** brewpub owned by Sinebrychoff in a pavilion on Eteläesplanadi has an interesting range of unfiltered lagers, and seasonal specialties have included a bock and a German-style wheat; **Hartwall's** widely available Lapin Kulta (two strengths: 4.5% and 5.2%), a pale, malty-dry, unpasteurized beer named after a gold mine, plus Weizen Fest, a Bavarian-style wheat beer; from **Lappeenrannan Panimo** brewery in Lappeenranta there are two versions of a newish brown ale called Husaari (4.3%, malty fruity, and another at 5.7%); the **Wanha Posti** (Old Post Office) microbrewery on Hämeenkatu street, Tampere, offers Postin oma (5.7%), a full-bodied, malty-dry, brown ale; and Finland's third largest brewery **Olvi** brews two seasonal beers, pale and dark, for summer and winter, under the name Vuosiolut (4.5%).

Many of the new micros are tiny backyard businesses but under more relaxed laws they are finding ready markets in nearby restaurants. Brewing locations include: Espoo, Kiiminki, Loppi, Oulu, Raahe, Rautalampi, Suomenlinna, near Helsinki, and Vaasa. The biggest sahti producer is in Lammi (**Lamin Sahti Co**).

RUSSIA

Russians are the world's greatest consumers of alcohol – annually downing the equivalent of about four liters (seven UK pints) of pure alcohol per capita, mostly in the form of vodka and strong sweet wines.

But new, better brewed and packaged beer is increasingly seen as a more moderate, and sophisticated, drink. High-priced imported foreign brands have become fashionable among the new rich in Moscow and St Petersburg, where beer consumption is twice the national average of 16 liters (28 UK pints) per year.

In other parts of Russia, beer is often still a weak, reddish-brown brew made with a mix of barley, rye, and maize and served rather unsophisticatedly from street tankers to householders who queue with teapots, buckets, and kettles. State-owned breweries produce a standard generic brand called Zhigulevskoe, but this is giving way to the new beers from privatized breweries.

With a population of 147 million, Russia is seen (along with China) as one of the last great untapped beer markets.

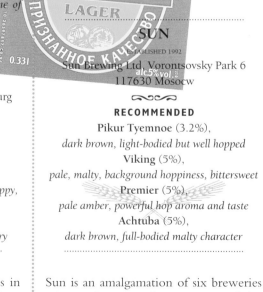

BALTIKA

ESTABLISHED 1978

6 Proezd, Parnas-4, 194292 St Petersburg

RECOMMENDED

Classic (4.8%),

golden, light hop aroma and taste

Original (5.6%),

dark brown, malt sweetness balanced by hoppy, slightly bitter edge

Baltika Porter (7%),

black, roasted malt flavors, fruity edge, dry

This is the biggest of four breweries in St Petersburg and since its takeover by a Scandinavian consortium in 1993 a new range of quality beers has been produced, including the powerful Porter in 1995. Baltika brews about 900,000hl (767,000 US barrels, 550,000 UK barrels) a year; it now commands more than half the lucrative market in the St Petersburg area.

Russian barley and hops are used. A sharp rise in the cost of malted barley led in 1996 to Baltika building its own malthouse. Modernization has included fast fermentation techniques and pasteurization, but some Baltika beers still enjoy a slow, traditional conditioning. Classic is the most popular brand. The new owners, Baltic Beverage Holdings, is a partnership of Norway's Ringnes, Sweden's Pripps, and Hartwall of Finland.

SUN

ESTABLISHED 1992

Sun Brewing Ltd, Vorontsovsky Park 6 117630 Mosocw

RECOMMENDED

Pikur Tyemnoe (3.2%),

dark brown, light-bodied but well hopped

Viking (5%),

pale, malty, background hoppiness, bittersweet

Premier (5%),

pale amber, powerful hop aroma and taste

Achtuba (5%),

dark brown, full-bodied malty character

Sun is an amalgamation of six breweries scattered across the vastness of the Russian Federation. It is Russia's biggest brewing group with a combined annual production of 4.2 million hl (3.6 million US barrels, 2.56 million UK barrels). It is an independent company of private investors, including foreign banks, and draws on western, notably British, technical expertise.

Sun maintains its own maltings at five of the breweries; emphasis is laid on hop flavor. Most of the beers are bottled and have been given longer shelf life through better filtration or pasteurization.

The breweries are at Ivano, northeast of Moscow, producing Viking and Premier among others; Kursk, south of Moscow near the Ukrainian border, brewing the Pikur range; the Saransk Brewery in the Moldova Republic; the Povolzhie Brewery in Volzhsky, 1,200km (750 miles) southeast of Moscow, and brewing Achtuba and several pale lagers; at Perm,1,400km (870 miles) to the east, also brewing Viking; and in Ekaterinburg beyond the Urals and European Russia, and notorious as the place where Tsar Nicholas II and his family were murdered during the civil war.

THE BALTIC REGION

There is a long tradition of brewing in Estonia, Latvia, and Lithuania, which together have about 30 breweries, but beer consumption slumped in the early 1990s in the wake of economic problems after the republics obtained independence from Moscow.

The Baltic region is noted for dark, strong beers stemming from a fashion for English porters and stouts which began in the late 18th century. Leading breweries in Estonia, Latvia, and Lithuania have been bought by a Scandinavian brewing partnership called Baltic Beverages Holdings, made up of Ringnes (Norway), Pripps (Sweden), and Hartwall (Finland).

ESTONIA

SAKU

ESTABLISHED 1820

Saku Brewery, EE 3400, Harju Maakond
Saku, Tallinn

RECOMMENDED

Hele (4.9%),
pale, big hop aroma and spicy dry taste
Tume (6.6%),
dark amber, vinous aroma, rich malt-fruit
Porter (7.4%),
dark ruby, fruity aroma, full-bodied, malty

The oldest brewery in the three Baltic states has undergone a major facelift since it was sold by the state in the early 1990s. Saku's main beers are pale lagers but the brewery maintains a traditional local taste for strong porter-style beer.

Three of Saku's eight beers are dark styles, although all are bottom-fermented. Slow maturation is still the rule for some, notably the Porter, which is released at Christmas – in the words of the brewery as 'a good companion for long and dark winter nights.' In 1995, a third dark beer was introduced to celebrate the brewery's 175th anniversary and named after founder Count Karl Friedrich Rehbinder (5%, black, coffeeish, bitter-dry). Saku's most popular beer though is a new light-flavored pale lager, Originaal (4.5%), which has overtaken Saku Pilsner (4.2%).

A 75 percent shareholding in Saku is held by Baltic Beverage Holdings (see above).

LATVIA

ALDARIS

ESTABLISHED 1865

Tvaika 44, LV-1005 Riga

RECOMMENDED
Baltijas (4.5%),
pale amber, firm hop flavor, malty background
Latvijas (6%),
amber, yeasty aroma, full-bodied malty taste
Aldara Porter (7.2%),
black, rich malt and licorice-like dryness

Aldaris has a truly international flavor. It was created by members of Riga's former German-speaking community, acquired Russian influences after World War II, and is now largely owned by Swedes and Finns from across the Baltic.

Latvia has a long tradition of beer drinking, although the biggest community of drinkers – ethnic Germans – were expelled in 1945. Until the early 1990s, beer was only roughly filtered and sometimes served in wooden casks.

Above: Aldaris has 50 percent of the Latvian market.

ALSO WORTH TRYING

In Moscow, **Moskovkoye** (4.5%, pale, hoppy) and **August** (4.5%, amber, fruity); in Estonia a new microbrewery in Sillamae has München (5.5%, dark brown, bittersweet); in Lithuania, where they sometimes use peas in brewing, **Kalnapilis** in Panevezys offers Radvilu (5.6%, red-brown, malty-dry).

EASTERN EUROPE

The favorite tipple is vodka, but past German influences have left a sizeable brewing industry in Poland that includes between 60 and 80 breweries; closures and micro openings obscure the exact number.

Australian entrepreneurs in association with the Dutch Grolsch Brewery have created Poland's large Elbrewery group, merging breweries at Elblag on the Baltic coast and the country's oldest brewery, Hevelius, in nearby Gdansk. But they are shadowed by Dutch giant Heineken which owns a 25 percent share in the noted Zywiec Brewery near Cracow.

Hungary has broken out in a rash of brewpubs, stimulated by the activities of German entrepreneurs, although the country's biggest brewery is now South African-owned (see below). Ukraine has dozens of state-owned breweries but, as in Russia, the market is undeveloped and large quantities of beer are still dispensed from street tankers. The Ukrainian Beer Lovers' Party urges people to drink 10 liters (18 UK pints) of beer a week.

POLAND

OKOCIM

ESTABLISHED 1845

Browar Okocim, ul Browarna 14
32-800 Brzesko

RECOMMENDED
Zagloba (4.8%),
pale amber, malty with some fruitiness, bittersweet finish
Okocim Pils (5.1%),
light-bodied, gentle hops aroma and flavor

This old established brewery in the south

Above: Poland's Okocim is now part German-owned.

near Cracow and the Czech Republic has brewing traditions firmly cast in the German–Czech mold: it was once part of the famous Austrian brewing dynasty Dreher. Since 1994, the German giant Brau und Brunnen has had a 25 percent stake and has installed German technical assistance as well as finance.

Okocim is the fourth largest brewery in Poland and is expanding to reach an annual capacity of 1.6 million hl (1.36 million US barrels, 975,000 UK barrels). At the end of 1995, the company bought the Amber Brewery in the north at Chociwei, near Szczecin and the German border.

Traditional Czech-style brewing methods are currently being replaced with faster conical fermenters. The hops are Czech and Polish from around the Lublin area. Okocim's yeast originates from Weihenstephan in Bavaria. Okocim is also a major malt producer.

UKRAINE

OBOLON

ESTABLISHED 1980

Bogatyrskaya str 3, 254655 Kiev 212

RECOMMENDED
Obolon Black (3.8%),
dark brown, malty flavor, dryish
Obolon Original (3.9%),
pale golden, lightly hopped, clean flavor
Special (5%),
deep golden, full-bodied, bittersweet taste

Obolon is Ukraine's most sophisticated brewery, with relatively modern equipment and the most popular beers. Before the break up of the Soviet Union, beer from Kiev was highly rated in Moscow and beyond.

The brewery is the biggest in the country, producing about 850,000hl (724,000 US barrels, 520,000 UK barrels) a year. All beers are bottom-fermented and lagered traditionally – the brewery was built with Czech technical help. Water is drawn from the brewery's own deep wells and local grain and hops are used. The weakest of four pale beers use rice as well as barley malt, but the stronger varieties are 100 percent barley malt and are lagered for two months. Obolon Black has some black malt plus caramel.

HUNGARY

KŐBÁNYA

ESTABLISHED 1854

Kőbányai Sörgyár, Maglódi út 17
1106 Budapest

RECOMMENDED

Dreher Pils (6%),
*strong for the style, good hoppiness, some
bitterness, crisp dry finish*
Dreher Export (6.2%),
*pale amber, full-bodied malt flavor, firm
hoppiness, malty-dry*
Dreher Bak (7.8%),
black, rich roasted malt aroma and flavor

Kőbánya was part of the influential Germanic brewing circle established through central Europe during the mid 19th century, linking Munich, Vienna, Pilsen, and Budapest. Peter Schmidt returned home in 1844 from Munich where he had been a student of pioneer brewer Gabriel Sedlmayr. He surprised established brewers by building a brewery outside the town among the hillside vineyards so he could utilize tunnels and caves dug in the Middle Ages to provide stone for defensive walls against Mongol invasions. The caves offered ideal, stable, cool conditions for the new concept of lagering. Schmidt also tapped new water supplies beneath the hills. The popularity of his beers led

Above: Traditional methods are favored at Kőbánya.

to a new brewery quarter – the district of Kőbánya. One of these breweries was bought in 1862 by the great Viennese brewer Anton Dreher, and Budapest became an important part of the Dreher beer empire.

All things Germanic were vilified after 1945, but the Dreher name was recently revived after archives containing old brewing recipes were discovered. Kőbánya says today's Dreher brands are a recreation of those recipes. Kőbánya was bought in 1993 by the South African Breweries group, but the Dreher heritage is seen as important. Barley for the Dreher brands is now being traditionally floor-malted in the caves again, open fermenters are used, and some beers enjoy long, traditional lagering, but all are pasteurized. Hops are from southern Hungary and Bohemia.

Kőbánya is Hungary's largest brewery, producing nearly 4 million hl (3.4 million US barrels, 2.4 million UK barrels) a year.

SLOVAKIA

HELL

ESTABLISHED 1473

Pivovar Vyhne, 96602 Vyhne

RECOMMENDED

Sitňan Sudové (4.1%),
very pale, light-bodied with a hoppy-dry finish
Sitňan Tmavé (4.8%),
dark brown, malty and fruity
Steiger (5.2%),
pale, firm hop aroma, crisply dry, slightly bitter

The oldest brewery in Slovakia traces its roots back to the rich order of religious Knights Templar whose influence survived in this part of Europe longer than elsewhere. The brewery is in the central Štiavnicky Hills – which rise to

1,000m (over 3,000ft) – and for centuries it quenched the thirsts of ethnic German miners who from the Middle Ages extracted gold, silver, copper, and later iron ore from the ground.

The newest beer, Steiger, recalls an earlier owner of the brewery. Hell is the name of the new owners following privatization in 1993. Water for brewing is drawn from nearby abandoned and flooded mines. The beers are traditionally brewed and conditioned for up to six weeks, but are pasteurized.

ALSO WORTH TRYING

In Poland, **Warka** Dark (5%, stout-like), **Zywiec** (5.2%, amber, malty-dry), Warsawski Porter (5.8%, ruby-black, chocolatey, bittersweet), **EB** (4.9%, pale, quite hoppy) from Elblag; in Ukraine, from Gorlovka, **Donetsk** Dark (4.3%, dark brown, malty-sweet) and **Zhigulevskoe** Special (4.5%, amber, malty); in Hungary, **Jäger** from Tiszafüred (5.2%, golden, malty), **Chicago** (5%, golden, hoppy-dry) from a brewpub adjoining Hotel Emke, Budapest; in Slovakia, **Cassovar** (5.8%, black, bitter porter-style) from Košice, and **Martin** Porter (8%, ruby-black, roasted malt, dry) in Martin.

SOUTHERN EUROPE

Brewing is no stranger to the wine lands, but there are no original styles indigenous to these regions, and beers are often light-bodied and light flavored. The oldest breweries are in the Balkan region of former Yugoslavia – some dating to the 18th century – and in Spain.

The Spanish are the biggest beer drinkers in the Mediterranean rim with a consumption of 71 liters (125 UK pints) per capita per year, followed by the Portuguese with 66 liters (116 UK pints) and the Greeks who drink 40 liters (70 UK pints). In Italy, imported beer is fashionable but Italians consume under 25 liters (44 UK pints) – one of the lowest per capita rates in Europe after Russia.

The north European brewing giants Heineken, Interbrew, Carlsberg, and Danone (France's former BSN), plus several German companies, have bought large slices of the south's beer industry; in Greece there are now no Greek-owned breweries. Heineken has captured about 75 percent of the Greek market and in tandem with Interbrew has been busily carving up the Italian industry. The result is Heineken, Amstel, and Stella über alles. Spain and Italy can muster about 20 breweries each, but perhaps the most unusual brewery in the south is on the island of Malta (see below).

Above: La Zaragozana's ceremonial drayman and his team.

SPAIN

LA ZARAGOZANA

ESTABLISHED 1900

Ramón Berenguer IV, 50007 Zaragoza

RECOMMENDED

Ambar (4.2%),
pale Pilsner-style, light hoppy aroma and taste, quite dry

Ambar Dos (5.2%),
amber, well balanced rich malt and hop character, malty-dry

Marlen (5.8%),
golden, fruity aroma, firm-bodied, some bitterness, finally bittersweet

Export (7%),
dark red, full-bodied, toasted malt and spicy flavors, bitterish finish

Full-bodied beer making in Spain is maintained by this independent, family-owned brewery in the provincial capital of the parched River Ebro valley plains, south of the Pyrenees. The medium-sized brewery (400,000hl, 340,000 US barrels, 250,000 UK barrels) maintains its own maltings and has a new, gleaming stainless steel brewhouse, but still adheres to traditional brewing methods including slow conditioning. A stable of dray horses is kept for ceremonial occasions and local festivals.

A variety of barley malts, from pale Pilsner to roasted, are used, plus small quanties of rice and corn. All the beers are bottom-fermented. The beers are particularly popular with local university students, but some of Zaragozana's specialties are exported to neighboring Portugal and as far afield as Australia.

MALTA

FARSONS

ESTABLISHED 1889

Simonds-Farsons-Cisk Ltd., Mriehel

RECOMMENDED

Hop Ale (3.8%),
pale ale in character, big hop flavor, bitter-dry

Milk Stout (4%),
dark, initial sweetness fades, malty-dry finish

Brewer's Choice (4.8%),
full-bodied and fruity, bittersweet end

Palm trees sway in the hot Mediterranean breeze outside, but most of the beers which leave the elegant, 1930s art deco building might be more at home in an English village pub.

Farsons is a pleasant hangover from yet another corner of the vanished British Empire where ales were produced to lubricate soldiers and administrators. Most such breweries that survive from Imperial days, particularly in India and southeast Asia, long ago converted to light lager brewing, but Farsons has maintained the old traditions, and its ales remain popular with tiny Malta's population. But Farsons also produces Cisk Lager, which it inherited after taking over the island's only other brewery in the late 1940s. Barley malt, hops, and top-fermenting yeast for the ales are imported from Britain.

ITALY

MORETTI

ESTABLISHED 1859

Birra Moretti, Viale Venezia 9, 33100 Udine

RECOMMENDED

Friulana (4.7%),
golden Pilsner, crisp, clean palate, hoppy nose and finish
Bruna (6%),
chestnut brown, strong version of Munich dunkel, malty, nutty, and dryish
La Rossa (7.5%),
copper red, Märzen-like, firm maltiness, slightly spicy and bittersweet

An endearing and enduring trademark is a special feature of this three-brewery company based near Venice. Since the 1940s, Moretti has featured a thirsty-looking moustachioed man about to draw a frothy golden beer to his lips. It's an industry classic to rank alongside Tuborg's thirsty man on a hot winding road advertisement which has been in use since 1900. The flowing walrus moustache is further celebrated in a beer of that name, Baffo d'Oro.

Moretti is no longer a family-owned brewery and it's to be hoped that new owners Heineken will not forsake the moustachioed man – nor undermine Moretti's broad range of beers in the classic German-Vienna mold. Several of the beers are made with 100 percent barley malt, a big taste plus in a country inclined to use adjuncts such as maize.

In a recent shuffling of the international ownership pack, Moretti was bought by Heineken from the Belgian Interbrew conglomerate, which in turn had inherited the Italian company with its purchase of Canada's Labatt.

Another endearing Moretti touch is the practice of serving an unfiltered beer during winter in the bar next to the Udine brewery. Appropriately, it is called Integrale – the whole thing. The two other Moretti breweries are in Bologna and, in the south, Baragiano.

PORTUGAL

CENTRAL DE CERVEJAS

ESTABLISHED 1881

Vialonga, Lisbon

RECOMMENDED

Sagres (4.7%),
pale, full-bodied malt flavors, quite hoppy-dry
Sagres dark/moreno (4.8%),
brown, rich roasted malt with dryish finish
Europa (5.2%),
amber, malty-dry in the German Export style, bittersweet finish

German and Danish brewing influences prevailed in Portugal during the formative years of large-scale commercial brewing in the mid 19th century, and the main brewery of this group was once called Germania – before being conveniently renamed Portugalia when war broke out between Britain, France, and Germany in 1914.

The Sagres brand name is confusingly used for two distinct beers, one pale the other dark in the Bavarian dunkel style.

Above: Central de Cervejas's main brewery at Vialonga.

Europa beer was first brewed to celebrate Portugal's membership of the European Union in 1986. The company has also recently ventured into ale brewing with the even more confusing name of Bohemia.

Central de Cervejas is the largest of two dominating brewing groups in Portugal; the other is based around Oporto (see below). Central has a second brewery at Coimbra.

ALSO WORTH TRYING

In Spain – **Damm** of Barcelona has Voll Damm (5.5%, amber malty-dry), **Aguila** of Madrid offers Master (5.5%, golden, bittersweet), while **San Miguel** provides the more hoppy Selecta (5.4%, amber).

In Portugal – **Unicer** of Oporto has a lightly hoppy pale lager and a stronger Bock (5.6%, amber, malty).

In Italy – **Forst** in the far north German-speaking Sud Tirol offers the most firm, hop accented beers, especially Pils (4.8% malty-dry); a light Pilsner style is **Peroni's** Nastro Azzuro (5.4%, softly hopped), Italy's biggest selling beer; while a much more full-bodied, flavorsome, and tongue-twisting Splügen Fumée (5.2%, copper red, smoky-dry) comes from **Poretti** of Varese near Milan.

AFRICA

Most beer styles in Africa today reflect European brewing developments, but brewing's roots extend back to north Africa's ancient civilizations. On a village scale, thick beers are still made using sorghum, millet, and herbs, and are fermented by wild yeasts.

Africa has more than 150 breweries. Nigeria has the most – about 30 – including three producing Guinness strong stout.

The two largest brewing groups are South African Breweries and the French-based Brasseries et Glacieres Internationales (BGI), which is particularly strong in west Africa. Maize often supplements barley malt. Hops are now grown in South Africa and Zimbabwe.

SOUTH AFRICAN BREWERIES

ESTABLISHED 1895

65 Park Lane, Sandown, Sandton 2146

RECOMMENDED
Castle Lager (5%),
pale, medium-bodied, light hoppiness, dryish
Lion Lager (5%),
amber, full-bodied, bittersweet
Ohlsson's (5%),
amber, light-bodied, some fruitiness, dry
Castle Milk Stout (6%),
full-bodied, sweet malt and licorice flavor

This is the largest brewing company in Africa and dominates not only the South African market but also neighboring countries such as Zimbabwe, where it also has breweries. SAB has eight breweries in South Africa and either owns or jointly operates another 18 elsewhere in the world.

The biggest one in South African is Rosslyn which produces 7.2 million hl (6.1 million US barrels, 4.4 million UK barrels) a year. The biggest brands are Castle and Lion; Ohlsson's is a reminder of one of southern Africa's early European brewers, a Norwegian who arrived on the scene in the 1860s. Today's SAB is the result of a merger in the 1950s between the Ohlsson group and a smaller SAB, originally created by an Englishman.

All beers are produced by high gravity brewing (high original strength which is then diluted). Maize is an adjunct to barley malt. Eighty per cent of SAB's hops are the bitter Southern Brewer, developed and grown in South Africa around George in the Cape. SAB has its own hop farms.

NIGERIAN BREWERIES

ESTABLISHED 1949

1 Abebe Village Road, Iganmu, Lagos

RECOMMENDED
Star (4.8%),
pale amber, gentle hoppiness, slightly fruity
Gulder (5%),
pale, hoppy aroma, malty character
Legend Stout (7%),
rich roasted malt flavor, slight bitterness, dry

Heineken's presence is felt throughout much of Africa, but nowhere as strongly as in Nigeria where the Dutch company

has a substantial share in Nigerian Breweries. The company operates four breweries within Nigeria and its beers are also produced under licence in neighboring countries.

Gulder is the most popular everyday brand. Heineken has brought in modern western brewing methods, but Nigerian Breweries is still resisting government attempts to make the country's breweries use a higher percentage of domestic cereals, such as maize, in order to help Nigerian farmers who have difficulty growing quality brewing barley in tropical west Africa. Barley malt forms about 75-80 percent of fermentable ingredients; hops come from Europe.

ALSO WORTH TRYING

Kenya Breweries' Tusker (4.8%, full-bodied, hoppy lager) and White Cap (4%, fruity-dry lager) are widely available in south-east Africa; from Benin, **BSI's** Castell (5%, amber, bittersweet) and La Beninoise Pils (4.5%, very pale, light-bodied, dryish); Nigeria's **Golden Guinea Brewery** has Eagle Stout (7%); while in South Africa, **Mitchell's** micros in Knysna, Cape Town and Johannesburg brew Raven Stout (6%) and several pale ales.

THE INDIAN SUB-CONTINENT

Despite prohibition in some states, India has a slowly growing, if small, brewing industry. Just 46 breweries cater for a population of 925 million people. Average per capita consumption is a mere 0.5 liters (0.9 UK pints) a year, and annual production is less than Germany's Bitburger Brewery.

Two companies – United Breweries and Mohan Meakin – own 20 of India's breweries. Most Indian beers are full-bodied; many are sweetish, but some are quite hoppy. Brewing has suffered in Pakistan because of increasing Islamic anti-alcohol influences. But in Sri Lanka, beer remains a popular drink and stout is still brewed.

UNITED BREWERIES

ESTABLISHED 1915

14 Cunningham Road, Bangalore-562 052

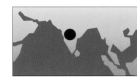

RECOMMENDED

Kingfisher (5%),

pale golden, hint of yeast, quite hoppy flavor, moderate bitterness

Kalyani Black Label (5%),

pale, smooth, fullsome malty-dryness, firm hoppy aftertaste

UB Export (5%),

deep golden, full-bodied, bittersweet

A Scotsman is credited with creating India's biggest brewing group, which today consists of 13 breweries. Originally, Thomas Leishman united five small breweries in southern India, the oldest of which – Castle Brewery – was founded in 1857.

Kingfisher is India's biggest selling beer with 25 percent of the total market. It began life as an ale, delivered around Madras in giant wooden hogshead casks pulled by bullock cart. Today it is a lager and is sold in 24 countries.

Barley malt is Indian grown, supplemented by maize and sugar, which are commonly used in Indian brewing. Hops are imported from Germany and New Zealand, since political unrest in the northern Jammu and Kashmir states has disrupted supplies of locally grown hops.

Until 1996, Flying Horse and Sun lagers were widely available domestically, but today they are brewed only for export markets. Two UB lagers, Bullet and Charger, have 8% ABV.

UB breweries are strung across the country from Shertally on the far southwest coast up to Ludhiana, north of New Delhi. Other breweries are in Calcutta, Pailan, Faridabad near Delhi, Bombay, Hyderabad, Goa, Bangalore, and Palghat.

MOHAN MEAKIN

ESTABLISHED 1955

15 Barakhamba Road, New Delhi 110001

RECOMMENDED

Lion (4.5%),

pale amber, light maltiness, dryish

Gymkhana Pilsner (4.5%),

lightly hopped, medium-bodied, bittersweet

The company is based in northern India, and one of its brewing centers is in the cool Simla Hills at Solan, north of Delhi. Mohan is an expanding brewing company, but it also produces a wide variety of other drinks, from apple juice to whisky and rum.

ALSO WORTH TRYING

In Sri Lanka, the **Ceylon Brewery** at Nuwara Eliya produces a top-fermented Lion Stout (7.5%, fruity); Sando Stout (6%, dark chocolatey) from **Three Coins** brewery in the capital Colombo is bottom-fermented. London Lager (4%, pale, sweetish) brewed in Rawalpindi is Pakistan's most widely known beer, but brewers **Murree** also produce a strong Stout (8%, bittersweet).

AUSTRALIA AND NEW ZEALAND

Brewing diversity in Australia and New Zealand has gone the way of their beer-drinking prowess – down. Twenty years ago Australians shared third place with the Czechs in the world league with 142 liters (250 UK pints) per head of population a year.

Today they are down to 95 liters (167 UK pints) and out of the top ten. New Zealand is a nose ahead.

The Australian wine industry flourishes, but brewing is the victim of an unbridled 'free' market. Two companies, Foster's Brewing Group and Lion Nathan (which is New Zealand-based), now dominate the Australian beer market with a 97.4 percent market share between them. In the 1970s Australia had 12 brewing companies. Coopers of Adelaide is the last old-established Australian independent.

In Australia, once popular pub drinking is in decline due to changing social habits and tough drink-drive laws in a car-orientated society. Three-quarters of all beer drunk is canned or bottled. What used to be ordinary beer (about 5% ABV) is 'Premium,' while beer under 3% – which has grown to 20 percent of the market – is dubbed 'Light.'

ADELAIDE

COOPERS

ESTABLISHED 1862

9 Statenborough Street
Leabrook, South Australia 5068

RECOMMENDED

Coopers Dark (4.5%),
ruby-black, mellow malt flavors, dryish
Original Pale Ale (4.5%),
hoppy and fruity
Sparkling Ale (5.8%),
amber, yeasty aroma with yeasty-fruity flavors
Extra Stout (6.8%),
black, full-bodied, roasty, fruity, and dry

Thomas Cooper was a puritanical shoemaker who saw alcohol as the demon drink. It's said he never once entered a bar. But when his wife Alice fell ill in 1862 she asked him to make her a tonic and gave him a brewing recipe from their English homeland in Yorkshire. The result made Alice feel better and launched Thomas on a new career.

Exports go to Japan, North America, Britain, Scandinavia, and even China. Expanded production and costs have led to changes in brewing methods – the 800 wooden puncheons (108-gallon, 491-liter casks) which were part of the

original fermentation process have been scrapped. They caused 15 percent wastage. Primary top-fermentation is now in closed metal tanks, followed by a week's storage after filtration before re-seeding with yeast in bottles or kegs. The bulk still goes into bottles which are then stored for another six weeks.

Coopers produces its own pale and black roasted malts. Cane sugar is also used. Tasmanian Pride of Ringwood hops are preferred and there is an old house yeast. In Adelaide, the range is on tap in the Rising Sun, Kensington – next door to where Thomas Cooper first brewed his wife's tonic.

WESTERN AUSTRALIA

SAIL & ANCHOR

ESTABLISHED 1984

64 Station Terrace, Fremantle

RECOMMENDED

Seven Seas (4.5%),
amber, fruity aroma and flavor, bittersweet
Brass Monkey Stout (6%),
black, slightly bitter roasted maltiness, dry

This was the first of a new breed of brewpubs in Australia and while some have fallen victim to economic recession in recent years, the Sail & Anchor has prospered. Founder Philip Sexton, a former brewer at the giant Swan Brewery in nearby Perth, went on to establish a microbrewery in the vicinity, Matilda Bay. That has expanded considerably and is now part of Foster's – giving that giant a toehold in Western Australia against rivals Lion Nathan, who own Swan.

The Sail & Anchor specializes in top-fermented ales in the English style, and even serves them English style via handpumps. The tiny brewery is housed in a typically traditional Australian 'pub,' a large turn-of-the-century corner building known as an hotel.

NEW SOUTH WALES

LORD NELSON

ESTABLISHED 1987

Kent Street, Sydney

RECOMMENDED

Trafalgar (3.7%),
pale amber, malt sweetness countered by hoppiness, bittersweet
Victory Bitter (4.6%),
amber, firm-bodied mellow maltiness, dryish
Old Admiral (5.8%),
brown, full-bodied maltiness with fruity notes

It doesn't take a great historian to link the names of these beers with the brewpub's title. The Lord Nelson holds claim to being the oldest pub in Australia, built in 1836 in Sydney's earliest settlement. Then, the district was a rough and ready port bustling with seafarers, immigrants, and numerous pubs. Today, it's a tourist haunt known as the Rocks, and still peppered with interesting pubs.

Above: Main St, Mudgee, NSW, and Foster's is there.

The beers are top-fermented, using local grain, Tasmanian hops, and an imported English ale yeast. The beers are English in style and are unfiltered and unpasteurized, although some are artificially carbonated to suit local tastes. Other brewhouse offerings have included a wheat beer.

The Nelson is not only a safe haven for beer drinkers seeking refuge from bland lagers, it has accommodation and is noted for classic Aussie beef steaks.

THE PUMPHOUSE

ESTABLISHED 1989

17 Little Pier Street, Darling Harbour, Sydney

RECOMMENDED

Federation (3.5%),
brown, firm maltiness, nutty-dry
Bull's Head Bitter (4.5%),
pale amber, very hoppy and crisply dry

Top-fermenting fruity ales are the preferred choice of the brewer at this small micro in an upmarket pub-restaurant, bordering Sydney's magnificently huge, natural deepwater harbor. The name Pumphouse has nothing to do with the method of dispensing beer however. It comes from an old water pumping station on the site, parts of which still form part of the present building.

Pumphouse beers are unusually hoppy

for Australia, drawing on flavors not only from Tasmania but also from England's Kent hop gardens. The Pumphouse's big beer garden is a popular social gathering place on hot summer evenings.

ALSO WORTH TRYING

In Sydney: the best pubs are in the Rocks district. The Australian Hotel offers **Scharer's** German-style beers from up-country Picton; **Hahn's** Sydney Bitter (4.3%, pale lager, hoppy), **Toohey's** Red Bitter(4.5%, amber lager, malty-dry); **Resch's** Draught (4.6%, golden, hoppy, dryish) and Resch's DA, or Dinner Ale (4%, dark amber-red, hoppy, bittersweet); **Tooth's** Sheaf Stout (5.7%, ruby-black, fruity, roasty); Tooth's Kent Old Brown (4.4%, malty brown ale).

In Adelaide: **Port Dock** brewpub's Lighthouse (4.2%, pale, malty ale); Southwark Bitter (4.6%, pale dry lager) and West End Premium (4.9%, malty lager) from **South Australian**.

In Perth: Dogbolter (5.2%, dark brown, malty lager) from **Matilda Bay Brewery**; **Swan Brewery's** Swan Draught (4.9%, very pale sweetish lager) and Emu Bitter (4.6%, pale hoppy lager).

In Melbourne: **Geebung Polo Club** brewpub's Pale Ale (4.6%, fruity ale); Abbots Invalid Stout (5.6%, fruity, light-bodied, bottom-fermented) from **Foster's** Abbotsford Brewery; **Redback** (4.7%, spicy, yeasty) from the Foster's-owned micro in Flemington Road, North Melbourne, an unfiltered version of the Redback Original now brewed at Matilda Bay, Perth, and named after a tiny but deadly spider which stalks Australia.

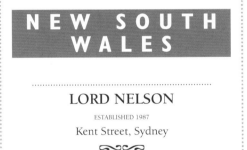

FOSTER'S

ESTABLISHED 1864 (AS CARLTON)

Foster's Brewing Group
77 Southbank Boulevard
Southbank, 3006 Victoria

〜〜〜

RECOMMENDED

Kent Old Brown (4.4%),
brown ale, some malt and fruitiness, bittersweet
Resch's Pilsner (4.6%),
full malt, crisp and dryish
Redback Original (4.7%),
pale amber, filtered wheat beer, gentle spiciness, fruity
Victorian Bitter (4.9%),
pale amber lager, light malty flavor, bittersweet
Cascade Stout (5.8%),
bottom-fermented, roasted malt flavor

Foster's is one of those beers which hype has intertwined with the national image of its home country. The archetypal rugged Australian male swigs from a 'tinnie' (aluminium can) of Foster's. Yet the name derives from two American brothers who lived briefly in Australia during the last century, and Foster's is not Australia's biggest-selling beer. That honor belongs to its stablemate, Victorian Bitter. The success of the image, however, has prompted the giant Carlton United Breweries to rename itself Foster's Brewing Group.

Above: A traditional Australian pub.

There are seven Foster's breweries in Australia commanding 54 percent of the domestic market. The biggest is in Melbourne – where nearly 6 million hl (5.1 million US barrels, 3.6 million UK barrels) are brewed per year, including Victorian Bitter, Foster's, and Carlton – followed by Sydney (Tooth's/Resch's) and Yatala in Queensland (Power's), with much smaller brewhouses in Hobart (Cascade) and Perth (Matilda Bay), plus micros in Melbourne (Redback) and Sanctuary Cove on Queensland's Gold Coast.

The handsome stone brewery in Hobart is Australia's oldest, dating from the 1820s. Its longtime sister brewery, Boag's of Launceston also in Tasmania, has become an independent company again. Matilda Bay and Power's started out as independent micros in the 1980s.

The Group brews 51 beer brands, although some are variations of a single type – there are six versions of Foster's – from Foster's Lager (4.9%, sweetish), down to low alcohol Light and Special (2.5%-2.8%). The gimmicky 303 Icegold offers the nonsensical marketing hype of 'a unique brewing process that brews the flavor in.' Do all other beers have their flavor brewed out? The breweries use their own house yeasts. Tasmanian Pride of Ringwood is the favored hop. Queensland cane sugar is a common ingredient. The term 'bitter' suggests ale, but most so-called are lager.

LION NATHAN

ESTABLISHED 1993

1 Macquarie Place, Sydney 2000

〜〜〜

RECOMMENDED

Toohey's Old (4.2%),
brown, light maltiness, bittersweet
Castlemaine XXXX (4.3%),
deep golden, some hoppiness, clean and dryish
Hahn's Premium (4.6%),
pale amber, rich malt and hop flavors, bitterish
West End Premium (5%),
golden, firm hoppy and malty-dry accent, hoppy
Old Australia Stout (7.2%),
bottom-fermented, full-bodied, rich, roasty

Lion Nathan is an aggressive newcomer onto the Australian beer scene, having hopped across the Tasman Sea from New Zealand to buy up the interests of entrepreneur Alan Bond, who over-extended himself in creating a rival to Carlton United (Foster's) by welding together the breweries of Swan, Toohey's, and Castlemaine.

Lion's now commands 56 percent of the beer market in New Zealand and 43.4 percent in Australia, where it has six breweries. These are in Brisbane (Castlemaine Perkins), Sydney (Toohey's, Hahn's), Grafton in New South Wales, Adelaide (South Australian), and Perth. They have their roots in the early/mid-19th century, and names such as Old and Bitter are reminders of their ale-brewing origins before they switched attention to

lager. Newer beer names have no such respect for brewing nomenclature – Toohey's Blue Bock is the opposite of a strong German-style beer. Hahn's is an expanded micro whose founder, American Chuck Hahn, is now Lion Nathan's chief brewer.

NEW ZEALAND

MAC'S

ESTABLISHED 1982

McCashin Malt & Brewhouse
642 Main Road, Stoke, South Island

RECOMMENDED

Black Mac (4.2%),
copper-brown, malty, some hop character
Mac's Ale (4.6%),
amber, firm-bodied, malty, bittersweet finish

International rugby player Terry McCashin was inspired by the real ale movement in Britain to join the world microbrewing trend and establish New Zealand's first new brewery for many years. His small brewery, near the town of Nelson, unusually has its own maltings, which may explain the darkish, malty character of most of the brews. Barley comes from nearby farms and the Motueka hops are locally grown.

Despite its name, the Ale is a bottom-fermented lager beer made even more schizophrenic by being dubbed 'real ale,' which it clearly is not. Still McCashin's pioneering business has inspired other New Zealanders to take up small-scale commercial brewing and offer a little more consumer choice.

LION NATHAN

ESTABLISHED 1923 (AS NEW ZEALAND BREWERIES)

Shortland Towers, Shortland Street, Auckland

RECOMMENDED

Lion Red (4%),
deep amber, malty, bittersweet
Canterbury Draught (4%),
copper-colored, malty-sweet
Speight's (4%),
copper, malty, light hoppiness, dryish and crisp
Steinlager Export (5%),
deep golden, flowery hop aroma, dryish

New Zealand is the Norway of the southern hemisphere, not least in its ambivalence to alcohol consumption. Its brewing diversity was undermined early this century when ten of the biggest breweries amalgamated to resist a vigorous temperance movement which twice came within a whisker of achieving total prohibition. The amalgamation created New Zealand Breweries, subsequently Lion Nathan. The group now commands 56 percent of the New Zealand beer market, while its only rival, Dominion Breweries, has 37 percent. Of the original ten breweries, four remain – Auckland and Hastings on North Island, Christchurch and Dunedin on South Island.

Lion Red is New Zealand's biggest brand, and in a country with a sweet palate it is regarded as quite bitter beer. But Steinlager Export, which has won major awards abroad, is really much hoppier and drier. Export is nicknamed 'Steinie Green' to distinguish it from its cousin Steinlager Blue (4%). Lion Red has a Brown (fruity-sweet) stablemate, and these two are most popular in North Island. Speight's, brewed in Dunedin, is the name of a brewery dating from 1876.

Opposition to alcohol is rooted in the attitude of mid-19th century immigrant Presbyterians who had retreated from a 'decadent' Britain. It has

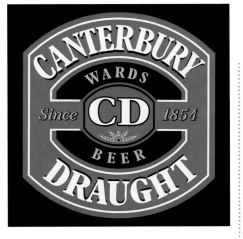

never quite left New Zealand where some restrictions on beer remain. And brewers have never lost their nervousness. Lion Nathan Chairman Sir Gordon Tait's observations on social behavior in his 1995 annual report seem more appropriate to Victorian England than the late 20th century: 'It is pleasing to note that beer's improved acceptability is coming at a time when social attitudes towards licensed drinks are improving...'

ALSO WORTH TRYING

Christchurch on South Island offers several new brewing ventures – the **Loaded Hog** brewpub in Dundas Street has a Bavarian-style, top-fermented Weissbier (5.2% pale, fruity-tart); the micro **Harrington's** produces another, sweeter wheat beer, while brewpub **Dux de Lux** in Hereford Street has full-bodied, top-fermented ales, notably Souwester (7%, dark and rich) and Norwester (7%, pale, hoppy); in Auckland, the **Shakespeare** brewpub in Albert Street offers Falstaff Ale (4.3%, amber, hoppy-bitter) and Stout (3.9%, light-bodied, dryish); at the base of North Island, Petone near Wellington has the micro **Strongcroft**. **Dominion**, with three breweries, offers Kiwi Lager (5%, pale, lightly hopped), DB Draft (4.2%, pale, malty) and Double Brown.

JAPAN

Beer drinking in Japan is now more colorful following a shake-up of the decades-long, cosy monopoly of the four major producers: Kirin, Asahi, Sapporo, and Suntory. First, a buoyant economy encouraged massive imports of foreign beer, then in 1994 the government scrapped a law which prohibited small breweries from being created.

Since then, Japan has joined the world microbrewery revolution with brewing kettles bubbling up in Kyoto, Tokyo, Sapporo, Yokohama, and several country towns. Top-fermenting ales predominate. This brings the total number of breweries to just under 60, of which Kirin owns 15, and Sapporo 10.

Most Japanese beer is now unpasteurized. Pale light-tasting beer is the staple, but even the big brewers have a tradition of producing some very tasty full-bodied stouts.

Japan is one of the world's top five beer-producing countries and Kirin one of the top five brewing companies, but competition with the rice drink sake and whisky means the Japanese rank only 22nd in the world beer-drinking table.

Above: Beer is officially Japan's 'national adult beverage.'

the big four Japanese brewers, but, unlike the others, it is not exclusively a brewer; another major activity is distilling. The company has three breweries, in Fuchu, near Tokyo, Nagaokakyo, and Chiyoda-cho in the east. The oldest, Fuchu, includes a microbrewery where exotic seasonal and trial brews are produced.

Like its chief competitors – all suffering from high production costs – Suntory seeks to make beers to compete with cut-price imports while at the same time meeting growing domestic demand for quality and unsullied products. Hence its new brew Daichi which means 'a gift from earth and water.' Daichi is 100 percent barley malt with spring water. The same cannot be said for another new brew called Hop's, which cannot be legally described as beer in Japan because it is made with less than 67 percent malted grains.

SUNTORY

.ESTABLISHED 1963

1-40 Dojimahama 2-chome
Kita-ku, Osaka 530

RECOMMENDED

Daichi to Mizu no Megumi (4.8%),
golden, light maltiness, clean, crisp aftertaste
Malt's (5%),
pale amber, gentle malt and hop flavors, dryish
Weizen (5.5%),
pale amber, fruity flavors and firmly tart
Black (5%),
bottom-fermented, malty, smooth

Suntory is the smallest and youngest of

CHOJUGURA

ESTABLISHED 1995

Chuo 3-4-15, Itami

RECOMMENDED
Blond (5%),
pale golden, good hop bouquet, hoppy dry taste
Dark (5.5%),
brown, some fruitiness with firm-bodied malty dryness

Sake maker Shintaro Konishi developed a taste for brewing beer after importing Belgian beers and seeing how well they went down among local people in the Osaka-Kyoto region. A change in brewing laws allowed sake producers – and anyone else – to move into brewing. Prior to 1994 a brewing licence was unobtainable without a minimum annual producton of 20,000hl (17,000 US barrels, 12,250 UK barrels), which effectively gave the four big brewers a total monopoly. Now the minimum is only 600hl (510 US barrels, 370 UK barrels). Mr Konishi's restaurant brewpub is in a converted warehouse.

ALSO WORTH TRYING

Asahi Stout (6.5%), full-bodied and bittersweet; from **Kirin**, Kirin Stout (8%), rich dark malty dryness, and Kyoto Alt (4.5%), gently hoppy and clean finishing.

SOUTHEAST ASIA

The microbrewing revolution has now moved into this corner of the globe, until now dominated by the giant San Miguel Corporation of the Philippines, which operates eight breweries.

Micros in Hong Kong and Manila started the trend, followed by Singapore and Bangkok. More are expected to follow along the Chinese seaboard. One of the new brewing entrepreneurs, the US-owned South China Brewing Co., says there are sound reasons for projecting an enormous growth curve for microbrewing throughout the Pacific Rim.

HONG KONG

SOUTH CHINA BREWING

ESTABLISHED 1995

Unit A1, 29 Wong Chuk Hang, Aberdeen, Hong Kong

❧

RECOMMENDED

Crooked Island Ale (5%),
golden, good balance of malt and hops, dryish
Signal 8 Stout (5%),
black, rich roasted malt flavor, bitter-dry
Lemongrass Ale (5%),
pale amber, gentle sweet-tart flavor
Dragon's Back India Pale Ale (6%),
full-bodied, well-hopped example of the style

The British are leaving and the Chinese taking over, but American microbrewery revolutionaries have just arrived. This 5,000 barrels–a–year brewery has the financial support of New Orleans distillers Sazerac Co, who are branching into brewing, especially round the Pacific rim.

Brewer Ted Miller – who worked previously at Hart Brewing – serves up a range of full-bodied, top-fermented ales; the well-hopped IPA is a reminder of brews originally sent out from England to quench tropical colonial thirsts. Lemongrass Ale innovatively draws on a spicy local ingredient commonly used in regional cooking. Fresh lemongrass is added at the boil with US hops Chinook and Cascade. The all-malt beers are filtered but not pasteurized and would be offered to Hong Kong as cask-conditioned real ale but for the climate and storage facilities, not to mention the lack of a true cellarman," says Miller.

South China's welcome alternatives to chilled, thin lager are in 70 Hong Kong bars and restaurants and are finding their way to Los Angeles. Locally the biggest selection is at BB's Bar, 114 Lockhart Road, Wanchai.

THAILAND

ROYAL HOFBRÄUHAUS

ESTABLISHED 1996

Terminal 2
Bangkok International Airport

❧

RECOMMENDED

Helles (5%)
unfiltered, pale amber, malty and slightly fruity

Lederhosen and laced dirndl dresses, sausages and sauerkraut are rare enough in east Asia. Add a Bavarian-style brewhouse and that's the scene which greets air travelers passing through Bangkok – home of the world's first 24-hour airport brewpub.

The project is financed by a Germanophile Thai businessman who has secured a franchise to use the famous Munich brewery name in Thailand. He even has a Bavarian brewer, Ulrich Martin, who uses imported Bavarian malt and hops and complies with the German Reinheitsgebot purity law. The Helles enjoys classical open fermentation and one month's cold conditioning in a building which looks as though it has been plucked from an Alpine meadow. The adjoining Munich-style restaurant overlooks lines of airline check-in counters. Even so, customers sometimes end up running for their plane. The pub also serves imported Hofbräu wheat beer.

ALSO WORTH TRYING

Bangkok's **Boon Rawd Brewery** has one of the hoppiest bitter beers in east Asia, Singha (5.6%+), named after an animal in Thai folklore; Singapore's **Tiger** is a firm-bodied 5.1% pale lager, while the city-state's **Paulaner** brewpub seeks to emulate its Munich namesake; the Filippino-brewed version of the widely available **San Miguel** Pilsner-style (5%) is generally considered superior to the Hong Kong or Vietnam-brewed versions; San Miguel's Dark (4.8%) is malty-sweet; Manila's 1995-established micro – in the Makati Business Center – brews pale ale, stout and a lager.

CHINA: THE SLEEPING GIANT?

Try if you can to imagine a country of 1,200,000,000 thirsty people where more than 600 breweries have been built since 1979 to meet demand but where annual per capita beer consumption is still only about 16 liters (28 UK pints) – just one tenth of the quantity drunk by the world-beating Czechs. This is China.

By the year 2000 China is expected have overtaken the United States as the world's biggest beer producer. Twenty years ago China was not even in the top 20 producing countries; ten years ago it ranked seventh.

Beer has been brewed in China since the beginning of this century when western countries established little commercial fiefdoms along the Pacific coast until Mao Tse Tung's revolution drove them out. Today, the best known Chinese beer in the west, and the biggest brand in China, is Tsingtao, which was first brewed by Germans in Qingdao in 1903 – when the city was called Tsingtao.

Western brewers are now being welcomed back with open arms as part of China's great market economy drive. The Chinese need their know-how and investment capital, and the foreigners (nicknamed 'Gweilos') want to tap into the world's last great beer bazaar. Major brewing companies already there include: Asahi (Japan), Anheuser-Busch (Budweiser), Bass, Beck's, Carlsberg, Foster's, Guinness, Heineken, Holsten, Interbrew (Belgium), Kirin (Japan), Lion Nathan (New Zealand), Miller (US), San Miguel (Philippines), South African Breweries, Suntory (Japan), and Britain's Whitbread.

Only a handful of Chinese breweries predate 1937 when the country was engulfed in war and revolution. These are Qingdao (Tsingtao, 1903 – the oldest), Beijing Shuanghesheng (1915), Shandong Yantai (1920), and Shenyang (1936). The second generation of breweries was built in the late 1950s, although curiously a Beijing brewery opened during the Japanese occupation, in 1943. But although the majority of China's estimated 850 breweries have been built since 1979, industry analysts say many are small and inefficient. Most are still state-owned. The biggest brewery is Tsingtao, in which Anheuser-Busch has a stake. China's two biggest brewing cities are Shanghai and Beijing.

Virtually all Chinese beer is a very pale lager style, but there are several dark brews and Qingdao reputedly has a porter-style

Above: Tsingtao's head brewer, Mr Wu, presides over China's best-known brand.

Above: The popularity of beer in China is rocketing, particularly among the young.

times the national average. The overall rise in beer drinking is phenomenal given that the Chinese averaged just one half-liter glass of beer each in 1979.

Because China is such a vast country, and road and rail networks are very poor by western standards, the beer industry is localized in a way that brewing generally was in Europe until after World War II. The practice of localized brewing and local consumption is further encouraged by the fact that China's 21 provinces are increasingly autonomous economically, often putting up trade protection barriers against 'imports' of competing raw materials and products from other regions. This seems likely to impede the development of national brands. The only beer which comes near to being nationally distributed is Tsingtao.

However, Britain's Bass plans to compete nationally with its Scottish Tennent lager. 'There is going to be a battle for China's beer market and at the end of the day there are going to be three or four national brands,' predicted a confident senior Bass executive Tony Portno when Bass announced their $40 million investment in the two-brewery Ginsber company in Siping in northeastern Jilin province. That seems over-optimistic given the marketing logistics and size of population which surpasses anything western businesses have tackled before – unless a single brand is brewed in numerous breweries across the entire country. To put things in perspective, Belgium's much bigger Interbrew (Stella Artois) signed a $24 million deal in 1996 with the popular Blue Sword brewery in China's most densely populated Sichuan province – which has over 100 million people. That's a population equal to Belgium, the Czech Republic, Denmark, Ireland, and Germany combined, five of the world's top ten beer-drinking countries.

beer. They are sometimes only roughly filtered, giving them a yeasty-fruity flavor. Their strength ranges between 3.5% and 5% ABV and they tend to be thin and lacking malt and hop character, although China is now the world's biggest grain producer, albeit of variable quality, and has developed a hop growing industry.

Perhaps there is a future for more dark beers – imported stout is sought after. 'Black in a Chinese context represents quality and extra ingredients,' says Guinness's regional director Brian Pate. 'Black has associations with wholesome healthy products.' The Chinese most certainly get a kick from Guinness: they drink the Foreign Extra Stout (8%), which is prepared in Putian with a concentrate sent out from Dublin. Another imported dark ale finding a foothold in China is Whitbread's Export version of Mackeson Stout (5%, fruity-dry) which is not available in Britain.

The biggest-selling Chinese brands are Tsingtao – which is reasonably hoppy when exported – Snowflake from Shenyang, and Five Star from Beijing. Others are simply named after the town or city where they are brewed; some have more exotic appeal, like Blue Sword. The most unoriginal name – or perhaps the most clever? – is Reeb, which is beer spelt backwards. Reeb comes from Shanghai.

The growing Chinese taste for beer parallels the rising prosperity of the populace. Beer drinking – especially foreign brands – is considered sophisticated. And China is a youthful country: more than 70 percent of the population is under 35. Beer bars are proliferating in the cities, while in the countryside the pleasures of a cool beer have grown as the refrigerator has become as commonplace as the bicycle. In the capital Beijing, anuual beer consumption has rocketed to 58 liters (102 UK pints) per person, nearly four

Two of the biggest foreign investors so far have been Anheuser-Busch, with more than $200 million in Qingdao and Wuhan (where the Budweiser Wuhan International Brewing Co has been established), and Australia's Foster's Brewing Group, with more than $140 million tied up in three projects. Heineken has joint venture plans to build up to ten new breweries of one million hectoliters (850,000 US barrels, 610,000 UK barrels) each.

There have been more than 40 buy-ins or joint venture deals undertaken by major foreign brewers in the past few years, estimated to total more than $1,000 million. According to Hong Kong investment analyst Helena Coles, buying breweries and brewing beer is the easy part. 'Distribution and marketing is going to sort the men from the boys,' she predicted.

BEER OWNERSHIP

Who owns your beer? That may seem a silly question as you sip a favorite brew you have just bought at the bar or in a shop. But it is a very pertinent question if you value choice because the ownership of beer is shrinking as the world of brewing falls prey to the concept of 'globalization.'

Ownership is often masked but, increasingly, quite disparate breweries and their beers can be traced back to a single parent company.

As beer drinkers in the main brewing countries become more fussy and seek alternatives to standard brews – particularly mass-produced pale lager – big brewing companies are finding it easier simply to buy 'off the shelf' a successful smaller brewery which is already producing the beer or beers missing from their own portfolios. This is a new twist in the battle to maintain market shares in countries where beer consumption has become static or is even declining.

Thus, for example, the anonymous Belgian Interbrew giant – parent of Stella Artois – is now also the owner of Belgium's de Kluis brewery which brews the increasingly popular Hoegaarden wheat beer. Britain's Whitbread company, having taken over and closed more than a dozen other breweries in England, discovered it needed a quality cult real ale and so bought the Boddington brewery in Manchester. The world's third largest bland lager brewer, Miller of the United States, has become an instant specialty provider by buying into the Celis wheat beer brewery in Texas, Leinenkugel of Wisconsin, and The Shipyard Breweries of Maine. Miller itself is owned by the tobacco giant Phillip Morris.

In Australia, Foster's owned four breweries across the country producing more than 40 brands, but still went out and bought three micros: Redback, Powers, and Matilda Bay, which had been successfully providing something different to beer drinkers.

Left: Hoegaarden began life as a small, independent Belgian specialty brewery; now it has the same parent as Stella Artois.

Above and left: What unites these three craftbrewers? They've all been courted by 'corporate' brewers. Leinenkugel and Celis are now linked up with American brewing giant Miller (who has also snapped up Maine's The Shipyard Breweries), while a substantial proportion of Redhook is in the hands of Anheuser-Busch.

The danger of this trend is that once a big company grows tired of its acquired specialties, or another beer trend develops, the once independent smaller brewery can end up on the scrap heap of business rationalization. Almost as bad is the risk of 'blandification' of a specialty beer as its new, big market-mentality owner seeks to expand demand by ironing out the very flavors which made it attractive in the first place.

Although statistically there are more breweries in some countries today than 10 or 20 years ago – notably in Britain and the North America – beer markets are inexorably concentrating into fewer hands.

In Britain, several hundred microbreweries have been created in recent years to feed the demand for traditional beer – real ale – but, despite that trend, 84 percent of the country's beer market is now controlled by just four giant companies – Scottish Courage, Bass, Carlsberg-Tetley, and Whitbread. And the prospect looms that it could soon be just three companies. Twenty years ago, six companies had a similar market share. The British micros have managed to muscle in on just over one percent of the beer market.

Monopoly legislation which is supposed to protect consumers from the inevitable consequences of market concentration is shown to be a sham in some countries.

One of the worst examples of monopoly is Australia where just two companies now control a crushing 97.4 percent of the beer market between them. Foster's Brewing Group and the New Zealand-based Lion Nathan own virtually all Australia's breweries – and beer brands – from the Pacific east coast 2,000 miles (3,200km) across the country to the west coast.

Just one major beer-drinking country, Germany, still has a genuinely diversified brewing industry where even the biggest company has only a small percentage share of the domestic market. But the trend there is also towards bigger groups and the hundreds of old established small breweries, especially in Bavaria, face increasingly harsh competition from bigger breweries which deliberately dump cheap beer to satisfy the big take-home market in an attempt to squeeze out the smaller competitiors. Ironically, Germany's biggest group, Brau und Brunnen, which spent the early 1990s building up an eight percent domestic market share by buying 14 breweries across the country is facing break-up by the banks, who recently called in debts.

Left: Australian-born Foster's is now brewed worldwide, although ambitions to 'Fosterize' the world seem to have faded somewhat in the last few years.

Right: A Brit, reading this label, would most likely be surprised to learn not only that one of 'their' well-known lagers is also brewed in South Africa by SAB, but also that it has such a 'lusty' reputation in America. In fact, Carling originates from Canada.

With beer markets in western Europe, north America, and Australia already saturated and stagnating, the bigger players are not satisfied with building bigger and broader domestic portfolios; they have to expand internationally.

For much of this century there have been perhaps half a dozen global beer brands, among them Guinness, Heineken, and Carlsberg-Tuborg. But these are now being joined and overtaken by others: Foster's, Miller, Coors of the US, San Miguel, Kronenbourg of France – now owned by a pasta manufacturer called Danone – and, most notably, the US's Anheuser-Busch with its mission to 'Budify' the world. American Budweiser is now sold or brewed under licence in 70 countries, and has become the world's largest selling beer through advertising and sponsorship promotions running into tens of millions of dollars. Together with its other brands such as Michelob, Anheuser-Busch has secured 44 percent of the United States' market. The company also purchased a substantial share in America's Redhook as a way of entering the blooming microbrew segment.

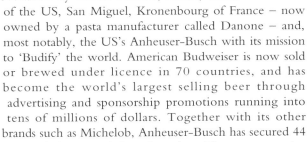

There are 50 or so brewing combines worldwide which are thirsting after ever bigger gulps of the global beer mug. They range from Anheuser-Busch, which has set huge targets – such as five percent of the Japanese market by 2001 – to United Breweries of India, and South African Breweries, both steadily pushing into Europe. And many of these combines are also making multi-million dollar investments in China, tipped to be the beer giant of the 21st century (see pages 174-5).

The pace of ownership change leaves some brewers themselves bewildered; none more so than Italy's Moretti brewing company. The former family-owned Italian business founded in 1859 went through several foreign owners during 1995-6 in buyouts and trade-offs between the international giants. First Moretti was bought by the Canadian group Labatt; then it became Belgian-owned when Interbrew swallowed up Labatt. But Interbrew didn't want all Labatt's acquisitions, so Moretti was sold on to Heineken. And since the Dutch giant already owned other breweries in Italy, Heineken now controls 38 percent of the Italian beer market.

Own up, you're confused!

INDEX